Groundwork

Groundwork

Local Black Freedom Movements in America

EDITED BY

Jeanne Theoharis and Komozi Woodard

WITH A FOREWORD BY CHARLES PAYNE

New York University Press

NEW YORK AND LONDON

NEW YORK UNIVERSITY PRESS
New York and London
www.nyupress.org

Library of Congress Cataloging-in-Publication Data
Groundwork : local black freedom movements in America /
edited by Jeanne F. Theoharis and Komozi Woodard ;
foreword by Charles Payne.
p. cm.
Includes bibliographical references and index.
ISBN 0–8147–8284–1 (cloth : alk. paper) —
ISBN 0–8147–8285–X (pbk. : alk. paper)
1. African Americans—Civil rights—History—20th century.
2. African American civil rights workers—History—20th century.
3. African American civil rights workers—Biography.
4. Civil rights movements—United States—History—20th century.
5. United States—Race relations—History—20th century.
6. United States—History, Local.
I. Theoharis, Jeanne.   II. Woodard, Komozi.
E185.61.G899   2004
323.1196'073—dc22   2004017053

New York University Press books are printed on acid-free paper,
and their binding materials are chosen for strength and durability.

c 10 9 8 7 6 5 4 3 2 1
p 10 9 8 7 6 5 4 3

Contents

Abbreviations

ASCS	Agricultural Stabilization and Conservation Service
BARTS	Black Arts Repertory Theater/ School [of Harlem]
BMCR	Black Methodists for Church Renewal
BPS	Boston Public Schools
BRP	Black Revolutionary Party
BSU	Black Student Union
CAP	Community Action Program
CCHR	Cincinnati (Citizens) Committee for Human Rights
CDGM	Child Development Group of Mississippi
CFUN	Committee for a United Newark
CHR	Conference on Human Relations
CIG	Civic Interest Group
CIO	Congress of Industrial Organizations
CNAC	Cambridge Nonviolent Action Committee
COFO	Council of Federated Organizations
CPUSA	Communist Party of the United States of America
CRC	Civic Rights Committee
CRF	Civil Rights Federation
HEW	Department of Health, Education, and Welfare
LCCM	Lowndes County Christian Movement [for Human Rights]
LCFO	Lowndes County Freedom Organization

LCTS	Lowndes County Training School
MAP	Mississippi Action for Progress
METCO	Metropolitan Council for Educational Opportunities
MFDP	Mississippi Freedom Democratic Party
MFRC	Mayor's Friendly Relations Committee
MUSIC	Milwaukee United School Integration Committee
NAACP	National Association for the Advancement of Colored People
NCNW	National Council of Negro Women
NHA	Newark Housing Authority
NNC	National Negro Congress
OCS	Oakland Community School
ODAC	Oakland Direct Action Committee
OEO	Office of Economic Opportunity
PAC	Project Area Committee
PCSP	Princeton Cooperative Schools Program
PDP	Progressive Democratic Party
ROAR	Restore Our Alienated Rights
SCLC	Southern Christian Leadership Conference
SNCC	Student Nonviolent Coordinating Committee
UAW-CIO	United Auto Workers—Congress of Industrial Organizations
ULGC	Urban League of Greater Cincinnati
UPWA	United Packinghouse Workers of America
USES	United States Employment Service
VEP	Voter Education Project
WHRC	West Side Human Relations Council (Detroit)
WMC	War Manpower Commission
WOPC	West Oakland Planning Committee
YC	Youth Council

Foreword

Much of what is important in John Dittmer's approach to the civil rights movement is present on the first page of his book *Local People*.[1] The time is July 1946, two years after the Supreme Court struck down the all-white primary, one of Mississippi's favorite devices for systematically disenfranchising its black citizens. Despite warnings of bloodshed and retribution, several thousand blacks across the state tried to vote in the 1946 primary. In Decatur Medgar Evers and a group of his friends, all veterans of the late war against fascism, put on their uniforms and marched to the courthouse, determined to vote like Americans. There they were met by a group of fifteen or twenty white men just as determined that they would not. The white men were armed, so Evers and his friends went back to get *their* guns. Again they drove to the courthouse, found the mob still there, and decided not to contest the issue further that day.

That brief vignette does some important work. It locates the "beginnings" of the movement story in the years surrounding World War II, revising the more traditional assumption, among both scholarly and popular audiences, that all that really mattered happened between the mid-fifties and mid-sixties, the Montgomery to Memphis framework. Much of the initiative that made the movement possible, much of the tactical innovation, and much of the persistence came from select local people like Evers and his friends. No national organization nor charismatic leader suggested that they try to register. As far as we know, they were acting on their own sense of what it meant to be a citizen, a sense undoubtedly strengthened by their service in the war. It is also significant that the incident concerns voting. As the Mississippi movement entered a new phase in the 1960s it maintained a focus on voting rights, and this was at the insistence of indigenous leaders like Amzie Moore who maintained that desegregating lunch counters and the like might be fine in other places but it made no sense in Mississippi.

While the initiative of a handful of individuals is central to the incident, Dittmer makes it clear that there is an important structural context to their actions. Absent the destruction of the white primary and the experience of the war, it is difficult to see the incident unfolding in the same way. This is not bottom-up history in any simple sense. Rather Dittmer, here and throughout his book, is writing about the collision between individual determination and structural opportunities and constraints, particularly economic and political ones. One strength of the book is the author's facility at weaving micro- and macro-analyses into one narrative. Finally, the incident suggests that nonviolence is not necessarily the way to understand the whole movement story. There were people who were willing to stick their necks out, but they were willing to defend themselves, too.

That the Mississippi story is a particularly important one should not be doubted. Deservedly or not, the state has long occupied a central place in America's racial imagination. In the 1940s, V. O. Key carefully documented the state's proclivity for extremism in all matters racial.[2] Some of the movement's most creative thinking took place in Mississippi, and some of its most arresting personalities did much of their work there. Whether the forces of racist repression were, in fact, any more brutal in Mississippi than, say, in Alabama or Southwest Georgia remains an open question, but there were moments—the killings of Emmett Till and Mack Charles Parker, the killings of Andrew Goodman, Mickey Schwerner, and James Chaney—when Mississippi's bloodlust captured the attention of the nation and the world, playing an important role in finally spurring the federal government to do something about racist violence. The Mississippi Summer Project of 1964—Freedom Summer, as it came to be called—provided thousands of young people who never came anywhere near Mississippi with a model of what activism could be, and many of those who did go to Mississippi left to become important leaders in the other movements that defined the sixties—the student power movement, the antiwar movement, the feminist movement.[3] Circumstances conspired in such a way that issues being played out across the South played out in Mississippi with particularly dramatic effect.

Giving local people a central place in the movement narrative changes how we think about historical agency, but it changes more than that. Take nonviolence, for example. The idea that nonviolence characterized black Americans generally or the movement in particular gave the movement a certain advantageous moral stature but at the cost of obscuring the complicated political currents swirling through black America after the Second World War. It is hard to see how a philosophy so out of step with American traditions could have rooted itself among more than a handful of people, although for a moment—1961–62, let us say—their thinking had an extraordinary impact on the movement. Still, the notion that the most important axis of choice among black Americans was the choice between violence and nonviolence probably tells us much more about the anxieties of white commentators on the movement than it does about the priorities of black people. What Stokely Carmichael was saying after 1966 probably resonated at least as deeply with the thinking of black communities across the country as did the words of Dr. King before then.

Posing matters as a choice between violence and nonviolence just seems wrongheaded from the viewpoint of Mississippi's indigenous leadership. Dittmer quotes E. J. Stringer, president of the state conference of the National Association for the Advancement of Colored People (NAACP) branches in 1954: "I had weapons in my house, and not only in my house. I had weapons on me when I went to my office, because I knew people were out to get me. I would take my revolver with me and put it in the drawer, right where I worked" (47). Ten years later the people who met "Sweets" Turnbow, from Holmes County, at the Democratic National Convention may have thought it odd that she always carried a small brown paper bag, but presumably no one guessed that she had a pistol in there. "Sweets" never left home without it (285–86). Turnbow and her husband Stringer, Amzie Moore, Medgar Evers, C. C. Bryant, E. W. Steptoe, T.R.M. Howard all habitually carried weapons to protect themselves or, in Howard's case, went about with armed guards. Bob Moses commented:

> I don't know if anyone in Mississippi preached to local Negroes that they shouldn't defend themselves. . . . Probably the closest is when I asked Mr. E. W. Steptoe not to carry guns when we go together at night. So, instead, he just hides his gun and then I find out later. . . . Self-defense is so deeply engrained in rural southern America that we as a small group can't affect it. It's not contradictory for a farmer to say that he's nonviolent and also to pledge to shoot a marauder's head off.[4]

A great many of the organizers attached to the Student Nonviolent Coordinating Committee (SNCC) or the Congress of Racial Equality (CORE) felt morally uncomfortable at the fact that they were living in homes guarded by local people, enough so that some of them felt they had to take a turn on guard duty themselves, notwithstanding organizational policies or personal beliefs. If not for the practical, nonideological attitude of many local people toward self-defense, it is not at all clear that the movement could have rooted itself in the rural Deep South. Moreover, the more one knows about those attitudes, the more difficult it is to present the late-sixties movement as a complete break with the early sixties. It is hardly coincidental that the Black Panther Party borrowed its logo from the Lowndes County Freedom Organization in Alabama.

It is appropriate that this book appears during the fortieth anniversary of the Mississippi Summer Project. Freedom Summer, as it came to be known, was so fraught with contradiction, so instantly mythologized, that it is a particularly difficult part of the history to write about effectively. Professor Dittmer's sophisticated framing of "That Summer" is one of the lasting contributions of *Local People*. He begins with the frustration many volunteers felt at not being immediately accepted as equals by SNCC and CORE veterans, but he frames that against what the veterans had been going through for the previous two years so that the volunteers come off as petulant, which is not the way that story is ordinarily spun. Dittmer's treatment of the racial and gender tensions during that summer is admirably balanced, but, true to the spirit of the book, he does not let those stories drive out the larger story of the summer. From an organizing perspective, the mere willingness of hundreds of black families to take in summer volunteers, knowing perfectly well that in doing so they exposed themselves to reprisals, would have been a significant victory in itself, but the summer accomplished much more than that. It brought an unprecedented level of national attention to Mississippi, which led to unprecedented pressure on the FBI to stop acting as if it were a branch of Southern law enforcement; it established Freedom Schools that served more than twenty-five hundred students and continue to be an influential model of alternative education; it provided health and legal services to some of the most impoverished communities in America; it facilitated the formation of the Freedom Democratic Party, which, until white liberals and black moderates undermined it, was a remarkable attempt to give voice and leverage to the poor themselves and not just to those who claimed to represent the poor.

The story of the summer is in part the story of the movement's radicalization, and Dittmer is at the other end of the spectrum from the school of thought that makes nonviolence the norm and problematizes radicalism. Radicals are pictured as hijacking what was a perfectly fine movement until they came along. Dittmer catalogues the sources of movement frustration with liberal America so fully, describes the emotional state of the activists so carefully, that by the time one comes to the speech given by CORE's Dave Dennis at the funeral of James Chaney, the depth of Dennis's anger seems not capricious but inevitable.

> I blame the people of Washington, D.C. and on down in the state of Mississippi for what happened just as much as I blame those who pulled the trigger. I don't grieve for James Chaney. He lived a fuller life than most of us will ever live. He's got his freedom, and we're still fighting for ours. I'm sick and tired of going to the funerals of black men who have been murdered by white men. I've got vengeance in my heart tonight, and I ask you to feel angry with me. . . . If you go back home and take what these white men in Mississippi are doing to us . . . if you take it and don't do something about it . . . then God Damn your souls. (284)

The 1964 Democratic National Convention is among the most important turning points in the process of radicalization. The basic story is well known. The Freedom Democratic Party came to the convention challenging the seating of the delegates from Mississippi since black Mississippians had been excluded from their selection. Lyndon Johnson, not wanting to alienate Southerners successfully undermined the challenge. Dittmer's treatment of the story is more detailed than any other I know, but the real contribution it makes is what it reveals about the extent of government spying, including wiretaps, on the activists. Bill Moyers was a central figure in the process and took some pride in having been of service to his president. That piece of treachery has to be understood in the context of other liberal organizations, organizations that did not necessarily have a history in the state nor any constituency but who abrogated unto themselves the right to tell the people of Mississippi who they could be represented by—not the Freedom Democratic Party, of course, and not SNCC. Even after forty years the sheer arrogance comes through clearly from Dittmer's accounting. The National Council of Churches, Americans for Democratic Action, several liberal foundations, the national office of the NAACP, some of the Old Guard of Mississippi NAAACP leaders, dissatisfied with the militant turn of the movement and with their loss of status to more grassroots leaders, openly conspired to neutralize grassroots leadership. At both the national and local levels, much of the movement's energy and dynamism was co-opted by people who, for the most part, had not been the people who made the sacrifices it took to bring the movement to the level of prominence it had attained by 1964. The liberals blew the moment, something that is still not properly appreciated.

Professor Dittmer's understanding of this period probably owes much to the fact that for twelve years, from the late 1960s through the end of the 1970s, he taught at Tougaloo College, an institution that was very much a part of the Mississippi movement. Dittmer is able to present nuanced portraits of dozens of individuals, without a false note that I can detect; he can convey the centrality of mass meetings to the movement in less than a page; and he can capture the complex and shifting class relationships of black Mississippi. One suspects that some of this is more than impeccable research; it is also the product of being immersed in a historical experience, and, further, some of Dittmer's discussions are the distillation of a hundred conversations beyond the formal research.

Professor Dittmer leads by example, not precept. *Local People* does what it does without talking about what it does. The text does not grapple much with previous historiographical literature—there is not much "Scholars have said unto you . . . but now *I* say unto you." One could argue this both ways. On the one hand, one could argue that the differences between what Dittmer is doing and the Master Narrative approach to the movement are so stark that pointing them out would be overkill. The story stands out more clearly because it is not loaded down with conceptual baggage. Furthermore, forcing the reader to do some of the work, to develop his or her own framework, is very much in the character of SNCC. On the other hand, a more formal situating of himself intellectually would have made the work even more broadly instructive in that it would have helped other readers develop a methodological toolkit for the investigation of other movements. Then, too, it is pretty clear that Dittmer's point of view was significantly affected by all his exposure to movement people. This presumably is, in part, a self-conscious attempt to write a history that reflected some of the intellectual concerns of its participants. Being more explicit about that part of the book's intellectual lineage would be another way to make the point that the legacy of the movement continues in ways that are often not recognized.

If Professor Dittmer missed a few points, it is almost a comfort to the rest of us. When one considers the depth and breadth of the research, the methodological and theoretical importance of the work, Dittmer's comprehensive knowledge of the "factions" both within and between the black and white communities, his refusal to reduce the defenders of segregation to one-dimensional racists, giving respect to the multiple viewpoints, his complete rejection of the triumphalism that has traditionally dominated civil rights scholarship, his almost ethnographic sense of the movement's particularity, the great variation in its character from place to place within Mississippi, this is arguably the single best book we have on the movement, and that it is influencing other scholars is all to the good. Still, the most important aspect of this book is that it is profoundly respectful, respectful of both the complexity of the people and the politics, and of the possibilities and limitations of historical situations. It is good that younger scholars are building on the modes of analysis exemplified by *Local People* but it may be even more important that they try to emulate his openness to complexity. Of the young people who came down for the Summer Project, Ms. Hamer said, "they done their share in Mississippi." Of Mr. Dittmer we can say that he has done more than his share to help us understand one of the defining American social movements.

Charles Payne
Duke University

NOTES

1. John Dittmer, *Local People: The Struggle for Civil Rights in Mississippi* (Urbana: University of Illinois Press, 1994). Hereafter, page numbers to this work are given in the text of the foreword.

2. Valdimer O. Key, *Southern Politics in State and Nation* (New York: Knopf, 1949), chap. 11.

3. Doug McAdam, *Freedom Summer* (New York: Oxford University Press, 1988).

4. Quoted in Charles Payne, *I've Got the Light of Freedom: The Organizing Tradition and the Mississippi Freedom Struggle* (Berkeley: University of California Press), 204–5.

Introduction

Jeanne Theoharis and Komozi Woodard

> Nowhere in America were the prospects for a black protest movement less encouraging. Despite the intensity of this white opposition, the Mississippi movement became the strongest and most far-reaching in the South. . . . Several explanations account for the character of the Mississippi movement. First, and foremost, were the local people themselves.
>
> —John Dittmer, *Local People: The Struggle for Civil Rights in Mississippi*

The crowds that filled church mass meetings in Birmingham; the somber procession marching over the Edmund Pettus Bridge on the road to Selma; the stoic formation of Black Panthers in their berets and black leather, rapt and standing at attention; the determined picket line of sanitation workers in Memphis carrying signs reading, "I Am A Man"[1]—all these are familiar images. Yet the people remain unknown, documented in myriad photographs and videos of the Black Freedom movement and, to some extent, heroicized for their roles in the struggle but unexplored, stripped of their political programs, their well-planned strategies, and their intellectual visions. Such iconography have often obscured the groundbreaking work of local people across the country who challenged the racial caste system in the United States. These local people drove the Black Freedom movement: they organized it, imagined it, mobilized and cultivated it; they did the daily work that made the struggle possible and endured the drudgery and retaliation, fear and anticipation, joy and comradeship that building a movement entails.

1

This volume seeks to return our gaze to these local activists, to look at grassroots struggles for racial justice and the people who organized them throughout the country from 1940 to 1980. In places as diverse as Des Moines, Iowa, and Brooklyn, New York, Charleston, South Carolina, and Cincinnati, Ohio, these struggles were protracted, often spanning decades, and prolific, springing up in towns and cities throughout the nation. This collection highlights thirteen local movements and the surprising similarities and sharp differences among them in tactic and direction, focus and origin. By exposing the local roots of tactics and ideologies such as nationalism, socialism, confrontational direct action, internationalism, and self-defense, the authors show how grassroots activists not only acted but theorized for themselves and tailored global ideas to suit their local circumstances. Local people, as many of these scholars demonstrate, were at the center of deliberation, and it was this melding of theory and action that built a movement for black liberation. They arrived at political positions step by step, as the result of the successes and failures of previous actions, the particular issues facing their communities, and their own politicization.

We use the term *local people* broadly but not loosely. For our purposes *local* does not mean provincial; it is not meant to contrast people who struggled with local issues with those who took on national or international matters. Indeed, community activists often saw the national import behind the local issues they faced and linked their immediate struggles with national and international concerns. *Local people* is not a racial code word. While many of the community leaders detailed in this book are black, these local struggles included whites, Latinos, Asian Americans, and Native Americans. Nor is *local people* a class signifier meant to distinguish real working-class activists from their middle-class "Uncle Tom" counterparts. Indeed, *Groundwork* is populated with a range of black leadership, from field hands to independent entrepreneurs, from teachers to high school students to people who made their money through the informal economy. Finally, while the term is fundamentally about struggles that come out of a particular place, *local* does not solely refer to geographic origins; some local activists were not born and raised in the place they organized even though that locality was considered their home by them and by others who lived there. Nor are we suggesting that the experience of growing up in a community within a family whose roots stretched back through this community naturally translated into a clearly defined philosophy or plan of action for how to mobilize for political change. For the local men and women who built these movements had to join their long-standing knowledges of their communities with a process of strategic analysis and sustained reflection and reassessment. By *local people*, then, we mean a political orientation, a sense of accountability and an ethical commitment to the community. As such, local people were those who struggled with, came out of, and were connected to the grassroots. And it was this groundwork across the decades—along with, and often above, national black leadership, the rise of white liberalism, and the new political imperatives introduced by the Cold War—that would change the racial landscape of the nation.

Groundwork threads the struggle for justice from the heart of Dixie to the Cradle of Liberty. It takes a long view of the movement and its geographical, temporal, and philosophical complexities, beginning the story in the 1930s and 1940s and extending well into the 1970s.[2] Foregrounding the interconnections between churches, unions, black self-help organizations, and earlier civil rights actions, these essays join a chorus of work documenting that the movement was not just a product of Martin Luther King, Rosa Parks, Stokely Carmichael, Bob Moses, Bobby Seale, and Angela Davis. They show that the Black Freedom movement was not just Southern, not led only by men, not simply a series of spontaneous urban uprisings, not started in 1955 nor ended in 1965. The essays also demonstrate the danger of making artificial and easy distinctions between "civil rights" and "Black Power" regionally, chronologically, and ideologically. Introducing a diverse set of characters previously relegated to the margins of history, this book begins a new story of postwar America and the ways that ordinary citizens pressed the nation to live up to its professed ideals of liberty, equality, and justice. The essays illustrate how local movements were built from scratch and inheritance, out of the labor movement, local churches, community groups, women's organizations, and organized self-defense movements, on the shoulders of longtime activists and teenage militants. Most important, this collection demonstrates that there were local movements across the nation, in big cities and small towns, far vaster, more philosophically complex, and longer in duration than has previously been acknowledged.

This story of the Black Freedom struggle as a web of local struggles contrasts with the still-enduring portrait of the movement dominated by Martin Luther King and Malcolm X. While an avalanche of scholarship has brought into public view a cast of different leaders,[3] such as Ella Baker and Bayard Rustin, there is nonetheless a prevailing sentiment that the struggle only became a Movement because of the emergence of an exceptional set of charismatic black visionaries in the postwar period. Indeed, many believe that there is no movement today because we have lost these great leaders and have developed no new comparable ones. This "Great Man" view of the movement, partly encouraged by the media of the time, was exacerbated by an early wave of scholarship that focused largely on individual leaders, particularly Martin Luther King, Jr. Pulitzer Prize–winning books by David Garrow in 1986 and Taylor Branch in 1988 broke important new ground with the detailed analysis they brought to the study of Martin Luther King and a vast array of his compatriots, the Southern Christian Leadership Conference, and the evolution of King's own philosophy and the movement itself.[4] Still, by framing the civil rights movement as Southern, male-led, and nonviolent, these works largely marginalized other Southern and Northern struggles and the pivotal groundwork laid by many local leaders. They implied, often unwittingly, that these leaders were the key to the movement, reduced a community struggle to personality and psychology, and provided only a narrow view of what it took to build and sustain a movement. Similarly the King holiday has now been sanitized into a celebration of a man and his dream, not a recognition of what King himself knew—that the movement made him, not that he made the movement. Any honor for him, as King acknowledged in his speech for the Nobel Prize, was "much more than for me personally" but actually an honor for the movement, for "the known pilots and the unknown ground crew."[5]

Early attention to black nationalist and militant revolutionary groups also largely fell into this paradigm, reducing organizations like the Black Panther Party to a handful of fiery male masterminds. Ideologies of self-defense, socialism, independent political action, and pan-Africanism were not understood as locally grown philosophies and strategies but instead were attributed to the charismatic brilliance (or "ideological rhetoric") of leaders such as Malcolm X, Huey Newton, and Eldridge Cleaver and the alienations of Northern black communities. Black Power, then, was often portrayed as an angry, largely spontaneous, and ultimately unsuccessful movement of apolitical ghetto dwellers.

Another problem with the "Great Man" paradigm is that it easily slips into binaries, King vs. Malcolm, Newton vs. Karenga. It contributes to an artificial distinction between civil rights and Black Power, between leaders and followers, between the heroic movement pre-1965 and its militant demise post-1965.[6] Numerous scholars have narrowly confined the Black

Power struggle to Northern cities and late 1960s activism, casting it as reactive and angry rather than as a continually theorized set of tactics and ideas.[7] Other theoreticians, not liking the messiness of movements that used self-defense tactics in the fight for equality and desegregation, have defined local Southern self-defense movements like those of NAACP leader Robert F. Williams and the Monroe movement, and Gloria Richardson and the Cambridge movement, beyond the pale of Black Power politics.

A second stream of scholarship, exemplified in the publication of John Dittmer's *Local People* (1994) and Charles Payne's *I've Got the Light of Freedom* (1995), among others, began to give face and texture to the local movement that produced the black liberation struggle. These works documented the import of local struggles in places like Mississippi in breaking the back of fear and violence in the state and in prompting federal transformations such as the Civil Rights Act, the Voting Rights Act, the Fair Housing Act, and the birth of Headstart. Emphasizing the prevalence of women organizers, the variety of tactics and ideologies at work in Mississippi, and the range of people who made these movements possible, this research on the South reshaped the paradigms of movement historiography. When Dittmer wrote *Local People*, these propositions were extremely controversial and, in some quarters, even disreputable. Some scholars argued that the Supreme Court was the main actor in Black Freedom; others argued for the White House and Congress as prime movers. Still others put the agency within the black community but then located it within a cadre of ministers and other leaders. Thus Dittmer's book did much more than simply add new characters to the story; it rewrote the story, changing the timing of the beginnings and endings, the gender and class composition of the social forces, the power dynamics, the aims of the struggle, and finally shifting the center of action from Washington, D.C., to the grassroots.[8]

Groundwork was born as a tribute to John Dittmer, to the dramatic impact his book has had on the research agenda and interpretation of civil rights history, and the new scholarship it has inspired.[9] Charles Payne's preface to this volume situates Dittmer's book, and Dittmer himself, in this broader civil rights historiography and shows how his work has acted and continues to function as a springboard for a new generation of scholarship. While Dittmer analyzed the Mississippi movement, a new cohort of scholars (many of them contributors to this book) is examining local struggles in various counties in the Magnolia State as well as in North

Carolina, Alabama, and Maryland, and branching outside of the South to California, Wisconsin, Michigan, Ohio, Massachusetts, New Jersey, and New York.

Dittmer's *Local People* was published at a time when most social science research had turned to underclass theory to explain local black communities in an era of "urban crisis."[10] Many social scientists portrayed black communities (especially those in Northern cities) as socially disintegrated, postindustrial wastelands[11] where people were too busy surviving and too alienated from "mainstream culture" to theorize and mobilize against their oppression. By portraying local black Mississippians as organized and organizing in the face of tremendous economic and social upheaval, Dittmer provided a fruitful contrast to underclass theory, sowing the seeds for some of the authors in this volume to take it up more extensively. These essays, then, lay out new ways of imagining the urban, of seeing street corners, crowded apartments, inner-city schools, and welfare offices not as proof of community collapse but as sites of organizing and community mobilization. These authors challenge more totalizing narratives that, in attempting to foreground political economy and the wages of whiteness in the racialization of postwar cities (in the North and South), ignore the existence of decades-long Black Freedom struggles carried out by local activists.

Like Dittmer, other authors in this collection complicate popular depictions of rural blacks who are often represented as salt-of-the-earth followers or premodern simple folk—not as thinkers—who needed a Martin Luther King or a Bob Moses or a Stokely Carmichael to show them the way politically and intellectually. Examining some of the intellectual roots of self-defense, pan-Africanism, independent political action, and socialism among rural blacks, a number of these essays show how local people, rural and urban, were acting on their own, that partnerships with nationally recognized leaders and organizations occurred only after these grassroots struggles were well established, and that, as often as not, these local activists pulled the movement in their ideological direction. Ultimately, then, this collection breaks down the more superficial divides between urban and rural, between Northern cities and Southern towns, showing the cross-fertilization, the similarities of space and economy, and the organizing visions and challenges that linked them.

Interestingly, even in 2004, to some scholars and analysts, a focus on grassroots activists risks romanticization by overplaying the significance of local activists or underplaying their shortcomings. This book takes issue with such a premise. By taking local people seriously, it accords them the same detailed analysis of a Malcolm X, a Thurgood Marshall, or a Martin Luther King. Contrary to the argument of many scholars, poor and working-class people were not simply spectators or consumers, mimicking the ideas around them or being swept up in the fervor of the times. They did not need a great leader to chart their path or to introduce them to more militant ideas, because they were already analyzing the social and economic forces of the time. They produced their own leadership, made and learned from their own mistakes, and educated themselves. They moved through and between issues—from education to voting to poverty to police brutality—not seeing these concerns as mutually exclusive but imagining and defining fuller possibilities of self-determination, justice, and citizenship.

This book is not intended as a critique of national organizing or national leaders, nor is it intended to reaffirm a binary opposition between the local and the national. We are not claiming the authenticity or purity of the local; some of the pieces analyze the ways that local movements were co-opted by community leaders who sought power for themselves. Indeed, many articles reveal the symbiosis between the local movement and the national, and, at times, the impossibility of marking the distinction between them. Part of the politicizing process for many people was moving from seeing issues as personal, or even as local problems, to viewing them as systemic and national. Thus in order to conceive of a movement and then to have the logistical support to enable it to continue over a significant duration, local activists made an essential connection between the local and the national. The organizing and solidarity work of celebrities, national leaders, and international figures underscored for many local people that the world was indeed watching, that what happened in their town or city did matter, that they were part of a broader struggle against racial injustice.

These essays challenge any simple local/national divide, showing at once how local activists came to see their struggle as national and international (that the problems they faced also affected black communities across the nation and the world); as federal (that these injustices demanded federal attention and redress); as local (that real political change could only come at the ground level); and as autonomous (that black people must provide solutions and avenues for liberation and self-determination within the black community itself). They reveal that the local is where the national and international are located—that national events

and policy outcomes are driven by local movements and grassroots people—and that often national mobilizations and even national organizations were created as a way to aid a local front. One of the key themes of
this collection is to explore the intersection of the local, national, and
global, to demonstrate the symbiotic relationship between what happened
in a place like Lowndes County, Alabama, or Cincinnati, Ohio, the national context, public policy, and international developments. Community
activists often saw no hard lines between a local school struggle in Boston,
a housing protest in Detroit, the antiwar movement, and independence
movements criss-crossing the continent of Africa.

These essays have been organized by region in order to highlight the
breadth of the Black Freedom movement, its existence throughout the nation, and the commonalties and differences between local struggles. The
regional breadth of these struggles substantiates what might otherwise
seem like a glib point—that it was local people that changed America.
They force us to rethink the Mason-Dixon line and assumptions about
what is Southern and what is Northern in terms of racial terrain, geography, and economic landscape. However, these pieces were not selected
based on region alone, and many places are not represented, notably the
Pacific Northwest and the Southwest. These thirteen essays are not a comprehensive survey of local movements but one that, by its very diversity,
suggests how much is yet to be learned about the Black Freedom struggle
more generally. This book is intended to foreground the diversity of local
movements, not to suggest that there was a local movement (or even a
paradigmatic one).

Thus this variety (and the movements detailed here only scratch the
surface) reflects the wide spectrum of geographical and social forces that
animated the Black Freedom movement. The three-decade movement for
educational equity that Ruth Batson headed in Boston looks significantly
different compared to the political trajectory of Septima Clark that led to
the organization of the citizenship schools or Mary Rem's founding of the
Des Moines Black Panther Party. In Newark the movement was led in part
by a poet and playwright, but even in Newark, as well as in Des Moines
and South Carolina, other key elements of the leadership were nearly illiterate. While the United Brothers and the Committee for a Unified Newark
(CFUN) were staunch black nationalists without any white membership,
the Milwaukee Black Power movement boasted Father Groppi, a white
Catholic priest, as the adult adviser to the militant NAACP youth group,
the Commandos.

We have included a cross-section of movements from the deep South as well as from the middle South, the West, the Midwest, and the Northeast, less-traveled places such as Claiborne County and less well-studied cities such as Cincinnati and Milwaukee—all of which reveal that the movement was indeed a national one. *Groundwork* demonstrates that the South was not the exclusive terrain of the civil rights struggle, that women's leadership was extensive but ideologically various from the womanist Christian organizing of Womanpower Unlimited in Jackson, Mississippi, to the direct-action-meets-self-defense approach of Gloria Richardson, that poor people were organizing long before the War on Poverty, not in episodic reaction but by building institutions and through decades-long mobilizations.[12] This book puts in conversation self defense in the South and non-violence in the North; it draws common ground between school struggles in postwar Detroit, 1950s Cincinnati, 1960s Lowndes County, and 1970s Boston, and it engages a much more explicit conversation about the ties between the local movement, a growing national consciousness, federal action, and international struggles.

Tracing the deep roots and extensive backdrop of local struggles that took on national significance such as busing in Boston or political power in Lowndes County reveals that movements do not appear overnight nor do they spontaneously erupt. Paying attention to the local, then, foregrounds the early phase of movement building that laid the groundwork often slowly and painstakingly (and sometimes with very little public attention or "success"). This book continues the task of expanding the periodization of the Black Freedom struggle, in particular by pushing the time line earlier, and highlighting the decades of struggle that were the necessary precursor to visible change.

Early indications of that foundation are found in South Carolina, Boston, and Cincinnati. In thoroughly segregated Cincinnati it took more than a decade of activism to desegregate Coney Island Amusement Park. As Michael Washington shows, CORE and other local activists waged a protracted struggle to end police brutality and to desegregate employment, schooling, and recreation that took up direct action and sustained mass protest, years before national attention would focus on direct action in Montgomery and despite the creation of the mayor's Friendly Relations Committee to thwart such action and advocacy within the city.

Katherine Mellen Charron traces the political education of Septima Clark, who helped found citizenship schools throughout the South. Mellen Charron shows the early Clark within the network of the black women's club movement, forging relations with Southern white liberals. However, when Clark takes what some of her white liberal friends considered the "slow route" of working with the barely literate lower classes, she and her fellow grassroots activists had to develop their own logic for the freedom movement. Katherine Charron's story of South Carolina takes us back to the gestation of the freedom movement, as does Jeanne Theoharis who begins her story in Boston in the 1940s. Theoharis traces the activism of Ruth Batson, a leader in the three-decade fight for educational equity in the city who then worked to preserve this movement as part of Boston's public history. Like Batson, local people understood the centrality of representation to their struggle—"culture of poverty" arguments became the justification for segregation of black children in the city. Thus local activists in Boston systematically and self-consciously fashioned a multifaceted movement to counter segregation, to challenge these pathologizing representations of themselves, and then to preserve the history of their movements.

A number of authors bring new theoretical understandings to the issue of violence and the movement. They show that anti-black violence that often accompanied integration sometimes spurred organizing within the black community. In Detroit Karen Miller finds the early shoots of the movement following racial clashes at the integrated Northwestern High School. Rather than anti-black violence demobilizing the black community, as some scholars have argued, such violence lent urgency to the early Black Freedom movement efforts to formulate collective means of advancing desegregation, increasingly based on mass mobilization and direct action. Moreover, a number of authors demonstrate that the movement was often charged with violence when it moved to confrontational nonviolent tactics. Brian Purnell takes us to Brooklyn and examines the decision by Brooklyn's CORE chapter, after years of direct action, to organize a stall-in for the opening day of the New York World's Fair. This decision led to strident criticism of this confrontational tactic as "violent" from many New Yorkers and black and white CORE members, including a suspension by the national office, but also catalyzed the move toward more militant nonviolent tactics, inspiring other such actions across the country.

These essays also offer a critique of charismatic leadership from a number of angles. Emilye Crosby examines the complex dynamics of the Mississippi movement in Claiborne County during the 1960 and 1970s, by following the rise and fall of the leadership of Charles Evers. Evers developed a charismatic style of leadership drawn from the grassroots and embraced by national leaders that ultimately had little accountability to his community. Crosby shows the ways that national actors, fearing the unwieldiness of grassroots movements, were attracted to such charismatic leaders, hoping that they might be seduced to set aside grassroots demands to play the political game. Tiyi Morris takes us to the backstage of the Freedom Rides to look at the organization of Womanpower Unlimited in Jackson, Mississippi. Womanpower formed to provide support, essential supplies, and dignity for Freedom Riders being jailed in Jackson and further developed to play a key role in the movement for voter registration and school desegregation in the state. Refocusing the gaze from the Riders to the "ground crew" who enabled their Ride, Morris reframes definitions of both who the leaders were and what effective, sustained political work entailed.

Another important observation revealed across the thirteen essays is that local people were struggling before the arrival of national groups, and many national mobilizations were actually confederations of local groups. For instance, by the time Amiri Baraka returned to his hometown of Newark in 1966, artists and writers, as well as productive cultural circles, had already begun doing the work of the Black Arts movement. Komozi Woodard explores the key leadership of several local activists in the Black Power movement in Newark, New Jersey. The myths associated with charismatic leadership die hard in both politics and scholarship. Therefore it is easy to believe that Black Power in Newark began and ended with the poet and playwright, Amiri Baraka. However, by changing the focus of the narrative to the development of such local leaders as Sultani Tarik and Harold Mhisani Wilson, the chapter on Newark suggests that one key to the distinctive Black freedom struggle in that city was the durable genius of collective grassroots leadership.

The rewriting of the history of places such as Cambridge, Maryland, and Lowndes County, Alabama, lifts them from being understood as simply outposts of SNCC and other national organizations to locally grown protests that drew national organizations to their struggle. Ultimately they show that neither the "civil rights" nor the "Black Power" banners fully capture the dynamics of the protracted Black Freedom struggle waged in the postwar period. Peter Levy's story of Gloria Richardson and the Cambridge movement in 1960s Maryland forces us to reexamine our understanding of the temporal and ideological contours of the Black Freedom movement. Employing elements of both nonviolence and self-defense, the Cambridge struggle focused on desegregation and economics, particularly jobs and housing; however, many in the movement refused to participate in a city referendum on desegregation, believing that rights should not be subject to polls. Cambridge became a formative experience for many of the important freedom movement leaders, including Malcolm X and leaders of SNCC, who cut their teeth in the midst of the "civil war" in Cambridge. Hasan Jeffries's analysis of the movement in Lowndes County, Alabama, complements this reexamination of the role of national civil rights organizations. The emergence of Black Power is credited to Stokely Carmichael and SNCC. Yet an analysis of the rise of political consciousness and activism in Lowndes County before the arrival of SNCC shows the local roots of Black Power and the ensuing partnership between the local movement and SNCC. Jeffries shows that the independent political movement forged in the county came out of years of activism and did not simply derive from the organizing inspiration of Carmichael and other SNCC leaders. Both Levy's and Jeffries's pieces, then, demonstrate that national groups such as SNCC were successful because they tapped into and enabled already existing local movements.

These essays also break new ground on Black Power research, demonstrating that Black Power was local as well as national, tactical as well as ideological, and garnered numerous local successes. Many of these articles document the native character and indigenous dimensions of Black Power organizations and the role of the NAACP, particularly the organization's Youth Councils, as incubators for militant activism in many cities. In Wisconsin, as Patrick Jones demonstrates, a distinct combination of social forces and activists merged to form the Milwaukee movement in the "Selma of the North." In the struggle for open housing and desegregated schools in Milwaukee, the NAACP Youth Council took on a new and militant posture when it embraced the white Catholic priest Father Groppi as its adult adviser. Black Power in Milwaukee embraced "not-violence" and did not see a contradiction in having a white leader of a Black Power movement.

Looking at Black Power at the local level gives us a much different view of its texture and tactics. The Black Panther Party, for instance, was an organization on the ground, stemming not only from the work of local militants but also from the social and cultural conditions in specific urban communities. Robyn Spencer examines the inner life of the Oakland Black Panther Party, including the communal lifestyle, local electoral politics, and daily work that was done to raise member consciousness about the race, class, and gender dimensions of black liberation. Many activists journeyed to Oakland to see what the Black Panther Party was doing; one of them was Mary Rem from Des Moines, Iowa. Reynaldo Anderson and Robyn Spencer show the difference that place makes. While Spencer shows how the Oakland Black Panthers were an expression of the cultural politics in the Bay Area, including sexual liberation, Anderson examines the very different struggle for self-definition and political education in Des Moines. In contrast to the popular image of local branches mimicking what was said and done in Oakland, Des Moines members educated themselves as they organized their community, taught themselves to read by using the Black Panther newspaper, and engaged in criticism and debate with the Oakland headquarters. The Des Moines Panthers took on, for example, the contradiction between the party position on women's liberation and passages in Eldridge Cleaver's *Soul On Ice* suggesting that rape was a revolutionary weapon.

Overall these essays provide an important reminder of the ways that local people imagined and took power for themselves. As one young activist explained, "I myself desegregated a lunch counter, not somebody else, not some big man, some powerful man, but little me. I walked the picket line and I sat in and the walls of segregation toppled. Now all people can eat there."[13] By demonstrating the myriad of actions and tactics taken by local people in the period from 1940 through 1980, this volume rewrites the history of the Black Freedom struggle in postwar America, showing that it was a movement across the nation (not one restricted to the South that met its death on the concrete of Northern cities) and that it was developed and realized by local people (not brought to them by movement leaders).

Unfortunately the battles for rights, justice, and equity explored in this volume are far from over. Today the language of racial justice has changed from "power and powerlessness, internal colonialism, repression, poverty, racial and ethnic discrimination, participatory democracy, and community control"[14] to that of angry and undeserving black people who benefit unfairly from affirmative action and other government programs,[15] of a different kind of black people—"the underclass"—a group that is somehow morally unfit for desegregated neighborhoods and unsuited for excellent and integrated schools. Race relations today are often viewed through the lens of individual pathologies, personal choices, and family values, and the forces of global capitalism, federal power, and structural inequity are perceived to be unfathomably complex and impenetrable to social change. It is easy to forget that activists in Des Moines and Milwaukee, in Lowndes County and Brooklyn, were also blamed for their own conditions, also struggled to find ways to tackle the enormity of the problem, and also were thought to be too small in number, not unified enough, up against a structure they could not possibly change. If we are to learn from them, it is to see that the work and visions of an exceedingly diverse group of individuals in a remarkable number of places ushered in a Second Reconstruction in America.

NOTES

1. We thank all the authors who contributed to this volume as well as Debbie Gershenowitz, Alejandra Marchevsky, Scott Dexter, Corey Robin, Arnold Franklin, Jason Elias, the Theoharis family, Tim Tyson, Charles Jones, Amiri Baraka, Amina Baraka, Askia Toure, Fanon Che Wilkins, David Barrett, Tim Holiday, Carmen Ashhurst-Woodard, Donna Murch, and especially John Dittmer.

2. We are defining the Black Freedom movement as the entirety of African American efforts to knock down the barriers to black equality in the United States and to overcome the obstacles to the social, cultural, and economic development of peoples of African descent. Therefore, the Black Freedom struggle is heterogeneous by nature; it is a common effort embracing a broad range of the different strategies and tactics, ideologies and philosophies, as well as social classes and political views in black America.

3. See, for instance, Joanne Grant, *Ella Baker: Freedom Bound* (New York: Wiley, 1999); Chana Kai Lee, *For Freedom's Sake: The Life of Fannie Lou Hamer* (Chicago: University of Illinois Press, 2000); Cynthia Fleming, *Soon We Will Not Cry: The Liberation of Ruby Doris Smith Robinson* (New York: Rowman and Littlefield, 1998); Bettye Collier Thomas and V. P. Franklin, eds., *Sisters in the Struggle* (New York: New York University Press, 2001); Belinda Robnett, *How Long, How Long: African American Women and the Struggle for Freedom and Justice* (New York: Oxford University Press, 1997); John D'Emilio, *Lost Prophet: The Life and Times of Bayard Rustin* (New York: Free Press, 2003); Joy James, *Shadowboxing: Representations of Black Feminist Politics* (New York: St. Martin's, 1999); Barbara Ransby, *Ella Baker and the Black Freedom Movement: A Radical Democratic Vision* (Chapel Hill: University of North Carolina Press, 2003); Tim Tyson, *Radio Free Dixie* (Chapel Hill: University of North Carolina Press, 1999); Peter Levy, *Civil War on Race Street: The Civil Rights Movement in Cambridge, Maryland* (Gainesville: University Press of Florida, 2003); Charles Jones, ed., *The Black Panther Party Reconsidered* (Baltimore, Md.: Black World Press, 1998); Kathleen Cleaver and George Katsiaficas, eds., *Liberation, Imagination, and the Black Panther Party: A New Look at the Panthers and Their Legacy* (New York: Routledge, 2001); Jeanne Theoharis and Komozi Woodard, eds., *Freedom North: Black Freedom Struggles outside the South,*

1940–1980 (New York: Palgrave Macmillan, 2003); Wendell Pritchett, *Brownsville, Brooklyn* (Chicago: University of Chicago Press, 2002); Martha Biondi, *To Stand and Fight* (Cambridge, Mass.: Harvard University Press, 2003); Charles Payne, *I've Got the Light of Freedom* (Berkeley: University of California Press, 1995); and Yohuru Williams, *Black Politics/White Politics* (New York: Brandywine, 2000).

4. Part of this stems from an issue of form. Biography narrates the movement through the life of one person; as biography moves increasingly into delving into the psychology and personality of the subject, it then personifies and psychologizes the movement, viz., David Garrow, *Bearing the Cross: Martin Luther King, Jr., and the Southern Christian Leadership Conference* (New York: William Morrow, 1986); Martin Duberman, *Paul Robeson: A Biography* (New York: New Press, 1995); D'Emilio, *Lost Prophet*; and David Levering Lewis, *W. E. B. Du Bois: Biography of a Race* (New York: Henry Holt, 1994). Tim Tyson's biography of Robert Williams, *Radio Free Dixie*, largely eschews this psychological tendency, frames Williams as emblematic of a generation of black grassroots workers, and thus has more space to explore the movement that Williams helped lead.

5. Martin Luther King Jr., "Nobel Prize Acceptance Speech," in *A Testament of Hope*, ed. Joseph Washington (New York: HarperCollins, 1986), 225.

6. As historian Eric Foner writes, "If the movement's first phase had produced a clear set of objectives, far-reaching accomplishments, a series of coherent if sometimes competitive organizations (SNCC, CORE, King's own Southern Christian Leadership Council), and a preeminent national leader, the second phase witnessed ideological and organizational fragmentation and few significant victories" (*The Story of American Freedom* [New York: Norton, 1998], 282).

7. William Van Deburg's *New Day in Babylon: The Black Power Movement and American Culture, 1965–1975* (Chicago: University of Chicago Press, 1992), one of the only extended studies of Black Power, only begins in 1965. In their broad studies of civil rights struggles, Adam Fairclough's *Better Day Coming* (New York: Viking, 2001) and Robert Weisbrot's *Freedom Bound* (New York: Penguin, 1990) also place Black Power largely in the North and start it in 1965. Even *Eyes on the Prize*, the acclaimed Blackside PBS documentary, only picks up the story of Black Power with the appearance of Malcolm X.

8. Harris Wofford, *Of Kennedys and Kings: Making Sense of the Sixties* (Pittsburgh: University of Pittsburgh Press, 1992); Carl Brauer, *John F. Kennedy and the Second Reconstruction* (New York: Columbia University Press, 1979); Robert Mann, *The Walls of Jericho: Lyndon Johnson, Hubert Humphrey, Richard Russell, and the Struggle for Civil Rights* (New York: Harcourt, 1996).

9. This is not to say that Dittmer was the first to bring careful attention to the local; William Chafe's seminal study of Greensboro, *Civilities and Civil Rights* (New York: Oxford University Press, 1981), for example, certainly predates it as do many others, such as George Lipsitz's biography of St. Louis's local activist Ivory Perry, *A Life in the Struggle* (Philadelphia: Temple University Press, 1988). A range

of important work has come out subsequently. A considered and complicating focus on the local has been taken up in works by Wendell Pritchett, Tim Tyson, Martha Biondi, Chana Kai Lee, Barbara Ransby, and Yohuru Williams, in collections such as *Sisters in the Struggle, The Black Panther Party Reconsidered,* and *Freedom North,* to name just a few.

10. William Julius Wilson has written, for instance, that "lower income blacks had little involvement in civil rights politics up to the mid-1960s."

11. The presence of sustained urban civil right movements disrupt current assumptions of a disintegrated and dysfunctional black community after the Great Migration of African Americans to the North. See Alice O'Connor, *Poverty Knowledge: Social Science, Social Policy, and the Poor in Twentieth-Century U.S. History* (Princeton, N.J.: Princeton University Press, 2001); Alejandra Marchevsky and Jeanne Theoharis, "Welfare Reform, Globalization, and the Racialization of Entitlement," *American Studies* 41, nos. 2/3 (summer/fall 2000): 235–65; and Alejandra Marchevsky, "Flexible Labor, Inflexible Citizenship: Latina Immigrants and the Politics of Welfare Reform" (Ph.D. dissertation, University of Michigan, 2004), for a more elaborated critique of underclass theory.

12. *Groundwork* expands on many of the concerns that we outlined in our earlier book, *Freedom North.*

13. Jeanne Theoharis and Athan Theoharis, *These Yet to Be United States: Civil Rights and Civil Liberties in America since 1945* (New York: Harcourt-Wadsworth, 2003), 59.

14. Ira Katznelson outlines the phases as follows: first, it was common to "speak dramatically of power and powerlessness, internal colonialism, repression, poverty, racial and ethnic discrimination, participatory democracy, and community control"; second, the political language retreated away from issues of "savage inequalities" to a discourse of "balancing budgets, bondholder confidence, service cutbacks, wage freezes, municipal employee layoffs, the erosion of the tax base, and making do with less (*City Trenches* [Chicago: University of Chicago Press, 1981], 4).

15. Historian Clayborne Carson writes, "The spontaneous urban uprisings of 1968 . . . failed to foster a strong enough sense of collective purpose to override the endemic selfish and vindictive motives that emerged in outbursts of racial spite. Black urban rebellions were too short-lived to transform personal anger and frustration into a sustained political movement (*In Struggle: SNCC and the Black Awakening of the 1960s* [Cambridge, Mass.: Harvard University Press, 1995 (1981), 287]). Gerald Horne corroborates this view, asserting that one of the causes of the Watts rebellion was that "few took pride in or care of their community, and that became a root of many of its social problems. . . . This treadmill of poor self-respect and external derision did much to produce the angry mood of blacks in Watts in 1965" ("Black Fire: 'Riot' and 'Revolt' in Los Angeles, 1965 and 1992," in *Seeking El Dorado: African Americans in California,* ed. Lawrence de Graafe et al. [Los Angeles: Autry Museum of Western Heritage, 2001], 382).

Chapter 1

"They Told Us Our Kids Were Stupid"
Ruth Batson and the Educational Movement in Boston

Jeanne Theoharis

In 1994 community activists in Boston held a conference at Northeastern University to document the history of grassroots struggle for racial justice and educational equity in the city.[1] The 1986 publication of J. Anthony Lukas's Pulitzer Prize–winning book *Common Ground* had galvanized many in Boston's black community to put forth their own histories of black families, community organizing, and the city's turmoil surrounding school desegregation. The dismissing of three decades of black activism and the dysfunctional portrayal of the book's main black family in Lukas's book was galling to local activists like Ruth Batson, who had spent the better part of their lives fighting for educational equity in Boston and against these pathologizing images of black families.[2] "JOHN ANTHONY LUKAS STOLE OUR MOVEMENT,"[3] she declared. Lukas's book examined Boston's busing crisis by tracing the experiences of three local Boston families—the working-class black Twymons, the working-class Irish McGoffs, and the middle-class Yankee Divers—from 1968 to 1978. Seven years in the writing, *Common Ground* still discounted black leaders as key players in this decade and focused on a black family who were not activists and whose children embodied a variety of social ills. Lukas's portrayal of local blacks as politically passive and culturally deprived bore a dangerous resemblance to the political ideologies that had maintained segregation in the city for decades. Determined that books like *Common Ground* would not dominate the historical record on Boston, Batson sent out questionnaires to movement participants asking for their recollections as well as any documents they had from the movement and called on them to attend the

Northeastern meetings.[4] Indeed, the struggle that Batson and other activists now waged to reclaim their history followed from the one they had fought in previous decades to get public officials and local citizens to recognize segregation as a problem in the Cradle of Liberty that had to be addressed.

Lukas's book embodied a consensus that had emerged among journalists and scholars about the failure of court-ordered "busing" in Boston. The recognized history of Boston's busing crisis had become one of a benevolent suburban judge, Judge W. Arthur Garrity, whose order to desegregate Boston Public Schools (BPS) in 1974 inflamed working-class white ethnics in the city, who protested "forced busing" in an effort to protect their "neighborhood schools."[5] Led by City Council member Louise Day Hicks, white parents took to the streets and kept their children out of school, sparking some of the largest, most violent protests of desegregation in the nation's history. Accounts of Boston's desegregation focused primarily on white resistance, making it a story of poor blacks against poor whites, while ignoring the twenty-five years of civil rights organizing prior to Judge Garrity's decision, the middle-class interests that had sustained segregation in the city for decades, and the many whites who did not oppose desegregation.[6]

Angered over the inequities and insufficiencies of her own daughters' educations, Batson had been one of the leading organizers since the late 1940s who had pressed the city through demonstrations and civil disobedience, lobbied for legislation, and formed independent black educational initiatives to remedy inequity in Boston's public schools. And throughout those decades Batson and other activists in the Roxbury and Dorchester communities had been met with an intransigent School Committee and other public officials who denied that segregation existed in Boston schools while pouring energy and money into solidifying racially differential education in the city. This activism, and Batson's story in particular, challenges the prevailing historiographical and sociological schools of thought that marginalize the entrenched and explicit structures of racism in Boston and erase a well-organized, protracted local movement constructed against racial injustice. This story of black women's activism in Boston counters the pathological view of black motherhood so exemplified in work like the Moynihan Report and taken up in more contemporary "underclass" theory. With their ideologies of righteous motherhood, self-determination, and radical democracy, their organized activism disrupts current assumptions of the disintegrations and dysfunctions of the black community after Northern migration.[7] Complicating the dichotomy between integration and Black Power, between the black poor and middle class, these women in Boston sought to claim a public position *as black mothers*. To do this meant challenging societal expectations grown over centuries of American reliance on black domestic labor that black women would put their own children second. And it meant refuting newer social theories made public through the Moynihan report that cast "the black matriarchy" as the cause of the "tangle of pathology" in the black community, that linked the failures of black children to ghetto culture, and that posited black women's power as disempowering for black men.[8]

Sociological theories of "cultures of poverty" and "ghetto behaviors,"[9] which were put forth by liberal social scientists and national political figures, and echoed by local citizens and city officials, sat at the heart of the defense of segregation in Northern cities like Boston. While World War II is understood to be a watershed period in terms of American race relations, the postwar period in Boston ushered in increasing segregation and racial inequity. This segregation was shielded from public condemnation by the city's reputation as the "Cradle of Liberty" where problems in black education were attributed to black students themselves. These theories of cultural deprivation contrasting "mainstream" and "ghetto" behaviors provided a way for school districts like BPS to locate the problem *within* black communities and avoid systemic change for decades. There was no governor at the schoolhouse door proclaiming "segregation now and forever" in Boston; rather, the School Committee asserted that there were "no inferior schools, just inferior students." These public officials claimed that what was wrong with the education of black students was their culture and motivation and spent millions of dollars creating special programs to uplift these culturally deprived students. In response, black Bostonians like Batson built a movement not only to unveil the injustices embedded within Boston's educational system but also to dismantle these formulations of themselves and their children. A study of Boston's movement reveals that sociological theories highlighting cultural deprivations and poor values had taken hold in Boston by the 1950s and that black community members took up a variety of strategies to counter them.

While many women turned to activism to improve their children's education, the ideologies that drove their work focused broadly on justice and self-determination for the black community. Ruth Batson is both unique in her unrelenting leadership of this struggle and emblematic of a generation of women in Boston who were taking matters into their own hands, whether to organize and pay for a bus to take their children to a less-crowded school, to call a sit-in at the School Committee building, or to file suit in federal court. As she declared in 1965, "We intend to fight with every means at our disposal to ensure the future of our children." This public claim to act as mothers was, in itself, an act of resistance because it stood as visible and direct opposition to prevalent ideologies of black community disrepair and declining values. Putting Ruth Batson squarely in the center of Boston's history, then, reveals that black women's activism was neither exceptional nor episodic but rather a fundamental and sustained repudiation of the politics and economics of race in the city. Finally, such a study shows the ways in which community leaders like Batson understood popular and scholarly ideologies that posited them as the problem and then self-consciously and systematically sought to repudiate them.

Even before the landmark Supreme Court decision *Brown vs. Board of Education*—and more than twenty years before Judge Garrity would order the desegregation of the city's schools—a group of black parents and community activists led by Batson attacked the educational disparities within Boston Public Schools.[10] Born on August 3, 1921, to politically active, West Indian parents,[11] Ruth Batson grew up in segregated housing in the Roxbury section of Boston. Her mother was active in Marcus Garvey's Back-to-Africa movement and taught Ruth not to "stand by" in the face of injustice. She also instilled in Ruth a devotion to education.

> My mother was a single parent. She constantly lectured my brother and me about the importance of education. She set the example by returning to school herself to complete her grammar school education. I was eleven years old at the time and to this day I cherish the memory of my mother walking to the podium to accept her diploma . . . [at] Everett Grammar School on Northampton Street in Boston. At the time, I was a sixth grader at this very school.[12]

Batson completed high school, married John Batson at age nineteen, and had three daughters—Cassandra, Dorothy, and Susan.[13] In 1949, on the invitation of a friend, she attended a meeting of the Parents' Federation, a local activist group made up primarily of white women. "I was amazed to learn . . . that the oldest school buildings in Boston were located in the black communities, and these buildings were unsafe. These facilities also lacked the amenities found in other school districts, such as lunch rooms, libraries, and gymnasiums."[14] Black children typically went to overwhelmingly black schools that received less funding, but segregation was not total nor publicly pronounced which made it more difficult to see. The Parents' Federation politicized Batson's involvement in her children's education, "expand[ing] our minds beyond my expectation";[15] it was not enough to encourage her children in their schooling, she now believed, without also fighting to remedy the serious disparities faced by all black children in BPS.[16] Batson's first action with the Parents' Federation took place on November 30, 1950, when a delegation protested Mayor John Hynes's opposition to building a new school in the South End, a predominantly black neighborhood "whose children are entitled to as many privileges as any other children living in this city."[17] Soon after this campaign the Parents' Federation, like many organizations pushing for racial equality in this period, was red-baited and two members accused of being Communist sympathizers. "These disclosures soon forced the end of the Parents' Federation. . . . In time I came to believe that these were premeditated and organized attempts to plant in the public's mind a Communist conspiracy." Thus the politics of anti-Communism played out on the local level as a way to stymie Boston's interracial movement.

Batson needed to find another political outlet. In 1951 she decided to run for school committee, becoming the first black person to run in the twentieth century.[18] Batson's campaign literature urged voters "for your children's sake, elect a mother," promising the replacement of old, unsafe buildings, a hot lunch program for elementary schoolers, better working conditions for teachers, democratic home and school associations, and "interracial understanding and responsible citizenship." Running in a city-wide election with an at-large voting system, she lost. Still, she garnered 15,154 votes, and the black newspaper, the Boston *Chronicle,* described her "in the vanguard of our political leaders."[19] Batson's personal experience and early political work laid the foundation for a much broader movement to emerge in Boston. Her own daughters had been shifted from school to school.[20] Then, after finding out that the son of a white friend from the Parents' Federation had science in his school but her daughter Susan did not, Batson talked to the principal who assured her that her daughter would have science later that year. Sure enough, her daughter soon had a science project—but she was the only one in class to be given one. When Batson went back to the school, the principal flatly denied that her daughter was receiving different work. "At first, I shrugged it off, because, when you have three little kids, you get busy, and you don't have any money, and you just have enough problems trying to live; never mind getting into other things. But I couldn't shake it; I couldn't shake this thing."[21]

Having seen an ad for the NAACP that instructed local residents to bring their complaints to the organization, Batson called the Roxbury office but was told that they did not have a committee to deal with the public schools. The next day she received a phone call from the NAACP asking her to chair a new subcommittee around the issue. After this call, "my life changed profoundly. . . . Some black citizens scolded me for raising the issue of segregation and discrimination in Boston, the seat of culture and the home of abolitionists. . . . Some white citizens—usually officials and press representatives—argued my declarations to be without foundation."[22] From the outset in 1950 the NAACP Public School subcommittee composed of parents and other community activists[23] focused on educational equity and the allocation of resources within the system. And also from the outset it faced opposition over whether segregation even existed in the Cradle of Liberty.

The subcommittee saw firsthand that keeping black students in separate schools allowed the School Committee to provide them with an inferior education.[24] According to Batson, "We decided that where there were a large number of white students, that's where the care went. That's where the books went. That's where the money went."[25] Their investigation revealed that many black schools, including six of the nine black elementary schools, were overcrowded. Of the thirteen predominantly black schools, at least four had been recommended to be closed because of health and safety reasons but remained open, and eight were in need of repairs to meet present city standards.[26] Per-pupil spending averaged $340 for white students but only $240 for black students. The city spent 10 percent less on textbooks, 19 percent less on libraries, and 27 percent less on health care for black students than they did for white students. The curriculum at many black schools was outdated and often blatantly racist, and black students were often tracked into manual and vocational classes rather than college preparatory ones. Teachers at predominantly black schools were less permanent and often had less teaching experience than those assigned to white schools. Segregation was most consciously evidenced by the fact that white and black children from the same neighborhood were often tracked into different junior high schools. As parent activist Ellen Jackson explained, "You could live on the same street and have a white neighbor, as I did, and you went to one junior high school and she went to another junior high school. . . . It was not de facto at all."[27] And because predominantly black junior high schools ended in eighth grade whereas white junior high schools ended in ninth grade, black students were effectively channeled into black high schools.

Segregation also ensured the overwhelming majority of teaching and administrative jobs in the district for whites. Many schools had no black teachers (blacks made up only .5 percent of the city's teachers), and there were no black principals in the system. As Mel King, a member of the subcommittee, observed, "The teachers were either Irish or Yankee. . . . I didn't see my first black teacher until I was in the seventh grade." Thus neither black nor white children were being educated by black teachers, and an important career avenue into the middle class was being monopolized by white people in the city.

Batson also noted that they found a "general consensus" among principals that "black parents did not care about education and that black students did not do as well as white."[28] Already in the early 1950s, at the outset of this organizing, black children's motivation and their parents' values were being framed as the problem. By isolating black students in meager schools that created conditions under which most students could not succeed, the school system then blamed black parents for the limited academic performance of their children. The schools came to represent the quality of the students, as if the students could determine the structure of the school. As Batson explained,

> It angers me when I hear and read that black parents do not help their children—do not participate in their educational growth . . . what black parents wanted was to get their children to schools where there were the best resources for educational growth—smaller class sizes, up-to-date books. They wanted their children in a good school building, where there was an allocation of funds which exceeded those in the black schools; where there were sufficient books and equipment for all students. Is that too much to ask for?[29]

Black parents were regularly told by school officials (and people throughout the city) that the problem was not with racial injustice within the system but with their own children, further justifying limited resources in schools educating black children.

When the Supreme Court made its historic decision in *Brown v. Board of Education* in May 1954, Batson "sat down to savor this historic victory and said to myself, 'Everything is going to be fine now. Our kids will get a decent education.'"[30] But in the years following *Brown*, partly because the national NAACP was focusing its efforts on the South, Batson and the Public School Committee found it "difficult to keep the momentum going on the education issues [within the city]."[31] As Mel King observed, "In the fifties people opposed to our activism would say, 'This is Boston, not Birmingham.' Yet, in fact, this city is to be compared in every way to the most entrenched opposition to civil rights in the South."[32] Batson became the first woman president of the New England Regional NAACP in May 1957,[33] declaring in 1960: "Negroes in Boston are second class citizens because they are always fighting the subtle opposition of the Northern bigot." Batson's role as a political organizer entailed showing people how Boston's racial politics, although more veiled, were quite similar to the more highlighted politics of the South.

In 1961 the Education Committee of the NAACP appealed to the Massachusetts Commission Against Discrimination (MCAD) to recognize segregation in Boston's schools. MCAD refused, alleging that racial segregation was not a problem in the schools. Moreover, at the MCAD hearing the Boston superintendent maintained that they kept no records of the race of students in the public schools, further blocking the NAACP's efforts.[34] Access to comprehensive information would be a critical obstacle and a crucial weapon in the fight for racial justice in Boston. Given MCAD's unwillingness to pursue the issue, the NAACP decided to publish its findings itself. This report prompted School Committee member and former teacher Louise Day Hicks (who was, at this point, considered a friend of the black community) to meet with NAACP members and grant them a hearing with the School Committee.

Community activists took their case en masse to the School Committee in June 1963, packing the hearing in order to demand changes. More than eight hundred desegregation supporters were turned away and congregated instead outside the building and in front of City Hall, singing freedom songs.[35] Laying out the NAACP's fourteen-point program, Batson decried the existence of de facto segregation in BPS, the lack of permanent teachers in black schools, the stereotypical ideas many teachers held about black students, the racism embedded in the curriculum, the tracking of black children into certain vocational programs, and discrimination in the hiring and assigning of teachers and administrators.[36] "I know that the word demand is a word that is disliked by many public officials, but I am afraid that it is too late for pleading, begging, requesting, or even reasoning."[37] Community leaders expected an ordinary meeting where they would present their issues to be discussed. Instead, according to Batson, "We were insulted. We were told our kids were stupid and this was why they didn't learn. We were completely rejected that night."[38] The School Committee refused to acknowledge any form of de facto segregation[39] or differential hiring within the schools; that is, they would not acknowledge any role in perpetuating an unequal educational system in the city. (The NAACP, at this point, was not arguing that the School Committee had deliberately segregated the schools, but simply that the Committee had to acknowledge the problem and take steps to remedy it.)[40]

As evidenced at the hearing, school and city officials sought to deflect charges of racial injustice by blaming black parents and students. On January 6, 1964, William O'Connor became the new School Committee Chair, declaring, "We have no inferior education in our schools. What we have been getting is an inferior type of student."[41] Evidently while school officials did not feel at liberty to embrace segregation, they were comfortable calling black students inferior, unmotivated, and stupid. Identifying the problem as the deficiencies within individual students, they began creating special programs and services for "culturally deprived students" called Operation Counterpoise. It was more palatable in a liberal city like Boston to use a sociological language of "culture" to separate out black students. Indeed, there came to be a public elision between the phrase "culturally deprived students" and black students.[42]

The assumptions behind such programs reflect the slipperiness of racial politics in Boston: black children and ultimately black parents were believed to be culturally inferior, and thus programs needed to be set up especially for these children. In his exposé of Boston's schools in the 1960s, *Death at an Early Age*, Jonathan Kozol, a white schoolteacher, wrote: "Only after it has divested itself of prior responsibility, does the school administration come forward to profess a willingness to do what it can. . . . It suggests that the child will be granted full mercy, high pardon, and even a certain amount of compassion just so long as it is made absolutely clear ahead of time that the heart of the problem is the lack of values of his parents."[43] While many Bostonians could easily identify the hypocrisy of white Southerners who said blacks liked their second-class status, such dissimulation was much more difficult to see in their own backyard. According to Kozol, "many of the staunchest bigots of the city could convince themselves that they were acting and speaking out of decent feelings."[44] Through this cultural deficit approach, the school district reduced demands of black parents for equity and desegregation to osmosis and cultural remediation, as if it were whiteness itself that black children needed and blackness that black parents sought to escape. Black parents were quick to counter. Eloise Barros remarked, "It's not that I want my child sitting next to a white child. All I want is an equal education for her. In the Roxbury school they used to have French classes but not anymore. They cut that out because the neighborhood was becoming Negro and when the neighborhood becomes a Negro ghetto, they are not going to give you the same things."[45]

To continue the pressure on the School Committee, community leaders turned to direct action, holding school boycotts and sit-ins. The first school boycott occurred a week after the School Committee meeting. Nearly half the black high school students participated in the Stay-Out-For-Freedom boycott and attended Freedom Schools.[46] The School Committee then granted the NAACP a second hearing. This meeting on August 15, like the first in June, was filled with civil rights supporters, once again with hundreds of demonstrators out in the street. However, the School Committee ended the meeting after fifteen minutes when Batson began a presentation on de facto segregation within the school system.

The NAACP turned to direct action, organizing numerous sit-ins and pickets against the School Committee. Many organizers were arrested. The School Committee treated the demonstrations and school boycotts not as an indictment of the educational system but rather as an indictment of those who protested. School Committeeman Joseph Lee's reaction was telling: "The Negro can make their schools the best in the city if they attend schools more often, on time and apply themselves."[47]

Community activists focused their attention on electing a more responsive School Committee. Two days before the primary ten thousand people marched on Roxbury, ending their protest at the decrepit Sherwin School. Yet with the exception of Arthur Gartland, the only incumbent endorsed by civil rights groups, none of their candidates won.[48] As Batson summed up,

> 1963 was a difficult year. While we expected opposition, we were completely unprepared for the reaction to the NAACP charge of de facto segregation.
> . . . We cannot claim that the black community in toto, supported the NAACP Education Committee's efforts to eliminate de facto segregation in the Boston schools but it was heartening to see community support for the

NAACP grow especially among just ordinary citizens. . . . The NAACP's membership in 1963 was the largest in NAACP history at the time. The NAACP was constantly being accused of demanding busing. . . . The term "busing" never appeared in the fourteen points presented to the School Committee. Busing became a code word, and when the term "forced" was annexed to the word, "forced busing" became widely used, especially by political candidates and the media.[49]

Interestingly, then, the term "busing" was already being used in 1963 as a racial scare word to deflect attention from constitutional issues of equity and to mobilize support for political candidates such as Louise Day Hicks. The arsenal of strategies that activists in Boston drew upon in the early to mid-1960s—sit-ins, boycotts, freedom schools, marches, and civil disobedience—contained many of the same weapons that characterized the Southern civil rights movement. Yet unlike their Southern counterparts (whose opposition publicly embraced segregation), blacks in Boston fought to have the reality of segregation recognized and to challenge the prevailing assumption that they were bad parents and their children inferior students. Already in 1963 parents were struggling over the ways that their demands for equity and justice in Boston were being twisted into a language of "forced busing," "maintaining standards," and "culturally deprived children."

A second boycott of schools was called for February 26, 1964, to coincide with a nationwide campaign organized by the Student Nonviolent Coordinating Committee to dramatize segregation in the nation's schools.[50] The national NAACP came out against the boycott (saying that it would not align itself with any group that would interfere with the progress of education), but the local branch voted unanimously to support it: "We have no other alternative, but demonstration. The School Committee is responsible for the actions of the people."[51] The School Committee met with the Boston NAACP hoping to derail the boycott, but the group refused. Organizers emphasized the ways that the Boston School Committee, unlike political leaders in most Northern cities, had not even admitted that the problem of segregation even existed.[52] Drawing between 22 and 40 percent of all black students and nearly twenty thousand people throughout the city, this successful boycott prompted action at the state level.[53] Governor Owen Peabody convened a blue-ribbon committee to study discrimination in the schools. The committee's report found that

Boston's schools were indeed racially imbalanced (racial imbalance being the more palatable Northern word for segregation) and that such imbalance was harmful to students' educations. Racial imbalance was defined as schools that had more than a 50 percent non-white student body; thus an *all-white* school was considered a *racially balanced* school. Still, the state had affirmed that the segregation of black students had a deleterious effect on their education. The lobbying efforts of the black community and its white allies led to the passage of the Racial Imbalance Act in August 1965, which forbade the Commonwealth from supporting any school that was more than 50 percent non-white. The Act provided that a district that was denied funding could seek judicial review of their situation. After trying unsuccessfully to challenge the legality of the Act in court, the School Committee tried to have it repealed by the legislature and used the judicial review to delay obeying the law for the next decade.[54]

Martin Luther King Jr. came to Boston in April 1965, attempted to meet with the School Committee who rebuffed his efforts, and led a march twenty-two-thousand-strong to protest school segregation. "I have no specific memory of what Dr. King said," Batson recounted. "It was the spirit of the day and fervor of the crowd which overwhelmed me."[55] Batson also spoke at the rally: "This cradle of liberty has lulled too many into a state of apathy—into a state of smug false security where we had really come to believe that all was well. But all was not well and all is not well—but unlike our co-workers in Selma, we were never too sure of what and how to fight, for our enemy was not visible and what opposition we had was polite and tactful."[56] Even in 1965, after more than fifteen years of activism, Batson was still contending with the prevalent idea that racism was not a problem in the city. (Batson herself was receiving all sorts of racist hate mail and threatening phone calls.)

The city's reaction to the Racial Imbalance Act was demoralizing for many activists. Hicks called the Racial Imbalance Act "unfair, ridiculous, unworkable, and unconstitutional." By the mid-1960s the School Committee was taking more deliberate and costly actions to avoid any desegregation. They decided to buy an old synagogue, Beth El (which cost $125,000 to buy, $10,000 to repair, and $90,000 a year to operate) rather than bus 150 to 200 black students from the crowded Endicott District to white schools (which would have cost $40,000). Claiming that busing was an infringement on the rights of (white) taxpaying families, the School Committee then moved to institute double-session days in black schools rather than bus black children from overcrowded schools to white schools—even though they were busing white children to other white schools to eliminate overcrowding. When black parents protested the double-session day, the Committee gave up the idea but did nothing to alleviate the overcrowding.

Unwilling to wait for state legislative action, parents founded their own busing organizations in the mid-1960s to bus black children to open seats in city schools with Operation Exodus and to suburban schools through Metropolitan Council for Educational Opportunity (METCO). This independent action—unparalleled in other cities—exemplifies the marriage of separatist and integrationist strategies that characterized much of the Boston movement. As social worker Kenneth Haskins noted, "After many attempts at trying to appeal to the 'hearts and minds' for equality . . . and to raise questions about continually blaming the victim for his condition—black people began to put into the arena a different set of definitions."[57] In 1965 a number of parents led by Ellen Jackson,[58] who had five children in BPS, formed the North Dorchester–Roxbury Parent Association, believing that BPS might respond better to a group explicitly made up of black parents. The group's attempts to secure change from within the school bureaucracy were largely thwarted. The School Committee forbade the use of school funds to bus children to the seven thousand open seats throughout the city, even though Boston's open-enrollment policy, which had started in 1961, allowed students to attend any school as long as there were open seats.[59] While open enrollment was designed to enable black students to attend white schools, numerous barriers made it extremely difficult for black families to use. Serving largely as a symbolic shield against charges of racial privilege within BPS, open enrollment was used primarily by white students to transfer out of schools in transitional neighborhoods.

Parent Betty Johnson explained the genesis of Operation Exodus: "Parents from Roxbury went down to the meeting of the Boston School Committee to find out how they were going to deal with the problem and instead heard them talking about the Negro child as being culturally deprived and inferior. So the parents decided to do something themselves."[60] Since the city refused to make it possible for black students to fill the open seats, the Parent Association decided to do it themselves by bringing their children to vacant spaces in many white schools.[61] Experienced in grassroots organizing, the vast majority of these mothers had been active in Headstart, school strikes, and tutorial programs. They researched where the open seats were and, on the first day of school, arranged buses and cars to "open" these schools to black children. According to Jackson, that first day a reporter asked her what their initiative was called. She explained. "'Casting our children out to reap,' you know, the benefits, so that they could come home and sow the oats at home. . . . 'That's sort of an exodus because we don't mean to stay out there.'" And so the program became known as Operation Exodus.

Batson was "overwhelmed by the determination of Operation Exodus parents to get the best possible education for their children. . . . They gave lie to the stereotypes applied to them: 'deprived . . . lack of educational interest . . . laziness . . . lack of ambition' and worse, 'a disregard for their children's future.'"[62] Over and over, as Batson points out, the continuous action of black parents in Boston sought to disprove what was being said about them: that they did not care about their children's schooling, and therefore their children's education had suffered. These mothers acted decisively and self-consciously, understanding that part of the social change they desired required overturning prevalent images about black families themselves. One mother saw Exodus as a way to counter the School Committee's "ideas as to what they'd do with our 'poor, culturally deprived children.' . . . if I can help it, no one that lacks the sensitivity or real concern will have the say as to what kind of an education my children will get."[63]

The Parent Association believed that if they began busing black students to these open seats, they would shame the school district into complying with the state law and taking over the operation and funding of the buses. They were wrong. The school district never did, despite publicly endorsing the program as part of its attempts to look legally compliant.[64] Nor did the district's open-enrollment policy ensure welcome for Exodus students. At some schools black students were locked out, segregated into separate classes, or relegated to the back of the classroom. Yet students in Exodus did make substantial improvement in reading. As Johnson explained, "Before Operation Exodus, the children never had homework; now they have. They have school libraries for the first time too."[65] Operation Exodus bused 250 students in 1965, 450 in 1966, 600 in 1967, and then decreased to 500 in 1967 (in part because of the formation of METCO). Holding bake sales, benefit concerts, and dances to keep its efforts afloat, Exodus expanded to include tutoring programs, black history classes, political advocacy, and other community outreach. As Audrey Butler, one of the organizers of Exodus, made clear, "Our efforts in Busing were good but there were so many black children left in those rotten schools in Roxbury that we've got to concentrate more on them."[66]

METCO took a different tactic from Operation Exodus, bringing black students from the city to predominantly white suburbs for schooling.[67] METCO's purpose was not integration, however, but quality education. Batson became director of METCO while continuing to fight for desegregation within the city,[68] explaining, "We've taken parents out to see other schools in the suburban areas because we've been put in a very bad position here in Boston. Parents have been put in the position of only being against something. They have not been put in a position where they can say what they're for."[69] A way to involve suburbanites concerned about the educational situation in Boston, METCO demonstrated the interconnections between the city and its suburbs. Like Operation Exodus, founders of METCO saw the program as temporary and thought it would force the city to deal with racial equity within the city. As Batson explained, "When Metco started . . . I know I thought 'We'll take the kids out and embarrass them [the Boston School Committee] . . . Nobody expected it to go on and on."[70] The METCO board consciously picked students from a range of family income and academic success. Resenting the implication that METCO took the "cream of the crop," Batson asked, "Were 220 students all of the cream?"[71]

METCO was largely successful. Of the first 220 children bused to seven suburbs, only one dropped out in the first year. METCO had an easier time raising funds than Exodus did because the suburban districts with which it paired requested money from the federal government, while the Boston School Committee refused to do this for Exodus. The School Committee publicly endorsed METCO but refused any expenditure of money on it. By the mid 1970s, with help from the U.S. Office for Education, METCO was busing nearly 2,500 students to thirty-eight suburbs.[72] While METCO hoped to destroy the negative stereotypes of urban blacks, organizers never saw this as a systemic solution to remedy the deficits within the educational system in Boston more generally. Batson concluded in 1967, "All in all, none of us are doing a very good job about making a dent in the total population of school children who need the help."[73]

Community initiatives like Exodus and METCO, the founding of independent black schools (Highland Park Free School, Roxbury Community School, and the New School) in 1966–68, tutoring and summer programs, the Bridge (which helped black students be admitted into private schools), and Upward Bound demonstrate the vigorous activity of Boston's black community in the mid- to late 1960s. As Batson observed, "To those white onlookers who constantly complain that 'they (the Negroes) should help themselves,' the black community, in virtual unison responds: 'STOP THE LIES ABOUT US!'"[74] They also demonstrate the frustration of community leaders with how they were being constructed as not being committed to education. Troubled by the slanted media coverage around these issues and the "liberal use of stereotypes, i.e., culturally deprived, agitators, forced busing," activists held a roundtable meeting with media representatives to address the issue.[75]

These relentless community efforts, while providing proof that black students desired and benefited amply with increased educational opportunities, still had not addressed the larger problems inherent in BPS. One major issue continued to be the hiring of black teachers. In 1968 nearly 30 percent of Boston's student body but only 4.98 percent of the teachers were black. There were only four black principals and no black superintendents or assistant superintendents (unlike in other large cities).[76] Extolling "neighborhood schools" and their quality across the board in the city, William Cunningham, associate superintendent of Boston schools, echoed the School Committee's reasoning and set policy accordingly. Ignoring the success of Operation Exodus, he claimed "that parents don't want their children bused"; "Negro parents are happier with their own."[77]

In 1969, although 35 percent of the elementary school population were black, only 10 percent of those graduating high school were African Americans.[78] Growing frustration among black students led to the creation of a Black Student Union, and in February 1971 the Black Student Union organized a citywide demonstration as black students asserted their right to wear dashikis and to be taught the history of black peoples. They had five demands: recruit black teachers, recruit black guidance counselors, commission an independent study of racial patterns in the city's schools, end harassment of black students, and grant amnesty to all striking students. Seventeen years after the *Brown* decision, Mel King observed, "They protested the very same issues that had prompted their parents to call the Freedom Stay Outs and the March on Roxbury in 1963."[79]

By the end of 1969, according to Batson, "more and more the rumblings in the black community center around legal action. Black activists continue to contribute their energies to new programs of all kinds . . . innovative and self-help organizing and fundraising. It soon becomes clear that none of these massive endeavors can provide long-term solutions."[80] In

1969 Bill Owens, who later became the first black state senator in Massachusetts, filed suit against the at-large voting system that elected the School Committee.[81] Then in March 1972 the NAACP, on behalf of black parents, filed a federal suit against the School Committee in *Tallulah Morgan v. James W. Hennigan.*[82] Despite the Racial Imbalance Act, 59 of the 201 schools in BPS had a majority of black students, and there were only 356 black teachers in a school system comprising 4,500 teachers.[83]

In February 1974 City Councilwoman Louise Day Hicks convened a group of her supporters who opposed desegregation and any enforcement of the Racial Imbalance Act. First known as the "Save Boston Committee" and then renamed ROAR (Restore Our Alienated Rights), they were given office space in City Hall. The message to the black community, according to Batson, was that "the Mayor of the City of Boston and the Boston City Council support lawlessness and racism."[84] Then, on June 21, 1974, Judge Garrity ruled that Boston's schools were intentionally segregated and ordered the Boston School Committee to begin desegregation in September. Explicitly rejecting the School Committee's argument that BPS was a neighborhood school system, Garrity's decision[85] cited the following as *intentional* segregation and cause for legal action: patterns of overcrowding and underutilization, the drawing of district lines, the creation of a dual system of secondary education through feeder systems, the use of less-qualified and lower-paid teachers to predominantly black schools, and the restricting of black teachers largely to black schools.[86]

ROAR began a furious mobilization against Garrity's decision, drawing support from white parents, politicians, teachers, police officers, and other concerned citizens. Political attention focused little on the constitutional issues of desegregation or the perspectives of the black community.[87] According to Ellen Jackson, "The mood in the black community was one of confusion, concern, and fear because the elected officials during that summer of 1974 . . . were very often making statements that this would not happen."[88] But there was also jubilation over finally having a systemic solution; a *Bay State Banner* cartoon celebrated this legal victory after years of struggle with the caption: "It's all over but the shouting."[89]

In late 1973 the Freedom House Institute on Schools and Education was formed to work with parents, students, and concerned citizens around the desegregation process, and to "help Black community members explode the myth about the inferiority of children."[90] Ellen Jackson became the director of this new project and helped to coordinate efforts within the black community to prepare for desegregation—once again, having to "explode the myths about black students." Working at Boston University as Director of Consultation and Education,[91] Batson enabled the Freedom House effort by developing a program to train people from various local groups on riding on the buses, dealing with white harassment, and working with kids after school. Concerned over issues of mental health, Batson was serving as the director of community mental health at Boston University's medical school in an effort to get psychologists and psychiatrists, who tended to treat their working-class and poor clients as pathological, to adjust their treatment. Freedom House also set up a hotline for parents to call about desegregation, which received hundreds of calls before school began. Along with the Roxbury Multi-Service Center and the Lena Park Community Development Corporation, a coalition was formed to protect white children who were being bused into black schools and to support black children going into white schools.

There was little leadership within the city to enable desegregation as most of the City Council, School Committee, home and school associations, the Boston Teacher's Union, and the Police Patrolmen's Association came out in active opposition to Garrity's decision. In describing Mayor White's response, Batson said, "YOU WOULD THINK THAT ALIENS WERE COMING."[92] Given this leadership, the start of school on September 12, 1974, provoked some of the ugliest anti-desegregation demonstrations in American history, even though desegregation happened in most Boston schools without incident.[93] As the first bus from Roxbury arrived at South Boston, the twenty black kids riding the bus were met by a crowd of whites throwing rocks, bottles, eggs, and rotten tomatoes, and yelling "Niggers Go Home." Phyllis Ellison, one of the students who attended school that day, described "people on the corners holding bananas like we were apes, monkeys. 'Monkeys get out, get them out of our neighborhood. We don't want you in our schools.'"[94] Leaving school that day, the buses were again pelted with stones. At Roxbury High ROAR's boycott proved effective as only 10 percent of the 525 whites assigned there showed up for the first day of school.[95] Nor was the violence and harassment confined to working-class enclaves like South Boston. Some of the worst harassment and violence occurred in the middle-class neighborhoods known as the High Wards, particularly at Hyde Park High School. On October 9, 1974, President Gerald Ford weighed in, opposing "forced busing and "respectfully disagree[ing] with the judge's order." "The President's statement is greeted with jubilation by anti-busing forces," Batson explained. "Those in support of equal educational opportunity, while cognizant that Gerald

Ford is not a civil rights proponent, are still shocked that the President of the United States would make such a statement."[96] October 1974 was a difficult time for civil rights activists. "Incidents continue on a daily basis. When we gather at the many meetings, we feel hung out to dry."[97] One black student eloquently explained her decision to continue attending South Boston High School, "If they run us out of that school, they can run us out of the city. They will be able to stop access wherever they want."[98]

While white violence received much of the media attention, pro-busing meetings, rallies, and marches turned out significant support but little mainstream media coverage. Decrying the violence infecting the city, black Communist Angela Davis spoke at a packed workshop in October.[99] Freedom House also organized an "assembly for justice" in early October, bringing together a coalition of black community groups. On November 30, 1974, Coretta Scott King led a march of twenty-five hundred people. And two weeks later an antiracist demonstration drew twelve thousand including Ralph Abernathy, Dick Gregory, and Amiri Baraka, while a ROAR demonstration drew only three thousand. Yet media coverage continued to focus on white resistance. On May 17, 1975, about forty thousand people marched to show their public—and organized—support for desegregation. "We wanted to show Boston," Ellen Jackson explained, "that there are a number of people who have fought for busing, some for over 20 years. We hoped to express the concerns of many people who have not seen themselves, only seeing the anti-busing demonstrations in the media." Jackson's comment reveals the ways that black organizers struggled to keep the issue of racial justice in public view; media attention to white resistance shaped how desegregation was being and would continue to be understood.[100]

Understanding the nature of Boston politics, Batson, Jackson, and other black leaders believed that the only solution was to take the Boston Public Schools from the disposition of the School Committee and put it under the jurisdiction of the court and an outside administration. NAACP head Thomas Atkins had testified to the U.S. Commission on Civil Rights at the end of the first year regarding the "vacuum" of leadership in the white community.[101] In a letter to Judge Garrity, Batson wrote of the need to disabuse South Bostonians of the idea that "South Boston High School belongs to them and them alone."[102] On December 9, 1975, Judge Garrity took the school system out of the control of the School Committee, ousted the principal of South Boston High School and seven other administrators, and put the system into receivership. That day the NAACP office was firebombed.[103] Many black leaders felt receivership was the real turning point when white opponents realized that the judge meant business. Hicks lost her seat on the City Council in 1977, and a black man, John O'Bryant, was elected to the School Committee, the first in seventy-six years.[104]

While many have labeled the judge's orders for Boston's school desegregation ill-conceived and ineffective, a broader analysis reveals tempered success.[105] In an interview in 1991 Batson foregrounded the twenty-five-year efforts of blacks. "The black people in this city, we saved this city. If we thought things were bad, God knows what would have happened [without our efforts for desegregation]."[106] While black activists in Boston "miscalculated white rage and white hate," Batson argued that she would certainly do it again. There should be "no place where black people can't go." The U.S. Commission on Civil Rights echoed her assessment in 1975: "Throughout the Nation the prevailing view is that court-ordered desegregation of the public schools in Boston proved to be a disaster during the school year 1974–75. We take issue with this conclusion . . . substantial progress was made in Boston in . . . upholding and implementing the constitutional rights of children."[107] On December 30, 1976, Garrity wrote Batson a "note of thanks . . . for helping the Boston public school system to pass the severest test in its history. While many other civil leaders looked the other way, you became involved with no expectation of reward, in efforts to implement unpopular court orders. . . . I am encouraged by the progress . . . in reducing racial discrimination in the schools and in enhancing their accessibility and accountability to parents and citizens generally."[108]

Yet this history of a local movement that reduced racial discrimination in the city faded from view as Boston's desegregation became a story of white resistance to busing and the continuing cultural dysfunctions of the black community. The Northeastern Conference that Ruth Batson and other community leaders organized shows the ways in which local people mobilized to challenge this faulty and incomplete history and the ongoing misrepresentations of their community. Highlighting issues of racial equity and black community action was not only about righting the historical record; it was also about a continued struggle over justice and equity in the city, a struggle that was still being thwarted by casting black children as lacking the proper values and culture to succeed. Racially inequitable education had been maintained in Boston by denying the existence of segregation in the city while blaming black parents and students for black educational outcomes. Crucial to the goal of racial justice, then, was challenging inaccurate and racially motivated representations of the black community and preserving a history of this long-standing political struggle against segregation and discrimination in the city's schools.

CODA: Ruth M. Batson died on October 28, 2003, at the age of eighty-two. She had directed the revitalized Museum of Afro American History on Beacon Hill until 1990; her nine-hundred-page chronology The Black Educational Movement in Boston: A Sequence of Historical Events (1638–1975) *was published by Northeastern University in October 2001, and she had donated her extensive papers to the Schlesinger Library for Research on Women at Harvard University.*

NOTES

1. The writing of this essay was supported by funding from the National Endowment for the Humanities, the Professional Staff Congress–City University of New York Research Award, Brooklyn College, and the Radcliffe Institute for Advanced Study Schlesinger Research Award. I am also grateful to the members of the "Writing Lives" Mellon Seminar at the Center for Humanities at CUNY for their ample encouragement, thoughtful feedback, and support for this research. This piece also grows out of earlier work supported by the Undergraduate Research Opportunity Program at the University of Michigan.

2. "Over the years, I have taken every opportunity to dispel the myths in *Common Ground* and to expose Lukas as a faulty historian" (Ruth Batson, *A Chronology of the Educational Movement in Boston,* manuscript in Ruth Batson's papers, 2001-M194 Box 1, Schlesinger Library, Radcliffe Institute [hereafter, Chronology], 15). Batson assembled this manuscript—an annotated chronology of the history of struggles for education in Boston complete with primary documents—from her own archives and the materials she had collected from others.

3. Chronology, 13.

4. The question "As you look back from the perspective of the 1990s, how do you now feel about your activities to improve the Boston Schools?" met with the following response: 69 movement activists answered "a lot of impact"; 53, "some impact"; 4, "no impact"; and 33 had no response.

5. Amy Offner has offered a powerful critique of the ways that Boston's desegregation has come to be understood as a "sudden crisis [rather] than a slow transformation of society and law." See idem, *"Too Late for Pleading": Black Boston and the Struggle for School Desegregation, 1963–1976,* unpublished senior honors thesis, Harvard University, 2001.

6. Portraying anti-busing whites as victims of liberal good intentions, most

writers see their job as to contextualize white resistance to busing as a class-based ethnic struggle. Such books include Anthony Lukas, *Common Ground* (New York: Knopf, 1985); Alan Lupo, *Liberty's Chosen Home* (Boston: Little, Brown, 1977); George Metcalf, *From Little Rock to Boston* (Westport, Conn.: Greenwood, 1983); Ronald Formisano, *Boston against Busing: Race, Class, and Ethnicity in the 1960s and 1970s* (Chapel Hill: University of North Carolina Press, 1991); and Michael Ross and William Berg, *"I Respectfully Disagree with the Judge's Order": The Boston School Desegregation Controversy* (Washington, D.C.: University Press of America, 1981), all of which portray blacks largely as passive actors in the drama. Even Steven Taylor's *Desegregation in Boston and Buffalo: The Influence of Local Leaders* (Albany: State University of New York Press, 1998), which claims to examine the role of local leadership, focuses decisively on white resistance.

7. This approach is exemplified in Nicholas Lemann, *The Promised Land* (New York: Knopf, 1991), but these theories have their roots in the work of earlier scholars such as E. Franklin Frazier and Oscar Lewis.

8. These theories were brought to national attention in "The Negro Family: The Case for National Action" prepared by Democratic policy maker Daniel Patrick Moynihan and released in 1965. Its conclusions echoed those found in black sociologist E. Franklin Frazier's 1939 book *The Negro Family in the United States* (Chicago: University of Chicago Press, 1939) and St. Clair Drake and Horace Cayton's *Black Metropolis* (Chicago: University of Chicago Press, 1945). A spate of liberal ghetto sociologists continued this line of work in the 1960s, notably Herbert Gans, *The Urban Villagers* (New York: Free Press, 1962); Ulf Hannerz, *Soulside* (New York: Columbia University Press, 1969); Lee Rainwater, *Behind Ghetto Walls* (New York: Aldine de Gruyter, 1970); and Elliot Liebow, *Tally's Corner* (New York: Little, Brown, 1967). Even these more sympathetic portraits of black culture framed black ghettos as operating under a different set of norms and values as a response to the larger racial landscape of the city, with urban blacks removed from and often indifferent to politics.

9. This language is the forerunner to the Moynihan Report and subsequently "underclass" theory.

10. While this essay focuses on postwar school desegregation campaigns, black Bostonians have a long history of activism around schools. Black people petitioned for their own school in 1781, and in 1806 the city agreed to help fund an existing school in the African Meetinghouse. They then pressured the city to allow blacks into white schools. In 1855 the legislature passed a bill disallowing racial and religious distinctions for enrolling students in public schools (Emmett Buell, *School Desegregation and Defended Neighborhoods* [Lexington, Mass.: Lexington Books, 1982], 59–60).

11. Batson's mother immigrated to the United States at the age of sixteen and worked as a domestic, the first in her family to immigrate but later bringing over the rest of her siblings. Ruth Batson notes, "Usually, when there are stories of im-

migrants to this country, we talk only about white immigrant history. . . . But there were black people who came to this country as immigrants. . . . But the black immigrants faced a more rocky future—just because they were black" (Ruth Batson "Black History Celebration" speech, State House, February 9, 1994, 2–3, found in Ruth Batson's papers, Schlesinger Library, Radcliffe Institute).

12. Chronology, 2.

13. When her youngest turned three, Batson went back to school at the Nursery Training School of Boston where she took classes in nursery school education.

14. The Strayer Report, released on January 25, 1944, documented these disparities within Boston Public Schools; most schoolhouses were not good buildings and schools in Roxbury and the South End, where most black people lived, were the oldest and unsafest. Furthermore, the Report noted that the School Committee had become a political springboard and often interfered with the sound administration of the public schools.

15. Chronology, 4.

16. Ibid., 6–7.

17. Ibid., 44.

18. Jon Hillson, *The Battle of Boston* (New York: Pathfinder, 1977), 65. Tahi Mottl, "Social Conflict and Social Movements: An Exploratory Study of the Black Community of Boston Attempting to Change the Boston Public Schools" (Ph.D. dissertation, Brandeis University, 1976), 174.

19. Chronology, 45.

20. Interview of Ruth Batson in the Civil Rights Documentation Project, Moorland Spingarn Research Center, Howard University (hereafter, CRDP).

21. CRDP, 2.

22. Chronology, 9–10

23. They included Batson, Erna Ballantine, Barbara Elam, Mel King, Leon Lomax, Paul Parks, Charles Pinderhughes, and Elizabeth Price.

24. Such widespread segregation was a relatively new phenomenon in Boston. The city's black population had hovered around 3 percent of the city's population until World War II. It was not until after the war that blacks began moving to the city in large numbers. By 1960 blacks made up nearly 10 percent of Boston's population and by 1970 formed 16.3 percent of the population, an increase, from 1940 to 1970, of 354 percent. Thus while discriminatory treatment had plagued blacks in the city for centuries, it was during this period from 1940 to 1970 that the Boston School Committee expanded and solidified its system of grossly unequal schools for blacks and whites.

25. Henry Hampton, *Voices of Freedom* (New York: Bantam, 1990), 588–89.

26. Ruth Batson "Statement to the Boston School Committee," in *Eyes on the Prize Civil Rights Reader* (New York: Penguin, 1991), 598.

27. Hill, Black Women's Oral History Project.

28. Chronology, 48.

29. Ruth Batson, "Black History Celebration" speech, 7–9. When many authors write about desegregation being misguided because Boston's schools were not good across the board, they miss the larger import of these battles—that they were pressing for equal access, justice, and educational excellence. And part of the School Committee's resistance to desegregation for twenty years entailed degrading education overall in the city.

30. Chronology, 47, 58.

31. Ibid., 58.

32. King, *Chain of Change*, 166.

33. Even with the national NAACP's middle-class base, Batson was not part of the black middle class at this point in her life, which was true of a number of other Boston NAACP activists (Chronology, 57). Batson also ran for the Democratic Primary state committee woman in 1956 and was the first black person to be elected to the position. Her election was subsequently contested, since these wards—12, 14, and 18—had always been represented by someone from the white Hyde Park, but the recount certified her victory.

34. Interestingly Batson was named Commissioner of MCAD from 1963 to 1966, perhaps as a way publicly to take Boston's black community seriously while co-opting one of their leading voices, given that MCAD was not vested with a great deal of power. Taking this position, however, did not divert Batson's activism.

35. King, *Chain of Change*, 33.

36. Ruth Batson, "Statement to the Boston School Committee," 597–98.

37. Chronology, Addendum 88a.

38. Hampton, *Voices of Freedom*, 589.

39. The NAACP newsletter defined de facto segregation as follows: "It would be the same as if a man's hands were tied behind his back and he were the told that it was his legal right to seek any kind of employment he desired. Or if a man's feet were tied together and he then was told he was free to walk wherever he wanted. This too would be a de facto condition. For, despite that he is legally able to go wherever he wants, he IN FACT cannot. A third example might be the case of a man whose mouth was shut with adhesive tape and who then was told he was free to speak his mind. Again, legally he may be free to speak; IN FACT he certainly is not able to do so. These are all DE FACTO conditions" (Chronology, 83).

40. Batson concluded, "We found out that this was an issue that was going to give their political careers stability for a long time to come" (Hampton, *Voices of Freedom*, 589).

41. Chronology, 134.

42. Even the newspapers engaged in this slippage, identifying schools with predominantly black student populations as culturally deprived and understanding that when the district called a school "culturally deprived" it meant there was a majority of black students.

43. Jonathan Kozol, *Death at an Early Age: The Destruction of the Hearts and Minds of Negro Children in the Boston Public Schools* (Boston: Houghton Mifflin, 1967), 184–85. The publication of Kozol's best-selling *Death at an Early Age* cheered many activists, validating many of their criticisms of Boston schools. A fourth grade teacher in BPS who was dismissed for teaching a Langston Hughes poem to his class, Kozol amply documented the poor conditions, administrative neglect, substandard curriculum, and marginal learning environment in many black public schools in Boston.

44. Ibid., 140.

45. Massachusetts State Advisory Committee to the U.S. Commission on Civil Rights, "The Voice of the Ghetto," July 1967, 22–23.

46. Ross and Berg, *I Respectfully Disagree*, 49. The national NAACP had been critical of the Stay-Out-For-Freedom boycott, but the local chapter followed the lead of the community activists such as Noel Day and James Breeden.

47. Chronology, 116.

48. As Mel King noted, "The re-election of the School Committee made it abundantly clear that the hardest work lay ahead, and we were forced to abandon our naive notion that Boston whites wanted integration" (*Chain of Change*, 36).

49. Chronology, 128–29.

50. Boston's activists saw their actions as part of the larger freedom struggle unfolding across the nation and wanted their fight to be seen as part of this national civil rights movement.

51. Chronology, Addendum 137a, 2.

52. Ibid., Addendum 152b.

53. Ross and Berg, *I Respectfully Disagree*, 49; Brian Sheehan, *The Boston School Desegregation Dispute* (New York: Columbia University Press, 1984), 70.

54. Chief Justice Wilkins wrote in his decision, "The committee seems bent on stifling the act before it has a fair chance to become fully operative. The objections it makes are numerous and . . . bluntly proclaimed as if the committee could by the force of its own word make the burden fall upon the 'Commonwealth' to 'establish a compelling justification' for the legislation" (Chronology, 281).

55. Ibid., 201.

56. Ruth Batson, "Statement made at King march on April 23, 1965," found in Ruth Batson's papers, Schlesinger Library, Radcliffe Institute, 1.

57. Chronology, 230.

58. Born in Boston on October 29, 1935, Ellen Jackson had grown up in Roxbury and had been active as a teenager in the NAACP Youth Council whose militant tactics and use of civil disobedience angered the national NAACP.

59. U.S. Commission, *Desegregating the Boston Public Schools*, xiv; Taylor, *Desegregation in Boston and Buffalo*, 43–44.

60. Massachusetts State Advisory Committee to the U.S. Commission on Civil Rights, "The Voice of the Ghetto," July 1967, 20.

61. When Batson's husband first saw Jackson on television, he saw an immediate likeness: "My husband answered the puzzled expression on my face: 'She talks just like you do.' After watching and listening, I was flattered by my husband's comparison. On the TV was a beautiful slim, young woman. She was speaking at a press conference. I said to myself, 'This is a wonderful new leader for the cause'" (Chronology, 217–18).

62. Ibid., 221–22.

63. Ibid., Addendum 221a.

64. Hicks publicly called Operation Exodus "Operation Disruption" (Offner, "Too Late for Pleading," 40).

65. Ibid.

66. Peggy Lamson, interview of Ellen Jackson, on file at the Schlesinger Library, Radcliffe Institute, 35.

67. Black activists have been criticized in works like Alan Lupo's *Liberty's Chosen Home* for focusing their efforts solely within the city, another example of how scholars have ignored the larger movement around Boston's desegregation.

68. Batson left the directorship of METCO in 1969 because of her husband's diminishing health. John Batson died in 1971.

69. CRDP, 13–14.

70. Nicholas Paleologos, "Wrong Plan and Wrong Place," *Boston Globe*, July 15, 1988.

71. Chronology, Addendum 265a, 5.

72. By 1969 the state legislature took over the funding for METCO, and by 1972 the state was spending $2 million on METCO (Formisano, *Boston Against Busing*, 38). According to Susan Eaton's broad-ranging study of METCO, "It wasn't long before busing in Boston became a popular symbol of . . . the futility of trying to legislate racial equality and racial harmony. Meanwhile, though, few onlookers noticed an irony not too many miles away. As the rocks flew, the tempers flared, and the fears escalated in Boston, black city kids were strolling with little incident into lily-white suburban schools" (*The Other Boston Busing Story: What's Won and Lost across the Boundary Line* [New Haven: Yale University Press, 2001], 23–24).

73. CRDP, 28–29.

74. Chronology, 319.

75. Ibid., 264. What led to this meeting between black leaders and a range of print and radio media was the inflammatory and negative coverage when Reverend Virgil Woods, a leader of the Southern Christian Leadership Conference (SCLC), protested Louise Day Hicks's provocative decision to attend the graduation of the predominantly black Patrick Campbell Junior High School in June 1966. Activists were also concerned that most media organizations employed few black writers, photographers, and editors.

76. Ibid., 300.

77. Ibid., Addendum 237b.

78. King, *Chain of Change*, 120.

79. Ibid., 122.

80. Chronology, 332–33.

81. The suit claimed violations of the 15th Amendment which "prevented [the black community] from pressing its special interest and concerns in the making of decisions governing the operation of the public schools in their community" (Chronology, Addendum 333a).

82. The first federal agency to investigate Boston was the Department of Health, Education, and Welfare (HEW). HEW confirmed Boston's worsening segregation and threatened to slash the $10 million of the city's money because it was in violation of Title VI. Political pressure—coming in part from Mayor Kevin White, who blamed the inflexibility of the new law and not the School Committee—resulted in HEW letting the city off the hook (Metcalf, *From Little Rock to Boston*, 198). In 1970 MCAD also took legal action against the School Committee based on the difficulties black students encountered in using the open-enrollment policy.

83. Robert Dentler and Marvin Scott, *Schools on Trial: An Inside Account of the Boston Desegregation Case* (Cambridge, Mass.: ABT Books, 1981), 5.

84. Chronology, 373.

85. The decision withstood numerous appeals and was given a bar association award the next year (Dentler and Scott, *Schools on Trial*, 4).

86. In 81 of Boston's 201 schools, no black teachers had ever been assigned and an additional 35 had only 1 black teacher (Metcalf, *From Little Rock to Boston*, 201).

87. As Mel King noted, "The term 'desegregation' seems to have disappeared from the language—the news media's persistent use of 'busing' has helped divert attention from the constitutional basis of the issue" (King, *Chain of Change*, 155).

88. Hampton, *Voices of Freedom*, 599.

89. Offner, *"Too Late for Pleading,"* 56.

90. Hillson, *Battle of Boston*, 63. "When a public school system fails children and continues to receive public tax dollars to operate, people begin to believe that the children are somehow inherently poor performers and responsible for their own failure. The attention gets shifted away from the school system's poor performance to the 'problem children'" (Chronology, 372).

91. Batson was associate professor of psychiatry at Boston University from 1970 to 1986. Concerned over the lack of preparedness within the city for the mental health and counseling needs associated with desegregation, Batson spent the better part of 1974 and 1975 agitating for these services. She ultimately succeeded in getting a National Institute of Mental Health grant to address the mental health aspects of desegregation.

92. Chronology, 378.

93. It is difficult to get an accurate sense of the attitudes of the majority of whites in Boston. While most sources agree that a majority of whites opposed

"forced busing," many whites were willing to go along with it. A *Boston Globe* poll in April 1975 showed that 57 percent of whites disapproved of school boycotts, 63 percent disapproved of demonstrations outside the schools, and 87 percent disapproved of the use of force to stop busing (Formisano, *Boston Against Busing*, 91).

94. Hampton, *Voices of Freedom*, 601.

95. Metcalf, *From Little Rock to Boston*, 206.

96. Chronology, 382.

97. Ibid.

98. King, *Chain of Change*, 163.

99. *Bay State Banner*, October 10, 1974, 1.

100. Christine Rossell's study of the *Boston Globe* shows that the media's focus on anti-desegregation whites and desegregation-related conflicts led the public to have an overinflated sense of the costs and problems with desegregation, and thus the public was more likely to oppose it (Taylor, *Desegregation in Boston and Buffalo*, 85).

101. U.S. Commission, *Desegregating the Boston Public Schools*, 13.

102. Chronology, Addendum 415a. The U.S. Commission on Civil Rights had also recommended receivership. U.S. Commission, *Desegregating the Boston Public Schools*, 63.

103. Hillson, *Battle of Boston*, 5–6.

104. Once blacks were elected to the School Committee, the procedure changed to having members appointed.

105. Desegregation, according to Emmett Buell's 1982 study of Boston, "virtually eliminated the less than 1 percent [of black] and 75 percent or more black enrollments so common before busing. Moreover, despite dwindling white enrollments, his [Garrity's] programs have drastically reduced racial isolation in the Boston schools—for the time being." Buell also listed, as gains from the decision, building renovations, greater black and Latino parental involvement in schools, and better and more merit-based teacher recruitment. The case also succeeded in introducing bilingual education and special education in Boston Public Schools on a widespread level. Finally, there were definite gains in black school performance initially following desegregation.

106. Batson, phone interview.

107. U.S. Commission, *Desegregating the Boston Public Schools*, v.

108. Chronology, 439.

Chapter 2

"Drive Awhile for Freedom"

Brooklyn CORE's 1964 Stall-In and Public Discourses on Protest Violence

Brian Purnell

Unfortunately, too often our standards for evaluating social movements pivot around whether or not they "succeed" in realizing their visions rather than on the merits
or power of the visions themselves. By such a measure,
virtually every radical movement failed because the basic
power relations they sought to change remain pretty
much intact. And yet it is precisely these alternative visions and dreams that inspire new generations to continue to struggle for change.
—Robin D. G. Kelley, *Freedom Dreams,* 2002

During the twenty years after World War II, some of the country's most
significant campaigns to end racial discrimination in housing, education
and employment; to stop police brutality against black citizens; and to improve the environmental conditions of poor, mostly black and Puerto
Rican neighborhoods took place in New York City.[1] In the late 1940s the
city's Black Popular Front brought together many different organizations
and activists—labor unions, religious institutions, fraternal organizations,
women's groups, Democratic and third-party politicians, Communists,
Socialists, and others—and pushed an antiracist agenda into mainstream
municipal and state policy debates. The Black Popular Front dissolved

under the tremendous pressures of anticommunism, which branded any call for social or economic justice as support for the Soviet Union. However, antiracist activists shaped social movements against racial segregation and inequality during the postwar era with a searing critique of America's claim to spread democracy around the world while its citizens of color lived in poverty and terror from the threat of police officers and violent mobs. Northern, urban communities, especially those in New York City, were at the forefront of this movement and achieved some of the most important legislative victories against racial discrimination before the 1960s.[2]

Despite what New York City has meant to the postwar Black Freedom Movement, very few historians engage the ways in which its local antiracist activists, particularly in Brooklyn, developed a protest movement that affected other activist communities throughout the country or the ways that its local people influenced the national discourse on civil rights during the 1960s. In 1964 the Brooklyn chapter of the Congress of Racial Equality (CORE) planned a protest tactic it called the "stall-in" for the opening day of the 1964–65 World's Fair. The action would bring attention to a broad range of issues by stalling cars and blocking subways on all major routes leading to the Fair. Using "street theater" to dramatize protestors' calls for social change was rare in 1964. In the late 1960s and 1970s groups like the Young Lords and the Black Panther Party made what historian Johanna Fernandez calls "urban guerrilla actions" a more common tactic; yet, with the stall-in, Brooklyn CORE was ahead of its time and helped to spur other groups toward this type of action.[3]

The aftermath of the stall-in—a demonstration that in some ways never actually occurred—reverberated throughout the country at a level achieved by few other protests of the civil rights movement. Brooklyn CORE sparked national debate over acceptable methods of protest. National CORE leadership officially censured and temporarily suspended the Brooklyn chapter. The stall-in inspired copycat protests by other local activists. Even more, it generated a citywide panic that reflected citizens' and politicians' fears and fantasies of protest groups that used tactics—like the creation of a massive traffic jam—to subvert the everyday normalcy of modern urban life in the fight to end racial discrimination. Brooklyn CORE's stall-in demonstrates the ways that local protest movements have national effects and how they potentially influence larger discourses on what constitutes acceptable forms of public challenges to status quo power relations.

During this period, popular opinion limited acceptable forms of protest to seemingly "nonviolent" acts of civil disobedience that targeted institutions that overtly practiced racial segregation. The stall-in reveals ways in which politicians, citizens, and editorialists characterized demonstrations that challenged systemic patterns of institutional racism throughout society as "violent" and "irresponsible." Nonviolent acts, such as the stall-in, which raised fundamental questions about the ways that racism shaped every inch of social life in America, were labeled as violent, unacceptable forms of protest. Its participants became known as directionless fanatics bent on destroying peaceful existence in the city. These were the tactics opponents used to evade and ignore the issues raised by the stall-in.

For the most part historians have taken this interpretation of the stall-in as gospel.[4] They write about it as a failure, an example of the "crisis of victory," that affected direct-action protest organizations like CORE in the mid-1960s. This argument claims that nonviolent direct action protest was successful when it targeted segregated public accommodations like lunch counters, water fountains, and bathroom facilities. According to historian Craig Turnbull, one of the few scholars to analyze the stall-in, "complex forms of racial discrimination in employment, housing, and schools proved to be less vulnerable when subjected to this approach. . . . CORE's use of direct action tactics in pursuit of these objectives enjoyed less legitimacy amongst previously sympathetic supporters, and produced unpopular 'symbolic' protests that were removed from the location of the discrimination they sought to eradicate."[5] This "crisis of victory" argument fails to consider the ways in which local protest organizations created tactics and demonstrations that successfully tapped oppressed people's frustrations and desires for political and social change. Turnbull does not examine why "previously sympathetic supporters" reacted negatively to demonstrations like the stall-in and ignored its attack on the entire system of racial discrimination. Nor does the "crisis of victory" theory consider ways that seemingly unsuccessful demonstrations attracted new followers to social movements and affected protest tactics in other parts of the country (or world).

Manhattan Institute Senior Fellow Tamar Jacoby also follows this path with her analysis of the stall-in. She writes that, "the anticipated stall-in on the city's roadways fizzled. . . . The expected twenty-five hundred cars did not appear, and those that did were vastly outnumbered by policemen and police towtrucks." Her account is so driven by a quest for finding the failures of integration, which she considers "the great achievement of the civil rights era—the hopeful consensus . . . of a single, shared community," that Jacoby fails to consider the seemingly indomitable social and political structures that made and continue to make "integration" so difficult to achieve.[6] The vision of the stall-in was less about Jacoby's ideal of "integration" and more about creating a truly free society by ending all forms of racism, which debates between activists and intellectuals have proven are not necessarily synonymous goals. Few historians grapple with this, nor with how the stall-in succeeded in demonstrating the power of ordinary people to influence and alter business as usual by merely threatening to shut down the city. It is the "alternative visions and dreams" of protest movements, as Robin Kelley writes, and the women and men who articulated them, that should be our main focus when we analyze social movements and demonstrations like the stall-in.[7]

Thus the stall-in invites historians to reexamine conventional notions of successful social movements. By the spring of 1964 New York City's antiracist activist communities had sustained more than four years of continuous protest activity. Some local activists decided to plan a dramatic protest on the opening day of the World's Fair, Wednesday, April 22, 1964. Media accounts and critics of the stall-in conjured images of unmitigated chaos and, through a public discourse of protest violence, turned an inherently nonviolent demonstration of civil disobedience into a violent, criminal, immature, and retrogressive act. What frightened people and produced such a strong reactionary response was not the actual protest but the imagined violence caused by the subversion of everyday normalcy. This subversion also constituted the power behind acts of civil disobedience, which is why the stall-in captured the imagination of activists throughout the country, including many who rallied to defend and support Brooklyn CORE and some who even reproduced the stall-in tactic in their own local movements.

By the spring of 1964 minimal advancements from previous campaigns led activists in Brooklyn CORE to plan a disruption on the opening day of the World's Fair. The 1964–65 World's Fair, which was being held in Flushing Meadows Park, Queens, was one of New York City's largest public works projects in the twentieth century. Its master builder, Parks Commissioner Robert Moses, received more than $1 billion to finance the redevelopment of Flushing Meadows, a one-time notorious dumping ground for Brooklyn's garbage, into a new "Central Park" for the city, which was rapidly expanding east into the suburbs of Queens and Nassau counties.[8] Planners for the event projected that it would attract around seventy million visitors on the first day.[9] A caption in the *New York World-Telegram and Sun* summarizes what the Fair meant in the imaginations of most New Yorkers:

It's an epic event for the city and for guests from all over the world. Sixteen million residents of the metropolitan area, with an unofficial but deep-seated interest in the exposition, invite fellow countrymen and people of other lands to this fair of fairs. To a large degree it was New Yorkers who planned and designed when there was nothing but an open field and untouched blueprint paper. Then other New Yorkers built the shining towers, the architecturally exciting buildings and the exhibits. Now it is done and all New York says—"Welcome!"[10]

Clearly "all New York" was not welcomed. Planners of the Fair knew that extending subway lines to Flushing Meadows would be necessary to attract the city's poorer families who did not own cars. However, as noted by Robert Caro, Robert Moses's biographer, the park that Moses envisioned would remain after the Fair closed was not designed for low-income people, "particularly the Negro and Puerto Rican people who made up so large a percentage of the city's lower-income families. So Moses vetoed the Transit Authority's proposed new subway extensions to the Fair."[11]

The plan for the traffic-snarling stall-in was to have participants' cars run out of gas and block traffic on major roadways leading to the park. Other demonstrators would lie down in front of subway cars and buses, effectively shutting down all means of travel to the Fair. One motivation for the stall-in was to create a large enough traffic jam so that women and men trapped on highways that ran through some of New York City's most impoverished areas would be forced to observe, up close, the effects of institutional racism on New York City's black and Puerto Rican citizens. Stall-in organizers believed that such an experience would prevent people from continuing to ignore the plight of the urban poor. As Oliver Leeds, a member of Brooklyn CORE, told reporters at a press conference, "Our objective is to have our own civil rights exhibit at the World's Fair. We do not see why people should enjoy themselves when Negroes are suffering all over the country."[12]

The stall-in expanded Brooklyn CORE's attack on American racism. Whereas in the past its members focused entirely on local problems of housing, employment, and schools, with the stall-in they articulated a protest that would target racism throughout the entire city and, on a symbolic level, the entire country. Women and men in Brooklyn CORE arrived at the ideas behind the stall-in after years of consistent local-level protest in the Bedford-Stuyvesant section of Brooklyn and throughout the city. Oliver Leeds, his wife Marjorie, and Rioghan Kirchner were three of the earliest members of Brooklyn CORE. Oliver Leeds, a leader in Brooklyn CORE since its beginnings in 1960, had seen the local movement reach a point where a tactic like the stall-in seemed viable and necessary.[13] In its early months, Brooklyn CORE was not very active in local protests. Marjorie Leeds was one of Brooklyn CORE's first members; she encouraged her husband to join when she saw that the current leadership, under the chairmanship of a man named Dr. Robert Palmer, was not interested in an active chapter. Mr. Leeds remembers that Dr. Palmer "was an NAACP type," which meant that "he didn't mind negotiating but he certainly looked at direct action with a jaundiced eye."[14] Rioghan Kirchner joined Brooklyn CORE shortly after it formed under Dr. Palmer's leadership. An émigré from England who had recently moved from Montreal to Brooklyn, Kirchner became a "white tester," whose job it was to expose discriminatory practices of landlords and housing realtors who refused to rent apartments or homes to African Americans. She remembers Dr. Palmer as a "charming man. He had a lot of great schemes, but it was always someone else had to do it. When we had a march or a sit-in, he wasn't there. After a while it began to sink into us that this guy was not a real leader. Unfortunately, when it came to the nitty-gritty, he led from behind."[15] This aversion to direct action protest was probably one of the reasons Brooklyn CORE failed to attract more people to its ranks early on, especially from the working-class African American community; another may have been its seemingly middle-class social events. Some of the first social activities the group sponsored in order to attract members were a "cocktail sip, X-Mass party, debutant ball and a spring dance."[16]

By 1964 Brooklyn CORE had developed considerably since the days of Dr. Palmer's leadership in early 1960. The stall-in represented a culmination of its involvement in Brooklyn's black community, its familiarity with the ways that local black people encountered day-to-day racism, and its use of the media as a tool of social protest. The chapter's first major protest campaign was against Woolworth stores to show support for the black student-led sit-ins, which spread throughout the South in February and March 1960.[17] These types of public demonstrations (probably unlike the cocktail sip and debutant ball) attracted local, working-class black folks to the ranks of Brooklyn CORE. The chapter's first action was a picket line in front of the store at 408 Fulton Street in Bedford-Stuyvesant. Msemaji Weusi remembered that those demonstrations inspired him and his wife, Nandi Weusi, to join the local group.[18]

> I was just impressed by how these young people were very disciplined, he recalled. They were very forceful. They were very articulate. They had a line going and they were voicing their concerns against the hiring policy of the store. This was an all black area and at that time you found very few blacks that even worked at those stores, let alone ownership of those stores. I was impressed by their militancy. I was impressed by their demeanor. They were clean. They were neat. They were forceful in what they had to say. We were just attracted by this, so we walked with them because some of them invited us. At the end of the demonstration we spoke to the fella that was in charge. His name was Oliver Leeds. We asked questions and he and his wife told us when they (CORE) met and where. We went to the next meeting.[19]

The Weusis exemplify the staunch members of Brooklyn CORE. Although neither served as a chairperson of a committee or held any "official" leadership title, they led through their commitment to the chapter's activities and the local Black Freedom movement, regularly attending CORE meetings, hosting fund-raising parties in their home, and participating in as many demonstrations as their jobs and family obligations would allow. As Msemaji states, "we weren't leaders. We were foot soldiers for freedom!"[20]

It was the countless "foot soldiers" like Nandi and Msemaji, many of them still unrecognized in the historical record, whose commitment and courage gave life and meaning to the Black Freedom movement. The stall-in emerged from these people's frustrations with the gradual gains of previous protest campaigns. Historians of the Black Freedom movement cannot forget that it was "local people," as John Dittmer has called them, who comprised the picket lines, sometimes risked their jobs to spend time in prison, and often saw the movement as a direct extension of their everyday lives. Oliver Leeds described how members of the Bedford-Stuyvesant community were more important to the local movement and the Brooklyn chapter than were national civil rights leaders, even those in CORE.

> For the eight or nine years [my wife and I] were involved with CORE, the only problems we ever had were at the top levels of CORE. They had very little to do with or were involved with the activities of the chapters, at least

in what we used to call the ghetto areas. They were obviously in control of college chapters of CORE, but the community chapters were more or less run by people like myself and local citizens.[21]

These local citizens were parents like Jerome and Elaine Bibuld, an interracial couple that became active members of Brooklyn CORE and participated in protests for better public education because they wanted more opportunities for their children. Some whites that joined Brooklyn CORE, like Arnold Goldwag, were young college students, fighting a paradoxical American political ideology that claimed to be democratic and free even as it allowed racial discrimination to thrive in domestic policies. Interracial couples like the Bibulds, Oliver and Marjorie Leeds, and Paul and Rita Heinegg probably became involved in Brooklyn CORE specifically because of its philosophy of interracial organizing. Others, black and white, may have joined the movement in the 1960s because of their personal history as antiracist activists in leftist organizations, especially the Communist Party of the United States of America (CPUSA), during the 1930s. After the purges of McCarthyism, many leftists dropped off the activist radar, but some resurfaced in community organizations like Brooklyn CORE.

"Local people" and their myriad motivations for participating in antiracist activism determined (and continue to shape) the direction of the Black Freedom movement with tactics like the stall-in. The protest politics they articulated and the movements they formed were direct reflections of their everyday experiences, personal contradictions, political ideologies, and dreams and desires for more free and just societies. Governmental decrees and national leadership do affect social movements, but prominent leaders and politicians are often temporary visitors to the communities and neighborhoods that experience the day-to-day struggles against oppression. Legislation often exists only on paper until people fight to ensure that the laws have real meaning in their lives. Indeed, we can only fully comprehend the historical significance of social movements if we study them in such a way as to highlight the relationships between local and national (and international) influences: how people shaped social movement cultures and politics from their own everyday experiences and concerns; how spokespersons and politicians of national movement organizations were sometimes in accord with the concerns of local people and sometimes at odds; and how local movements shape and are shaped by national and international influences like the passing of new laws or the politics of war.[22]

· · ·

The stall-in would bring together all the issues on the agenda of the Northern, urban, antiracist movement—namely, unemployment, racist hiring practices in unions, overcrowded and underfunded schools, housing discrimination, and urban decay. In a telegram addressed to Robert F. Wagner, mayor of New York City, and the governor, Nelson Rockefeller, the planners of the stall-in articulated their reasons for such a demonstration.

> For many years you have given lip service to the just demands of Black people of this city for equal jobs, decent housing, first class education and the right to live in peace and dignity—and for just as long, you and your agency heads, have done everything in your power to thwart these demands. . . . You have disregarded the rampant discrimination in the building trades, the brewery industry and even in your own office. You have acquiesced in the jailing of civil rights demonstrators, but have never seen fit to imprison or indict those who discriminate.
>
> The people of this community are fed up with empty promises and pious pronouncements. Unless you formulate and begin to implement a comprehensive program, by April 20th, which will end police brutality, abolish slum housing and provide integrated quality education for all—we will fully support and help organize a community backed plan to immobilize all traffic leading to the World's Fair on opening day Wednesday, April 22nd. [23]

The idea for a stall-in grew from past demonstrations in which Brooklyn CORE and other local activists created disruptions that disabled targeted institutions or sites from conducting business as usual. Probably the most famous and effective campaign was against the Ebinger bakery stores in Brooklyn, New York.[24] Protesting the company's racially discriminatory hiring practices, seven Brooklyn CORE members were arrested for blocking delivery trucks at the Ebinger company garage. While Brooklyn CORE was proud that its efforts won thirteen jobs for local black women and men, national CORE leaders were in conflict over the use of tactics that disrupted and disturbed public space. National CORE director James Farmer openly disapproved of such tactics, but at the same time other national leaders contemplated their usefulness in the urban North. Members of CORE's field staff thought "more controversial techniques will have to be adopted as the problems become more subtle, i.e., housing and employment. . . . People might have to resort to more shocking methods of protesting."[25] The types of protest tactics that national CORE officials pondered and of which Farmer disapproved were the very tactics that Brooklyn CORE cultivated in its movement culture and public persona.

As successful as the Ebinger campaign was in forcing an intransigent institution to reverse its practices of racial discrimination, thirteen jobs were rather small in number. Other campaigns achieved few tangible results and mostly ended in paper victories: changes in policies with little actual progress in the number of jobs created. Protests from the summer of 1963 illustrate Brooklyn activists' frustrations with token advancements. Little, besides negotiations and promises for change, resulted from activists' picket lines and demonstrations of nonviolent civil disobedience at many sites around the city.[26] The biggest letdown was the six-week demonstration at the construction site of the Downstate Medical Center in Brooklyn. Protestors, led by Brooklyn CORE and local black church leaders, demanded that 25 percent of the site's construction workers be black and Puerto Rican because the $25 million project was in the middle of a predominantly black residential area and yet had practically no black workers on the job.[27] After weeks of picketing and several hundred arrests related to civil disobedience, the governor agreed to negotiate with the ministers. Municipal and union officials made lists with the names of local blacks seeking employment at the site. Gilbert Banks, an experienced heavy equipment operator and diesel mechanic, participated in the demonstrations at Downstate Medical with Brooklyn CORE and was arrested for disorderly conduct.[28] Banks remembers:

> We had qualified people in the community and [city and union officials] got a construction team to review the 2000 names who applied for these jobs. There were 600 who were fully qualified who could do anything they wanted: electrician, plumbers, carpenters, steamfitters, all that stuff. And the deputy mayor got this committee together to find out if we were capable for doing this work and two years later, nobody was hired. So we had struggled in vain.[29]

Ollie Leeds was conflicted over the results of the Downstate campaign: "It was my judgment that while the accord was less than satisfactory, it was nevertheless, a good beginning. However, neither the membership of CORE nor [other participants] felt this way." Brooklyn CORE viewed the outcome as "a simple reaffirmation of a promise to enforce state laws against discrimination."[30]

The Downstate campaign was a precursor to the stall-in because it foreshadowed Brooklyn CORE's increasingly uncompromising stance toward campaigns that resulted in gradual, token advancements, and it signaled that Brooklyn CORE was becoming averse to negotiating with government and union politicians who had no interest in disrupting the status quo. Also, protest violence intensified during the summer of 1963 as increased police presence at demonstrations like Downstate resulted in numerous physical altercations between cops and protestors. The likelihood of violence affected participants' ideas about what their demonstrations meant, and it shaped the ways in which mainstream media reported protest activity, which invariably influenced public opinion on the movement as a whole. Speaking on the upcoming protest at Downstate, Reverend Gardner Taylor, one of the minister organizers, declared that "Revolution has come to Brooklyn . . . whatever the cost, we will set the nation straight (and) if the ruling white power structure brings it about, our blood will fill the streets."[31] These changes in protest discourse and increased media attention greatly affected mainstream support for the future campaigns of Brooklyn CORE like the 1964 stall-in.

These previous campaigns created a strategic impasse for Brooklyn's activists. Protests that brought the city's power structures to the bargaining table did not create substantial numbers of jobs, improve predominantly black and Puerto Rican schools, or ameliorate quality-of-life conditions in the ghettos of New York City. Thus Brooklyn CORE was preparing to use the 1964–65 World's Fair to expose the city's racist treatment of its black and Puerto Rican citizens. One of the first mentions of the stall-in in local newspapers was an article in the *New York Journal-American* that covered a speech made by Louis E. Lomax, the renowned African American journalist and author. In July 1963 Lomax, during a lecture at Queens College, insinuated that a "stall-in" might disrupt the forthcoming World's Fair. He told an audience of 1,000, "imagine the confusion which might result if 500 people get in their cars, drive towards the Fair grounds, and run out of gas."[32] The next day a *New York Journal-American* editorial denounced the proposed stall-in as "going too far." The paper's editors believed that "stalling hundreds of autos on crowded highways is not peaceful assembly. It is a clear threat to law and order which must be prevented. . . . What [these activists] are proposing would only harm their cause by alienating the innocent citizens who would suffer untold hardship."[33]

Later editorials that appeared closer to the date of the stall-in echoed this belief that the demonstration was inherently violent and the work of a mischievous group. The *New York Journal-American* asked, "How irresponsible can some civil rights leaders get? The answer is: very. As reflected in the threat of the Brooklyn chapter of CORE to paralyze every highway to the World's Fair . . . A spokesman for national CORE repudiates the plan as 'extremely childish and silly.'"[34] The *New York Post* ruminated on essential characteristics of a proper and productive demonstration:

> It is axiomatic that any effective civil rights demonstration must have both tangible and symbolic meaning plainly intelligible to the unaware bystander. Otherwise it merely serves to crystallize hostility without mobilizing any body of sympathy. It becomes an exercise in futility, or worse. [. . .] The projected traffic tie-up can win few converts to the civil rights banner. It will provide new ammunition for the racists—here and in Washington and in many other cities. It will create dangers as well as harassment for many innocent citizens who are not adversaries of the Freedom movement. It will leave a residue of rancor and confusion. It will in short be a form of sound and fury, carrying no clear message to most of the populace.[35]

Radio station WMCA acknowledged that "not enough progress has been made" in the struggle for Black Freedom, and claimed it "would favor any plan that would help to wipe out bias in any part of our city and nation. But we have to oppose the plan . . . to create a mammoth traffic jam on highways leading to the World's Fair. . . . The proposed 'stall-in' would only cause an irksome, and possibly dangerous, disorder on the highways without making any civil rights advances."[36] WLIB, "Harlem Radio Center," commented that "most demonstrations for civil rights have been carried out with dignity and singleness of purpose. The March on Washington last August 28th was, of course, the greatest. It was distinguished by thoughtful planning that focused clearly on the struggle for human rights." Knowing that in some ways the March on Washington was more reflective of the movement's national leadership and not its rank and file, WLIB went on to say that "there have been other demonstrations for equality, well planned and executed. Noteworthy was the recent March on Albany which gave citizens at the grass-roots level an opportunity to be seen and heard by their legislators." They then went on to lambaste Brooklyn CORE:

We believe that the traffic stall-in proposed to block arteries to the World's Fair on opening day Wednesday could have disastrous, even tragic, consequences.

We doubt seriously that the Brooklyn chapter of the Congress of Racial Equality, in announcing this move, considered all the ramifications. For example, did Brooklyn CORE consider that the ordinary citizen, white or Negro, has the right to travel to the fair free of any harassment?

Did Brooklyn CORE consider that on March 3rd just one car stalled on the East River drive and caused a 34–car collision?

In other words, what is Brooklyn CORE's purpose? Is tying up traffic on expressways with possible loss of life and limbs to innocent persons calculated to improve race relations in this city? We think not.[37]

At the same time the idea of a stall-in foreshadowed what would become a radical shift in the nonviolent tactics that activists used in New York City's Black Freedom movement. Frustrated by the ineffectiveness of gradualist protest techniques to effect meaningful change, CORE stall-in organizers planned to disregard national CORE's rules for direct action protest.[38] They abandoned the prolonged investigations and negotiations that national CORE believed must precede nonviolent direct action. With the stall-in Brooklyn CORE attempted to circumvent municipal reform mechanisms and effect change on their own terms.[39] Organizers wanted "the Mayor and City Council [to] take immediate action to right the wrongs that have been perpetrated upon Negro and Puerto Rican people for so long as a result of the apathy and callousness of the city of New York."[40] While the national civil rights movement, particularly in the South, concentrated on securing black voting rights and eradicating racism via participatory democracy, local activists in New York determined that staging an act of civil disobedience that affected the entire city was the only way to transform a power structure that disadvantaged black and Puerto Rican citizens. New forms of activism were needed to end the cycle of conciliatory tokenism that failed to change permanently racist imbalances. Such a shift in tactics created openings for critics to label this confrontational but nonviolent approach as being violent. The stall-in also attracted support from other frustrated individuals and activist communities.

A press release to the officials of New York City and the general public from the Bronx and Brooklyn chapters of CORE summarized local frustration and ushered in a more antagonistic approach to fighting racist power structures. "More severe direct action methods" were needed to bring attention to the city's inferior, segregated schools and inadequate housing in black and Puerto Rican neighborhoods. The press release continued to demand that,

> The officials of this city must also realize that they can no longer let citizens be subjugated to beatings by "criminals" who hide behind a badge—not if there is to be any peace in this city. *There will be no peace or rest* until every child is afforded an opportunity to obtain high-quality education, and until significant changes are made in all areas mentioned. The World's Fair cannot be permitted to operate without protests from those who are angered by conditions which have been permitted to exist for so long—conditions which deny millions of Americans rights guaranteed them by the Constitution of the United States. We want all our freedom!!! We want it here!!! We want it Now!!![41]

This philosophy also attracted younger, more militant neighborhood activists to the movement. Sonny Carson, who went on to become a major figure in Brooklyn's Black Nationalist politics and was a spokesperson for the community control movement that surrounded the Ocean Hill–Brownsville school protests of 1967–68, first became involved in organized protest with Brooklyn CORE. A small-time hustler on the streets of Bedford-Stuyvesant, Carson was a member of a local gang called "The Bishops" and, at one point, was sent to a juvenile detention institution for robbing a Western Union messenger. Enamored with Malcolm X in the early 1960s, Carson was looking to join a militant black organization and decided against the Nation of Islam after Malcolm X left the group. He joined Brooklyn CORE because, as he remembers, "Brooklyn CORE was in the papers more than anybody else. They were doing things that I thought were more suitable for the liberation of our people."[42] What most attracted Carson was Brooklyn CORE's unorthodox, confrontational style, its demonstration tactics, and its willingness to challenge seemingly "acceptable" practices of protest behavior.

> [Brooklyn CORE's] sit-ins weren't all together nonviolent. [Nonviolence] prevented me from joining many groups because I just didn't believe in the nonviolent concept. And at some of the Congress of Racial Equality's sit-ins or programs that were challenged by the white folks, it became confrontational, and some of them fought back. And that caused me to look

longer at them then to look at some of the others like the NAACP and all those organizations that were talking about—when he hits you, don't hit him back—because I'm not one of those kinds of people because when he hits me I'm *going* to hit him back. So the only group that I'd seen that could stand the way I felt, more so than anybody else, was CORE. And I meant Brooklyn CORE, because there were some CORE chapters that I didn't want anything to do with because of their leadership. But I think Brooklyn CORE was more suitable and appropriate for me at that moment. And as I began to get more involved, the more I got involved, the more I began to see that there was room for new thought, a newer thinking, to be introduced to those present folks who were caught up with we shall overcome, but nobody was hearing what Malcolm was saying and that was, "By any means necessary," and sometimes you have to think about not doing so much singing and sometimes doing some swinging. And I just felt more in tuned with the swinging back concept.[43]

This shift in tactics would also appear in later localized community struggles that disavowed "integration" as the mantra for equality, most notably in the Ocean Hill–Brownsville school battles of 1968, and the creation of an African Nationalist community cultural center in 1969 in Bedford-Stuyvesant called "The East."[44]

The premise of the stall-in was simple: cars would jam all major highways leading to the World's Fair on its opening day, April 22, 1964. Leaflets encouraged people to "drive awhile for freedom" and "take only enough gas to get your car on EXHIBIT." While the World's Fair showcased the country's technological and social progress, the stall-in would exhibit the power of the grassroots to draw attention to the government's negligence regarding urban poverty and racism. The demands of the protesters were listed on flyers that organizers handed out on street corners throughout New York City: "We want jobs now, integrated quality education, [and an] end [to] slum housing."[45] Ed Miller was one of CORE's volunteers that distributed flyers around Bedford-Stuyvesant. A white high school student who volunteered in numerous Brooklyn CORE projects, Miller was born in Bedford-Stuyvesant, and his family later moved around the New York City Housing Authority low-income projects in the Brownsville section of Brooklyn. Miller also joined CORE after seeing the organization's picket lines at the local Woolworth stores in Bedford-Stuyvesant. During the buildup for the stall-in, Miller remembers that the media attention excited many people in the community and brought, "lots of unsolicited phone calls and drop-ins from people who simply liked the idea and wanted to be part of the stall-in. I did a lot of the mimeographing and sign painting, lots of putting up posters and distributing leaflets along Nostrand Avenue and at the Subway stations and distributed a lot of leaflets at the Projects where I lived."[46]

Brooklyn CORE's stall-in generated an enormous response on both local and national levels, much of it shaped by the dominant discourse of the national movement. As Congress debated civil rights legislation, and national organizations such as CORE and the Student Nonviolent Coordinating Committee (SNCC) prepared to intensify the voter registration movement in the Deep South with a campaign called "Freedom Summer," Brooklyn CORE's stall-in appeared as a radical anomaly that threatened to hurt the Black Freedom movement.

A letter from Mary R. MacArthur, a white resident of Glen Ridge, New Jersey, and a self-defined "active participant in the Civil Rights movement," warned of the repercussions that the stall-in would have on the national struggle for Black Freedom:

> I feel very strongly that the recent actions of the Brooklyn chapter of CORE may set the civil rights movement back from 2 to 4 years . . . there are certainly hundreds of thousands of people who believe as I do . . . and among them may be MANY workers in this struggle whose support you may lose if you continue along this path.[47]

John Keating from Yonkers, New York, echoed these sentiments. He wrote Isaiah Brunson, the chairperson of Brooklyn CORE after Ollie Leeds:

> I am a white man. I was all for the Civil Rights Bill to help the colored people. I don't like the violence that's being used now such as the Stall-In. If I had to vote now, I would vote against it. It shows by the actions of your people they are not ready for us to accept them as equal. P.S. I shall write to Washington hoping to stall the Civil Rights Bill now.[48]

Black citizens also encouraged Brooklyn CORE to rethink their plans for the "Stall-In." Myra Zuckerman, whose daughter died en route to a hospital because of traffic tie-ups, wrote:

> After hearing your threats to stall cars on roads . . . I can only feel shock and fear. I am a Negro myself, and I know and understand what you're

fighting for . . . These demonstrations you proposed can only cause other Americans to call and think us unpatriotic and unfit for the rights of citizens. . . . Many times the end justifies the means but in this case the means will only bring the Negro further from his goal.[49]

Other letters reflected more violent and racist opposition to the stall-in. An unsigned letter to the Brooklyn CORE office told Arnold Goldwag, the chapter's community relations director, "it is Communist kikes such as you that cause the hatred by so many for law abiding Jewish people. Watch out!"[50] Margaret V. Martyn, the chair of White Teachers of American Inc., wrote: "Why you miserable black sonofabitch! How dare you threaten the Worlds Fair and the Christian White Power structure of this City? You nigger bastards belong in Africa not here among genteel white Christian folk! We hope the police break your black ape heads on Wednesday! So drop dead!"[51]

Letters to local papers were equally reactionary. Jerry H. Gumpert wrote to the *Post* that "close to half a million people from all corners of the globe are expected to witness the opening of the New York World's Fair and a group of fanatics plan to shame us all with their stall-in."[52] "A. White" wrote to the *Daily News*: "To the Negro voices who write 'We shall overcome,' all I can say is that you might have a very long wait, like maybe another 100 years. These current animalistic tactics will only set you big bunch of idiots back about that much."[53] L. W. from Queens pleaded with the *New York World-Telegram and Sun* that "it is time for your newspaper to cease giving so much space to the little dictators of the Brooklyn CORE. Having magnified their position by the continuous limelight you give them, it is difficult for them to back down without losing 'face.'"[54] However, Charles T. Jackson from Woodmere, New York, wrote to the *New York Herald-Tribune and Sun* and voiced a need for cooperation from both protesters and government officials. He also foreshadowed the repercussions that would result if politicians failed to make good on their promises to ameliorate conditions afflicting a majority of the city's poor black and Puerto Rican citizens. "For Brooklyn CORE the moral would seem that the wisest course is negotiation spurred by non-violent demonstrations relevant to specific grievances. The authorities must see that the need for sympathetic negotiations followed by effective action is urgent—before frustration does lead to such attacks as are now just beginning to be advocated."[55]

From editorials and letters we can discern a public discourse on protest violence that demonizes stall-in supporters and marginalizes any of their legitimate critiques of racist policies and demands for political change. Social movement theorist Donatella della Porta, borrowing from the work of sociologists David Snow and Pamela Oliver, defines a public discourse as "an *interactive* process: movements, parties, media, governments and state apparatuses (including the police) engage in a . . . struggle to have certain meanings and understanding gain ascendance over others, or at least move up some existing hierarchy of credibility."[56] During the postwar Black Freedom movement, a national public discourse, which supported nonviolent civil disobedience, developed after televised images showed police and white citizens committing violent suppression of a peaceful demonstration in the South. In the context of the Cold War, the White House feared the ways these incidents would be seen around the world, especially as communist propagandists used them to expose lies behind American claims to spread freedom and democracy among former European colonies in Africa, Asia, and Latin America. Thus, at the national level, the Kennedy and later the Johnson administrations reluctantly supported the calls for protection of voter registration workers and nonviolent protests to desegregate public facilities in the South. Newspapers and television stations also shaped this public discourse with their dramatic portrayals of police dogs mauling peaceful demonstrators and fire hoses blasting nonviolent protesters to the ground. In analyzing a public discourse, della Porta cautions that we "focus not only on the reality but also on the *perception* of the reality—assuming that the latter is one of the relevant intervening variables between structure and action."[57] The dominant public discourse placed the stall-in at the lowest end of a hierarchy of acceptable protest tactics. People perceived the stall-in as being violent and its participants as being irresponsible and reckless. For many editorialists, citizens, and politicians and national civil rights leaders, these perceptions became a reality and shaped the ways that they dealt with Brooklyn CORE.

There was nothing "violent" about the idea of a stall-in. Large traffic jams are practically part of everyday life in modern megalopolises. It was not the traffic jam of the stall-in that was "violent." Rather, when compared to other protests and demonstrations of the era, the rhetoric and tactics of the stall-in were an aberration. Pictures of events in the South defined the "reality" of antiracist protest for most people in 1964 (and even still today). The movement was black school children being turned away from schools or black citizens being terrorized for attempting to eat in a diner or to vote. The meaning of the movement was (and is) probably most commonly associated with the August 1963 March on Washington and Martin Luther King's mantra, "I Have a Dream!" According to the dominant televised discourse in 1964, it was also about whites committing *real* violence against protesters. With the stall-in, Brooklyn CORE planned to affect as many people as possible because of its belief that all members of society were responsible for maintaining racist structures *and* for eventually eradicating them. Social protest advocated this idea in theory but did not often incorporate it into its public demonstrations, which were mostly limited to economic boycotts and civil disobedience that targeted specific institutions: department stores, diner lunch counters, schools, voter registration. Thus most stall-in critics felt that they were being unfairly targeted in a citywide traffic jam. To those people the World's Fair and American racism had nothing to do with each other. The idea of sitting in miles and miles of traffic "violently" intruded on most people's belief that the effort to remedy racism was someone else's problem, namely the government's.

Some of the most vocal critics of the stall-in came from moderate leaders of national civil rights organizations and from politicians, who viewed the stall-in as a threat to the movement. Roy Wilkins of the NAACP dismissed the stall-in and marginalized its organizers as "strictly Brooklynese,"[58] and James Farmer, national director of CORE, suspended the Brooklyn chapter for its plans to go through with the stall-in. In a telegram sent to Isaiah Brunson, Farmer stated, "Your chapter and all members thereof are immediately ordered to refrain from making any public statements and any news releases or taking any actions in the name of CORE."[59] In a newspaper article Farmer commented that the stall-in would "merely create confusion and thus damage the fight for freedom." The city traffic commissioner said that the stall-in would "paralyze the whole city. It would take a week to untangle the mess"; and the police commissioner commented that the stall-in "ignored the civil rights of others to work and play without interference."[60] Senators Hubert H. Humphries (Minnesota) and Thomas Kuchel (California), the floor managers for the civil rights legislation in Congress, expressed concern over the white resentment and violence that the stall-in would generate. "Violence," they said, "is the very antithesis of law and order. Illegal disturbances, demonstrations which lead to violence or to injury, strike grievous blows at the cause of decent civil rights legislation." They felt that the fight for black equality would be furthered if rights advocates conducted "their peaceful crusade with the same good manners, forbearance and devotion so abundantly displayed in last August 28th's civil rights march on Washington."[61] These critics failed to see that the message behind the stall-in was more in touch with the sufferings of a majority of the country's urban poor and that it signaled a change in how this population would fight for social equality.

Brooklyn CORE did not waver in its radical plans. In fact, members reveled in their status as a radical chapter in the seemingly conservative national CORE organization. A staunch member of Brooklyn CORE and a black army veteran, Gilbert Banks had been unable to gain employment in construction unions despite his expertise as a mechanic and heavy equipment operator. He explained that "Brooklyn CORE was a very radical CORE. National CORE didn't want us to do the World's Fair in 64 and they wanted to kick us out of National CORE and we took the blows. We don't care what you do."[62] The rogue chapter did receive support from other CORE chapters in Manhattan and the Bronx, who claimed that they would help stall cars on the highways leading to the Fair. The Camden, New Jersey, chapter of CORE sent a telegram to National CORE that "urgently requests that every effort be made . . . to settle the differences with the Brooklyn chapter so that national unity will be maintained."[63] A group called "Seattle Friends of the Student Nonviolent Coordinating Committee," declared its "heartiest support" to Brooklyn CORE, "for your plans at the World's Fair. Your courageous action is a fine example to others across the country. You do not stand alone." Indeed, in the city Brooklyn CORE did not stand alone. Some municipal labor organizations even went against city officials and supported the stall-in. John J. Delury, president of the Sanitation Men's Local 831, said that all ten thousand of his men would stay home on April 22 if they were asked to tow cars. "We're not going to scab on anyone fighting for freedom or civil rights," he said.[64]

Brooklyn CORE stayed focused on their constituents and the objective. Arnold Goldwag—a Jewish Brooklynite who, as noted earlier, joined Brooklyn CORE shortly after the chapter's rejuvenation in 1960, and was one of the last white members to leave after the group's leadership abandoned interracial organizing in 1965[65]—unequivocally reminded critics that Brooklyn CORE had an "ultimate responsibility to the people of this community who look to us for leadership and for solutions to the long-standing problem of discrimination and exploitation." Oliver Leeds emphasized the role that Brooklyn's black citizens would play in the stall-in: "It's not so much that CORE is planning (the stall-in) but that the man in the street is going to do it. From what I've heard in Bedford-Stuyvesant, neither CORE nor anyone else is going to be able to stop him. That's the beauty of this whole operation."[66] Isaiah Brunson, the young new chair-man, had moved to Brooklyn from Sumter, South Carolina, while in his early twenties. Before serving as full-time chairman, Brunson worked as an auto mechanic but quit to join CORE's national rent-strike committee in New York. He was described as an unpretentious, soft-spoken man, "who smiles easily and who appears wholly unruffled by the nation-wide storm of protest surrounding him."[67] He summarized the need for the radical nature of the stall-in in letters that responded to people who wrote to the Brooklyn office:

> As you are obviously aware, we have up until this very day used every means at our disposal to awaken the City Fathers of New York to the crying needs of their city. We have picketed, boycotted, sat-in, lied-in, etc. All of our efforts have been in vain.
>
> The time has come. The Power structure of this city, state, and country must be made to realize that we will accept palliation no longer. Empty promises, investigative committees, and such have done nothing to alleviate the problems that exist.
>
> We have, therefore, been forced into the position of using the only path left open to us. Our demands are simple. They can be instituted immedi-ately, and do not necessitate the passage of any new laws. Rather all we are actually asking is that all existing laws are enforced."[68]

Fear, along with an unseasonably chilly drizzle, dampened the mood in Flushing Meadows Park on April 22, 1964. Only 49,642 people attended the first day of the World's Fair, a number far short of the quarter million ex-pected by the World Fair's master builder Robert Moses. City officials said that the threat of the stall-in, combined with the cold weather, kept people away. Moses, according to Robert Caro, "ascribed that to over-dramatiza-tion" of the stall-in "and to chilly drizzly weather. But attendance the next day, clear and warm, was 88,130. On the first weekend there were crowds each day of 170,000. But during the following week, the fatal figures read: 45,000; 53,000; 38,000."[69] Many who attended the opening day of the World's Fair opted to take public transportation, and thus there were few cars on the roads. The one thousand patrolmen working that day probably did not see much traffic.[70] Police arrested twenty-three protesters for lying down on subway tracks at the 74th Street IRT station in Queens and delay-ing trains bound for the World's Fair. Transit Authority and city police in-flicted severe head injuries on five subway demonstrators after beating them with nightsticks. While the stall-in disrupted the opening day of the World's Fair by generating high levels of fear and anxiety, there were no paralyzing traffic jams. Gilbert Banks was reportedly the only person who disrupted traffic with a stalled car on the Fair's opening day.[71] The organizers seemed far better at publicizing this action than coordinating it.

This does not signify failure; rather, it is indicative of one of history's silent successes. According to Frances Phipps Crayton, the chapter vice chairman during the stall-in, one major reason Brooklyn CORE did not mobilize a significant number of automobiles to stall was because organizers feared that the police had infiltrated the chapter and potentially could use a list of specific names of people who volunteered to stall their cars on the highways to thwart the entire campaign. Therefore Brooklyn CORE did not organize a specific roster of participants out of fear of government retaliation against stall-in volunteers. Those who would stall their cars would do so on their own, at random, and in such a way as to have no clear connection to the planned protest. In the end few decided to stall their cars.[72]

But they really did not have to because, as numerous former Brooklyn CORE members remember, there were few cars traveling to the World's Fair, or anywhere in New York City, on the advertised day of the stall-in. The success of the stall-in cannot be quantified in the numbers of cars that were backed up on highways or of participants who tied up traffic. As far as my research reveals, answers to those questions are obscured by biased newspaper reporters, a panicked city administration, and the faulty, selective memory of Brooklyn CORE organizers. Yet the silent responses from these questions allow other markers of the stall-in's impact to speak: the pervasive assumptions of violence directed at a completely nonviolent act; the ability for community activists to choose an issue and a tactic that evoked such an emotional response from both friends and foes; the courage of a local affiliate, Brooklyn CORE, to risk ostracism from the larger, national CORE organization. These results of the stall-in, while camouflaged, reveal the ways that local activism conflicted with national agendas and yet spoke to the needs and frustrations of everyday people.

The historical significance of the stall-in lies in the grassroots organizers' refusal to work within a system which they felt gave them nothing for their efforts. As activists engaged the city's liberal reform mechanism on its own terms, real change for poor citizens of color remained an illusion. Thus Brooklyn CORE decided that it had to go outside liberalism's tactical rules of engagement. As civil rights legislation passed on the national level in June 1964, little actually changed in the streets of Bedford-Stuyvesant and Harlem. One Harlem resident remarked that the Civil Rights Bill was "still a piece of paper. Let's wait until the letter of the law is carried out."[73] Brooklyn CORE's threat to create havoc throughout the city on the opening day of the World's Fair spoke directly to these issues and signaled a new direction in the local and national struggle for Black Freedom. If the laws and liberal institutions could not improve the lives of struggling citizens, community activists would employ more antagonistic and radical measures to exert power over their lives, and thus change the direction of their freedom movement.

The stall-in captured the national imagination at a time when the Black Freedom movement was on the cusp of change. Civil rights groups and liberal politicians were making headway in their advocacy for a national civil rights law; local movements in the South, especially Mississippi, were gaining national attention as white college students volunteered to spend the summer of 1964 working in Freedom schools and participating in voter registration drives. Violence against movement workers in the South and murders in Birmingham and Philadelphia, Mississippi, also attracted newspaper and television cameras, as well as the FBI and Justice departments.

However, there is a tendency to view these local incidents as isolated pieces of the movement and not as parts of a larger, connected story. Brooklyn CORE's stall-in demonstrates how local movements have the ability to spread and inspire other activists' protest tactics and ideas about what is an effective way to bring about social change. Ivory Perry, of St. Louis CORE, responded to National CORE's request that members come to New York City and help with the picket lines that Farmer would lead outside the Fair grounds. While in New York, Perry came in contact with members of the Brooklyn chapter and learned about their stall-in. He supported the tactic, because he "felt that the life-and-death issues facing black people, and their exclusion from access to political power, justified obstructive actions like the stall-in." Eleven months after Brooklyn CORE's stall-in, Perry brought the tactic to St. Louis in order to focus attention on the recent string of violence against blacks and movement workers in Selma, Alabama. On March 15, 1965, along with Ernest Gilkey, another of St. Louis's "local people," Perry stalled a truck at one of the busiest exit ramps. His intent was to create a massive traffic tie-up that would paralyze the city.[74]

Activist comedian Dick Gregory joked about the stall-in in a 1964 stand-up performance, "So you see . . . we all have problems." He told a Midwestern audience: "I was in New York City for the stall-in. Got there early that morning, was walking through Harlem, and right next to a filling station, a cat walked up to me and said, 'Hey baby, can you loan me three pennies? I want to buy some gas. I'm driving to the World's Fair.' One cat pulled into the filling station, looked at the attendant and said, 'Empty me up!'" The crowd responded with vociferous laughter and applause. Gregory even commented on the accusations that the stall-in and other demonstrations were total failures, a position that failed to see how the stall-in effectively prevented the city and Fair organizers from profiting from discriminatory practices. "And at the Fair, you know the attendance was down so low on opening day of the Fair," Gregory said, that "they had big signs out in front of the World's Fair that said, 'Welcome picketers.'" In an interview with *Playboy*, Dick Gregory accentuated the contradictions in people's quick condemnation of the stall-in and uncritical (but often filibustering) support for legislative processes as a means of ending racism in America. To the question, "Do you feel that such extreme tactics are either wise or justified?" Gregory said, "Yes. If the duly elected senior citizens of this country, the United States Senators, can hold a stall-in in the sacred halls of Congress, a second-class citizen ought to be able to hold one on a bloody American highway."[75]

Indeed, while we can and should debate the effectiveness of the stall-in and of similar disruptive tactics in social movements that challenge the status quo of power dynamics in society, those that dismiss them outright as immature and foolhardy miss the ways that such antagonistic measures are meant to create disturbances that force *all* citizens to consider their complicity in the maintenance of structural racism. The history of the stall-in demonstrates the ways that public discourses shape "acceptable" forms of social protest, which, in effect, puts limitations on activists' abilities to illuminate disparate social conditions brought on by racism, class exploitation, gender oppression, and sexual violence. Labeling the stall-in as inherently "violent" automatically placed it outside conventional methods of direct action protest, which allowed citizens, politicians, and editorialists to ignore its call to end all forms of racial exploitation.

NOTES

1. I extend my thanks to those who co-authored this essay by sharing their ideas, friendship, and history: members of the Brooklyn CORE community, especially Gilda and Arnold Goldwag; Jeffrey T. Sammons, Mark Naison, Robin D. G. Kelley, Angela Dillard, Adam Green, Craig Steven Wilder, Martha Hodes, Erik Mc-Duffie, Orlando Plaza; special thanks to Clarence Taylor for his comments on earlier drafts and for generously sharing sources; much love and thanks to Harold, Elizabeth, and Matthew Purnell; and tremendous thanks to Jeanne Theoharis and Komozi Woodard, who are both historians, editors, and friends par excellence.

2. For a comprehensive discussion of the Black Popular Front and postwar civil rights activism, see Martha Biondi, *To Stand and Fight: The Struggle for Civil Rights in Postwar New York City* (Cambridge, Mass.: Harvard University Press, 2003). For an analysis of Cold War ideology and the civil rights movement, see Mary Dudziak, *Cold War Civil Rights: Race and the Image of American Democracy* (Princeton, N.J.: Princeton University Press, 2000).

3. Johanna Fernandez, "Between Social Service Reform and Revolutionary Politics: The Young Lords, Late Sixties Radicalism, and Community Organizing in New York City," in Jeanne Theoharis and Komozi Woodard, eds., *Freedom North: Black Freedom Struggles outside the South, 1940–1980* (New York: Palgrave Macmillan, 2003), 255–85.

4. One exception is Craig Steven Wilder in the epilogue to his expansive study of Brooklyn history, *A Covenant with Color: Race and Social Power in Brooklyn* (New York: Columbia University Press, 2000), 235–42. Wilder is the only historian to analyze the stall-in, arguing that "although many issues collided in the Fair crisis, it is worth noting that the authority of the state could be marshaled so easily and effectively to stop a protest of racial inequalities but was not available to prevent those injuries" (238).

5. Craig Turnbull, "'Please Make No Demonstrations Tomorrow': The Brooklyn Congress of Racial Equality and Symbolic Protest at the 1964–1965 World's Fair," *Australasian Journal of American Studies* (New Zealand) 17, no. 1 (1998): 22. The term "crisis of victory" comes from A. Philip Randolph's opening remarks at the Conference of Negro Leaders, New York, January 30–31, 1965. See Turnbull, "'Please Make No Demonstrations Tomorrow,'" 38 n. 3; and August Meier and Elliot Rudwick, *CORE: A Study in the Civil Rights Movement, 1942–1968* (New York: Oxford University Press, 1973), 329, 513 n. 1.

6. Tamar Jacoby, *Someone Else's House: America's Unfinished Struggle for Integration* (New York: Free Press, 1998), 3, 30.

7. Robin D. G. Kelley, *Freedom Dreams: The Black Radical Imagination* (Boston: Beacon, 2002), ix.

8. On the 1964–65 World's Fair, see Robert Caro, *The Power Broker: Robert Moses and the Fall of New York* (New York: Vintage, 1974), 1082–1116; Robert

Rosenblum et al., *Remembering the Future: The New York World's Fair from 1939–1964* (New York: Rizzoli, 1989); Bruce Nicholson, *Hi, Ho, Come to the Fair* (Huntington Beach, Calif.: Pelagian, 1989). Documentaries on the 1964 World's Fair include *New York World's Fair: Memories of 1964*, directed by Alexander Hammid and Wheaton Galentine (Orland Park, Ill.: Moviecraft, 1991); *The 1964 World's Fair: Relive the Wonder*, produced by Connecticut Public Television (Hannington Park, N.J.: Janson Video, 1996); and *The World That Moses Built*, produced by Ovenhaus Films (Alexandria, Va.: PBS Video, 1988). Thanks to Sharyn Jackson for graciously sharing her knowledge of sources on the 1964 World's Fair.

9. The *New York Journal-American* and the *New York World-Telegram and Sun*, both newspapers that gave extensive coverage to the World's Fair in the hopes of boosting its slumping sales, offered special souvenir sections that promoted the World's Fair with maps, guides, and lists of the numerous pavilions and attractions planned for the Fair. See the *New York World-Telegram and Sun*, April 20, 1964; and the *New York Journal-American*, April 22, 1964.

10. *New York World-Telegram and Sun*, April 20, 1964.

11. Robert Caro, *Power Broker*, 1087.

12. *New York Post*, April 10, 1964.

13. After more than a decade of fits and starts, CORE took hold in Brooklyn in February 1960. A copy of the chapter's application for affiliation, dated October 7, 1960, lists only nine active members, thirty-two associate members, and forty people on a mailing list. The group had committees to organize membership drives, to investigate discrimination in housing and public schools, and to coordinate youth programs and chapter socials. Dr. Robert Palmer, an African American Brooklynite, was the first chairman of Brooklyn CORE. He ran meetings from his home at 603 Eastern Parkway.

14. Clarence Taylor interview with Oliver and Marjorie Leeds, August 11, 1988 (in author's possession). The Leeds met during their participation in Communist Party–led employment drives in Harlem during the 1930s and were both involved in the Party's campaign to elect Ben Davis to the City Council in 1943. Oliver Leeds, who went by the nickname Ollie, also ran, unsuccessfully, for Congress on the American Labor Party ticket in 1955. For information on the Ben Davis campaign, see Biondi, *To Stand and Fight*, 42–47. For information on Oliver Leeds, see "Obituaries: Oliver H. Leeds, 68, Civil Rights Leader," *New York Newsday*, February 22, 1989, 35.

15. Interview with Rioghan Kirchner, September 29, 2000; interview with Mary Ellen Phifer Kirton, Elaine Bibuld, Rioghan Kirchner, and Nandi and Msemaji Weusi, April 7, 2000.

16. Congress of Racial Equality, *The Papers of the Congress of Racial Equality, 1941–1967* (microform) (Stanford, N.C.: Microfilming Corporation of American, 1980), series 1, file 1, reel 12, frames 782 and 783. Hereafter, *The Papers of the Congress of Racial Equality*, with series, file, reel, and frame numbers.

17. See Clayborne Carson, *In Struggle: SNCC and the Black Awakening of the 1960s* (Cambridge, Mass.: Harvard University Press, 1981), chap. 1.

18. During the early 1960s when the Weusis first joined Brooklyn CORE, they were known as Winnie and Maurice Fredericks. They changed their names to Nandi and Msemaji in the late 1960s, after joining a local black cultural nationalist organization called "The East." Both were born in Manhattan and courted as teenagers. After Maurice served in the navy he and Winnie moved to Brooklyn in 1950, where Maurice worked as a mail carrier in and around Bedford-Stuyvesant.

19. Interview with Mary Ellen Phifer Kirton, Elaine Bibuld, Rioghan Kirchner and Nandi and Msemaji Weusi, April 7,2000. Interview with Nandi and Msemaji Weusi, March 9, 2001.

20. Conversation with Msemaji Weusi, January 20, 2002.

21. Clarence Taylor interview with Oliver and Marjorie Leeds, August 11, 1988 (in author's possession).

22. The argument for the importance of "local people" to the history of the Black Freedom movement is made most strongly in John Dittmer's groundbreaking monograph *Local People: The Struggle for Civil Rights in Mississippi* (Chicago: University of Illinois Press, 1994). Charles M. Payne also offers an exciting historical narrative of local movement activity in Mississippi in *I've Got the Light of Freedom: The Organizing Tradition and the Mississippi Struggle* (Los Angeles: University or California Press, 1995). For more local histories of the Black Freedom movement in the South, see William H. Chafe, *Civilities and Civil Rights: Greensboro, North Carolina, and the Black Struggle for Freedom* (New York: Oxford University Press, 1980); Robert J. Norrell, *Reaping the Whirlwind: The Civil Rights Movement in Tuskegee* (New York: Knopf, 1985); and Aldon D. Morris, *The Origins of the Civil Rights Movement: Black Communities Organizing for Change* (New York: Free Press, 1984). See also, Clayborne Carson, "Civil Rights Reform and the Black Freedom Struggle"; and Steven F. Lawson, "Comment," in *The Civil Rights Movement in America,* ed. Charles Eagles, 19–37 (Jackson: University Press of Mississippi, 1986). Steven Lawson has been a longtime advocate for a synthesis history of the Black Freedom movement, one that is both local *and* national in focus. See his "Freedom Then, Freedom Now: The Historiography of the Civil Rights Movement," in *American Historical Review* 96, no. 2 (April 1991): 456–71; and Steven Lawson and Charles Payne, *Debating the Civil Rights Movement* (New York: Rowman and Littlefield, 1998). The scholarship that engages this type of analysis is growing. See Biondi, *To Stand and Fight;* Timothy Tyson, *Radio Free Dixie: Robert F. Williams and the Roots of Black Power* (Chapel Hill: University of North Carolina Press, 1999); and Komozi Woodard, *A Nation within a Nation: Amiri Baraka (LeRoi Jones) and Black Power Politics* (Chapel Hill: University of North Carolina Press, 1999). Tremendously important studies on gender and women and the Black Freedom movement are growing. See Vicki L. Crawford et al., eds., *Women in the Civil Rights Movement: Trailblazers and Torchbearers, 1941–1965* (Indianapolis:

Indiana University Press, 1990); Belinda Robnett, *How Long? How Long? African-American Women in the Struggle for Civil Rights* (New York: Oxford University Press, 1997); Bettye Collier-Thomas and V.P. Franklin, eds., *Sisters in the Struggle: African American Women in the Civil Rights–Black Power Movement* (New York: New York University Press, 2001). Barbara Ransby, *Ella Baker and the Black Freedom Movement: A Radical Democratic Vision* (Chapel Hill: University of North Carolina Press, 2003).

23. Arnold Goldwag papers, Western Union telegram to Governor Nelson Rockefeller and Robert F. Wagner, April 9, 1964 (in author's possession).

24. After several months of negotiations and organizing a boycott of the chain, which Brooklyn CORE investigated for racially discriminatory hiring practices, activists adopted a protest technique that at the time seemed radical to the leadership of National CORE. One of them was Arnold Goldwag, who later became Brooklyn CORE's community relations chairperson and was a key organizer of the stall-in. Some of the protesters went limp and had to be carried by the police, which marked the first time a CORE affiliate had used this technique since a 1953 demonstration in Cincinnati. See Meier and Rudwick, *CORE*, 193, 201–2. For information on the Brooklyn CORE campaign against Ebinger bakeries, see *Ebony* (March 1963). See also State Historical Society of Wisconsin, Congress of Racial Equality, Brooklyn Chapter (N.Y.) Records 1959–1978 (mss. 947), box 1, folder 6.

25. See Meier and Rudwick, *CORE*, 201–2.

26. June through August 1963 was one of New York City's "long hot summers" of the 1960s. Demonstrations took place at several construction projects throughout the city: the Rutgers Houses on the Lower East Side of Manhattan, Harlem Hospital, and Downstate Medical in Brooklyn. Further, a coalition of activists, which included members of Brooklyn CORE, staged several days of round-the-clock sit-ins at the offices of the mayor and governor to demand the immediate stoppage of $2.5 billion in city and state construction projects pending the hiring of more black and Puerto Rican workers. In the Bronx, Bronx CORE demonstrated against racial discrimination in hiring practices at local White Castle restaurants, which had 4 black workers out of 126 employees. White youths verbally harassed protesters and pelted them with eggs and rocks. A police office described the situation as "a bomb. And it may explode any minute." On July 15 just such an explosion seemed possible as eight members of the National Renaissance Party, a neo-Nazi organization, were charged with conspiracy to incite rioting at two Bronx White Castles after police uncovered their cache of arms. See *New York Times*, July 7, 10, 11, 12, 16, 1963; *New York Amsterdam News*, July 13, 1963; and Brian Purnell, "A Movement Grows in Brooklyn" (Ph.D. dissertation, New York University, forthcoming).

27. *New York Times*, July 16, 1963.

28. Ibid., July 11, 1963

29. Author's interview with Gilbert Banks, April 1, 2000, and April 2, 2000.

30. Quoted in Clarence Taylor, "'Whatever the Cost, We Will Set the Nation Straight,'" *Long Island Historical Journal* 1, no. 2, 143.

31. *New York Times,* July 22, 1963; *Amsterdam News,* July 27, 1963; quoted in Taylor, "'Whatever the Cost,'" 140.

32. "Queens Traffic Jam Threatened in Racial Protest," *New York Journal-American,* July 11, 1963, 1.

33. Ibid., July 12, 1963.

34. Ibid., April 10, 1964.

35. *New York Post,* April 12, 1964.

36. Arnold Goldwag papers, WMCA "Radio Editorials," April 14–15, 1964 (copy in author's possession).

37. Ibid., WLIB, Editorial Point of View, "What Is the Purpose," April 18–19, 1964 (copy in author's possession).

38. Turnbull, "'Please Make No Demonstrations Tomorrow,'" 23–24.

39. Martha Biondi provides an in-depth study of the creation of liberal institutions to combat racial employment discrimination on the municipal and state levels in New York. See Biondi, *To Stand and Fight,* 17–37.

40. Arnold Goldwag papers, "Statement of Demands," n.d. (copy in author's possession).

41. Ibid., "Press Release from Bronx CORE, 1301 Boston Road, and Brooklyn CORE, 319 Nostrand Avenue, to the Officials of New York City and the General Public," April 4, 1964 (copy in author's possession).

42. Sonny Carson's observation that Brooklyn CORE "was in the papers more than anybody else" was probably reflective of the chapter's almost constant stream of high-profile local protest activities. The campaign against the Ebinger's bakery chain was covered in *Ebony* magazine (March 1963) as well as in the local press. In April 1962 Brooklyn CORE led a demonstration called "Operation Cleansweep," in which they collected garbage from the streets of Bedford-Stuyvesant, dumped it on the steps of Borough Hall, and staged a picket. That protest also garnered a lot of press, as did Elaine and Jerry Bibuld's campaign against the New York City Board of Education and Brooklyn CORE's leadership during the Downstate Medical campaign. Often these demonstrations were done in collaboration with other protest groups, like CORE chapters and local ministers. However, Brooklyn CORE's charismatic leadership and simultaneous involvement in multiple antiracist campaigns caused that organization to stand out in the press coverage. In the summer of 1963 alone, Brooklyn CORE was in the local papers for its leadership in campaigns against housing discrimination, construction union biases, and poor public schools. See Purnell, "A Movement Grows in Brooklyn," forthcoming.

43. Author's interview with Sonny Carson (in author's possession). For more on Carson, see Obituaries, *New York Times,* December 23, 2002; and *New York Amsterdam News,* January 2–8, 2003; Claire Jean Kim, *Bitter Fruit: The Politics of Black-Korean Conflict in New York City* (New Haven: Yale University Press, 2000);

and Mwlina Imiri Abubadika (Sonny Carson), *The Education of Sonny Carson* (New York: Norton, 1972). On Ocean Hill–Brownsville, see Jerald Podair, *The Strike That Changed New York: Blacks, Whites, and the Ocean Hill–Brownsville Crisis* (New Haven: Yale University Press, 2002); and Diane Ravitch, *The Great School Wars: New York City, 1805–1973: A History of the Public Schools as Battlefields for Social Change* (New York: Basic Books, 1974).

44. Very little has been written about "The East." The most detailed study to date is Kalonji Lasana Niamke's "The Legacy of 'The East': An Analysis of a Case Experience in Independent Institution and Nation(alist) Building, 1969–1986" (Master's thesis, Cornell University, 1999). Snippets of information can be found in Jim Sleeper, *The Closest of Strangers: Liberalism and the Politics of Race in New York* (New York: Norton, 1990), 210–13. For information on the grassroots movement behind the Ocean Hill–Brownsville protests, see Clarence Taylor, *Knocking at Our Own Door: Milton A. Galamison and the Struggle to Integrate New York City Schools* (New York: Columbia University Press, 1997), 176–207.

45. *The Papers of the Congress of Racial Equality,* series 1, file 1, reel 12, frames 907, 908.

46. Interview with Ed Miller (e-mail), March 3, 2001.

47. Arnold Goldwag papers, "Letter to Arnold Goldwag, April 14, 1964" (copy in author's possession).

48. Ibid., "Postcard to Isiah Brunson, April 20, 1964" (copy in author's possession).

49. Ibid., "Letter to Brooklyn CORE office, April 13, 1964" (copy in author's possession).

50. Ibid., "Letter to Arnold Goldwag, April 15, 1964" (copy in author's possession).

51. Ibid., "Letter to Brooklyn CORE office from Margaret V. Martyn, written on Board of Education of the City of New York letterhead, April 17, 1964" (copy in author's possession).

52. *New York Post,* n.d.

53. *New York Daily News,* April 26, 1964.

54. *New York World-Telegram and Sun,* April 21, 1964.

55. *New York Herald-Tribune and Sun,* April 19, 1964, 22.

56. Donatella della Porta, "Protest, Protesters, and Protest Policing: Public Discourses in Italy and Germany from the 1960s to the 1980s," in *How Social Movements Matter,* ed. Marco Giugni, Doug McAdam, and Charles Tilly, 66–95 (Minneapolis: University of Minnesota Press, 1998), quote at 69. See also David A. Snow and Pamela E. Oliver, "Social Movements and Collective Behavior: Social Psychological Dimensions and Considerations," in *Sociological Perspectives on Social Psychology,* ed. Karen Cook et al. (Boston: Allyn and Bacon, 1995), 571–99.

57. Ibid., 67.

58. *New York Times,* April 11, 1964.

59. *The Papers of the Congress of Racial Equality,* series 1, file 1, reel 12, frame 879.

60. *New York Post,* April 10, 1964.

61. *New York Herald-Tribune,* April 16, 1964.

62. Author's interview with Gilbert Banks, April 1–2, 2000.

63. *The Papers of the Congress of Racial Equality,* series 1, file 1, reel 12, frame 909.

64. *New York Times,* April 15, 1964.

65. Interview with Arnold Goldwag.

66. *New York Post,* April 10, 1964.

67. *Baltimore Afro-American,* April 25, 1964, 17.

68. Arnold Goldwag papers, "Letter from Isiah Brunson, chairman of Brooklyn CORE, to Mr. and Mrs. Thurow, 19 April 1964" (copy in author's possession).

69. Caro, *Power Broker,* 1102.

70. Craig Turnbull, "'Please Make No Demonstrations Tomorrow,'" 31.

71. *New York Journal-American,* April 22, 1964.

72. Interview with Frances Phipps Crayton, November 27, 2003. Frances Crayton, a native of North Carolina, moved to Brooklyn as a teenager and joined Brooklyn CORE after graduating high school in 1963. On police infiltration of urban protest movements, see Frank Donner, *Protectors of Privilege: Red Squads and Police Repression in Urban America* (Los Angeles: University of California Press, 1990).

73. *New York Times,* June 20, 1964.

74. George Lipsitz, *A Life in the Struggle* (Philadelphia: Temple University Press, 1995), 81–83, 87–89.

75. Dick Gregory, "So You See . . . We All Have Problems" (1964), and "Playboy Interview," in *Playboy,* August 1964. Special thanks to Justin T. Lorts for generously sharing these sources with me and hipping me to the importance of seeing comedians as powerful communicators of social movement ideologies.

A 1974 Committee for a Unified Newark (CFUN) demonstration on the right to establish a taxi drivers' union. *Photo courtesy of Komozi Woodard.*

Chapter 3

Message from the Grassroots
The Black Power Experiment in Newark, New Jersey

Komozi Woodard

> You and I want to create an organization that will give us
> so much power we can sit down and do as we please.
> Once we can sit down and think as we please, speak as
> we please, and do as we please, we will show people what
> pleases us. And what pleases us won't always please
> them. So you've got to get some power before you can be
> yourself. *Do you understand that?* You've got to get some
> power before you can be yourself. Once you get power
> and you be yourself, why, you're gone, you've got it and
> gone. You create a new society and make some heaven
> right here on this earth.
> —Malcolm X, *By Any Means Necessary,* 1970

In late 1969, in the midst of the struggles of the Black Power movement three twenty–year-old college students went to the headquarters of the controversial grassroots organization, the Committee for a Unified NewArk (CFUN), in the heart of Newark, New Jersey's Central Ward ghetto to inquire about the nature of its political program. Each of them had been in black student unions; one had been involved in Newark's Black Youth Organization; and each one knew of the Student Nonviolent Coordinating Committee (SNCC) and the Black Panther Party—but they were searching for a serious grassroots organization that addressed the tremendous problems in their own communities. One student was Eric Dillard who grew up in the Hayes Homes public housing projects in

Newark's Central Ward and was a basketball star at South Side High School as well as a martial arts expert. He had attended Southern University in Baton Rouge, Louisiana, the same college that the militant Black Power leader H. Rap Brown had attended. Leon Herron was raised in a cold-water flat on Whiton Street in the Lafayette working-class section in nearby Jersey City; he attended Lincoln University in Pennsylvania, the same college that Ghanaian President Kwame Nkrumah had attended and where Herron met his classmate Gil Scott Heron. Tim "Doc" Holiday was also from one of Jersey City's working-class neighborhoods in the Bergen-Lafayette section. Doc Holiday had attended Rutgers University in New Brunswick and the "totally bourgeois" intellectual, social, and cultural environment had turned him off. When they were sixteen years of age both Holiday and Herron had studied at Princeton University as part of the Princeton Cooperative Schools Program (PCSP), a forerunner to the Upward Bound program. At Princeton, Holiday had listened to Malcolm X's "Message to the Grassroots" speech for the first time, and it had been a life-changing experience. Since then he had been searching for answers to burning issues of identity, purpose, and direction.

At the front desk of the militant headquarters they met the leader of one of the youth divisions of CFUN, the Young Lions. At fifteen years of age the handsome Sultani Tarik was already one of the proudest symbols of the Black Cultural Revolution. Not only did Tarik boast a bold and beautiful Afro, but he also wore the uniform of the Young Lions: immaculately clean green and black military boots, black slacks, a green African shirt, and, around his neck, an elaborately hand-carved wooden "talisimu"[1] representing his cultural and spiritual connection to the mythical first African ancestor, *Nkula Nkula*.[2] Tarik explained to the students that the red-, black-, and green-colored bans on his talisimu, as well as those colors on the black nationalist flag, articulated red for the blood of their people (that was not shed in vain), black for their faces, and green for their youth and new ideas.[3] Telling the students his background, Tarik said that he had joined the Black Revolution at age twelve when the Spirit House Theater (once a Muslim Mosque) and community center opened down the block from his tenement apartment on Stirling Street in the heart of the Central Ward. The writers and actors of the Spirit House and the Black Arts movement became a second family to him. The Spirit House established not only a theater and cultural center but also the African Free School where children learned reading, history, math, and science.

Tarik had been groomed for leadership. In fact, Kaimu Sonni, a marine veteran of the Korean War in charge of training the Young Lions, provided Tarik with daily guidance and shared with him what he had learned about the arts of leadership and group discipline. Within CFUN, another elder was in charge of Tarik's martial arts training. Sultani Tarik was both fervent and articulate about the aims of the Black Power movement: self-determination, self-respect, and self-defense. He had traveled from coast to coast in the United States (and later to Guinea in West Africa), and he had met a number of the leaders of the insurgency. Tarik described what he had seen of the structure and dynamics of the Oakland Black Panther Party and the Los Angeles US Organization, and he outlined the emerging distinctions and conflicts between "revolutionary nationalism" and "cultural nationalism." The three students were in awe of this teenager who was already a "veteran" at fifteen. Tarik was not only trained in the martial arts but was also the leader of the charismatic Boot Dancers, who performed the dynamic and sensuous South African step dance at marches, demonstrations, and Black Power programs throughout the country. Sultani Tarik's political, cultural, and social development represented a deadly blow to the prevalent myths concerning culturally deprived street youth devoid of social and educational potential. After hearing Tarik's story, the college students asked one question, "*Where do we sign up?*"[4]

What happened when those working-class college students joined with revolutionary Tarik in the heart of the ghetto to develop a liberation organization for the grassroots? What can we make of those complex psychological, social, and political dynamics in the process of fusion that occurred when a powerful black united front would require addressing "its programs" to the cultural tastes, social milieu, and aspirations of the grassroots? And, above all, what did it mean for those young people to "come home" or "to give something back" to their communities? Was their spiritual journey any less meaningful or transformative than that of the activists who joined SNCC and CORE in the Deep South because the activists under study were in Northern urban centers? In the midst of the temptations of "underclass" theory it has become "all too easy" to paint that whole experience of the Black Revolt as part of the processes of urban corruption, of a waste of the talents of black college youth in the hopeless ghettos of America—even of a loss of "social capital," some might say. Who were those grassroots activists whom they joined with and what was that experience about?

In the midst of the urban crisis, the *fusion* of grassroots community residents, student activists, artists, and progressive intellectuals into one struggle produced a fruitful and explosive blend that fueled the Black Power movement of the 1960s and 1970s. With the collective leadership of the Black Power movement in Newark, CFUN developed an innovative way to develop a substantial political program to attack the postwar ghetto crisis in the shape of the Modern Black Convention movement and its black agenda. As new recruits flooded CFUN during the political mobilization to seize power, the organization thrived and developed into departments of specialization in community building: Communications, Economics, Security, Community Organization, Education, and Politics. CFUN organized numerous political conventions and community assemblies where a grassroots process of agenda building unfolded in order to set its own political and community priorities regardless of what the two major political parties had in mind. In essence, agenda building was a counter-hegemonic strategy that meant changing the political discourse on not only local but also national issues. Instead of black communities passively awaiting whatever political candidates might decide were the pressing issues just before the elections, whether there were elections or not, black grassroots assemblies took the initiative in their own hands to determine and define the issues they felt were most important, speaking in their own language. In order to enact their priorities, CFUN ran candidates for public office, fashioned public policies, advocated reforms, mobilized huge demonstrations to resist President Richard Nixon's political reaction, and, above all, established an elaborate network of institutions, programs, and business operations to carry through their black agenda in the heart of the ghetto: the Spirit House Movers and Players, for drama and poetry; the African Free School, for early childhood education; the *Black NewArk* newspaper, for local communication; the *Unity & Struggle* newspaper, for national politics; Events, Inc., for public relations; Proposals, for development grants; and Kawaida Towers and the NJR-32 Project Area Committee, for urban planning and community development.

While the Newark movement included a charismatic leader, poet and writer Amiri Baraka (LeRoi Jones), he did not dominate the movement. The crucial difference in the case of Newark was that Baraka merged with a brilliant and innovative local grassroots leadership that was already in place when he returned to Newark in the aftermath of the collapse of the Harlem Black Arts Repertory Theater/School (BARTS). This chapter begins to examine the rich combination of genius and experience that was pooled within that collective grassroots leadership in order to navigate CFUN through the hidden traps that wrecked many other organizations in their first years.

One more word of advice before the discussion begins. The social history of persistent poverty and the urban crisis has introduced great caution about the intellectual habit of dividing the poor into two moral groupings, the deserving and undeserving poor.[5] According to Michael B. Katz, tragically that "[predisposition] toward moral definitions of poverty found support . . . in the work of Darwin and early hereditarian theory," and it was so "deeply embedded in Western culture . . . that even writers on the Left invoked it automatically or translated it into their own vocabulary."[6] Thus we need to reconsider even Karl Marx's ideologically charged "lumpen-proletariat" class in the same ways that in the context of colonial revolution we had to rethink the way Marx and Engels misunderstood the vast political potential of the world's peasants.[7] In short, we need to stop talking about "social constructs" and attempt to talk about some of the real people in those communities, in those political movements, and in our research. Let us begin to see who those grassroots leaders were.

"What's Gonna Happen? / The Lands Gonna Change Hands!"

The Black Power agenda of CFUN and its political arm, the United Brothers, addressed the social, political, and economic challenges for African Americans of the postwar urban crisis. While the United Brothers was a tight-knit Black Power political organization that formed in 1967 in the aftermath of the Newark uprisings, CFUN emerged later as a broader Black Power group during the 1968 electoral campaign in Newark representing an umbrella group, or what Aldon Morris calls a "movement center" that embraced not only the United Brothers (politics) but also the Spirit House (culture), the Young Lions (youth), the African Free School (education), Jihad Productions (publishing), *Black NewArk* newspaper, and several other groups.[8] When the United Brothers entered the electoral arena, one political adviser from Los Angeles, Maulana Karenga, suggested that the original name sounded too racial and too "sinister," and proposed the new name without any racial markers, emphasizing political unity. Over time CFUN replaced the United Brothers as the larger group's namesake, and the United Brothers became that group of pioneering veterans who founded the original movement.

At public assemblies CFUN and its allies discussed the specter of Newark's urban crisis: a black unemployment rate of 11.5 percent contrasting with a 6 percent white rate; a median income for black and Puerto Rican households of only $3,839 compared to one of $6,858 for white families; a ten thousand shortage of pupil stations and a drop-out rate of 32 percent in the school system; the highest maternal mortality and venereal disease rate in the country, as well as the highest rate of new tuberculosis cases for all cities; a drug crisis ranking seventh and an air pollution problem ranking ninth in the nation; and a housing crisis that involved over 75 percent of the city's old and rapidly aging structures. Thus the challenge before the Black Power movement was to develop the kind of politics that would address the horrors of the urban crisis, the demands of the urban social movement, the development of black and Puerto Rican unity, and the requirements of self-determination.[9]

At the foundation of Newark's Black Power movement was an African American and Puerto Rican alliance and mutual defense pact, joining them against white terror. The terrorism, vigilantism, and police brutality in Newark had deep roots in a lethal combination of racism, capitalism, and fascism. African Americans and other oppressed groups had been attacked on Newark's streets since the 1930s with the rise of white groups that supported Hitler and Mussolini. In Newark's North Ward many whites paraded to commemorate Mussolini's rise to power, and the crowd roared, "Ethiopia is Italian!"[10] Later, when the Nazis in Newark fomented anti-Semitism and racism, Jewish and African American groups fought against Hitler's thugs in the streets, supported by street organizations and sports clubs, particularly amateur boxers.[11] By the 1960s, when Black Power groups mobilized to support African liberation groups and the Young Lords advocated Puerto Rican independence, extremist Newark police officers and Anthony Imperiale's vigilantes attacked both African Americans and Puerto Ricans. In response, a distinct solidarity developed in Newark, New Jersey, marking an important political path toward the Black and Puerto Rican Political Convention in 1969.

The troubles of African Americans were not limited to the violent police and vigilante groups. They were also political problems, because there was a raw monopoly of political power in the hands of the Italian-American Mayor Hugh J. Addonizio in the 1960s. While Anthony Imperiale openly represented reactionary politics as he became a Newark City Councilman, including support for Alabama governor George Wallace and Klan leaders, Mayor Hugh J. Addonizio was nominally a white liberal.

However, under Addonizio, Newark's urban crisis exploded in part because he attempted to stifle any genuine black protest by buying out civil rights leadership or by putting a few of the leaders on the city payroll. This is part of a larger pattern in which liberal civility was used as a means of social control; thus community protests became increasingly hostile and disruptive in order to be heard.[12] Similarly New Haven's mayor Richard Lee had combined buying out the leadership of the local branch of the NAACP with massive urban renewal.[13] Thus, when Newark's Congress of Racial Equality (CORE) demonstrated against employment discrimination in the city, the head of the Newark National Association for the Advancement of Colored People (NAACP) condemned CORE and supported Mayor Addonizio.[14]

Since Democratic mayor Addonizio climbed to power with an African American and Italian American coalition, the plans for widespread urban renewal in the heart of Newark's black belt split the Central Ward Democratic Party, particularly in what was known as the Medical School Crisis and NJR-32 controversy. The black Central Ward councilman Irvine Turner, a political maverick turned machine boss, backed Mayor Addonizio and the Newark Housing Authority (NHA) in their plans to level several neighborhoods in the Central Ward in order to build the proposed New Jersey College of Medicine and Dentistry and more high-rise public housing in a nearby neighborhood designated as NJR-32.[15] By contrast, Mhisani Harold Wilson, a local political activist and merchant, led a community movement in the heart of the Central Ward that opposed the City Hall and NHA plans to destroy their community in order to construct high-rise public housing projects. The NHA had already built one of the highest concentrations of segregated public housing in that part of the Central Ward by building five public housing projects in the area.[16] With that unprecedented concentration of poverty, the community institutions had been severely strained, and ordinary people began to feel the pressure in their neighborhood. The leadership produced by that Central Ward community joined with the efforts of Amiri Baraka in the struggle for Black Power; however, in joining with the writer they changed the meaning of the movement in order to reflect the fight for the power to redefine urban space.

When a local merchant, Mhisani Harold Wilson, and other militants joined Amiri Baraka in founding CFUN, it caused a major political realignment in favor of the black militants. CFUN was an organization of organizers, meaning that at the head of that group was a council of local organizers, leaders representing several segments of Newark's community, including tenants, social clubs, teachers, neighborhood youth, mothers, community organizations, veterans, reform-oriented black police caucuses, low-level civil servants, militant welfare mothers, high school students, women's clubs, progressive welfare department and housing authority social workers, families of inmates, relatives of victims of police brutality, musicians, dancers, poets, and actors. They discussed political and community issues from many different angles, and sometimes they fought behind closed doors until they fashioned a united front for the wider political arena. They were involved in cases of police brutality, tenant evictions, rallies against urban renewal plans, and, on one occasion, a community protest against a furniture merchant who took advantage of a welfare mother, selling her a flimsy living room suite. In addition to daily protests in front of the store, the Spirit House actors developed "anti-commercials" on the *Black Newark* program on WNJR-AM radio, dramatizing the shoddy furniture sold by that store. The campaign lasted until the media-shy and uncomfortable merchant replaced the first living room suite with one that was much better. Thus CFUN slogans, tactics, programs, press releases, and direct action initiatives were created in that process of discussion of problems and tactics, planning, experimentation, collaboration, and street demonstrations.

This collective dynamic required those in the CFUN leadership council to talk to one another with mutual respect. When that failed, tempers sometimes flared: at one point Eulius "Honey" Ward, a former golden gloves champion, knocked out a young lawyer in the group, leaving him laid out on a large conference table. Despite those flare-ups, the group held together through battle after battle in the political arena.

Mhisani Harold Wilson is a good example of CFUN's grassroots leadership. While Wilson would eventually became a district leader in the Central Ward Democratic Party in 1972, he had already emerged as an independent grassroots political leader who belonged to a number of organizations ranging from the NAACP to the Nation of Islam. Wilson represented key dimensions of the Central Ward's grassroots culture, including social sectors ranging from the Masonic Temple crowd to the "duce and a quarter" set of working-class men who drove powerful cars and held regular jobs.[17] Wilson was especially respected because he knew how "to take care of business." Like his father, who was a grocer killed at the hands of Newark policemen, Wilson had won some measure of psychological, social, economic, and political independence as a small merchant who owned a series of enterprises, alternating between a furniture, clothing, and grocery store. Instead of using that independence to stand aloof from his community, Wilson provided community members with jobs, apartments, and access to credit.

Since Wilson knew that women staffed most of the community organizations and grassroots struggles, he developed an understanding of their deep concerns for personal safety, including street crime and domestic violence. Over time, Wilson was able to articulate some of the social responsibilities discussed within CFUN collective leadership to his male constituency in the streets in a way they could understand—and when he criticized their lack of respect for black women, his peers listened. He sponsored programs that provided safe evening transportation for women and children in the Central Ward community when public transportation closed down. The standard operating procedures included instructions for the drivers to wait until women and children were safely in their apartments. If it was a dangerous building, the family was escorted to the door. Wilson also sponsored a fleet of cars with which the United Brothers responded to calls regarding domestic quarrels in working-class districts and in the public housing projects; indeed, a number of women preferred the United Brothers and CFUN to intervene instead of trigger-happy policemen.

As African clothing emerged as the style in black America, Wilson sponsored a community "fashion show" where ordinary women and men, large and small, light and dark, did a jazz step across the stage of Weequahic High School showing off their colorful new outfits.[18] Not wanting to be excluded from that dimension of the Black Cultural Revolution, the welfare, tenant, community, and workplace activists of the CFUN Community Council enjoyed celebrating their bodies and resisting commercial fashion culture that required them to look thin like "Twiggy" as they participated in the show to raise funds for their political work. Similarly they held soul food dinners to raise funds for African liberation movements.

Wilson also introduced new political ideas to his community, becoming a vital bridge between local and national struggles. Wilson passed on the word of Malcolm X from his "Message to the Grassroots" that President John F. Kennedy and the *man* in the Democratic Party had made chumps out of them; that blacks had put them *first* by voting for the Democrats, but "their party" had put them *last* by making civil rights a low priority on the White House political agenda. Furthermore, he taught that the go-slow gradualist and reformist leaders were being used to take the fight out of them: "It's just like when you've got some coffee that's too black, which means it's too strong. What do you do? You integrate it with cream, you make it weak. But if you pour too much cream in it, you won't even know you ever had coffee. It used to be hot, it becomes cool. It used to be strong, it becomes weak. It used to wake you up, now it puts you to sleep."[19] One of the things that Wilson remembered from the last days of Malcolm X was that the struggle was about *land*. And at the head of the struggle to stop high-rise public housing in the NJR-32 neighborhood, the land issue slowly began to take on a very concrete form: if not public housing, then what would be developed in that space?

Mhisani Harold Wilson was an impressive community leader because he was a great fighter for his people; he had *heart* in the heat of battle: he never backed down from the power structure at the Newark Housing Authority and City Hall. For many who followed him, he seemed fearless. Of course, even Mhisani had his own fears, but he was the type of person who possessed enormous courage in physical confrontations. During the very early days of CFUN, at the worst moments, Mhisani was Amiri Baraka's bodyguard when he would go to the North Ward—deep into the lion's mouth—for heated "debates" with vigilante Anthony Imperiale; in this regard, he had the type of reputation in the streets since childhood that earned him everyone's respect. What made people recognize him, whether friend or foe, was that he believed in what he was doing, and he was willing to die for the cause. Thus his leadership was distinctive because he was unmatched in his devotion to the cause, unrivaled in his link to the masses in his community, and consummate in his ability to find his own bearings.

With those instincts, when Mhisani heard what had happened to his childhood friend, Amiri Baraka, being beaten by the police in the midst of the Newark uprising of July 1967, like many other men and women he rushed to the Spirit House where Baraka lived upstairs above the theater. A number of people were discussing a legal defense committee for Baraka, some were proposing that the answer was to have the Spirit House become a Muslim Mosque. Others suggested that Newark Black Power needed an army. However, Mhisani was singular in that he came up with the idea for a new kind of political organization rooted in the community struggles he had been waging with others in the Central Ward ghetto, which he believed was the way to rally people around the cause of Black Power. This idea struck everyone's imagination. It would not be a bureaucratic organization but something based on an intimate mutual dedication and kinship in the struggle, on people being concerned about one another, and on taking care of one another as they spoke for their community. He envisioned a group so dedicated to the liberation of its people that it would run its operations seven days a week and nearly twenty-four hours each day. Indeed, the group would eat, sleep, and dream about getting power into the hands of African Americans, not for the purpose of putting black faces in high places but rather to help those in the grassroots seize power with their own hands in order to make change. Thus he dreamed of a group that would seize power for the benefit of the majority, not the minority, whether black or white. In line with that thinking, one of the first measures of community control was that Wilson's Black Power group would take back control of the local branch of the NAACP.[20] How would they begin? They decided to call the Newark Black Political Convention. Later, in the political arena, the United Brothers flowered into a larger umbrella group, the Committee for a Unified NewArk, or CFUN.

By 1966 Amiri Baraka had withdrawn from the Harlem Black Arts and returned to Newark. His early writings suggest that black communities like the one in Newark had *no organization.* However, surrounded by Mhisani Wilson and other key advisers at the helm of CFUN and the United Brothers, Baraka soon realized that he had landed in the midst of a black Newark with hundreds of social clubs and neighborhood organizations. One of his key advisers was Russell Bingham who had helped organize in the Central Ward since the 1950s. Bingham became Baraka's chief political adviser, probably the only one more important than Mhisani Wilson. Russell Bingham would become *Baba Mshauri,* the Father Counselor. In his eulogy at Baba's funeral Baraka would refer to him affectionately as his consigliere, his most trusted adviser, and a second father who counseled him about controlling his unmanageable rage against racism and forced him to think strategically and politically. That collective leadership helped Baraka see what had been invisible to outsiders: that there was a plethora of organizations and networks in the African American community with their own leadership.[21]

During one of the early political assignments, when a tired political worker looking forward to the early end of what was developing into one of many all-night assignments, he asked Baba Mshauri, *What time is it?* And with singular wit and authority Mshauri answered bluntly, *"It's Nation Time!"*—meaning that the work had to get done no matter how long it might take; doing so was their responsibility in a difficult and protracted struggle.[22] When the United Brothers heard the story, "It's Nation Time" became an inside yarn, then a legend, and later a local slogan and then a chant developed by Baraka's drama group, speaking to the larger issue of the urgency of black national self-determination. A few years later Baraka unveiled it as an epic poem at the 1970 Atlanta Congress of African People summit, his signature poem of that period.[23] In that collective fashion, step by step, they developed a combination of work, determination, and ethos to make a distinct grassroots political culture. Obviously fusion is a two-way process, and, in this case, with a great deal coming from below.

For Baraka, another early discovery was that Newark had its own homegrown Black Arts movement, particularly artists influenced by the Cellar and the Jazz Arts Society.[24] Thus the key issue would become how to unite those groups, not how to start them. For example, he found that the hotel manager at his temporary residence, Ben Caldwell, was an artist and playwright originally from Harlem. Caldwell had not only developed a distinct Afrocentric drawing style that gave the impression of African woodcuts, but he had also written a one-act play, *The First Militant Preacher*, that spread like wildfire in both the Black Arts movement and in the Black Student movement. The Newark Black Arts movement was developing a new militant jazz idiom in pace with the increasing militancy of the Black Freedom movement, and that new language would inform not only Baraka's poetry but also his developing political oratory.

A club called the Cellar in Newark housed the Jazz Arts Society, which hosted musical and dance acts as well as poetry readings by local people such as Nettie Rogers and Sylvia Robinson, both of whom would eventually form the core of CFUN. At times Rogers and Robinson danced to poetry and music at the Jazz Arts Society; at other times Sylvia Robinson, who had done some modeling, acted on stage. Both women had attended Newark schools: Rogers graduated from a vocational high school, Robinson from Arts High. Amiri Baraka was meeting the neighborhood leaders, activists, and artists who would form the heart of the phenomenal Black Arts and Black Power movement in Newark. Eventually he leased a wood frame building at 33 Stirling Street in the Central Ward. Since it was both a cultural and at one point Muslim religious center, it became known as the Spirit House, the new home of Newark's Black Arts movement.[25] During performances at the Spirit House the poets developed call-and-response chants with the audience, including this one:

> What time is it?
> It's Nation Time!

And what's gonna happen?
The *land's* gonna change *hands*!

By the time Amiri Baraka was attacked by the police in the midst of Newark's July 1967 black uprising, he and Sylvia Robinson were married. The summer night that Baraka was nearly beaten to death by the police, Sylvia Jones left her baby at the Spirit House and ran to the city hospital where she was shocked to find her husband handcuffed to a wheelchair, his clothing soaked in blood.

The Newark Rebellion of 1967

Beginning on July 12, 1967, the Newark Rebellion was a major turning point for Amiri Baraka, Sylvia Jones, Mhisani Harold Wilson as well as black Newark in general; as far as they were concerned it was a declaration of war. That was the night that fighting erupted in the Central Ward at the Fourth Police Precinct, after some people in the black community caught a glimpse of a badly beaten black cab driver named John Smith, as the police dragged him into the police station, supposedly for a minor traffic violation. The Fourth Precinct station house on the corner of 17th Avenue and Livingston Street faced Hayes Homes, one of the largest public housing projects in the ghetto. Word of the arrest spread quickly throughout black Newark, along with alarm over Smith's beating. A large and angry crowd gathered in front of the Fourth Precinct station house.

While Smith was being beaten, the black community was gathering outside, fearing that the worst had happened to Smith, and demanding to see him. Eventually the mood of the crowd turned ugly. Before long, a hail of bricks, bottles, and Molotov cocktails hit the side of the police station. Seventy-five riot police, wearing helmets, stormed out of the station house, clubbing anyone within reach. Indeed, journalist Robert Allen reports, "The cops beat everyone and anyone with black skin, including a black policeman in civilian clothes and several black newsmen. Cursing and mouthing racial slurs, the club-swinging cops indiscriminately smashed into the throng."[26]

After laying siege to the Fourth Police Precinct in the Central Ward, black people attacked a mile-long section of the Springfield Avenue shopping area, and then headed downtown. The local newspaper reported that the weapons they used were bricks and slabs of concrete that they threw at the police.[27] After the uprising waned, the National Guard riddled Harold Wilson's furniture store with bullets.

Amiri Baraka was beaten on the second night of the disturbance, after being stopped by police while traveling in a van with other community activists. After they were viciously beaten, they were charged with unlawfully carrying firearms and resisting arrest. Baraka was scarred for life; a photo in *Jet* magazine, showing the poet in police custody, pictured him handcuffed to a wheelchair, covered in his own blood.

The situation was wretched for both men and women. Baraka's wife Sylvia explained that, fearing attack by the police during the insurrection, the women in the Spirit House boiled large pots of water and lye and waited for the assault at the top of the third floor stairwell. That is where she was positioned when her neighbors told her that she had better go to the hospital to see what the police had done to her husband. In a panic, she ran through the streets barefoot until she reached the hospital, and then she screamed when she saw Amiri Baraka in shackles. She protested that he was bleeding but receiving no medical attention.

Nonetheless, the Black Power movement rose like Phoenix out of the ashes of the Newark Rebellion. CFUN came to symbolize the politics born of the urban uprisings. With that momentum, the idea of the United Brothers was born, when Mhisani Wilson began working with Amiri Baraka at the Spirit House. With his extensive network of contacts in Newark, Wilson began to mobilize resources and recruit people to form the nucleus of a new organization to struggle for power; he would be elected the first president of the group. The first recruit, John Bugg, dubbed the organization with a name that evoked a close kinship in struggle for the new organization, the United Brothers.

In November 1967 Baraka, Bugg, and Wilson began their movement for political power with the following letter:

The United Brothers of Newark would like you to attend the initial meeting of interested citizens coming together to form a steering committee that would issue a call to Black Leaders for a citywide unity meeting.

The meeting to form a steering committee will take place at Abyssinian Baptist Church—W. Kinney Street, 8.00 P.M. Friday, December 8, 1967. You are urged to attend. Don't let your people down!

In Unity,
The United Brothers[28]

More than a dozen men and women answered the call, and together they were determined to change the complexion of Newark politics. The United Brothers began discussing a new political agenda that was not on the usual radar screen, one embedded in mass resistance to urban renewal and a style of community organizing involving tenant strikes, eviction resistance, welfare and unemployed protests, wildcat actions in the factories, student protests in communities and schools, parents' and teachers' struggles for educational equality, construction stoppages by unemployed workers demanding jobs, and demonstrations against police brutality. By making those issues "political," the United Brothers changed the content of politics, making black communities in the political arena "unmanageable" and "ungovernable" for the political establishment.[29] With that organizing tradition, the United Brothers began planning the 1968 Black Political Convention to be an assemblage of all those grassroots activists and their constituencies.

From those same grassroots developments, the United Brothers made mutual defense treaties with the Young Lords and other Puerto Rican activists to resist racist vigilante attacks, an alliance that flowered into the 1969 Black and Puerto Rican Political Convention. In fact, it was in the midst of the Black Convention movement that the United Brothers developed into a larger umbrella organization, CFUN. Thereafter the organization was not solely the political department but was also the cultural, communications, community organizing, public relations, economic development, educational reform, militant women's, and youth divisions all in one central headquarters in the Central Ward at 502 High Street, only one block from the Spirit House. The basic strategy of CFUN's politics of cultural nationalism reflected a radical sense of the urban crisis of the 1960s. The black nationalists of the 1960s viewed the liberation movement members in the Caribbean, Africa, Asia, and Latin America not only as allies but also as brothers and sisters in the struggle. Identifying with the global battles for self-determination, their Black Power politics proposed a strategy of black liberation involving struggles for regional and spatial autonomy in urban centers, in alliance with oppressed people of color in the United States, particularly Puerto Ricans and Mexican Americans. Tactically this stratagem involved mass social mobilization for black self-government at the municipal level and for proportional representation at higher levels of government in coalition with progressive whites. In Newark that included CFUN's successful litigation for congressional redistricting and eventually the election of U.S. Representative Donald Payne, who became a specialist in African affairs. From these semi-autonomous urban enclaves, CFUN sought to accelerate the process of black nationality formation (otherwise known as nation building) through the rapid spread of independent black economic, institutional, cultural, social, and political development. By such political work, they expanded the demand for self-determination to mean the transformation of urban space, particularly to change the social and material meaning of the "ghetto" into that of a community. One important driving force in that process was the utter collapse of basic government and commercial services in the postwar ghetto. The cultural nationalist strategy of African American militants was to develop parallel black institutions in that void left by the urban crisis, emphasizing the failure of the American government and mainstream capitalist economy to provide basic services and to offer black nationalism, Pan-Africanism, and cooperative economics as rational alternatives to the political and economic vacuum left by "benign neglect."[30]

In the midst of that black cultural revolution many of the founders changed their names: LeRoi Jones became Imamu Amiri Baraka; his wife Sylvia, Bibi Amina Baraka; Nettie Rogers, Muminina Salimu; and Harold Wilson, Kasisi Mhisani. In 1969, when those three college students entered CFUN's headquarters to join Sultani Tarik, Eric Dillard became Jeledi Majadi; Leon Herron, Saidi Subira; and Doc Holiday, Mwanafunzi Taalamu—all three to be trained by Baba Mshauri and Mhisani Wilson to become first-rate political organizers. Muminina Salimu would become the first full-time salaried organizer in CFUN, and using her organizational genius she revolutionized the central headquarters so that it served as the headquarters for several local, statewide, and national organizations, including the Congress of African People, the African Liberation Support Committee, and the National Black Assembly. Alongside Salimu and the sisterhood in CFUN, Amina Baraka founded the African Free School that became a leading model for alternative black independent education in the United States. Majadi, Subira, and Taalamu joined with other young men and women in direct action campaigns to win a number of community struggles and tenant strikes as well as several local, county, and anti-poverty elections and to gain democratic representation for African Americans and Puerto Ricans in that area. They led struggles for prison reform and promoted a local and then national "Stop Killer Cop" campaign. Mhisani became the executive director of the NJR-32 Project Area Committee (PAC) that planned and ultimately redeveloped that one-hundred–acre community that included a park, a medical center, a shop-

ping center, and a radio and cable television communications and conference hub, as well as affordable garden apartments. Residents explained
that high-rises with long hallways made them feel like prisoners; they also
did not like the abandoned railroad spur that the General Electric plant
maintained in the midst of their neighborhood. NJR-32 PAC and its partners, Pilgrim Baptist Church and the Temple of Kawaida, won funding
from a number of government sources, but there was never the federal
and private funding for the medical center that they had planned next to
the senior citizens' building or for the Nat Turner Community Park that
was designed for neighborhood recreation. Nonetheless, the NJR-32 PAC
helped set the pace for African American community developers who had
been totally excluded from the building, construction, and management
processes. In a community that began at the bottom of the city's housing
crisis suffering from hazardous and degrading tenement structures, as well
as from the overconcentration of ominous high-rise public housing, NJR-
32 PAC fashioned new zoning ordinances to guard against overcrowding
and developed government subsidized garden apartments, many of which
are owned by residents and community groups. The one high-rise allowed
was the senior citizen tower that was planned by the community elders in
consultation with the NJR-32 PAC architect.

For many CFUN organizers, the Black Revolt was the high point in
their lives.[31] They recall the pride with which they walked through the
community, and the exhilaration of winning grassroots battles with the
power structure. With great pride, they stand shoulder to shoulder with
the veterans of SNCC, CORE, and the Black Panther Party. None of them
felt that they had been corrupted by their experience in the Black Liberation movement. And none of the college students or graduates felt that
they had wasted their talents in a "hopeless ghetto." All of them knew that
Newark was a better place because of the mass struggles during a time
when people took their destiny into their own hands.

The Newark Black Power experiment sent a message *from* the grassroots. It was "Nation Time" and the land changed hands. The grassroots
organizations built housing, cooperative businesses, schools, and numerous institutions; they fought many battles that they tell their children
about. Above all, the Black Power struggles in Newark made new women
and men: it did not make them rich, but it made them self-governing.

By March 1972 when Sultani Tarik, Baba Mshauri, and Mhisani Wilson
stood with Newark's delegation to the National Black Political Convention
in Gary, Indiana, it was widely acknowledged that CFUN had developed

into one of the most formidable Black Power groups in the world; and alongside its twenty-five branches in the Congress of African People (CAP), CFUN established its hegemony at the Gary Convention.[32] A central force at the convention, CFUN's work in Newark proved that a local organization could unleash creative ideas and energies at the grassroots level and use self-determination to redefine urban space, turning a slum and a ghetto back into a community. Together, CFUN and the United Brothers organized their community and in the process articulated an urban vision for a liberated zone, a *New Ark.*

NOTES

1. The "talisimu" was a hand-carved figure of Maulana Karenga's mythical first African ancestor, Nkula Nkula.

2. According to Maulana Karenga's doctrine Kawaida, the first ancestor was Nkula Nkula whose image is at the center of the talisimu.

3. Of course, this is not the same definition that Marcus Garvey gave to that flag. His colors represented red for the blood, black for the African people, and green for the land. But Karenga's youthful group improvised and attempted to modernize those terms.

4. Author's eyewitness account.

5. See Michael B. Katz, *The Undeserving Poor* (New York: Pantheon, 1989); idem, ed., *The "Underclass" Debate: Views from History* (Princeton, N.J.: Princeton University Press, 1993).

6. Katz, *Undeserving Poor,* 15.

7. See, for example, Amir Samin, *Class and Nation* (New York: Monthly Review Press, 1981); and idem, *The Arab Nation* (London: Zed, 1978).

8. See Aldon Morris, *The Origins of the Civil Rights Movement: Black Communities Organizing for Change* (New York: Free Press, 1984).

9. See more on that political agenda and summit meeting in Komozi Woodard, *A Nation within a Nation,* (Chapel Hill: University of North Carolina Press, 1999), 143.

10. Michael Immerso, *Newark's Little Italy: The Vanished First Ward* (New Brunswick, N.J.: Rutgers University Press, 1997), 134. Unfortunately Immerso is uncritical of those developments.

11. Ibid.; Warren Grover, *Nazi's in Newark* (New Brunswick, N.J.: Transaction, 2003).

12. See similar dynamics in William Chafe, *Civilities and Civil Rights* (New York: Oxford University Press, 1980).

13. Yohuru Williams, *Black Politics/White Power: Civil Rights, Black Power, and Black Panthers in New Haven* (St. James, N.Y.: Brandywine Press, 2000).

14. Robert Curvin, "The Persistent Minority" (Ph.D. dissertation, Princeton University, 1975).

15. Curvin's "The Persistent Minority" is the definitive study of that bossism.

16. Komozi Woodard, "The Making of the New Ark" (Ph.D. dissertation, University of Pennsylvania, 1991), 89; Harold Kaplan, *Urban Renewal Politics: Slum Clearance in Newark* (New York: Columbia University Press, 1963); Curvin, "The Persistent Minority," 15.

17. See Elijah Anderson, *A Place on the Corner* (Chicago: University of Chicago Press, 1978); and *Streetwise: Race, Class, and Change in an Urban Community* (Chicago: University of Chicago Press, 1990).

18. See reports and photos in CFUN Newsletters in Komozi Woodard, ed., *The Black Power Movement Part 1, Amiri Baraka: From Black Arts to Black Radicalism and Beyond* (Lexis-Nexis microfilms, 2000).

19. Malcolm X, *Malcolm X Speaks*, George Breitman, ed. (New York: Pathfinder, 1989), 16

20. The local branch of the NAACP was flooded with new members from the United Brothers and the CFUN Community Council, and elected several new leaders that were in step with political change, including Sally Carroll, who was a delegate at the 1969 Black and Puerto Rican Political Convention. See Woodard, *A Nation within a Nation*, 142.

21. In *A Place on the Corner,* Elijah Anderson also suggests that there is an indigenous sense of social order based on working-class community values.

22. Russell Bingham/Baba Mshauri, interview by author.

23. Imamu Amiri Baraka, *It's Nation Time* (Chicago: Third World Press, 1970).

24. Amiri Baraka, *The Autobiography of LeRoi Jones* (New York: Freundlich, 1984), 236.

25. See the discussion of Baraka's work with Kamiel Wadud in Baraka, *The Autobiography of LeRoi Jones,* 266.

26. Robert Allen, *Black Awakening in Capitalist America* (New York: Anchor, 1970), 132.

27. "New Violence in Newark: Stores Burned and Looted," *Star Ledger,* July 14, 1967, 1.

28. Woodard, *A Nation within a Nation,* 88–89.

29. For a similar discussion, see Ira Katznelson, *City Trenches: Urban Politics and the Patterning of Class in the United States* (Chicago: University of Chicago Press, 1981); for a view from one city hall, see Douglas Yates, *The Ungovernable City: The Politics of Urban Problems and Policy Making* (Cambridge, Mass.: MIT Press, 1984 [1977]).

30. Tanzanian President Julius Nyerere published an important article which argued that socialism was not a radical option but a "rational choice" for African

countries ravaged by colonialism, and here I have borrowed the spirit of that argument. CFUN republished Nyerere's paper in the United States. "Benign neglect" refers to Moynihan's controversial policy memo to President Nixon recommending that as a guiding principle in the black and Puerto Rican urban centers.

31. Interviews by author with Muminina Akiba, Shakoor Aljuwani, Tamu Aljuwani, Sam Anderson, Amina Baraka, Amiri Baraka, Tamu Bess, Baba Mshauri, John Henrik Clarke, Larry Hamm, Curtis Hayes, Harry Haywood, Wynona Holman, Malaika Imarisha, Maisha Jackson, Ndugu Kamau, Maulana Karenga, Jeledi Majadi, Cheo Mfalme, Kasisi Nakawa, Muminina Salimu, Mwanafunzi Taalamu, and Malaika Thazabu.

32. Paul Delany, "Conciliator at Black Parley," *New York Times*, March 13, 1972, 30.

Chapter 4

Gloria Richardson and the Civil Rights Movement in Cambridge, Maryland

Peter B. Levy

This essay examines Gloria Richardson, one of the heroines of the civil rights movement, within the context of the history of Cambridge, Maryland, and the civil rights movement that arose there in the 1960s. It focuses on answering two interrelated questions: First, why do so *few* people know who Gloria Richardson is? Second, in what ways does her story enhance our understanding of the modern struggle for civil rights? The key to answering both these questions has less to do with the public's ignorance about the civil rights years, or the fact that male civil rights activists have received the lion's share of Clio's gaze, than it does with the place where Gloria Richardson gained fleeting fame—namely Cambridge, Maryland—and the nature of the struggle that took place there. Most simply stated, Richardson has been largely forgotten because the civil rights movement in Cambridge does not fit neatly into the standard rendition of the civil rights years. According to the established canon, the civil rights movement began in the South in the mid-1950s as a fight to overturn Jim Crow and obtain citizenship rights, and then, after it had completed these tasks, moved north. As it did, so the story goes, it shed its commitment to nonviolence and its dream of creating a color-blind society, and turned instead to "black power." Prod nearly any American, one who grew up in the 1950s and 1960s or one of their children, and they will be able to identify a common litany of figures, places, and events associated with this seminal episode in their nation's experience: *Brown v. Board of Education*; Rosa Parks; Greensboro, North Carolina; Birmingham and Selma, Alabama—followed lamentably by Watts, Detroit, and, last but not least, the assassination of Martin Luther King, Jr.[1]

Black leaders meet in Chester, Pennsylvania, to form Associated Community Teams (ACT), March 14, 1964. *From left to right:* Lawrence Landry, Chicago school boycott leader; Gloria Richardson; comedian Dick Gregory; Malcolm X; and Stanley Branche, Chesterton, Pennsylvania, NAACP. © *Bettmann/CORBIS.*

In terms of our geographic, chronological, and ideological conceptualization of the civil rights years, Cambridge appears out of place. The willingness of blacks in Cambridge to defend themselves with guns and Richardson's militancy, particularly her call for blacks to boycott a special election aimed at eliminating segregation, at a time when the nation's attention was riveted on struggles to topple Jim Crow and win the vote in the South, cast Richardson outside the accepted understanding of the movement. That blacks even had the opportunity to vote on a referendum to integrate lunch counters—and chose not to—seemed so out of place to contemporaries that it led President John F. Kennedy and *New York Times* reporter Anthony Lewis, among others, to portray Richardson as a betrayer of the movement. Looking backward, historians have not figured out where to situate the movement that Richardson led in Cambridge on the geographic and chronological time line. While H. Rap Brown and the riot he allegedly sparked in 1967 in Cambridge often finds a place in the master narrative, because it meshes with the traditional discussion of the turn to black power in the latter part of the decade, Richardson's and the Cambridge Nonviolent Action Committee's militancy are left untold because they complicate the image we have of the movement as one that was nonviolent, focused on toppling Jim Crow, and largely unified until conflicts over the seating of the Mississippi Democratic Party and whether to turn back on the Edmund Pettus bridge began to tear the movement apart.[2]

Of course, Richardson has received some attention at conferences dedicated to exploring the role women played in the civil rights movement.[3] Ironically, for some contemporaries, the fact that Richardson *was* a middle-aged woman explained her and Cambridge's alleged deviancy. Accustomed to seeing men, such as Martin Luther King, Jr., James Farmer, and John Lewis, as the titular leaders of their respective civil rights organizations, reporters jumped to the conclusion that the movement in Cambridge was different because it was led by a woman who, to put it simply, did not know any better. Even fellow activist, NAACP official Phillip Savage, lambasted her as the most "fickle woman that you can imagine." Liberal reporters, who otherwise supported the movement, described her as a "live wire," "irrational," "temperamental," and "insecure."[4] Other notable female middle-aged activists, including Rosa Parks and Myrlie Evers, avoided such derisive labels, largely because they more neatly fit the prevailing mold of femininity. Parks, for instance, was admired for her quiet yet firm refusal to give up her seat. But contemporaries cast her action as a measured response to injustice and noted that men, like King and Ralph Abernathy, led the protests against segregation in Montgomery.

Even though students of women's roles in the struggle for racial equality, as well as the authors of a plethora of community and regional studies, have enriched our understanding of the civil rights movement, stretching its origins back in time and challenging the notion that the movement was a national effort, primarily led by men, especially preachers, which took as its purpose winning legal equality from the federal government, the framework of the orthodox interpretation of the civil rights years remains essentially the same as when it was first established. By locating Richardson in Cambridge and by describing the ways in which the community shaped her views, we can better understand where to place her in the history of the civil rights movement and how to adjust the master narrative. Put somewhat differently, only by locating Richardson in the locale of Cambridge can we truly understand her, and, conversely, once we do so we will better appreciate the need to see the relationship between the location of various local or community-based civil rights movements and the course they took.

Given the limits of time and space, I focus on three aspects of this story: a brief survey of the black community in Cambridge in the twentieth century in the years preceding the rise of the modern civil rights movement; the structural forces that destabilized the community and help explain the timing and concerns of the local movement; and the relationship between Richardson and ordinary men and women. By examining these three themes we will find, I contend, that Richardson shared much in common with the movement as a whole.

Like nearly every other community that served as a locale of the civil rights movement, Cambridge was populated by a sizable black community. (Approximately four thousand of Cambridge's twelve thousand residents were black.) By the 1960s blacks in Cambridge had accumulated the resources and skills necessary to launch and sustain a struggle for racial equality. Building on a modicum of gains made by the Eastern Shore's free blacks, they built churches, schools, small businesses, fraternal organizations, and cultural establishments in the decades that followed the Civil War. By World War II, a walk along Pine Street, in the heart of the all-black Second Ward, would have revealed some of these accomplishments, from barber and butcher shop to the Green Savoy, a combination hotel and entertainment spot owned and operated by Hansel Greene. There were funeral homes, and churches, pool halls, and drug stores, the Elks' lodge and schools, where black teachers taught black schoolchildren the three R's and about Harriet Tubman, a heroine from nearby Buckstown. On the Fourth of July blacks would gather on one side of Race Street, the road that literally separated the Second Ward from the white sections of the city, and watch with pride as veteran black soldiers and the Merry Concert Band paraded down the street, the latter playing, at least in the estimation of those on the black side of the street, the best music in town.[5]

Throughout most of the first half of the twentieth century Cambridge's leading black citizen was H. Maynadier St. Clair. The son of Cyrus St. Clair, a successful butcher, Maynadier represented the Second Ward on the town council for all but two years between 1894 and 1946. A disciple, so to speak, of Booker T. Washington, St. Clair entertained such notables as Mordecai Johnson, president of Howard University, and Duke Ellington. Although St. Clair accommodated himself to segregation, he was also a "race man," who raised his family to give back to the community and to work for the betterment of all blacks.[6] One family member who learned this lesson well was his granddaughter Gloria Richardson.

Born in Baltimore, Maryland, in 1922, Richardson moved to Cambridge with her mother, Mabel St. Clair, the daughter of Maynadier and Mamie St. Claire, and father, John Edward Hayes, a native of Virginia, in 1931. Richardson spent most of her teenage years in her grandfather's home, where she learned important lessons about politics and had instilled in her the faith that she could become anything she wanted to. In the fall of 1938 she enrolled at Howard University, where she studied with Rayford Logan, E. Franklin Frazier, and other giants of black scholarship, and experienced her first taste of civil rights protest, namely, against the discriminatory practices of Washington D.C.'s segregated establishments. Upon graduation, with a degree in sociology, she returned to Cambridge and married Harry Richardson, a schoolteacher. Unable to find employment as a social worker, because of racial discrimination, she worked in her family's drugstore and raised her two daughters, tasks that became increasingly arduous following her divorce.[7]

In many ways Richardson's experience illustrated the cruel hand dealt to middle-class blacks across America. She enjoyed the benefits of education, relatively high social standing in her community, and a family environment that nurtured her personal development. Yet prevailing racial caste barriers restricted her real-life opportunities. Arguably some middle-class blacks found social and economic opportunities in bigger cities with larger black communities, cities that could support a broader black professional class. But for middle-class blacks, who resided in mid-sized and small towns like Cambridge, opportunities remained extremely limited.

Before turning to Richardson's rise as a civil rights leader, however, we must first examine some of the broader forces that played a key role in shaping the nature of the civil rights movement in Cambridge, Maryland, particularly the rise and fall of the Phillips Packing Company. Established in 1902 by three local white businessmen, Albanus and Levi Phillips and William Winterbottom, the Phillips Packing Company, which canned vegetables and other food products, grew into the dominant industry in the region. By 1950 it owned and operated nineteen separate plants on the Delmarva Peninsula and employed approximately four thousand workers, about half of them in Cambridge. During World War II Phillips was the leading producer of C-rations. Phillips made good profits even during the depression.[8]

The Phillips Company's political power paralleled its economic fortunes. Augustus and Levi Phillips were power brokers within Maryland's Republican Party; Winterbottom enjoyed nearly as much power within the Democratic Party. The *FTA News*, the newspaper of the Food and Tobacco Workers, the union which unsuccessfully attempted to organize Phillips's workers after World War II, aptly captured the company's prowess: "Cambridge might well be named Phillipsburg," the paper observed. "The Phillips family dominates the city politically and economically. In addition to the packing plants . . . Phillips owns the city's largest wholesale and retail hardware store and the city's largest gasoline and fuel-oil distributing service. Phillips workers, under fear of punishment, are expected to eat Phillips soup, feed their pets Phillips Dog Food, burn Phillips Vim Pep gas, split their wood with a Phillips axe and decorate their homes with Phillips paint. The present Dorchester County sheriff is ex-captain of the Phillips guards, and most other office holders . . . owe their election to Phillips backing."[9]

For blacks, the growth of the Phillips Packing Company was a mixed blessing. Even though whites were hired for the better jobs, at least there were jobs to be found. In contrast, blacks in the Deep South faced a crumbling cotton economy during the same years. Moreover, in part because of the Phillips Packing Company's political influence, blacks not only retained the right to vote in the twentieth century, they maintained a seat on the city council. While we must resist romanticizing life for blacks in Cambridge during the heyday of the Phillips Packing Company, the salient point is that the company's collapse during the 1950s created an economic and political crisis in the community, the very type of conditions which J. Mills Thornton has theorized served as one of the necessary preconditions for the emergence of the civil rights movement in numerous locales.[10]

Between 1947 and 1956, years in which the nation enjoyed an economic boom, Phillips saw its earnings plummet from $3.64 a share to 2 cents a share. In 1957 Consolidated Foods (now Sara Lee) acquired Phillips and began to close its plants. As a result, by 1962 the former Phillips Packing Company plants in the region employed only between two hundred and four hundred people. Blacks were particularly hard hit by the company's troubles. In 1963 the unemployment rates for the city stood above 7 percent, about twice the national average. For blacks, however, the unemployment rate topped 29 percent! These conditions thus created the context out of which the civil rights movement in Cambridge would grow and shaped the demands of the local movement.[11]

A second, unrelated development during the same period influenced the nascent civil rights movement and the reception it received from the white community—namely, the completion of the Chesapeake Bay Bridge. Historically the Eastern Shore of Maryland, particularly the lower Eastern Shore where Cambridge is located, had been, as John Wennersten writes, "one of the most isolated regions" in the nation. "It was difficult to get to and difficult to leave." Over the years the region attracted few new-comers, grew slowly, and matured as a separate society. Many communities across America shared Cambridge's provincialism, but modernity came to these other communities gradually. It arrived in Cambridge in a hurry. Long a remote town, Cambridge *suddenly* became the neighbor of Washington, D.C., Philadelphia, New York, and Baltimore, in easy reach of college students, the mass media, and government officials, many of whom would be viewed as foreign agitators when the civil rights move-ment erupted. Like the collapse of the Phillips Packing Company, the completion of the Bay Bridge did not cause the civil rights movement in Cambridge. But it contributed to the context of the movement that burst onto the scene in January 1962 with the arrival of "freedom riders" led by activists aligned with the Civic Interest Group (CIG) of Baltimore and the Student Nonviolent Coordinating Committee (SNCC).[12]

Consumed with work at her family's drugstore and with her duties as a mother of two young girls, Gloria Richardson was *not* one of the first indi-viduals to be galvanized into action by these freedom rides. But several of her family members were. Frederick St. Clair, her cousin, who worked as a bail bondsman, first suggested to CIG and SNCC activists that they should "investigate" the situation in Cambridge. William Hansen and Reginald Robinson, two SNCC stalwarts, accepted his invitation and took up resi-dence at Herbert St. Clair's home prior to organizing the first protests. Following the first "rides," where activists "tested" various public establish-ments, local blacks gathered to form the Cambridge Nonviolent Action Committee (CNAC). Frederick St. Clair was elected as one of its co-chairs; Herbert St. Clair agreed to serve as an adult adviser. (Over the course of the next couple of years Gloria's mother would join the protests as well.) One other family member who played an active role from early on was Donna Richardson, Gloria's oldest daughter. Like many other young blacks across the country, Donna felt that the time had come to challenge the racial status quo. Hence she participated in sit-ins organized by SNCC and CIG and defied school authorities who sought to squelch such ac-tivism with threats of suspension and other penalties. When little change occurred, because of the insistence on the part of white leaders that Cambridge had a progressive racial record, Donna and many of her cohorts grew disillusioned. This development, her daughter's despondency, helped convince Gloria Richardson that she had to become more actively involved in the local movement. In the late spring of 1962 she agreed to become adult supervisor of CNAC, and traveled to Atlanta with Yolanda St. Clair, Frederick's wife, to attend a SNCC conference, whereby CNAC became the only adult-led affiliate of the student-led group.[13]

The relationship between Richardson and SNCC can best be described as synergistic. Drawing on the teachings of Ella Baker, SNCC sought to catalyze grassroots community-based movements. To this end, SNCC field workers, like Reginald Robinson and William Hansen in Cambridge, identified and supported the development of indigenous leaders and provided logistical support where necessary. In the best of all worlds, SNCC would become superfluous. In many ways this happened in Cambridge. Without any great knowledge about the history of race relations in Cambridge or the role played by the St. Clair family, Hansen and Robinson were successful enough that by late spring 1962 they were turning away requests from college students to come to Cambridge to help the movement there, because the local movement no longer needed outside help. Hansen and Robinson remained in Cambridge but spent much of their time and attention on organizing blacks in surrounding communities up and down the Eastern Shore.

Whether Richardson could have worked with other civil rights organizations will never be known, but clearly the SNCC philosophy and temperament meshed very well with hers. Unlike the Southern Christian Leadership Conference (SCLC), SNCC was a secular organization. It used churches and religious traditions but was not led by ministers, and it sought, in Richardson's words, to involve both the "saved" and the "sinners." While Richardson and CNAC cooperated with the local branch of the National Association for the Advancement of Colored People (NAACP), which was moribund until SNCC arrived, the national NAACP's dislike of direct action protest and its largely middle-class constituency ensured that its relations with CNAC remained strained. In contrast, even though Richardson was almost old enough to be the mother of many SNCC members, they saw her as a fellow colleague, and she soon became one of SNCC's most legendary members.

From the start, what distinguished the movement in Cambridge, however, was not that it was led by a middle-aged black woman (after all, historians have revealed that many middle-aged women led movements, from Daisy Bates in Little Rock, Arkansas, to Amelia Platts Boynton in Selma, Alabama) or that it was aligned with SNCC but rather that it enjoyed strong support from poor and working-class blacks. It did so in part because of Richardson's leadership skills. She shunned conciliatory or "Tom-ish" black leaders in Cambridge, most importantly Charles Cornish, who had won the Second Ward's seat on the Town Council following the retirement of Richardson's grandfather, and Helen Waters, the only black member of the school board. (Waters owned a beauty shop that catered to an all-white clientele.) While Cornish and Waters sought to avert protest and touted the line that Cambridge had a progressive racial record, Richardson insisted that the city's reputation was largely a farce and that direct action protest remained the black community's best form of leverage for attaining real reform. Put somewhat differently, she garnered support by refusing to kowtow to the whims of the white community so as not to risk an open split with "moderate" whites. Richardson won working-class support by including working-class men and women on CNAC's executive committee, including Marva Banks, the wife of a union organizer, and a welfare recipient, and involving them in the decision-making process. She gained the admiration of many through the sheer strength of her personality and by her willingness to sacrifice and risk imprisonment and bodily harm, rather than, as one Cambridge activist recalled, to stay "within the confines of her upper-middle-class life." But perhaps most important, Richardson helped mold a broad-based and vibrant movement in Cambridge by addressing the two specific issues that mattered most to blacks in the community, jobs and housing.[14]

Richardson's leadership skills and style exploded into public view in the spring of 1963. After organizing a voter education drive aimed at raising the political consciousness of blacks in Cambridge, Richardson and CNAC initiated an ongoing campaign of direct action protests and a boycott of downtown businesses. (While the standard interpretation of the civil rights years contends that SCLC's protests in Birmingham spawned the mass wave of demonstrations that swept across the nation in the spring of 1963, which in turn prompted President John F. Kennedy to call for civil rights legislation, the protests in Cambridge began shortly before "Project C" in Birmingham.) With the help of students from Baltimore, Philadelphia, and other eastern seaboard cities, CNAC organized sit-ins at public establishments that remained segregated, picketed the offices of the Board of Education and Employment in order to demand the desegregation of schools and an end to employment discrimination, and rallied outside the county courthouse and jail in sympathy with activists who had been arrested and placed in jail. These demonstrations were often preceded by mass meetings held at local churches or at other black establishments such as the Elk's Lodge. At times Richardson remained behind the scenes. Yet on other occasions, despite threats against her life, she joined the protests and faced violence and arrest.

In late April, for example, Richardson and her mother were arrested for participating in a sit-in. Along with fifty-three other defendants, Richardson was tried in the court of Judge W. Laird Henry Jr., one of the most prominent whites in the community. (He was a descendant of one of the signers of the Declaration of Independence.) After finding them guilty of disorderly conduct (they all waved their right to a jury trial), Henry fined all fifty-three one penny and then proceeded to single out Richardson for a personal reprimand, exclaiming that she was disgracing her family's good name. Evidently Henry hoped that Richardson would retreat in the face of his paternalistic lecture. Instead, she countered with a barbed retort, arguing that Cambridge's reputation as a community with good race relations was ill-founded, that the city was worse than even Salisbury, Maryland, the site of an infamous lynching in the 1930s. SNCC veteran Courtland Cox later recalled that Richardson's response to the so-called "penny trials" sent shockwaves through the elite white community. Accustomed to seeing black leaders accommodate themselves to its wishes, the white elite now feared that working-and lower-class blacks would explode since middle-class blacks like Richardson were in open rebellion. Put somewhat differently, Richardson's militancy symbolized that whites had lost their black middle-class buffer, a development that boded poorly for the maintenance of the social order.

Indeed, in spite of Judge Henry's efforts to mediate a peaceful resolution to the city's racial problems, which white small-business owners refused to abide by, the rift between blacks and whites intensified. The arrest of two black youths, Dwight Cromwell and Dinez White, and their subsequent imprisonment for an indefinite period in the state institution for juvenile delinquents by Judge F. McMaster Duer, a symbol of white supremacy, particularly angered the black community. Their "crime" was praying peacefully outside an all-white bowling alley. Articulating the views of many, Richardson declared that their prosecution "makes us wonder if we are really dealing with Christian people or heathens." In response to white night riders and clashes with white mobs, many blacks began to arm themselves—with at least the implicit support of CNAC. Herbert St. Clair explained: "We are not going to initiate violence. But if we are attacked, we are not going to turn the other cheek."[15]

Ultimately violence erupted; white-owned stores were firebombed, guns were fired, and individuals were injured—miraculously no one was killed. As a result, Maryland Governor J. Millard Tawes ordered the Maryland National Guard to restore order in Cambridge. Encamping themselves on Race Street, which as noted above was the name of the main street that literally divided the white and black sections of town, the Guard remained for nearly a year, one of the longest occupations of a community in peace time in American history. (Technically the Guard left Cambridge briefly, but another round of violence prompted their rapid redeployment.) The turmoil in Cambridge also prompted Robert F. Kennedy to convene a meeting to which he invited Richardson, political leaders from Cambridge and the state of Maryland, and an assortment of other figures.

Richardson approached the meeting with a cynical eye, having grown to distrust the Kennedy administration, as had many SNCC activists. Nonetheless, Richardson made an impression on Robert Kennedy by sharing with him the findings of a detailed study that CNAC had completed earlier that summer. Drawing on a door-to-door questionnaire, administered by Swarthmore College students and answered by nearly every resident of the Second Ward, the study documented that jobs and housing mattered much more to blacks in Cambridge than did the desegregation of public accommodations. Along with Richardson's steadfast approach to the meeting, the study also demonstrated that blacks wanted respect and a real shift in power—not just token change. As SNCC chairman John Lewis, who participated in the negotiations recalled, Richardson and the study made a strong impact on RFK, contributing to his budding concern with battling poverty.[16]

Ironically the meeting also ultimately contributed to Richardson's marginalization by contemporary analysts and historians. Richardson and RFK emerged from the meeting with a unprecedented agreement, whereby local, state, and federal authorities pledged to speed up the construction of public housing and the desegregation of schools, establish a bona fide biracial human relations committee, implement an innovative federally funded job-training program, to be administered by Morgan State College, and to amend the city's charter to make racial discrimination in public accommodations illegal. In other words, they agreed to implement nearly all of CNAC's demands. Arguably the agreement marked the most significant intervention of the federal government in the affairs of a single community with regard to civil rights, paling similar agreements in Birmingham, Alabama, and Jackson, Mississippi. However, while Richardson saw the concessions on jobs, housing, and school desegregation as the keys to the agreement, local authorities, and many liberals nationwide, saw the public accommodations amendment as the centerpiece of the pact. When conservative whites, who had not been party to the negotiations, challenged the promise to make discrimination in public accommodations illegal, by placing a referendum before the city's voters, these different perceptions over the relative priorities of the movement came to the fore.[17]

Earlier, in the spring of 1963, Richardson and CNAC had rejected an offer to call off protests in exchange for an amendment to the city charter banning discrimination in public accommodations, on the grounds that such an amendment could be repealed by means of a referendum. Instead, CNAC insisted that the town should pass an ordinance which could not be so reversed. But when the amendment was packaged with the aforementioned other reforms, all of which the referendum did not affect, she signed on to the pact. Nonetheless, shortly before the referendum, Richardson held a press conference where she announced that CNAC favored boycotting the election. Constitutional rights cannot be given or taken away at the polls, she explained. "A first-class citizen does not beg for freedom. A first-class citizen does not plead to the white power structure to give him something that the whites have no power to give or take away. Human rights are human rights, not white rights."[18]

Local authorities, who were engaged in a concerted effort to defeat the referendum and uphold the ban on discriminating in public accommodations, and liberal whites, nationwide, expressed their shock at Richardson's call for a boycott. So, too, did Cambridge's black moderates. Reverend T. Murray, the president of the local chapter of the NAACP, and most of Cambridge's other black ministers, denied CNAC access to their churches. The NAACP's national office sent field secretaries to Cambridge to urge blacks to defy Richardson's and CNAC's call. On the day of the referendum, about 50 percent of registered voters of the Second Ward voted overwhelmingly in favor of making segregation in public accommodations illegal. But record-high turnouts in the all-white wards of the city, reaching 85 percent, resulted in the passage of the referendum and the annulment of the agreement to desegregate public establishments.

The impact of Richardson and CNAC on the final results are difficult to gauge. Since whites outnumbered blacks more than two to one, and since the vast majority of whites voted to maintain segregation, it is not clear that the referendum would have been defeated even if blacks had voted in the same record numbers as whites had. Nonetheless, in Cambridge and in the national press, Richardson got nearly all the blame for the defeat. As suggested above, the national press decried Richardson as a zealot, claimed she acted as she had because she wanted power and because she did not know better. Hoping to undercut her appeal, the local NAACP invited Daisy Bates to speak at its annual meeting. Emphasizing the need for "togetherness," Bates called on the "more moderate elements [to] assert themselves."[19]

Ironically, not long before the NAACP invited Bates to Cambridge to counter Richardson's influence, the two women shared a spot with eight other "women of the movement" on the dais at the March on Washington. At the last minute, organizers of this historic demonstration realized that all the speakers were men. Hence they put together a list of black female civil rights notables, including Richardson, and invited them to attend and be recognized at the March. Richardson's inclusion signified her rise to national prominence. Yet at the same time the organizers of the event did not provide Richardson (or any woman) the opportunity to address the crowd and, by some accounts, did their best to marginalize her. (One historian reports that they did not even provide her with a chair.)

While this slight might be interpreted as an unintentional act, it was suggestive of a growing rift within the civil rights movement. Richardson largely felt that the March on Washington was a waste of time and, like many SNCC members, was angered over the fact that moderates had co-opted the demonstration by prohibiting any form of civil disobedience and overt protest against the Kennedy administration. This included the censoring of a speech by SNCC chairman John Lewis. While the public remained unaware of the tensions that existed within the movement, clearly these tensions grew in significance over the course of the next few years, exploding into the open with Stokely Carmichael's call for "black power" during the "Meredith march" in 1966. In retrospect, the decision of Richardson and CNAC to call for a boycott of the vote on the public accommodations referendum in Cambridge can be seen as one of the first signs of this broader development, as SNCC, CORE, and a loose collection of independent radicals, including Robert Williams and Malcolm X, distanced themselves from the mainstream civil rights organizations that counseled a more moderate course.

Back in Cambridge, calls for moderation largely fell on deaf ears. In the spring of 1964, in response to an appearance of Alabama Governor George Wallace at the all-white Rescue and Fire Company's arena attended by fifteen hundred to three thousand wildly appreciative supporters, CNAC sponsored counterdemonstrations that attracted civil rights activists from up and down the East Coast. These counterdemonstrations culminated in a showdown with the National Guard, with Richardson refusing to turn away from the confrontation, as would Martin Luther King Jr. in Selma, Alabama, the following year. (Richardson refused to obey the orders of the National Guard that she command members of CNAC to disband, leading to her arrest and a brief skirmish with the National Guard.) Her bravery left a lasting impression on Cleveland Sellers and Stokely Carmichael, two rising SNCC leaders. Carmichael, for instance, vowed never to be gassed again following the anti-Wallace protests in Cambridge. In spite of pleas for moderation, CNAC and Richardson also invited a string of independent black activists to Cambridge to speak and participate in protests, including Fannie Lou Hamer, Adam Clayton Powell, and Dick Gregory. In an essay published in the left-wing journal *Freedomways*, Richardson warned that the nonviolent battle for equality "could turn into a civil war" if the nation did not deliver "*here and now!*" There is no evidence that Richardson's militant words and actions, or pleas for moderation by national and local leaders, weakened the support she enjoyed from working-class blacks in Cambridge. On the contrary, the United Packinghouse Workers of America (UPWA) enjoyed several unprecedented successful organizing drives in the remaining packing plants in Cambridge in 1963 and 1964. To display its appreciation for the help that Richardson and CNAC lent to these campaigns, the UPWA invited Richardson to its annual convention in New York City, where delegates joined her in singing the civil rights anthem "We Shall Overcome." Richardson also forged ties with other independent black radicals at this time, from Chicago, New York, and Philadelphia, including Malcolm X.[20]

Nonetheless Richardson has largely been forgotten, because, as argued above, she did not fit neatly into the contemporary and historical account of the civil rights movement. Her insistence that jobs and housing take priority, that blacks should refuse to sacrifice their dignity in order to enjoy human rights, her refusal to accommodate moderates and local authorities for the sake of unity itself, her forging of a movement that enjoyed the support of poor and working-class blacks, appeared out of place. Ironically, if the movement in Cambridge had emerged in the way it did just a few years later, Richardson's and CNAC's stance and concerns would have seemed far less unusual. Contemporaries and historians could have incorporated Cambridge's story into their discussion of black power, if only the community had exhibited its militant brand of activism after the clash over the Mississippi Freedom Democratic Party in Atlantic City in August 1964 or after President Lyndon Johnson signed the Voting Rights Act. Perhaps not, though—that Richardson was a woman made the task of integrating her into the traditional narrative all the more difficult, since the established canon generally equated black power with men.

In a final irony, one that probably sealed her fate of historical oblivion, in 1964 Richardson remarried and moved with her husband to New York City. She continued to struggle for equality, focusing particularly on the social and economic conditions of the urban poor. Yet she could not compete for the historical limelight with the likes of H. Rap Brown, Bobby Seale, and other figures who enraptured the media. (Why militancy is largely confined in the American imagination to men is a subject worthy of consideration but too large and complex an issue to tackle here.) In one of the most astounding coincidences of history, Richardson moved into the same building where I once resided or, more accurately, I moved into the apartment complex where she lived. Unfortunately, like most Americans, I had no idea who she was, even though I had already consumed a load of works on the civil rights movement. As a result, not until after I had moved to Maryland and started my investigation of the movement in Cambridge, which I wrongly was led to believe was headed by H. Rap Brown, did I realize that Richardson and I had once lived only a few floors from each other.[21]

In closing, let me suggest some of the ways that Richardson's story can be incorporated into the history of the civil rights years and some of the ways that her story can enhance our understanding of the movement. First, Richardson's story, like that of the civil rights movement, is best understood if we root it in the history of the black communities out of which it arose. Top-down histories that emphasize the role played by the black elite or the courts or the federal government misrepresent the civil rights movement, which was, after all, only one phase in a long-term black struggle for freedom. While it is important that we not romanticize life for blacks during the era of Jim Crow, it is equally important that we show the connections between eras and how resources accumulated during one era could and were used in subsequent eras. This does not mean writing leaders like Martin Luther King Jr. and Thurgood Marshall out of the textbooks. On the contrary, King and Marshall make more sense when we see them as individuals who drew on and galvanized community resources to foster equality rather than as charismatic figures who achieved gains through the sheer strength of their individual efforts.[22]

Second, in understanding why the civil rights movement took place when it did and in the way it did, we must avoid the temptation to see it as an idea whose time had come. In so far as the ideal of equality was established at the time of the American Revolution and cemented by the Civil War, it was an idea whose time was long overdue. As the Cambridge story shows, significant changes in the political and economic conditions created the context out of which the movement arose. Shifts in the spatial relationship of provincial communities like Cambridge to the larger metropolitan world help explain the timing of the modern civil rights movement. Enough theoretical work has been done to suggest that Cambridge was not the exception. Broad structural forces, from the great migration to the collapse of the cotton economy, underlay the rise of the modern civil rights movement in the South; deindustrialization, combined with long-term institutional discrimination, helps explain its appearance in the North.[23] In addition, in Cambridge as elsewhere, individual agency mattered. Brave men and women took risks; they took advantage of opportunities. They had no guarantees of success and risked their livelihoods and lives in the quest to make American ideals real for all its citizens.

Finally, if we avoid the mistake contemporaries made, who viewed Richardson as out of step with the movement, and instead see that her views were rooted in the desires of the black community, we may be able to see that there were many others like her. The key here is to recognize that different communities gave rise to different demands and priorities, and leadership styles. The African American community in the late 1950s and early 1960s was not a monolith. Discussions of the civil rights movement that avoid compartmentalizing the movement into neat chronological, geographic, and ideological categories will do a much better job of accurately reflecting the past than those that focus on nonviolence and the struggle for integration and voting rights in the South and then jump to the black power drive for jobs, housing, and dignity located largely in the North.

Reared and raised watching Hollywood films, perhaps it is impossible to break from the urge to write stories that have an easily identifiable beginning, middle, and end, that follow a cogent plot line, and that include a cast of characters where everyone knows his or her part. But the history of the Black Freedom struggle was not like the movies. Instead, it was more like a film festival, where different actions, loosely related but tied together, in this case primarily by a shared history of racism and inequality, took place simultaneously. As a result, the chronology, geography, and ideology of the movement was not linear but crooked and uneven. Just as important, Richardson's story helps us better understand the movement because she so forcefully articulated the essential goal of the movement, to overcome racism, even if she did it in a way and at a time that made her appear out of place.

NOTES

1. The best-known narratives of the civil rights years are Taylor Branch, *Parting the Waters: America in the King Years, 1954–1963* (New York: Simon and Schuster, 1988); Taylor Branch, *Pillar of Fire: America in the King Years, 1963–1965* (New York: Simon and Schuster, 1998); Harvard Sitkoff, *The Struggle for Black Equality, 1954–1992* (New York: Hill and Wang, 1993); Robert Weisbrot, *Freedom Bound: A History of America's Civil Rights Movement* (New York: Norton, 1990); Juan Williams, *Eyes on the Prize: America's Civil Rights Years, 1954–1965* (New York: Viking, 1987); and, of course, the multipart film series by the same name, *Eyes on the Prize.*

2. As Anthony Lewis put it in one of the first and otherwise sympathetic histories of the civil rights years, Richardson had betrayed the principles of the movement (Anthony Lewis, *Portrait of a Decade: The Second American Revolution* [New York: Times Books, 1965], 100–103).

3. An early version of this paper was presented at the conference "Sisters in Struggle: Women and the Civil Rights Movement," Sarah Lawrence College, March 2002.

4. Murray Kempton, "Gloria, Gloria," *New Republic,* November 11, 1963, 15–17; Robert Liston, "Who Can We Surrender To?" *Saturday Evening Post,* October 5, 1963, 78–80.

5. Much of the material for this essay is drawn from Peter B. Levy, *Civil War on Race Street: The Civil Rights Movement in Cambridge, Maryland* (Gainesville: University Press of Florida, 2003). Three valuable unpublished sources on the history of the black community in Cambridge are: Kay McElvay, "Early Black Dorchester, 1776–1870" (Ed.D. dissertation, University of Maryland, 1991); Enez Grubb et al., *In Spite Of* (Cambridge, Maryland, 1999), photocopy at Dorchester County Public Library; and C. Christopher Brown, "Cambridge at Early 20th Century," in the author's possession.

6. George B. Kent, "The Negro in Politics in Dorchester County, Maryland" (Master's thesis, University of Maryland, 1961); author interviews of Gloria Richardson, March 21, 1993, May 13, 2000, and May 18, 2002.

7. Annette K. Brock, "Gloria Richardson and the Cambridge Movement," in *Trailblazers and Torchbearers: Women in the Civil Rights Movement,* ed. Vicki Crawford et al. (Bloomington: Indiana University Press, 1993), 121–44; Anita K. Foeman, "Gloria Richardson: Breaking the Mold," *Journal of Black Studies* 26 (1996): 604–15; Sandra Y. Millner, "Recasting Civil Rights Leadership," *Journal of Black Studies* 26 (1996): 668–87; Peter Szabo, "An Interview with Gloria Richardson Dandridge," *Maryland Historical Magazine* 89 (fall 1994): 347–49; Jenny Walker, "The 'Gun-Toting' Gloria Richardson: Black Violence in Cambridge, Maryland," in *Gender in the Civil Rights Movement,* ed. Peter J. Ling and Sharon Monteith (New York: Garland, 1999), 169–85; and Belinda Robnet, *How Long? How Long? African-American Women in the Struggle for Civil Rights* (New York: Oxford University Pres, 1998).

8. Philips Packing Company, "Annual Report," 1939–1956; Phillips Packing Company, Vertical file, Enoch Pratt Free Library, Baltimore, Maryland.

9. *FTA News,* January 15 and February 1, 1946, and January 8, 1947.

10. J. Mills Thornton, "Municipal Politics and the Course of the Civil Rights Movement," in *New Directions in Civil Rights Studies,* ed. Armstead Robinson and Patricia Sullivan (Charlottesville: University Press of Virginia, 1991), 38–64.

11. U.S. Department of Commerce, *1960 Census of U.S. Population: General Social and Economic Characteristics of Maryland* (Washington, D.C.: Government Printing Office, 1962); Memo to Attorney General (Regarding Employment in Cambridge), June 18, 1963, in *Civil Rights during the Kennedy Administration, 1961–1963, The Papers of Burke Marshall, Assistant Attorney General for Civil Rights* (Frederick, Md.: University Publications of America, 1984), microfilm edition, reel 26 (hereafter Burke Marshall Papers).

12. John Wennersten, *Maryland's Eastern Shore: A Journey in Time and Place* (Centerville, Md.: Tidewater, 1992), chaps. 3–4; Bill Newhouse, *Maryland Lost and Found* (Centerville:, Md.: Tidewater, 2000).

13. Author interviews with Gloria Richardson; author interview (written) with William Hansen, April 2, 1992; Donna Richardson, interview by Sandra Harney, August 6, 1997 (in author's possession); author interviews with Enez Grubb, February 11, 2000, and August 24, 2001; Clarence Logan, Notes and clipping file (partial copy in author's possession).

14. Author interviews with Gloria Richardson; Lemuel Chester, interview by Sandra Harney, August 2, 1997 (in author's possession); Millner, "Recasting Civil Rights Leadership"; Grubb, *In Spite Of;* CNAC, "Study," State Historical Society of Wisconsin, Madison; "Cambridge Report," CORE Papers, Martin Luther King Jr., Center for Nonviolent Social Change (Frederick, Md.: University Publications of America, 1984), microfilm edition, reel 40.

15. Cambridge *Daily Banner,* June 5, 8, 10, 11, 1963; *Afro-American,* May 18, 1963.

16. CNAC, "Study"; John Lewis with Michael D'Orso, *Walking with the Wind: A Memoir of the Movement* (New York: Simon and Schuster, 1998), 211–12; Author interviews with Gloria Richardson.

17. "Agreement," July 22, 1963, Burke Marshall Papers.

18. Gloria Richardson, "Press Release," Burke Marshall Papers; *Cambridge Daily Banner,* July 24–26, August 2, 4, 9, 10, and September 1, 3, 10, 12, 13, 20, 25, 28, 1963; *Afro-American,* July 20 and September 28, 1963.

19. Murray Kempton, "Gloria, Gloria," *New Republic,* November 11, 1963, 15–17; Robert Liston, "Who Can We Surrender To?" *Saturday Evening Post,* October 5, 1963, 78–80; "Daisy Bates Speaks at A.M.E.," *Cambridge Daily Banner,* November 11, 1963; NAACP Papers, Library of Congress, Washington, D.C., esp. Philip Savage folders, 1962–65.

20. Peter Szabo, "Interview with Gloria Richardson"; Cleveland Sellers, *The River of No Return* (New York: William Morrow, 1973), 71; author interview with Courtland Cox, March 24, 2000; *Cambridge Daily Banner,* May 27, 28, 1964; John Britton, interview of Gloria Richardson, 1967, Civil Rights Documentation Project, Howard University, Washington, D.C.; *Afro-American,* October 5, 1963; Gloria Richardson, "Freedom—Here and Now," *Freedomways* 4 (winter 1964): 32–34; *Packinghouse Worker,* April and May 1964.

21. Cambridge is often associated with Brown because in 1967 he delivered an incendiary address there. Shortly after the address, a fire broke out and Brown was subsequently indicted on charges of having incited a riot. The most famous account of this is James A. Michener, *Chesapeake* (New York: Random House, 1978), 792–93. Fairly typical descriptions of the "Brown riot" can be found in Weisbrot, *Freedom Bound,* 264–65; and Sitkoff, *Struggle for Black Equality,* 203–4. In my book, *Civil War on Race Street,* I suggest that a riot never even took place.

22. Others who have similarly argued that the civil rights movement is best understood from the bottom up are William Chafe, David Colburn, John Dittmer, Adam Fairclough, Robert Norell, and Charles Payne, in their studies of Greensboro, Mississippi, Louisiana, Tuskegee, and the Mississippi Delta, respectively.

23. For instance, see Aldon Morris, *The Origins of the Civil Rights Movement* (New York: Free Press, 1984); David Lewis, "The Origins and Causes of the Civil Rights Movement," in *The Civil Rights Movement in America,* ed. Charles Eagles (Jackson: University of Mississippi Press, 1986), 3–18.

Chapter 5

We've Come a Long Way

Septima Clark, the Warings, and the Changing Civil Rights Movement

Katherine Mellen Charron

January 7, 1957, signaled a quiet new beginning in the civil rights revolution in South Carolina. That evening fourteen adults on Johns Island, a rural Sea Island six miles outside Charleston, enrolled in the first Citizenship School class, pedagogically developed by Septima Clark. Citizenship Schools taught disfranchised African Americans how to read and write so that they might register to vote. The three men and eleven women who gathered in the classroom that night wanted to exercise a right that had been guaranteed for them by federal judge J. Waties Waring a decade earlier. But they thirsted more for the ability to act on their own behalf, a feeling of self-reliance and independence, privileges they had never enjoyed because they lacked formal education. When Esau Jenkins, a neighbor and trusted community leader who had completed the fourth grade, approached them inquiring if they wanted to learn how to register and vote, they responded because he also spoke to their more personal desires. "Do you *want* to read the letter that's coming from your daughter in New York? Do you *want* to be able to fill out a money order? Do you *want* to be able to pay your own taxes?" Jenkins asked.[1] Such practical concerns formed an equally important part of Septima Clark's Citizenship School curriculum; a second-step political education that empowered new voters to understand, through the lens of their own experience, how to transform the quality of their relationship to the wider society.

From New York two months later, Judge Waring's wife, Elizabeth, expressed her disapproval of Clark's latest endeavors to their mutual friend,

Ruby Cornwell: "I wrote her that her pursuits and methods were old past era ones that had proved to be useless—the road she is taking seems to be walking away from the issue, treading old trodden paths of words and not deeds—worthy words but substitutes for the reality of action."[2] Perhaps Waring's critique is understandable, given that ten years earlier her husband had upheld the right of black Carolinians to vote in the Democratic primary.[3] Certainly this served as one of the more dramatic inaugurations of the civil rights era in the Palmetto State. To the impatient Elizabeth Waring, her friend's less dramatic educational approach looked too much like the gradualism preached by white Southern moderates. By any conventional definition of the word "political," what Clark pursued through the classes on Johns Island was not bold or even realistic.

Yet as subsequent decades of unfolding activism would reveal, it was Elizabeth Waring who was clinging to "old trodden paths," and Septima Clark and her Johns Island colleagues who began charting a new world in 1957. From the South Carolina Low Country, Citizenship School classes spread into several Southern states under the aegis of the Highlander Folk School, an interracial adult education center in Tennessee, until attempts by the state to revoke its charter forced Highlander to transfer the program to the Southern Christian Leadership Conference (SCLC) in 1961. That same year Clark left her position as educational director at Highlander and went to work for SCLC, where she continued to train a network of Citizenship School teachers, "people with Ph.D. minds who never had the chance to get an education," to conduct classes in their communities. During the first two years of SCLC's administration, 9,575 Citizenship School graduates registered to vote, and by 1963 3,692 pupils studied in 277 classes in eleven Southern states. According to Andrew Young, the Citizenship Schools "really became a foundation for Martin Luther King's non-violent movement," with graduates playing "a very strong role" in most of SCLC's campaigns.[4] Because they incorporated more than teaching students how to register and vote, Citizenship Schools also fostered a shift in local civil rights movements as ordinary people gained the training and confidence to act when and where traditional community leaders would not. These adult students were among the core of "local people" John Dittmer described a decade ago.[5]

It is possible that Septima Clark could have never succeeded where so many had failed had she not befriended the Warings during the earliest years of the civil rights era, but the alliance cost her dearly. A wealthy, white, Charleston aristocrat, Waties Waring's decisions on behalf of

African American plaintiffs placed him in the vanguard of the post–World War II civil rights struggle. Elizabeth, his second wife, positioned herself similarly when she gave an incendiary speech at the black branch of the Young Women's Christian Association (YWCA) in 1950 and then took her message to a national audience. Their brave stand won them the approbation of the black community and the enmity of whites. With the exception of Septima Clark, Ruby Cornwell, and a few others, African American public support for the Warings proved short-lived, and those who feared association with the couple also distanced themselves from Clark, whom they increasingly considered too radical. Unlike most of her colleagues, Clark refused to compromise with either white paternalism or white repression, which led to her dismissal as a teacher in the city's public schools in 1956.[6]

More broadly, the friendship between Septima Clark and the Warings serves as a useful starting point for understanding the ways in which race and class privilege shaped perspectives of appropriate tactical strategies at a transitional moment in the Low Country civil rights movement. While the iconoclastic Waties and Elizabeth Waring believed that only the force of federal law could bend the will of the white supremacist South, the professional members of Charleston's black community—educators, ministers, independent businessmen, and clubwomen—usually defined the parameters for action on the local level.[7] Because of their education and respectable social standing, they saw themselves as the best positioned to obtain concessions from the city's white fathers on behalf of their neighbors. The greatest obstacle these leaders faced after African Americans won the right to vote revolved around their inability to marshal the power of the ballot effectively. Preferring top-down organizational and legal remedies, neither they nor the Warings could imagine a movement—or perhaps a society—thriving in which the "masses" led and the leaders followed.

Septima Clark had a more holistic vision, and the success of the Citizenship Schools stemmed partially from what she gleaned through her disappointment with the established black leadership in Charleston during the 1950s. Their reluctance to join her led Clark to the realization that "the people in the masses do better" because "they're willing to fight anyhow."[8] She discovered that the critical difference was not that the "masses" had less to lose materially; rather, it was what they gained personally from citizenship education that made them willing to assume the risks of civil rights agitation. As a black teacher and civic activist in the segregated

South, Clark had spent her adult life "teaching citizenship" by helping people to help themselves. By 1957 this had come to mean more to her than instructing poor and disenfranchised African Americans to navigate the obstacles of Jim Crow; "teaching citizenship" meant a kind of politicization that drew upon everyday experience to confront the public world of politics. Whether at the voting booth, the courthouse, or the school board meeting, Clark's program provided students with the tools to effect lasting change. Septima Clark understood, where Elizabeth Waring and others did not, that this type of politicization was itself a more democratic form of direct action.[9]

Septima Clark took her first steps on the road to radicalism before she met the Warings. While living in Columbia, the state capital, during World War II, she had joined the teacher-salary equalization campaign of the National Association for the Advancement of Colored People's (NAACP), an act she characterized as her first "radical" act, "the first time I worked *against* people directing the system for which I was working."[10] Clark returned to Charleston in 1947 and, once there, resumed her teaching and her participation in civic affairs with vigor. With the exception of the NAACP, Clark's civic activism continued to express itself in woman-centered organizations such as the city Federation of Colored Women's Clubs, the local chapter of the National Council of Negro Women, the YWCA, and her sorority, Alpha Kappa Alpha.[11] Her tireless advocacy guaranteed that Septima Clark was well known among the cadre of black women busy in both intra-communal and interracial social welfare work. She belonged to a minority of local activists who assumed the responsibility for leading the postwar civil rights struggle.

The summer Clark arrived home, Judge Waties Waring sent seismic tremors rippling through the state's political community. The Supreme Court's 1944 decision in *Smith v. Allwright* had opened the Democratic primary to black voters—long tantamount to election in the one-party South—but three years later the Palmetto State still successfully skirted the ruling. George Elmore, a member of the black-led Progressive Democratic Party (PDP), filed suit against Democratic Party officials in Columbia after they denied him the right to vote in the 1946 primary. On July 12, 1947, Judge Waring ruled in Elmore's favor, but again confronted the issue of black registration in his court a year later because white officials in Beaufort County had reasoned that membership in the PDP conflicted with the rules of the regular party and purged the names of several African American PDP members from their rolls. In *Brown v. Baskin* the judge made himself clear: "I'm going to say to the people of South Carolina that the time has come when racial discrimination in political affairs has got to stop." He extended the registration deadline and threatened officials who obstructed black enrollment and any troublemakers with contempt of court and imprisonment.[12] The stakes in the civil rights movement in South Carolina had changed and, in the aftermath of this decision, Waring became a detested pariah in his hometown.

Charleston hated Waties Waring for another reason too. Three years before his controversial primary ruling, their blueblood native son had sent even greater shockwaves through the city's social community when he divorced Annie Gammell Waring, his wife of three decades, to marry Elizabeth Hoffman, a twice-divorced Yankee woman. That Elizabeth and her ex-husband had been bridge partners with the judge and Annie set tongues wagging. That the judge had asked Annie to go to Florida to terminate their marriage, since South Carolina law forbade divorce, proved scandalous, if not unethical. That the judge continued to live in the ancestral home of his first wife while she moved into a carriage house around the corner—affording Annie a clear view of the goings-on of her ex-husband and his new wife—was downright dishonorable and barbaric.[13] When some of Charleston's leading black citizens began socializing with the Warings, who lived in the peninsula's most exclusive neighborhood, below Broad Street, it only added fuel to the fire. Local whites sneered and claimed the couple forged these friendships to legitimate the civil rights resumé they had been building since 1947; in reality, social calls by whites dried up after *Brown v. Baskin*. To replace them, the quiet, subdued Waties and the more out-going, strong-willed Elizabeth reached out to the well-educated, economically successful, cultured, and accomplished members of the black community.[14] Such social integration violated the last preserve of separate and unequal. Thus when black Y women decided to invite Elizabeth Waring to speak at their 1950 annual meeting they unleashed a terrific storm.

Charleston's YWCA had two branches: the central branch on Society Street for whites and the Coming Street branch for African Americans. As word got out that the women of Coming Street had chosen Elizabeth Waring as their guest speaker, Society Street women immediately protested. Even if all of the Y women of Society Street did not travel in the south-of-Broad social world that hated Elizabeth Waring, they certainly followed its lead, and they found the idea of that Yankee harlot speaking to any group affiliated with their YWCA absolutely unacceptable. They called a meeting on January 12 to persuade the Coming Street women to rescind their invitation.[15]

Septima Clark, then serving as the latter's chairman of the Committee on Management, listened to their objections and offered an alternative argument. Black women, she reasoned, would know little or nothing of the gossip surrounding the Waring's social life. When Clark refused to un-invite the judge's wife, Society Street representatives threatened that she risked the chance of having an African American woman appointed to their board. "All of this work we have been doing to get this representation will be lost," one woman contended. Clark stood her ground but decided to inform Elizabeth Waring of the new developments. She visited the Warings' house for the first time that evening, aware that it was a delicate mission that led her to knock on the front door of 61 Meeting Street. While there, she made two requests: "If the white people ask you not to speak, will you please speak? And if the Negroes ask you not to speak, please let me know." Over the next few days local gossips had a field day with the controversy, and Septima Clark began receiving threatening phone calls at home.[16]

An audience of approximately 150 Charlestonians turned out to hear what Elizabeth Waring had to say four nights later. The few whites who attended took pains to avoid the featured guest. Expecting trouble from the Klan, Judge Waring had advised organizers to position men around the room and next to the light switches. Clark sat calmly on the dais as Waring delivered what she styled as her "shock treatment" speech. Most contemporary observers—and commentators since—have focused on her describing white Southerners as a "sick, confused, and decadent people," a statement that earned the judge's wife attention in the national press. But she said other things, too, words that reflected her bravery and defiance as much as they revealed the short-sightedness of her social privilege.[17]

In her introductory remarks Elizabeth Waring compared the judge and herself to the force of an atom bomb detonated to "DESTROY" her Southern neighbors' "SELFISH AND SAVAGE WHITE SUPREMACY WAY OF LIFE." She declared that a "NEW DAY" was "DAWNING" and that African Americans were "a truly fortunate people." Then she announced, "I mean to make clear to you now WHY you are fortunate." From there, Waring took the suggested topic, "Achievement," to heart and spoke as someone whose vantage point allowed her to see civil rights change in national and international trends. Outside the South she saw a "tremendous rolling up of forces for good in this country," and she urged black Charlestonians to harness that force to combat Southern white intransigence.[18]

What encouraged her most, however, was "the strength and courage, the purpose and self-respect and dignity" of "the man and woman on the street—particularly the Negro women." By this time, walking the streets of Charleston had become something of a challenge for the judge's wife. White Charlestonians no longer looked Elizabeth Waring in the eye; worse, they pretended not to see her. Refusing to concede them the slightest satisfaction, Waring parlayed her travails into a gift that had bequeathed a special insight: "There is a new look," she claimed, "in the eyes of the Negro women I pass on the streets." Equally palpable was "the rising tide of inspiration and self-assurance of the plain everyday person who has no desire or opportunity perhaps for public importance, but is spreading his influence all around." That influence, both the Warings believed, would be felt most effectively in the wise use of the ballot. "MORE POWER TO YOU AND I AM PROUD TO BE A PART OF YOUR MOVEMENT," she concluded.[19]

The civil rights movement Elizabeth Waring envisioned began with her husband's judicial activism. Indeed, she reserved a messianic role for the judge because it was he who had "rolled away the stone from the grave and brought life to our Negro people as people and human beings." At the same time she understood that African Americans had to walk through that open door, had to take the lead while she and the judge played supportive roles, and she denounced black Charlestonians who capitulated to segregation as harshly as she condemned white supremacists. In "this battle for Negro Rights we cannot weaken our stand and make exceptions"; those who would not toe the line "will have to be spanked," she informed Ruby Cornwell. Women, especially wives of prominent men engaged in the civil rights struggle, had a special mandate: as hostesses, it was their duty to hasten social integration by presiding over interracial gatherings in their home. At a time when moderate pro-Truman Democrats in South Carolina admitted that the state was not prepared "to discuss the abolition of segregation, much less abolish segregation," both of the Warings advocated immediate integration.[20] Given her own defiance and its consequences, Elizabeth Waring reasoned that black Charlestonians had no choice but to side with her and the judge; you were either for them 100 percent or against them to the same degree.[21]

Charleston's black leadership initially agreed with her approach but grew wary of Waring's insistence on action regardless of the consequences. Being the wealthy wife of a federal judge afforded Waring faith in a federal government that most blacks recognized had not yet fully committed to civil rights. It also guaranteed her the option of leaving town if things became unbearable. As an outcast in the heart of the Confederacy who had no respect for local tradition, Elizabeth Waring failed to fully comprehend the extent to which Jim Crow circumscribed African American options and the risks involved for those who attacked it directly. Most leading black Charlestonians, fearful of sacrificing a lifetime of hard-won negotiating power as well as their livelihoods, found the luxury of her impatience too expensive.

Before a month had passed Septima Clark had sipped tea at 61 Meeting Street, and she soon joined the Warings for luncheons and evening meals as well.[22] At first, associating with whites left her uneasy and self-conscious. "I know that having been reared in an environment away from all white people it has been hard to feel comfortable just sitting and talking together," she explained later to Waring. "I was conscious of my appearance and wanted something extraordinary to wear to your house with a fresh hair-do every time."[23] Clark surmounted her discomfort, however, because the experience held great educational potential. "I really felt that I could get a better insight into the political way of doing things and learn more of Charleston and South Carolina politics simply by going to the Waring home and listening to the talk there than I could in any other way," she confirmed.[24]

The Warings mentored Clark in a number of ways. Most significantly, they provided her with valuable advice regarding electoral politics and strategic voting. In an era when black political self-assertion and national civil rights trends forced Southern politicians to prove their segregationist credentials, African American voters had no good choice in the 1950 U.S. Senate race between incumbent Olin D. Johnston and former Dixiecrat presidential candidate Strom Thurmond.[25] During one interracial campaign rally in Charleston, blacks hissed in protest when Johnston accused Thurmond of appointing a "nigger physician" to the state medical board. In response, the senator demanded that someone "make those niggers keep quiet!" Yet during a political debate among black summer school faculty, Septima Clark stepped in and, as she wrote Elizabeth Waring, took "the opportunity of telling the group all the information you gave me about Johnston's seniority and the wisdom [in] back of defeating Thurmond."[26]

Moreover, as Clark divulged to Waring, "your friendship helped me to crash the caste system here." Because her father had been born a slave who then never received an education and her mother had worked as a washerwoman, Septima Clark remained outside the closed circle of black aristocracy. "I wasn't considered too well by that group," Clark admitted, "because they were very fair-skinned people with straight hair." Although her civic work brought her into contact with many of these local leaders, they did not extend social invitations to her. "They would not come to my house. I wasn't good enough. Neither could I go to their house," Clark maintained. Being included on the Warings' guest list made Clark feel that people she could not otherwise engage now listened when she spoke her mind about racial justice.[27] Yet the more timid majority of black Charlestonians soon resented her association with the couple. When the Warings paid a social call to Clark's house, her neighbors worried that she risked making trouble for them. The principal at her school warned her of the danger of socializing at 61 Meeting Street, while her black colleagues complained that Clark's actions legitimated segregationists' claim that "the real reason blacks wanted integration was to socialize with whites."[28]

By advocating complete integration, Septima Clark also distanced herself from the civic-minded black women whose value system she shared and with whom she had worked intimately for years. Coming Street Y women failed to support Clark when she protested the white branch's purchasing tickets in a segregated coach for black delegates traveling to an interracial YWCA conference in New York. After the trip an indignant Clark tried to find out who was responsible and to register her complaint. The result, she reported to the Warings, was "not a word of action taken" by either white or black Y women. "That makes me know," she continued, "that our people need quite an educational program. They will let you down flat and the women in that assembly were all college trained women."[29] Clark's relationship with the Warings had helped her to develop keen insight as far as discerning between empty gestures and concrete progress.

Charleston's 1951 mayoral race drove that lesson home. Incumbent mayor William Morrison squared off against state senator Oliver T. Wallace, the candidate favored by the Warings and their allies. In the days leading up to the election, however, several prominent black Charlestonians threw their weight behind Morrison, presumably in return for future favors. Elizabeth Waring labeled these folk and their ilk "segregation profiteers" and, without the slightest sense of historical irony, advised Ruby Cornwell that, "a more powerful weapon than words will have to be used to whip them into line."[30] Meanwhile, both candidates and much of white Charleston waited anxiously to see whether their black neighbors would vote as a bloc. African Americans constituted almost half the voting-age population in the city's upper wards, 9 through 12, where 60 percent of the population had registered to vote. On election day, as expected, Wallace carried these wards. Yet in ward 12 he beat Morrison by a mere ten votes, which shows how effective the Morrison machine had been in making up lost ground there. The mayor also picked up wards 1 and 2, below Broad Street, and thus won reelection.[31]

Septima Clark attributed Morrison's victory to the fact that he "gave away more money" in wards 11 and 12, which, in turn, had given him more votes the second time around. A few weeks later she confided to the Warings that, "the reports of the behavior of Negroes in the last election are appalling. Many of us are embarrassed greatly. They sold fine opportunities to establish worthwhile principals for chicken dinners, cokes, beer, and whiskey." More problematic to Clark in terms of the long haul was that "the members on the [NAACP] executive board," the city's leading civil rights organization, were "so greatly divided in their thinking."[32]

Disgusted, Elizabeth Waring wrote to Ruby Cornwell declaring dramatically that the election results led her and the judge "to this grave decision that our work in Charleston is done. It is finished. . . . From now on you Negro people will have to work your problems out for yourselves." The Warings also felt betrayed by their black friends who deserted them in the wake of increased harassment, and, less than six months after the election, they moved to New York.[33] Alone, Septima Clark continued to take a stand after they were gone. In the years immediately preceding and following the Supreme Court's ruling in *Brown v. Board of Education*, she informed Elizabeth Waring that she attended as many civic meetings as possible in order to "put in my word" on the subject of integration. People began to think she was pushy. When she transferred to Rhett Elementary School in 1955, a few teachers caustically surmised, "Now she comes over here to rule." "I will speak," Clark answered in her own defense. Still, a lack of familial support and the growing resentment of colleagues left Clark little room to maneuver in her hometown.[34]

Septima Clark's alienation from black Charleston also translated into a frustration with local leadership. "We say so much and do so little," she opined to her friends in early 1952, as efforts to get a new school built for black children went nowhere. Explaining the reason why the NAACP had difficulty recruiting new members that summer, she concluded, "The heart of the apple is rotten."[35] Clark believed that in every area of the struggle Charleston's leadership was shortsighted. When it came to elections, she lamented, "few of us have been trained to think profoundly or to weigh matters on all sides," and she worried over the NAACP's ambiguity in the school fight. "I do want them to be specific and say to the school board exactly what they want in no uncertain terms with sound facts to back them up."[36] Things hardly improved as the stakes rose. Clark judged efforts to petition the school board after the *Brown* decision as ill planned and unnecessarily vague. "Then too the follow up is out of the thinking of the petition leaders. We are back a few more years than when we started." The problem, she confided to the Warings, was that, inside city limits, both "those who have and those who have not are equally fearful."[37]

Seeking an alternative arena for action, Clark visited the Highlander Folk School for the first time in the summer of 1954 and found its approach a welcome change. Highlander based its educational philosophy on cooperative problem solving. Director Myles Horton and his staff began with the assumption that "oppressed people know the answers to their own problems" and proceeded to develop workshops geared toward discovering answers contained "within the experience and imagination of the group."[38] They reasoned that communities experienced oppression embedded in the social structure collectively, and if the source was larger than an individual oppressor, then the solution must also be greater than the answer posed by one individual. Moreover, the development of potential leaders was the key component of the Highlander program and the standard by which it measured its success. The school's concept of spreading leadership throughout a community depended upon ordinary people's taking part in the decision-making process and assuming the responsibility to get their neighbors involved.

Septima Clark had been moving toward the realization that an educational foundation was needed in civil rights work for some time. Her experience at Highlander validated this but also affirmed for her what she long believed: adult education could inform a larger process of politicization that led to individual and communal empowerment. She returned to Charleston determined to recruit some members of a local labor union to attend a Highlander session on school integration. As she explained to the Warings, "They constitute approximately two-thirds of our school patrons and can force the issue if they know how."[39] But Clark did not concentrate her recruitment efforts in the city alone. Through her church work among migrant workers on rural Johns Island and her efforts to get island children immunized, she had come to know Esau Jenkins and she also persuaded him to go to Highlander that summer.

Like countless other local leaders in the civil rights movement, Esau Jenkins owned a piece of land, which gave him a degree of protection from white economic reprisals, and, as a small farmer, he supported his wife and thirteen children. Realizing he would be unable to compete with the increased levels of production made possible by postwar farming mechanization, he decided to buy a bus and use it to transport Johns Island produce, workers, and high school students to Charleston. As Jenkins's bus lumbered toward the city one morning, a woman passenger struck up a conversation with its driver. Alice Wine had not finished the third grade, but aware that Low Country African Americans had started to vote, she wanted to learn about registration laws and promised Jenkins she would vote if he would help her learn how to register. Jenkins agreed, but this initial request gave him another idea. He typed copies of South Carolina's voting statutes and began passing them out to other passengers on the bus. Driving the twenty minutes between Johns Island and Charleston, Jenkins explained portions of the laws; waiting in the city to pick up passengers, he spent time going over relevant sections of the state constitution, and discussing their meaning, with those who could not read. Aside from the in-town stops, which mandated caution, the bus afforded Jenkins and his passengers an ideal opportunity to engage in the dangerous activity of voter education without fear of being caught. When Jenkins got to Highlander, he insisted that the immediate problem he faced was getting African Americans of his community registered to vote so that they might gain some voice in the affairs of the island. He needed help devising a course of action.[40]

Thus, in the early spring of 1955, Septima Clark informed Elizabeth Waring that she had been working secretly with Jenkins and the people he had organized on Johns Island, conducting research for Highlander by taperecording interviews with potential leaders. The results, she added, would be sent back to Highlander and used to develop a leadership-training course for rural areas. Clark predicted that the research stage of the project would take two years and that one-day workshops would be conducted in the meantime. By June, she noted, "This leadership training is really taking hold on the island" and predicted "those people are going to lead the city in a few more years."[41] She had to wait only four months to see the first fruit of her efforts. "The men from the countryside are now taking a part" in Charleston NAACP meetings, she wrote the Warings, while "those who have climbed the social ladder are still at the top . . . doing absolutely nothing."[42] The constituency of the organization was changing.

Both the Warings and Clark imagined a civil rights movement led by people who would act for change. The judge and Waring readily admitted that those who had less to lose showed more courage but still believed that "social betters" should lead the masses. By this time the failure to act had undermined Septima Clark's faith in Charleston's traditional leaders, but Highlander had helped her to imagine different possibilities of leadership.[43] As ever, she remained sensitive to the important role of education. "I do feel a period of interpretation should be the next step," she explained to the Warings in 1956, "conditioned apathetic individuals will need lots of educational discussions before they are aware of the inequalities or inadequacies affecting the race."[44]

She learned from her own personal shortcomings, too. When the City School Board fired her for refusing to conceal her membership in the NAACP, Clark tried to gather a large contingent of teachers to protest the actions of the school board. Only five accompanied her to meet with the superintendent. "I considered that [to be] one of the failures of my life because I think I tried to push them into something that they weren't ready for," she admitted in hindsight. "You always have to get the people with you. You can't just force them into things."[45] That day reminded Clark that even educated people needed specific kinds of training before they would risk their livelihood to agitate on their own behalf. Soon she would apply the same principle to her Citizenship School organizing among the grassroots. "When I went into Alabama and Mississippi, I stayed behind the scenes and tried to work with people, tried to get the people in the town to push forward and then I would come forth with ideas." She continued, "But I wouldn't do it at first because I knew it was detrimental."[46] Shortly after she failed to rally her colleagues behind her Clark moved to Highlander and went to work as its educational director full-time.

Septima Clark, Esau Jenkins, and Myles Horton spent the fall of 1956 preparing to open the first Citizenship School. When it came to selecting a teacher, they decided against professional educators. Clark's recent dismissal underscored for her the timidity of those who remained dependent on the state for employment. Their decision also revolved around the recognition that professionally trained educators would be too middle class in their outlook and therefore unable to resist the temptation of usurping key decision-making roles. Such factors could potentially alienate Johns Island students, some of whom lived in poverty, hewing the land for plantation owners; others who worked as maids and cooks in the city homes of whites; and still others who combined seasonal work in Charleston with farming to eke out a decent living—but all of whom could not read or write well enough to register to vote.[47] Instead, they chose Septima Clark's cousin, Bernice Robinson, a beautician who ran her own shop in Charleston. Robinson protested that she was not the right choice for the job because she had not been to college, but Clark and Jenkins reasoned that a college degree was irrelevant because she would be teaching the most basic subject matter. Clark later observed, "We felt she had the most important quality; the ability to listen to people."[48] Patience mattered, too, because teaching adults to read and write was a laborious, time-consuming task.

The first class of the Citizenship School met two hours a night, two nights a week, for two months during the agricultural off-season. Among the materials Robinson used in the class was a citizenship primer designed by Clark. "My Reading Booklet" contained reprinted sections of the state constitution and voting laws; a copy of a registration certificate; information on the Democratic and Republican parties; a section entitled "Taxes You Must Pay in South Carolina"; a description of Social Security and instructions on how to claim benefits; a list of Charleston health clinics; directions for how to address elected officials; and blank mail-order and money-order forms.[49] Because Septima Clark knew that acquiring citizenship meant acquiring the information that citizens needed to know, materials in the booklet stressed the importance of law and procedure. Like Jenkins's recruiting strategy, however, Clark's curriculum imagined a more complete citizenship that included students' physical and economic well-being. As Clark pointed out, "We need to think about taxes, social welfare programs, labor management relations, schools, and old age pensions. These affect our daily lives and are definitely tied to the vote."[50] At the end of the first Citizenship School, eight of the fourteen students successfully registered, and enrollment increased to thirty-seven. Word spread quickly, and by 1958 three new schools opened, one in North Charleston and one each on neighboring Sea Islands Wadmalaw and Edisto.

Family and community networks often pulled people into local civil rights movements. Esau Jenkins's daughter, Ethel Grimball, became the teacher on Wadmalaw Island. To recruit students she enlisted the help of Willie Smith, "the main person" who rallied "the people together so that when you have the meeting they will be there," and made announcements at meetings of existing, secular community organizations. She also relied on Anderson Mack, who would enroll in her first class. Whereas some could read a little bit before they got to class, Mack had never learned the alphabet and could not write his name. When the sessions ended two months later, "he could kind of scribble 'Anderson,'" Grimball recalled. Another student, Laura Johnson, wanted to learn how to sew, "because she had so many children she figured she could help herself." Grimball, who mainly focused on teaching reading and writing to get people registered, had someone come in to teach sewing and crocheting.[51]

Aside from learning about registration and voting, these more practical concerns drew students to the Citizenship Schools and point to the inherent genius of Clark's program. Graduates became registered voters, but they also transformed their everyday lives as they gained more personal dignity or a marketable skill that could lead to a greater degree of economic self-sufficiency. All the Wadmalaw Island students added their names to the voting rolls, including Anderson Mack, but his education did not end there. "From that literacy class, when we stopped it there, he went onto night school," so that he could learn more, Grimball noted. Her other students experienced similar life changes. "When our people went to the court house, they got better treatment; health care came as a result of all that; better educational condition came as a result of all of that," she testified. "I can just keep naming it because after the literacy school, after people started registering and voting, you got a change in attitudes."[52] Septima Clark added her own evaluation: "One thing spreading out starts others. It's like the pebble thrown in the mill pond."[53]

Ironically Elizabeth Waring could no longer see these ripples created in the wake of her husband's primary ruling. Distance obscured Waring's vision, but more concrete factors led her to erroneously label Clark's work as "substitutes for the reality of action." Defending herself, Septima Clark understood that she had to make her friend see what she could not see from New York, what perhaps Waring had never been able to see from her position of racial and economic privilege. Both women still agreed that complete integration was the goal, but Clark had come to a different conclusion about how it should be accomplished. She now realized that the training that would best arouse action had to begin in autonomous black spaces, away from whites.[54] Clark gently suggested that although Waring could imagine the "plain everyday person" described in her YWCA speech, she knew little of the reality of that life. In a long letter she reminded Waring "how uncomfortable Negroes have felt with white people, especially in the inter-racial meetings before 1954," when "neither would be intellectually honest with the other." "What I think you fail to realize," Clark continued, "is that now just sitting and talking to someone interested in the same ideas is the rarest privilege to people who have virtually been shut up in a prison." Septima Clark's friendship with the Warings had brought her to a new understanding by the time they left town: "A new creature had welled up within and I saw the future full of hazards but [had] no idea of turning back." This was what she sought to replicate for others in the program she had designed: "It's that kind of education that I'm talking about," Clark explained, "not books as such but the education that makes a man a man." She assured Waring that she knew her friend advocated "force in action," and now she wanted Waring to grasp that teaching illiterate adults to read and write was preparing them to become active. "They have to do these to register and vote" but, beyond that—and this point was critical—"to question power structures about housing rights, to know their strength and how to gather strength when presenting petitions."[55] Citizenship training encouraged pupils to raise their voices along with their votes.

Septima Clark had also seen that the personal empowerment they acquired decreased their fear of the white power structure. In February 1959 the Charleston *News and Courier* published an editorial disclosing the true nature of what was happening on the Sea Islands. That same week Clark told Myles Horton: "I'm sure the program will not be hurt because the editorial . . . and the radio broadcasts have failed to intimidate any of our students."[56] Later she wrote Elizabeth Waring, citing Esau Jenkins's lack of fear in talking to the newspaper's pro-segregationist editor—who also happened to be the judge's nephew—Thomas R. Waring Jr. Jenkins "did not put off his church meeting" to see Waring, "but told him where he would be, what he would be doing and the free time afterwards would be the time he could see him. A Negro in South Carolina speaking to one of South Carolina's aristocratic sons," Clark marveled, "<u>We've come a long long long way</u>."[57]

Septima Clark's willingness to use education as a first step to gain last-ing political power differed from the strategic attempts of both the War-ings and Charleston's black leaders. All agreed that increasing the number of "local people" at the polls would make politicians more accountable to the black community. The city's established African Americans believed that more voters would give them the leverage to broker concessions on behalf of the community, but Clark focused on how "local people" them-selves could continue advocating on their own behalf after they left the voting booth. Her Citizenship Schools promoted a transformation in local civil rights movements because where once leaders had determined the appropriate course and then worked to rally support from the "masses," the advent of citizenship education meant that the people decided what goals they wanted to pursue and then developed their own strategies for action.

In 1962 Ruby Cornwell affirmed the effectiveness of the change Septima Clark had helped to bring about in the Low Country civil rights move-ment. "It is ironic that a man from the 'hinterlands' who learned to read only a few short years ago," she wrote Elizabeth Waring of Esau Jenkins, "should be the one who is accomplishing more than anyone else here in the fight for Civil Rights and employment for Negroes."[58] Undoubtedly an organizing genius like Jenkins knew that he needed "the force" of the peo-ple behind him, and that is precisely what Clark's citizenship training pro-vided. In the end, Clark's citizenship training furnished a critical measure of success in the broader civil rights movement as well, and thereby helped to change forever the political landscape of the South.

NOTES

1. Esau Jenkins, quoted by his close associate and Johns Island native William Saunders. In relaying this story as an example of Jenkins's organizing genius, Saunders repeatedly stressed the word "want," and I have preserved that emphasis. See William Saunders's interview with Katherine Mellen Charron, 23 March 2002, Charleston, South Carolina. For a social and cultural background of Johns Island people, see Guy and Candie Carawan, *Ain't You Got a Right to the Tree of Life? The People of Johns Island, South Carolina—Their Faces, Their Words, and Their Songs* (New York: Simon and Schuster, 1966). On the first Citizenship School class, see Septima Clark, with LeGette Blythe, *Echo in My Soul* (New York: Dutton, 1962), 147; and Septima Clark, with Cynthia Stokes Brown, *Ready from Within: Septima Clark and the Civil Rights Movement* (Navarro, Calif.: Wild Tree, 1986), 51.

2. Elizabeth Waring to Ruby Cornwell, 12 March 1957, box 3, folder 2, Ruby Cornwell Collection, The Avery Research Center for African American History and Culture, Charleston, South Carolina (papers hereafter cited as Cornwell Collection; archive hereafter cited as ARC).

3. For an in-depth discussion of Judge Waring's 1947 decisions in *Elmore v. Rice* and the follow-up case, *Brown v. Baskin* (1948), see Tinsley E. Yarbrough, *A Passion for Justice: J. Waties Waring and Civil Rights* (New York: Oxford University Press, 1987), 62–66, 70–76, respectively.

4. Andrew Young interview with Katherine Mellen Charron, January 29, 2002, Atlanta, Georgia. Young also made the comment about people with "Ph.D. minds." On Citizenship School classes, see "Statistical Reports for the Citizenship Schools," box 38, folder 4; and "Semi-Annual Statistical Report, June 1963–November 1963, box 38, folder 14, the Highlander Research and Education Center Papers, 1917–1978, Social Action Collection, State Historical Society of Wisconsin, Madison (hereafter cited as Highlander Papers).

5. The groundbreaking work of both John Dittmer and Charles Payne re-mapped the historiographical terrain of the civil rights movement by placing grassroots activists at the center of their local studies of Mississippi. In terms of the Low Country movement, my argument substantiates Dittmer's that the mobilizing role of the black middle class was minimal at best and underscores Payne's insight about the importance of an organizing tradition. See John Dittmer, *Local People: The Struggle for Civil Rights in Mississippi* (Chicago: University of Illinois Press, 1994); and Charles Payne, *I've Got the Light of Freedom: The Organizing Tradition and the Mississippi Freedom Struggle* (Los Angeles: University of California Press, 1995).

6. On April 16, 1956, the South Carolina legislature passed a law that made affiliation with the National Association for the Advancement of Colored People (NAACP) illegal for city, county, and state employees. Such state repression cost Septima her job and enfeebled the power of the NAACP. See Grace Jordan McFadden, "Septima P. Clark and the Struggle for Human Rights," in *Women in the Civil Rights Movement: Trailblazers and Torchbearers, 1941–1965,* ed. Vicki L. Crawford, Jacqueline Rouse, and Barbara Woods (Bloomington: Indiana University Press, 1993), 85–97, esp. 89. For a broader view of the white South's response to civil rights gains during this era and how it created a fear of white reprisal among black activists, see Numan V. Bartley, *The Rise of Massive Resistance: Race and Politics in the South during the 1950s* (Baton Rouge: University of Louisiana Press, 1969); and Aldon D. Morris, *The Origins of the Civil Rights Movement: Black Communities Organizing for Change* (New York: Free Press, 1984).

7. After the war Charleston's traditional black leaders confronted challenges by new, more aggressive groups such as the Veterans Civic Organization, which appealed to a broader, working-class base and initiated independent actions of their

own. See Millicent Ellison Brown, "Civil Rights Activism in Charleston, South Carolina, 1940–1970 (Ph.D. dissertation, Florida State University, 1997), 138–48.

8. Septima Clark interview with Cynthia Stokes Brown, n.d., Charleston, South Carolina, tape 5, side A, in author's possession.

9. Here I am drawing on theories of critical literacy developed most notably by Paulo Friere. See Henry A. Giroux, "Literacy and the Pedagogy of Political Empowerment," in Paulo Friere and Donaldo Macedo, *Literacy: Reading the Word and the World* (South Hadley, Mass.: Bergin and Garvey, 1987), 1–27.

10. Clark, *Echo in My Soul*, 81, 82. Clark had moved to Columbia in 1929. Not incidentally, both of South Carolina's teacher salary equalization cases were argued in Judge Waring's court and he ruled in favor of the black plaintiffs.

11. Ibid., 90–91. In 1951 Septima wrote a protest letter to the *Pittsburgh Courier* in which she listed her civic affiliations below her signature, including Chairman of the Coordinating Committee of the local NAACP. See Septima Clark to Robert Vann, 2 November 1951, box 9, folder 224, Judge Julius Waties Waring Papers, Moorland-Spingarn Research Center, Howard University, Washington, D.C. {hereafter cited as Waring Papers). See also, "National Council of Negro Women Yearbook," 105, box 11, folder 38, Septima Poinsette Clark Papers, ARC (hereafter cited as Clark Papers); and "Fortieth Anniversary of the South Carolina Federation of Colored Women's Clubs, 1909–1949" (pamphlet), and "Minutes of the Forty-second Anniversary of the South Carolina Federation of Colored Women's Clubs, Cheraw, South Carolina, 4–5 May 1951," in Ethelyn Parker Collection, box 2, ARC. For a broader history of black women's organizational culture, see Evelyn Brooks Higgenbotham, *Righteous Discontent: The Women's Movement in the Black Baptist Church, 1880–1920* (Cambridge, Mass.: Harvard University Press, 1993); Glenda Elizabeth Gilmore, *Gender and Jim Crow: Women and the Politics of White Supremacy in North Carolina, 1896–1920* (Chapel Hill: University of North Carolina Press, 1994); and Deborah Gray White, *Too Heavy a Load: Black Women in Defense of Themselves, 1894–1994* (New York: Norton, 1999).

12. Yarbrough, *A Passion for Justice*, 62–64, 69–75; and *Charleston News and Courier*, 17 July 1948. On *Smith v. Allwright*, see Richard Kluger, *Simple Justice: The History of "Brown v. Board of Education" and Black America's Struggle for Equality* (New York: Vintage, 1977), 234–37. On the Progressive Democratic Party, which spearheaded the 1944 challenge to the seating of South Carolina's all-white delegation at the Democratic National Convention, see Patricia Sullivan, *Days of Hope: Race and Democracy in the New Deal Era* (Chapel Hill: University of North Carolina Press, 1996); and Kari Frederickson, *The Dixiecrat Revolt and the End of the Solid South, 1932–1968* (Chapel Hill: University of North Carolina Press, 2001).

13. Yarbrough, *A Passion for Justice*, 29–41. For her part, Septima believed that Waring's first wife could not abide by her husband's change of heart with regard to civil rights. See Septima Clark interview with Sue Thrasher, 20 June 1981, New Market, Tennessee. For an insightful discussion of how Judge Waring's civil rights

decisions and his divorce coalesced in the minds of white Southerners to signal the collapse of racial and gender hierarchies, see Kari Frederickson, "'As A Man, I Am Interested in States' Rights': Gender, Race, and the Family in the Dixiecrat Party, 1948–1950," in *Jumpin' Jim Crow: Southern Politics from Civil War to Civil Rights,* ed. Jane Dailey, Glenda Gilmore, and Bryant Simon (Princeton, N.J.: Princeton University Press, 2000), 260–74.

14. Yarbrough, *A Passion for Justice,* 110–13. I am greatly indebted to Charlestonian Miriam DeCosta-Willis, who knew the Warings personally, for additional observations on their contrasting personalities.

15. The Charleston Y lagged far behind YWCAs elsewhere in the South—even in upstate South Carolina—as far as embracing the interracialism promoted by the national Y in the late 1940s. See, for example, Eugene C. Hunt's historical play "A Journey in Faith and Courage: The Story of the Coming Street YWCA," Clark Papers, box 11, folder 39. Interestingly Hunt omits the 1950 Waring controversy from his narrative.

16. The YWCA fiasco and hatred for the Warings in general is described in several sources. Septima's version, which includes the quote about interracial representation on the central board and her two requests, appears in her *Echo in My Soul,* 95–99. See also Clark, *Ready from Within,* 25–26; Yarbrough, *A Passion for Justice,* 127–35; and Carl T. Rowan, *South of Freedom,* (New York: Knopf, 1952), 87–100.

17. A year later, writing the editor of *Christian Science Monitor,* Elizabeth Waring declared: "I wrote my shock treatment speech deliberately to break the stone wall of silence on the subject [of civil rights] which the velvet glove method had never penetrated." See Elizabeth Waring to Bicknell Eubanks, 3 January 1951, box 4, folder 12, Cornwell Collection. For examples of analytical commentary, see Yarbrough, *A Passion for Justice*; and Rowan, *South of Freedom.*

18. Copy of "YWCA Speech," in NAACP Papers (microfilm), part 4, reel 11. I have preserved Elizabeth Waring's punctuation and emphasis.

19. Ibid. I am grateful to Joanie Algar for providing me with additional insight into white Charleston's reactions.

20. For Elizabeth's characterization of the judge as a messianic figure, see Elizabeth Waring to Ruby Cornwell, 5 February 1954, box 1, folder 15; on "spanking," see Elizabeth Waring to Ruby Cornwell, 13 July 1951, box 1, folder 2, Cornwell Collection. The point on women becomes clear in another letter Waring wrote to Cornwell that described her impressions of Marion Wright and Alan Payton. "Both of them seem to have some aloofness in their relationship with their respective wives and *neither seem enthusiastic companions much less helpers in the life work of their husbands for Negro rights. This certainly increases the social difficulties.*" See Elizabeth Waring to Ruby Cornwell, 18 May 1955, box 2, folder 2, Cornwell Collection (my emphasis). Maxie Collins, the pro-Truman Democrat, quoted in Yarbrough, *A Passion for Justice,* 141.

21. Elizabeth's daughter, Ann Mills Hyde, made this observation: "My mother was very strong; 'you're either for me or against me'"; quoted in Yarbrough, *A Passion for Justice*, 245.

22. In her "thank you" letter to Ms. Waring, Clark claimed that, for her, the event had "forged a new link in the chain of progress." See Septima Clark to the Warings, 5 February 1950, box 4, folder 52, Waring Papers. Clark was also at the Waring home the day a journalist and photographer from *Colliers* magazine visited, and her picture appeared in their article, "Lonesomest Man in Town," in late April 1950. See Yarbrough, *A Passion for Justice*, 149.

23. Septima Clark to the Warings, 14 June 1959, box 9, folder 231, Waring Papers. More than thirty years later Clark reiterated this point when she noted, "I always had to have my hair straightened and I tried to have a new dress," when visiting the Warings. See Clark, *Ready from Within*, 27.

24. Clark, *Echo in My Soul*, 102.

25. After his death at the age of one hundred, the Thurmond family affirmed that he had fathered a daughter, Essie Mae Washington-Williams, with the family maid, sixteen-year-old Carrie Butler in Edgefield, South Carolina. His daughter was born in 1925 when the unmarried Thurmond was twenty-two and living in his parents' home.

26. Septima Clark to Elizabeth Waring, 30 July 1950, box 4, folder 52, Waring Papers. On a more practical level, the judge tutored his black associates in safeguarding themselves against white reprisals, specifically warning them against the dangers of outstanding debt. See Ruby Cornwell interview with Katherine Mellen Charron, 11 April 2002, James Island, South Carolina. Olin D. Johnston quoted in Yarbrough, *A Passion for Justice*, 153. Frederickson provides good detail on the 1950 U.S. Senate race, which Thurmond lost; see Frederickson, *Dixiecrat Revolt*, 207–9, 213–15.

27. On breaking the caste line in Charleston, see Septima Clark to the Warings, 7 November 1955, box 9, folder 227, Waring Papers; and Clark, *Ready from Within*, 27. For a historical overview of the black elite in Charleston, see Bernard E. Powers Jr., *Black Charlestonians: A Social History, 1822–1885* (Fayetteville: University of Arkansas Press, 1994), esp. chap. 6.

28. Clark, *Ready from Within*, 27–28.

29. Septima Clark to the Warings, 1 June 1955, box 9, folder 227, Waring Papers.

30. Elizabeth Waring to Ruby Cornwell, 25 February 1951, box 1, folder 2; and 2 August 1951, box 1, folder 3, Cornwell Collection.

31. On voting demographics, see A. J. Tamsberg to Mayor Morrison, 13 June 1949, William McGillivray Morrison Papers, box 1, Charleston City Archives, Charleston, South Carolina. For election results, see *Charleston News and Courier*, 24 and 25 July 1951.

32. Septima Clark to the Warings, 2 August 1951, box 9, folder 223, Waring Papers. Of her voting practices, Septima asserted, "I really did not take part in the

eating nor drinking. I did not want anyone to feel that I needed food to vote. I voted for a man whose platform I felt was solid and who would in turn deal fairly and justly with all peoples." See Septima Clark to Elizabeth Waring, 24 July 1951, box 4, folder 53, Waring Papers.

33. Elizabeth Waring to Ruby Cornwell, 12 August 1951, box 1, folder 3, Cornwell Collection. By this time harassment of the Warings had increased dramatically, climaxing when someone threw a large rock through their living room window in October 1950. For his part Judge Waring, who had reached retirement age, also admitted that he was disappointed with the failure of the NAACP to bring litigation before his court. He hoped that his departure would help local African Americans to realize "that they must be the instruments of their own salvation." See Yarbrough, *A Passion for Justice*, 154–71, 210–12.

34. On putting in her word, see Septima Clark to the Warings, 5 May 1954, box 9, folder 226; on comment by teachers of Rhett Elementary School, see Septima Clark to the Warings, 6 October 1955, box 4, folder 53, Waring Papers. Elizabeth Waring described Septima's lack of support in a letter to Ruby Cornwell, noting that Septima told her over the phone, "my family are fighting me." See Elizabeth Waring to Ruby Cornwell, 29 April 1956, box 2, folder 10, Cornwell Collection.

35. First quote about inaction and the building of the new school appears in Septima Clark to the Warings, 26 January 1952. The "rotten" core comment appears in Septima Clark to Judge Waring, 6 July 1952. Both letters are in box 9, folder 224, Waring Papers. To be fair, Septima was not always so pessimistic; her enthusiasm, like that of the Warings, ebbed and flowed throughout this period.

36. Septima Clark to Elizabeth Waring, 30 July 1950, box 4, folder 52; Septima Clark to Judge Waring, 6 July 1952 and Septima Clark to the Warings, 10 March 1952, box 9, folder 224, Waring Papers.

37. Septima Clark to the Warings, 18 January 1956, and 16 September 1956, box 9, folder 228, Waring Papers.

38. Morris, *Origins of the Civil Rights Movement*, 142. See also Payne, *I've Got the Light of Freedom*, 70–77. For a broader discussion of Highlander's educational philosophy, see Frank Adams with Myles Horton, *Unearthing Seeds of Fire: The Highlander Idea* (Winston-Salem, N.C.: John F. Blair, 1975). See also, Myles Horton, "Materials on a Highlander Workshop, 1958," box 82, folder 2, Highlander Papers.

39. Septima Clark to the Warings, 11 July 1954, box 9, folder 226, Waring Papers.

40. See Ethel Grimball interview with Katherine Mellen Charron, 26 February 2002, Wadmalaw Island, South Carolina; Clark, *Echo in My Soul*, 135–36; idem, *Ready from Within*, 46; and Morris, *Origins of the Civil Rights Movement*, 150. For an extended discussion of working-class black resistance, particularly on public transportation, see Robin D. G. Kelley, "We Are Not What We Seem: Rethinking Black Working-Class Opposition in the Jim Crow South," *Journal of American History* 80 (June 1993): 75–112.

41. Septima Clark to the Warings, 22 March 1955, 16 May 1955, and 1 June 1955, box 9, folder 227, Waring Papers.

42. Referring to two previous NAACP meetings, Septima also noted that, "There were only four teachers, not one principal and not one doctor at either of those meetings but the membership has climbed over 1,000 an increase of about 55%." See Septima Clark to the Warings, 6 October 1955, box 4, folder 53, Waring Papers.

43. In a post-retirement interview, Judge Waring expressed his impatience with "the weak-kneed colored people" in South Carolina and conceded that "poorer" African Americans "were the brave ones." Yet he also maintained that "they need stronger and surer support from the people who should be in positions of leadership . . . the Negro ministers, the Negro school teachers, the Negro professional people." Quoted in Yarbrough, *A Passion for Justice*, 212. On Clark's post-Highlander view, see Payne, *I've Got the Light of Freedom*, chap. 3, esp. 68.

44. Septima Clark to the Warings, 3 May 1956, box 9, folder 228, Waring Papers.

45. Clark, *Ready from Within*, 38.

46. Septima Clark interview with Cynthia Brown, n.d., tape 5, side A. Clark specifically connects this later organizing technique with what she learned from failing to get Charleston's teachers to support her in 1956.

47. On the lives and status of Johns Island people, see William Saunders interview with Katherine Mellen Charron, 23 March 2002. "A lot of these people were doing all right economically," Saunders maintained, "but they were not fulfilled because somebody had to tell them what they were getting in a letter and a lot of the time, those folk were lying to them." By contrast, the Carawans document the rural poverty of residents. See their *Ain't You Got a Right to the Tree of Life?* See also Sandra B. Oldendorf, "The South Carolina Sea Island Citizenship Schools, 1957–1961," in Crawford, Rouse, and Woods, *Women in the Civil Rights Movement*, 169–82.

48. Clark, *Ready from Within*, 49. See also Morris, *Origins of the Civil Rights Movement*, 152–54.

49. "My Reading Booklet," box 38, folder 13, Highlander Papers.

50. Septima Clark to Myles Horton, 24 September 1963, box 9, folder 12, Highlander Papers.

51. Ethel Grimball interview with Katherine Mellen Charron, 26 February 2002. On family and community networks leading to civil rights activism, see Payne, *I've Got the Light of Freedom*, esp. chap. 7.

52. Ibid.

53. Clark, *Echo in My Soul*, 162.

54. One of the larger goals of the Citizenship Schools included dispelling the myth of white supremacy, and so program directors agreed that black teachers would teach all classes. See Morris, *Origins of the Civil Rights Movement*, 153. Here I am also drawing on Lawrence Goodwyn's theory of developing a movement cul-

ture. See Lawrence Goodwyn, *The Populist Moment: A Short History of the Agrarian Revolt in America* (New York: Oxford University Press, 1978), introduction, esp. xviii–xix.

55. Septima Clark to the Warings, 14 June 1959, box 9, folder 231, Waring Papers.

56. Septima Clark to Myles Horton, 27 February 1959, box 9, folder 12, Highlander Papers.

57. Septima Clark to the Warings, 14 June 1959, box 9, folder 231, Waring Papers. In the original Septima underlined the last phrase three times.

58. Ruby Cornwell to the Warings, 4 May 1962, box 10, folder 242. Waring Papers. By that time Cornwell was working with Esau's Citizens Committee.

Chapter 6

Organizing for More Than the Vote

The Political Radicalization of Local People in Lowndes County, Alabama, 1965–1966

Hasan Kwame Jeffries

At the start of 1965, in Lowndes County, Alabama, racist voting registrars and the state's voter registration exam guaranteed the exclusion of African Americans from the ballot box. Of the county's 5,122 African Americans of voting age, precisely none were registered to vote. At the same time, more whites were registered to vote than the 1,900 who were eligible. Absolute disenfranchisement reflected the thoroughness with which whites kept African Americans out of politics. So complete was this exclusion that not a single African American had held public office in the county in the twentieth century.[1]

Things began to change in March 1965 when a handful of working poor black residents launched a voter registration drive. The pace of progress, however, was slow. During the first month of agitation, Lowndes activists added only two African Americans to the voting list. Nevertheless their work generated significant movement momentum, resulting in the formation of the Lowndes County Christian Movement for Human Rights (LCCM), through which they coordinated future voter registration tries.[2]

Lived experience ignited the desire of black residents to fight for the vote. A lifetime without the ballot had made clear to them the importance of having a say in who set public policy and enforced the law, especially at the local level. Meanwhile, the Selma voting rights movement, which had started in January 1965, determined the timing of the campaign by serving as an example of the new kind of collective protest that was possible.[3]

The folk who started the Lowndes movement were permanent residents of the county. They were homegrown activists who labored not only to change the place where they lived but also the place where they intended to live for the remainder of their lives. Literally they were local people. Their status as local people was derived partly from the moment—their current place of residence—and partly from the future—where they planned to reside in years to come. It was also a function of the past. Almost all these folk had been born in Lowndes, and many of their parents, grandparents, and great grandparents had been born in the county as well. Thus their local roots were intergenerational, extending as far back as the Reconstruction and Antebellum eras. Their bloodlines, therefore, linked their activism directly and concretely to the struggle for freedom, justice, and equality that the county's black residents had waged since the daybreak of freedom.

Field secretaries of the Student Nonviolent Coordinating Committee (SNCC), led by Stokely Carmichael, partnered with Lowndes activists at the end of March 1965.[4] Although they joined a movement already under way, the myth persists that the struggle in Lowndes did not begin until they arrived. This misconception reflects the tendency of mainstream narratives of the civil rights movement to subsume the activism of local people to that of activists affiliated with national organizations. It also echoes the mistaken belief that black Southerners, particularly those in the rural black belt, had become so accustomed to Jim Crow and cowered by white violence that they had lost the will to fight. The implication is that neither the Lowndes movement nor the larger civil rights movement could have occurred without outside organizers.

The myth of movement messiahs obscures the symbiotic relationship that existed between local people and activists associated with national civil rights groups. Outside organizers brought to the partnership with local people an organizing expertise that allowed the latter to challenge white power in previously unimaginable ways. SNCC organizers, for example, introduced Lowndes County residents to the idea of forming a countywide third party, which resulted in the formation of the original Black Panther Party. Local people, meanwhile, challenged white power in ways that validated new organizing models. SNCC's brand of Black Power, for instance, drew heavily on Lowndes activists' tactical approaches to change.

By mid-summer 1965 the partnership between Lowndes activists and SNCC organizers had prompted more than one thousand black residents to file voter registration applications. The determination of African Americans to secure the franchise, however, did not break the will of whites to keep the ballot out of black hands. Five months into the voting rights campaign, county registrars had added only two hundred African Americans to the voter list, and these they added only to avoid federal intervention.[5]

Despite the nominal increase in the number of black registered voters, the mobilization effort was worthwhile because it put movement activists in perfect position to take advantage of the Voting Rights Act, which President Lyndon Johnson signed into law on August 6, 1965. It also forced the Justice Department to send federal registrars to the county, a notable accomplishment since Attorney General Nicholas Katzenbach dispatched registrars to less than 1 percent of the counties that, by law, ought to have received them. It is important to note that although the Voting Rights Act unlocked the door to black participation in electoral politics, it did not open it. This door remained closed until local people pushed it open by forcing the federal government to dispatch registrars, and by registering with them even though it remained dangerous to do so. In these ways, movement leaders and everyday people gave meaning to federal legislation.[6]

African American re-enfranchisement created new political opportunities that local people exploited. In December 1965 movement leaders announced the formation of the Lowndes County Freedom Organization (LCFO), an independent, countywide third party that the press dubbed the Black Panther Party because local activists had selected a snarling black panther as the party's ballot symbol. In the November 1966 general election, the LCFO ran a full slate of African American candidates for local office against white Democrats and Republicans.[7]

Forming an all-black independent party in the heart of Dixie was a remarkable accomplishment given the depth of black political exclusion. Six months earlier, registering eligible black voters even in small numbers was inconceivable. Even more remarkable, however, was the party's embrace of democratic politics. LCFO supporters worked hard to democratize political participation. Dissatisfied with simply mobilizing eligible black voters, they labored to expand the politically educated electorate by arming black voters with knowledge of the legal limits and obligations of officeholders. This prepared black residents to critically evaluate candidates. They also made available to black voters everything they needed to know about Alabama election law and county government, from how to get on the ballot to how to mark one. This helped residents avoid being bamboozled on

Election Day. In addition, LCFO supporters committed themselves to democratizing office holding. Party activists sought to pave the way for public officials who eschewed personal agendas in favor of a people's agenda by deemphasizing political experience and expertise as prerequisites for holding office. Finally, party supporters embraced a democratic platform. The LCFO policy agenda, for example, included fighting poverty by redistributing white wealth through major tax reform. "Tax the rich to feed the poor" was the campaign slogan of LCFO candidate for tax assessor Alice Moore, which captured the essence of the party's democratic program.[8]

By the November 1966 election, African Americans in Lowndes County had reached levels of political awareness rarely achieved by others in the civil rights movement. Life experiences greatly informed their political sophistication. When Frank Miles Jr., one of the first county residents to become active in the movement, was asked why local people had formed the party, he explained, "it didn't make sense for us to join the Democratic Party when they were the people who had done the killing in the county and had beat our heads." Life experiences, however, do not adequately explain grassroots political radicalization. Local people throughout the South, in counties identical to Lowndes, did not form democratic third parties at the moment of re-enfranchisement. Rather than life experiences, the political radicalization of local people in Lowndes County resulted from specific movement experiences that began, but did not end, with trying to register to vote.[9]

The movement in Lowndes was about more than the vote. In addition to access to the ballot box, local activists agitated for quality education by boycotting segregated African American schools and transferring African American students to white schools. They fought to lessen the economic distress of the working poor by developing a job-training program. They worked to help black farmers break free of cyclical debt by forming a farmers' cooperative and organizing for control of the county committees that set farm assistance policy. They sought to improve quality of life by bringing War on Poverty programs to the county. They also waged war against jury discrimination and courtroom corruption by filing federal lawsuits against the county's jury commission clerk and a justice-of-the-peace. The victories, and even more so the defeats, that accompanied these struggles taught local people valuable lessons that pointed them and the local movement in the direction of independent politics.

The uncommon degree of political insightfulness exhibited by the black residents of Lowndes County was as much a result of their having participated in political education workshops designed specifically for them by SNCC organizers, as it was a product of lessons learned from organizing for social and economic justice. Starting in December 1965 SNCC workers hosted a series of workshops for the residents of Lowndes at which they discussed the guidelines that governed third parties and independent candidates, and the duties associated with the offices up for election. These workshops helped local people make informed decisions about what to do with the vote and, in doing so, laid the foundation for the LCFO's democratic structure and policy agenda.

Scrutinizing local people's experiences organizing for social and economic justice, and their participation in a structured political education program, makes clear the process that radicalized their politics. The efforts of Lowndes County residents to improve the quality of black schools, bring the War on Poverty to the county, and control the committees that assisted and regulated farmers, along with their participation in SNCC's workshops, heightened their level of political awareness, leading them to create an all-black, democratic third party as their primary political solution to racial injustice. Studying this process also illuminates important aspects of the larger civil rights movement. It shows that local people organized for more than the vote, underscores the way in which they gave meaning to federal legislation, and demonstrates the ability of America's most forgotten and forsaken citizens to formulate and organize around their own critique of society. Moreover, it shines new light on the give-and-take relationship that existed between local people and outside organizers. SNCC field secretaries had a significant influence on the political solutions pursued by local people, and local people, through their organizing activities, had a profound effect on SNCC's ideological approach to social change.

A decade after the U.S. Supreme Court ordered school desegregation with "all deliberate speed," Lowndes County schools remained completely segregated. The county board of education maintained the dual system by shamelessly diverting resources away from black schools to white schools. In this way, white elected officials denied African Americans the quality education they deserved. One indicator of the poor state of black education was the African American adult illiteracy rate, which neared 80 percent.[10]

Shortly after the county's black residents mobilized to register to vote, they organized to improve the quality of black education. Young people were the catalysts behind this push. In April 1965 John Jackson and Timothy Mayes, neighbors and upperclassmen at Lowndes County Training School (LCTS), the county's oldest and largest public high school for African Americans, petitioned superintendent of education Hulda Coleman to increase the school's library holdings, extend the library's hours of operation, ban mandatory extracurricular activities during class hours, and add a breakfast program. Predictably Coleman dismissed the appeal without discussion. Her arbitrary decision, however, did not deter the two friends. On the contrary, they moved forward by calling for a school boycott, and turned to the leaders of the Lowndes County Christian Movement for Human Rights to help them execute the protest.[11]

LCCM leaders rallied substantial community support for the school boycott. The protest unraveled, however, when word spread that the local law "ain't going to let nobody register" until the students returned to school. Knowing that whites in power would make good on the threat, and realizing that black residents had more faith in registering to vote as a means to create change than in boycotting a high school, movement leaders called off the protest. At the same time, however, they agreed to renew it in the fall. In the interim, they planned to broaden the base of support for the boycott by having voter registration workers discuss its importance as they canvassed. The need to increase people's awareness of the possibility of change through protest other than voter registration had become clear.[12]

LCCM leaders announced their intention to renew the boycott at a mass meeting on August 29, just days before the start of the 1965 school year. As planned, they had discussed the merits of boycotting LCTS with parents during the summer as they knocked on doors encouraging folk to register. This political education work helped the boycott last longer than the first one but was not enough to keep it from disintegrating in less than a month. Once again, parents withdrew their support prematurely. School board intransigence had made it painfully obvious that parents would have to keep their children out of school indefinitely, which they were unwilling to do; poor schooling was better than no schooling. Their unwillingness to sustain the boycott led local leaders to create the county's first freedom schools. Former public school teachers who had been fired because they supported the movement, and SNCC volunteers, taught math, reading, French, and black history at the schools, which met in church sanctuaries and household living rooms. With an alternative in place, LCCM leaders, in mid-October, launched a third school sit-out. At first participation was high, but only a handful held true to the protest for an extended period. The freedom schools, as a temporary stopgap measure, were not enough to allay parents' worries about their children losing classroom time.[13]

Although ineffective, the boycotts provided movement leaders with valuable insights. First, local activists learned the importance of political education, not to raise consciousness about oppression (local people knew all about oppression from lived experience) but rather to raise awareness of the potential of collective action other than voter registration. Second, through the freedom schools, local activists glimpsed the potential of parallel structures to help sustain struggle. Later, when Stokely Carmichael suggested that they create a third party, the idea of working outside existing structures did not seem strange. Third, local leaders began to see that asking for change, even demanding it through organized protest, was not enough to create new public policy. With increasing clarity, movement leaders saw the need to control the school board. There was even talk of "running the county themselves," recalled LCCM chairman John Hulett, a thirty-seven-year-old father and husband who farmed land that had been purchased by his grandfather, a former Lowndes County slave.[14]

Concurrent with the fight to improve education was the effort to raise the standard of living of the county's working poor. By the 1960s agricultural mechanization and the conversion to dairy farming had sharply curtailed labor opportunities, enabling obscene levels of poverty to persist. In 1965 Lowndes County was the poorest county in Alabama, ranking dead last in per capita income. Not surprisingly, conditions for African Americans were the worst. While the median income for the county's white families was $4,400, the median income for the county's African American families was $935. According to the federal government, the minimum income necessary for a family to maintain a decent standard of living was $3,000.[15]

LCCM leaders looked to the War on Poverty to help alleviate the prevailing condition of poverty. In early August 1965, in a letter to Sargent Shriver, the director of the Office of Economic Opportunity (OEO), movement leaders explained: "The war against poverty offers hope for the future to Negroes in Alabama's black belt." Local activists were particularly impressed with the War on Poverty's Community Action Program (CAP), which, on paper, allowed ordinary people to plan and implement federally funded programs designed to improve quality of life. Programs established elsewhere provided poor black folk with preschools, adult education, job training, legal aid, and health clinics.[16]

LCCM leaders launched the effort to bring the War on Poverty to the county by hosting a series of neighborhood meetings at which they asked black residents to identify their most pressing problems and suggest possible solutions. A consensus soon emerged that first they ought to address the wretched state of housing. Dilapidated and deteriorating housing was a key component of poverty in Lowndes. Nine of ten African American homes lacked bathrooms and indoor plumbing. LCCM secretary Lillian McGill, a thirty-three-year-old single mother who had given up a decent-paying clerical job in Montgomery to work for the movement full-time, explained that most black residents had to haul water in coverless, sixty-gallon barrels once a week, from as far as fifteen miles away, to meet their household needs. The only alternative was to draw water from ponds used by cattle.[17]

Members of the LCCM executive committee also held neighborhood elections for representatives to a CAP planning committee. They opted to elect representatives rather than appoint them to ensure that the committee was a "broadly based representative group of Negro citizens." Acting on these same democratic sensibilities, they reserved a minority of the seats on the committee for representatives from the white community. They were willing to work with whites but unwilling to surrender their right to make decisions.[18]

The county's white power brokers, however, were unilaterally uninterested in working with African Americans and secretly organized to make sure that they did not have to. In early June 1965 members of the Board of Education and the Board of Revenue, together with a group of leading businessmen, joined with counterparts from three predominantly white counties to file an application for a CAP planning grant under the name Area 22. White power brokers wanted to win recognition as the county's OEO representative before African Americans had a chance to organize, and sought to neutralize the potential strength of the county's black majority by allying with majority white counties. In another shrewd move, they named a single African American, William "Sam" Bradley, a small farmer and businessman who had taken no interest in the movement, to the governing board of Area 22. Bradley's appointment was nothing more than a calculated attempt to dupe the OEO into believing that Area 22 represented African Americans.[19]

When local people discovered that a white group had submitted a CAP proposal and that the group was masquerading as a "biracial committee" they were stunned. In a letter to the OEO protesting the "formation and maneuverings" of Area 22, LCCM leaders wrote: "We are willing to work with the white community but [unwilling to] let them totally represent us. . . . We no longer wish to be spoken for without being asked what is best for poor people and how we will be governed in relation to Federal funds."[20]

White disinterest in interracial cooperation did not stop black residents from forming a CAP planning committee. It did stop the OEO from approving their grant application, as well as the application of Area 22. In both instances, OEO officials cited a failure of the planning committees to adequately meet the criteria for fair racial representation.[21]

Attempts by white power brokers to block supporters of the freedom movement from bringing a CAP to Lowndes County was a key experiential component of the political radicalization of local people. The covert formation of Area 22 provided activists with a snapshot of the extent to which whites in power would resort to political trickery and deception to maintain the status quo. In addition, the refusal by whites to recognize the right of African Americans to have the determining say in programs that would affect them most underscored white unwillingness to allow African Americans to make the decisions that shaped their lives.

Black farmers, especially black tenant farmers, felt keenly the economic distress that movement activists sought to alleviate through the War on Poverty. Some eighty-six white families, accounting for less than 3 percent of the population, owned almost all the land in the county. LaRue Haigler was typical of this class. Haigler owned approximately five thousand acres and contracted with thirty-five African American tenants to work a portion of it. By Haigler's own estimate, his tenants owed him between $100,000 and $150,000; some owed on loans that were thirty-five and forty years old. Debt of this sort was widespread, even among black landowners; they, too, had to borrow heavily from white financiers to run the agricultural year. Unfortunately overcoming privately financed debt was virtually impossible because white landowners controlled the county's Agricultural Stabilization and Conservation Service (ASCS), which offered the only alternative to borrowing from local white financiers.[22]

ASCS was the division of the Department of Agriculture that provided farmers with price supports in the form of loans and direct cash payments. It also decided the amount of cotton, peanuts, and tobacco that a farmer could plant, set penalties for those who exceeded their allotments, and determined eligibility for participation in conservation programs. In assessing the power of ASCS, one astute news reporter observed that it alone could decide a farmer's annual earnings.[23]

Committees of local farmers elected by their neighbors set ASCS policy at the county level. Theoretically ASCS elections were open to any farmer above the age of twenty-one. Unfortunately nominal federal oversight enabled large landowning whites to dictate election outcomes. Not a single African American had ever been elected to an ASCS county committee (the local policy-making board) in the entire South, and in 1964, of the thirty-seven thousand committeemen elected to the South's seven thousand community committees (the groups that selected county committeemen), only seventy-five were African American.[24]

In July 1965 SNCC field secretaries organized a series of ASCS education workshops for groups of ten to fifteen farmers in each ASCS community in the county. At the workshops, SNCC workers shared everything they knew about ASCS programs and electoral procedure. Providing local people with information that whites traditionally withheld helped black residents understand the support structure that undergird the status quo and envision new ways of undermining it. The tremendous value of having access to previously denied information was not lost on local people. They absorbed what SNCC workers uncovered and enthusiastically shared it with friends, family, and neighbors. Mathew Jackson Sr., a landowning farmer and the father of high school student John Jackson, was one of more than two dozen local people who canvassed the county and spoke at churches to increase ASCS awareness. "I'd do it in practically every church I went to," he said. "I just explained to them as I went along . . . [that] it was time out for letting white people make a monkey out of us. In other words, [letting them] use us for working tools."[25]

In September twenty-five African American farmers agreed to run for ASCS community committee seats. Mathew Jackson was one of those farmers. When asked why he chose to run, he explained: "I thought probably that I knew more about these people in here, their needs, more so than the people that were already in these offices."[26]

In years past, white farmers had manipulated the outcome of ASCS elections by refusing to nominate black farmers. "I've gotten one of those ASCS ballots in the mail for over five years now," explained a young black farmer. "I started voting but it was always the same kind of people on the ballot." In the October 1965 ASCS election, however, a new candidate nomination procedure mandated by Washington, which allowed any farmer to nominate a candidate simply by securing the signatures of six farmers who lived in the candidate's neighborhood, gave local people a fighting chance.[27]

Rather than submit to the democratic process, large landowning whites continued to subvert it. When black residents received their mail-in ballots they discovered that an additional 109 African American farmers had been listed alongside the 25 supported by the LCCM. In Mathew Jackson's district, white committeemen had added an extra 36 African Americans. In another district they had nominated an additional 68 black farmers. Obviously they were trying to split and dilute the African American vote by abusing a second federal mandate that instructed local ASCS officials to nominate African Americans in proportion to their percentage of the population.[28]

Lowndes County whites did not limit their effort to retain control of ASCS to ballot manipulation. According to SNCC field reports, whites physically threatened black candidates and those who signed their petitions, torched the home of candidate James Harris, and evicted candidate Threddie Lee Stewart, along with his wife and three children, from land that his family had worked for several generations.[29]

Through intimidation and ballot manipulation, white candidates won fifteen of the eighteen seats that carried voting privileges. In December these fifteen white farmers elected three of their own to the policy-making county committee.[30] Much like the outcome of the October vote, the result of this election was tremendously disheartening. The frustration born of both defeats prompted many local people to discontinue their affiliation with the freedom struggle. "Some of them," explained Elzie McGill, the stepmother of LCCM secretary Lillian McGill and a movement stalwart in her own right, "they wasn't strong enough to just go on, they just decided that you can't tell [white people] nothing." For others, the lessons learned were quite different. Some came to better appreciate the reach of white power. LCCM founding member Frank Miles Jr. observed: "When we had the ASCS election, we found out how we was tricked by the ASCS . . . the white people had control over that." For many, bearing witness to the shortcomings of democracy and the great lengths their white neighbors were willing to go to protect their power made clear that whites would neither share nor yield power without a dogged fight. This realization inspired them and others to redouble their support of the freedom movement. More important, it pushed more people squarely into the camp of independent politics. In retrospect, it was one of the most important experiential components of local people's political education. "The white folks tricked us in the ASCS election, that's when I started to get wise to the Democratic Party," explained Sidney Logan Jr., a World War II veteran and the imminent Freedom Party candidate for sheriff. "That's what gave me the idea I better stick with the Black Panther if I want to win. The Democratic Party is full of tricks. White people control it."[31]

The ASCS debacle confirmed what local people had learned from organizing to bring the War on Poverty to the county—white power brokers would use fraud, deception, and violence to maintain the status quo. In doing so, it extinguished what little possibility remained that supporters of the LCCM would cast their lot with the Democratic Party. LCCM chairman John Hulett explained, shortly after announcing the establishment of the LCFO, that "many people in the Christian Movement and SNCC felt that Lowndes County public officials threw away their last chance to court the Negro vote in this election."[32]

Meanwhile, significant black voter registration following the arrival of federal registrars in August 1965 prompted LCCM leaders to discuss the best ways to translate African American votes into political power. Stokely Carmichael, who had not forgotten the Democratic Party's duplicitous treatment of the Mississippi Freedom Democratic Party (MFDP) in Atlantic City in 1964, suggested that they take advantage of an obscure Alabama law left over from the post-Reconstruction era that allowed for the formation of countywide, independent political parties.[33] The suggestion captured the imagination of LCCM leaders. "We thought about what we were going to do with these 2,500 registered voters in the county, whether or not we were going to join Lyndon Baines Johnson's party," explained John Hulett. "Then we thought about the other people in the state of Alabama who were working in this party. We thought of the city commissioner of Birmingham, Eugene 'Bull' Connor; George Lingo, who gave orders to those who beat the people when they got ready to make the march from Selma to Montgomery; [and Jim Clark,] the sheriff of Dallas County." Upon reflection, it was painfully obvious that these were the people "who kept Negroes from voting in the South and in the State of Alabama." Simply stated, local people did not want to support a party that supported white supremacists. That the standard bearers of white supremacy in the county were Democratic Party leaders further diminished the appeal of the party.[34] Also, losing their political voice was a great concern. "If we went into the Democratic Party they would still control us," explained Hulett. "We would have to do the things they wanted us to do."

He added: "We had to find some ways or means to get our own people on the ballot." Thus, in September 1965, LCCM leaders voted to investigate the possibility of creating a third party.[35]

It is important to note that local people made the decision to pursue independent politics. As much as Stokely Carmichael and his fellow organizers may have wanted the county's black residents to develop a third party, it was not their decision to make. In true SNCC fashion, they provided information that revealed a new possibility for creating change, and then stepped aside to let local people decide the next move. "The SNCC workers brought the idea to us that we could organize our own political group if we wanted to," explained John Hulett. He added that the decision of whether to organize the party "was left entirely to the people of Lowndes County."[36]

As LCCM leaders assessed the viability of a third party, they turned to SNCC for help. They did so with a clear idea of the kind of assistance they wanted. The disappointing outcome of the ASCS crusade had taught them that winning political power required more than having the vote and fielding a slate of black candidates. They realized that they had to elevate political awareness, much as they had done during the school boycotts. Accordingly, they asked SNCC organizers to devise a political education program for their fellow residents that focused on local government. The thinking was that unless they knew the ins and outs of county government, trying to form a third party was pointless. They also believed that it made no sense to focus on "glamorous offices" such as the governorship that were too far removed from the local situation to make an immediate difference.[37]

In December 1965 SNCC organizers scheduled four weekend workshops for Lowndes activists at SNCC's Atlanta headquarters. The goal of the workshops was to teach local people everything they needed to know about Alabama election law and county government. To this end, each workshop began with a discussion of the statutory and constitutional guidelines for nominating third-party candidates and conducting elections. The focus then shifted to the legal powers associated with the positions up for election in November 1966, which included the offices of sheriff, tax assessor, tax collector, and coroner, as well as seats on the school board. It is important to note that SNCC facilitators purposefully steered talk away from abstract theories until, as they put it, "the participants had a clear idea of the statutory powers of the office." For example, they discussed theories of arrest and habeas corpus, differences between civil and criminal procedures, and dispossession and foreclosure only after everyone knew the statutory powers of the sheriff. By deconstructing political power and authority, they removed the mystery behind county government.[38] Also, by grounding political theory in actual Alabama law, they gave political power concrete meaning and demonstrated that local politics was an appropriate way to build the kind of society local people wanted. A conversation about the power and authority of the school board, for example, led to a discussion about physical plant necessities, curriculum change, and teacher requirements. This approach also brought into sharp focus the extent to which serious abuses of power were taking place. A SNCC report noted that, after discussing the duties of the coroner, "it became clear to everyone" that murder at the hands of persons unknown could not have gone "uninvestigated and unpunished" without the coroner's "connivance and collusion." Thus the workshops armed participants with valuable criteria for evaluating officeholders.[39]

Movement leaders learned enough at the initial workshops to announce the formation of the Lowndes County Freedom Organization at the end of December 1965. When a reporter asked an unnamed movement supporter about the new organization, she explained: "White folks think they can let a few of us vote and fool us. [But] we're starting to see how to use the vote to help ourselves instead of helping them."[40]

Although the Atlanta workshops helped local leaders to see the potential and practicality of independent politics, too few county residents made the trip to Atlanta for the workshops to have had a significant effect on the size of the politically educated electorate. Only twenty-five local people attended the first workshop in December, and no more than fifty people attended the last meeting in February. Local interest, however, was much greater than the attendance figures imply. From the outset, enthusiasm for the workshops ran high as participants returned from Atlanta and shared what they had learned with friends, family, and neighbors. Unfortunately the cost of traveling to Atlanta proved too burdensome for most. In response to this dilemma, SNCC organizers, at the end of February 1966, began conducting biweekly workshops in the county. At these workshops, just as at the Atlanta workshops, local people learned about electoral procedure, county government, and the duties of officeholders. In this way the workshops reached hundreds of people and dramatically increased the size of the politically educated electorate.[41]

Educating as many people as possible about county government was essential to building the independent party's democratic foundation. So, too, was increasing the number of residents who believed themselves qualified and capable of holding office. To boost the latter, workshop facilitators deemphasized experience and expertise, the twin pillars of political professionalization, as prerequisites for holding office. This not only increased the number of local people who believed that they could hold office but also elevated a people's agenda for socioeconomic empowerment above personal agendas. This explains why, on April 2, 1966, when some sixty ardent supporters of independent politics met to officially organize the LCFO, they did not discuss candidates. In a radically democratic way, candidates were irrelevant.[42]

Twelve potential LCFO candidates did eventually step forward. In this group of six men and six women were landowners and landless laborers, college graduates and elementary school dropouts, mothers of many and fathers of a few, and parishioners at large community churches and worshipers at small family churches. These fallible, fear-filled, yet determined people, who because of the fickleness of history had been born into an extreme situation at a unique time, very much reflected the core demographic of the Lowndes movement; they were the epitome of local people.

On Sunday, April 24, 1966, less than two weeks before the LCFO held its candidate nomination convention, each would-be nominee addressed party supporters at a countywide mass meeting. The high point of the meeting was the speech given by the lone candidate for tax assessor, Alice Moore, a forty-two-year-old wife and mother who divided her time between working on her farm with her husband, Joseph, caring for their seven children, and volunteering at Mt. Elam Baptist Church.[43] Holding the crowd's rapt attention, Moore declared: "Tax the rich to feed the poor—that's my slogan." The two hundred people in attendance applauded feverishly. "If everyone had been taxed their fare share," she continued, "we'd have better schools and good roads today." If elected, she promised to execute the duties of tax assessor in such a way as to provide the most benefit to all citizens. She pledged to be a servant of the people and committed herself to implementing a people's agenda rather than a personal agenda. Before taking her seat, she declared that it was time for black residents to take over county government.[44] Moore's speech revealed an understanding of the central significance of the unequal distribution of wealth to the problems plaguing local people, a firm grasp of the power of the office she sought, and knowledge of the extent to which white officeholders had been derelict in their duties. It also reflected the lessons local people had learned while organizing and attending workshops.

Grassroots enthusiasm for the LCFO persuaded SNCC organizers to make winning control of local government the centerpiece of their organizing work. In May 1966, at a staff meeting held in Kingston Springs, Tennessee, they voted to apply the political program developed in Lowndes to existing and future projects. This development is particularly noteworthy because it highlights the reciprocal relationship that existed between local people and outside organizers. The success of the political program that emerged in Lowndes validated Black Power—SNCC's new ideological and tactical approach to change. Indeed, the Lowndes County political program defined Black Power, which SNCC organizers understood to mean developing grassroots, independent political parties through which African Americans could win local office and secure a definitive say in the decisions that affected their lives. That Lowndes County was the seedbed from which Black Power sprang was not lost on SNCC organizers. "SNCC's Alabama experience was the immediate genesis of the concept of Black Power," wrote Ivanhoe Donaldson, the director of SNCC's New York office, in October 1966. Writing at the same time, Stokely Carmichael explained: "Our last year of work in Alabama added a new concrete possibility." That possibility was the creation of grassroots, independent political parties, and local people made it viable.[45]

Months of exhausting electoral preparation gave rise to high hopes for victory. Unfortunately, on November 8, 1966, LCFO candidates lost every race by a couple of hundred votes. African American nonparticipation hurt LCFO candidates considerably. Some 50 percent of the county's eligible black voters had not yet registered, and about 20 percent of those who had registered stayed at home on Election Day, fearing reprisals for voting.[46] The primary reason the party lost, however, was electoral fraud. In several communities, for instance, plantation owners handed employees marked sample ballots, trucked them to the polls, and commanded them to vote for the white candidates marked on the sample.[47] Despite the campaign of chicanery, LCFO candidates polled 40 percent of the total vote, an extraordinary accomplishment for a third party.[48]

SNCC's political education workshops deserve much of the credit for the LCFO's strong showing. The workshops dramatically increased the size of the politically educated electorate and, in the process, democratized political participation, a significant accomplishment given the history of exclusion in the county. Perhaps more extraordinary, however, was the contribution the workshops made to democratizing political decision making. By teaching local people everything they needed to know about Alabama election law and county government, the workshops armed black residents with knowledge of the legal limits and obligations of officeholders—information needed to critically evaluate candidates and curb the abuses of those already in office. Equally remarkable was the contribution the workshops made to democratizing office holding. By teaching movement activists about the procedures for forming a third party, promoting a people's agenda, and deemphasizing political experience and expertise as prerequisites for holding office, the workshops paved the way for candidates like Alice Moore who rejected personal politics in favor of what was best for the county's working-poor black residents.

The struggle of local people for social and economic justice radicalized their politics. The defeats and victories that accompanied their efforts to improve black education, ameliorate poverty, and gain access to new sources of capital revealed the importance of political education and the extent to which whites would fight to maintain the status quo. At the same time, information about county government, electoral law, and alternatives to the Democratic Party disseminated at SNCC workshops sharpened their political analysis and provided them with a blueprint for actualizing insights gained from organizing.

The radicalization of the grassroots in Lowndes makes clear that no single organizing endeavor, or individual, dictated local people's political beliefs and aspirations. Local people's political awareness was not a result of apocalyptic events or movement messiahs but was the product of a process of critical reflection that began with filtering movement experiences through a framework of premovement memories. This led local people to conceive of an entirely new social order, one in which the disenfranchised and dispossessed made the decisions that affected their lives, and local and federal government assumed a leading role in creating and sustaining equality of opportunity and outcome. Their participation in a structured political education program, meanwhile, unveiled the specific mechanics of their oppression and helped them translate their political insights into a concrete organizing program.

The radicalization of Lowndes County's black residents also illuminates the purpose of voting rights agitation. For local people, securing the vote was just one aspect of a much larger struggle. Rather than fighting solely for political inclusion, they fought to dramatically transform the society in which they lived. Voting rights agitation, therefore, was a means to an end that transcended legislation. More so than a voting bill, local people wanted the power to shape public policy. In Lowndes, local people sought the vote and created the LCFO to implement their broadly configured organizing agenda. This empowered them politically and gave meaning to the Voting Rights Act.

In addition, political radicalization in Lowndes underscores the symbiotic relationship that existed between local people and outside activists. Local people started the movement that took root in the county, and SNCC organizers contributed to its development by providing invaluable organizing assistance. Undoubtedly the Lowndes movement would have taken place without the participation of SNCC organizers. However, it would have evolved differently because the information and organizing expertise that SNCC field secretaries shared with local people significantly shaped the ways that local people prosecuted their struggle. It is highly unlikely, for instance, that county residents would have formed an independent party had SNCC not joined their struggle. At the same time, while SNCC organizers gave much to local people, they received much in return. The political program that developed in the county, for example, gave final form to SNCC's version of Black Power.

In Lowndes County the journey local people traveled as they organized for more than the vote determined their political destination to a greater degree than anything else. This was not unique. In local struggles across the country, organizing experiences shaped the political orientation and objectives of movement participants, which helps to explain the strikingly dissimilar outcomes of local movements that emerged in remarkably similar places. It also serves as a reminder of the importance of taking full measure of local people's organizing experiences when assessing movement aims and results.

NOTES

1. Lowndes County is located in south central Alabama, between Montgomery and Selma. It is the geographic buckle of the state's Black Belt region, which consists of a string of fifteen counties with fertile, black clay soil and majority African American populations stretching 170 miles, east to west, across the middle of the state. For voter registration statistics on Lowndes and other Alabama counties, see Pat Watters and Reese Cleghorn, *Climbing Jacob's Ladder* (New York: Harcourt, 1967), Appendix ii, "Voter Registration in the South—1962, 1964, 1966"; SNCC, "Special Report" (February 1965), 2, Martin Luther King Jr. Archives (hereafter, MLK Archives), *Student Nonviolent Coordinating Committee Papers* (hereafter,

SNCC Papers), box 35, folder 5; and Student Nonviolent Coordinating Committee, *The General Condition of the Alabama Negro* (Atlanta: SNCC, 1965), 24–26.

2. Lowndes County residents named the Lowndes County Christian Movement for Human Rights after Reverend Fred Shuttlesworth's Birmingham-based Alabama Christian Movement for Human Rights.

3. Interview with John Hulett by Stanley Smith, 30 May 1968, Howard University Archives (hereafter, HU Archives), *Civil Rights Documentation Project* (hereafter, *CRDP*); "Lowndes County Freedom Organization Leaders Talk about Their Party," *The Movement* (June 1966), in Clayborne Carson, ed., *The Student Voice, 1960–1965: Periodical of the Student Nonviolent Coordinating Committee* (Westport, Conn.: Meckler, 1990), 126; interview with John Hulett by Hardy T. Frye, 1973, Auburn University Archives, *Hardy T. Frye Oral History Collection*, RG 621, box 2, folder 27; interview with John Hulett by author, 17 July 2000; and Charles Eagles, *Outside Agitator: Jon Daniels and the Civil Rights Movement in Alabama* (Chapel Hill: University of North Carolina Press, 1993), 120–25.

4. SNCC organizers entered Lowndes County six months after the Mississippi Freedom Democratic Party failed to unseat the lily-white Mississippi delegation at the Democratic National Convention in Atlantic City in 1964. The defeat soured veteran organizers on the Democratic Party. At the same time it heightened their interest in independent politics. Soon after the challenge, several SNCC organizers discussed converting the MFDP into an independent party, but native Mississippi activists opposed the idea; they had not yet given up on liberal Democrats. Respecting their wishes, SNCC field secretaries withdrew from Mississippi and resettled in Selma, Alabama, where they worked with Southern Christian Leadership Conference (SCLC) organizers on the Selma voting rights drive. Tactical disagreements, however, made working with SCLC untenable and prompted SNCC organizers to relocate to Lowndes County, a place that they believed was too violent and oppressive to interest SCLC.

5. John Herbers, "9 Counties to Get Vote Aides Today," *New York Times*, 10 August 1965, 1; and SNCC WATS Report, 13 August 1965, 2, MLK Archives, *SNCC Papers*, box 40, folder 5.

6. By the end of October 1965 more than 40 percent of Lowndes County's eligible black voters had registered. SNCC WATS Report, 13 August 1965, 2, MLK Archives, *SNCC Papers*, box 40, folder 5; SNCC WATS Report, 24 October 1965, MLK Archives, *SNCC Papers*, box 41, folder 2; Gene Roberts, "Voting Officials Sign 1,444 Negroes First Day of Drive," *New York Times*, 11 August 1965, 1; U.S. Commission on Civil Rights, *The Voting Rights Act . . . The First Months* (Washington, D.C.: Government Printing Office, 1965), 16, 35; Gail Falk, "New Federal Examiners Register Negro Voters in Hale, Dallas, Marengo, Lowndes Counties," *Southern Courier*, 13 August 1965, 1; and Eagles, *Outside Agitator*, 197.

7. Alabama required political parties to have ballot symbols because of the high rate of adult illiteracy. The Democratic Party's ballot symbol was a white rooster.

Movement activists selected a panther because, as one local leader put it, cats chase roosters. Moreover, black panthers, when cornered, fought back with fury and without forgiveness. Black folk not only felt cornered but also felt the need to fight back. "Lowndes County Forms Local Political Group," *Student Voice,* 20 December 1965, 2, MLK Archives, *SNCC Papers,* box 51, folder 3; and Gene Roberts, "Student Rights Group Lacks Money and Help but Not Projects," *New York Times,* 10 December 1965, 37. For more on the selection of the black panther as the LCFO's ballot symbol, see Charlie Cobb, "Ready for Revolution," *Emerge* (June 1997): 43; and "Lowndes County Freedom Organization Leaders Talk about Their Party," 126.

8. "Mass Meeting Day Tuesday for Lowndes County Party," *Southern Courier,* 30 April–1 May 1966, 1; and "Lowndes County Freedom Organization Leaders Talk about Their Party," 126.

9. Frank Miles Jr., as quoted in "Lowndes County Freedom Organization Leaders Talk about Their Party," 126.

10. Plaintiff's complaint in *USA v. Lowndes County Board of Education et al.,* filed 11 January 1966, 3, Alabama Department of Archives and History (hereafter, ADAH), Alabama Governors' Papers 1963–1967, SG 20061, folder 22; and Alabama Department of Education, "Lowndes County Survey, 182," 1964, 12–13, ADAH, Alabama Department of Education, School System Surveys, SG 22324.

11. Edward Rudd, "Negro, White Lowndes Parents Wonder about School Integration," *Southern Courier,* 13 August 1965, 4; John Benson, "A New Freedom Party—Report from Alabama," *The Militant,* 2 May 1966, 1, 3; and *The Black Panther Party. Speech by John Hulett. Interview with Stokely Carmichael. Report from Lowndes County* (New York: Merit, 1966), 19.

12. Interview with Lillian McGill by Stanley Smith, 29 May 1968, HU Archives, *CRDP*; "Lowndes County Freedom Organization Leaders Talk about Their Party," 126; and "[Minutes of] Staff—People's Meeting [at Selma, Alabama, SNCC Office], 24 May 1965, 3, MLK Archives, *SNCC Papers,* box 94, folder 22.

13. Edward Rudd, "Lowndes Renews Boycott," *Southern Courier,* 25–26 September 1965, 1, 5; interview with Lillian McGill by Smith, 29 May 1968, HU Archives, *CRDP*; and SNCC WATS report, 24 October 1965, MLK Archives, *SNCC Papers,* box 41, folder 2.

14. John Hulett, as quoted in *The Black Panther Party. Speech by John Hulett. Interview with Stokely Carmichael. Report from Lowndes County,* 19.

15. SNCC, "Special Report," February 1965, 2, MLK Archives, *SNCC Papers,* box 35, folder 5; and Staff Report, "A Population, Employment, and Income Profile of Negroes in a 16–County Area of South Central Alabama," in U.S. Commission on Civil Rights, *Hearing before the United States Commission on Civil Rights: Montgomery, Alabama, 27 April–2 May 1968* (Washington, D.C.: Government Printing Office, 1968), 688–722.

16. Gail Falk, "Anti-poverty Programs Offer Many Chances for Progress," *Southern Courier,* 16–17 October 1965, 4; and John Hulett, Frank Miles, and Lillian

McGill to Sargent Shriver, 8 August 1965, and "Resident Participation," in application for OEO grant submitted by the Lowndes County Anti-Poverty Action Committee, November 1965, 3, Exhibit E, MLK Archives, *SCLC Papers,* box 148, folder 2.

17. In 1960 the U.S. Census Bureau defined dilapidated housing as that which "does not provide safe and adequate shelter and in its present condition endangers the health, safety, or well-being of the occupants." The same year census enumerators judged 28 percent of African American houses in rural Alabama dilapidated and another 34 percent deteriorating. SNCC, *The General Condition of the Alabama Negro,* 23. Testimony of Dr. Albert Wolf, in U.S. Commission on Civil Rights, *Hearing Held in Montgomery Alabama, 27 April–2 May 1968,* 251–55. Albert Wolf based his testimony on a 1965 survey of one thousand of the three thousand African American homes in Lowndes County. He also reported that less than 4 percent of white homes lacked indoor bathrooms and plumbing. Interview with Lillian McGill by Smith, 29 May 1968, HU Archives, *CRDP.*

18. "Resident Participation," in application for OEO grant submitted by the Lowndes County Anti-Poverty Action Committee, November 1965, 1–4, MLK Archives, *SCLC Papers,* box 148, folder 2.

19. Ibid., and M. E. Marlette Jr. to Senator John Sparkman, 18 July 1966, ADAH, Alabama Governors' Administrative File, SG 22400, folder 31 (2 of 2).

20. "Resident Participation," and John Hulett to Community Action Program, Office of Economic Opportunity, 22 August 1965, in application for OEO grant submitted by the Lowndes County Anti-Poverty Action Committee, November 1965, 6, Exhibit E, MLK Archives, *SCLC Papers,* box 148, folder 2.

21. Lowndes activists did succeed in securing a $240,640 OEO grant to develop a self-help housing and job-training program. For more on this award, see Nelson Lichtenstein and Robert Smith, "$500,000 to CR Groups," *Southern Courier,* 16–17 July 1966, 1. "Description of structure of Lowndes County Anti-Poverty Action Committee," in application for OEO grant submitted by the Lowndes County Anti-Poverty Action Committee, November 1965, 1, MLK Archives, *SCLC Papers,* box 148, folder 2; M. E. Marlette Jr., "Report of Attempts in Lowndes County, Alabama, to Organize an Interracial Community Action Program," 18 November 1966, 2–3; M. E. Marlette to Lister Hill, 5 December 1966, 2, ADAH, Alabama Governors' Administrative File, SG 22400, folder 31 (2 of 2); and Sargent Shriver to Lister Hill, 17 January 1967, 1, ADAH, Alabama Governors' Administrative File, SG 22400, folder 31 (2 of 2).

22. Testimony of L. R. Haigler in U.S. Commission on Civil Rights, *Hearing Held in Montgomery, Alabama, 27 April–2 May 1968,* 163–72; "Farm Talk: ASCS Committeemen Decide Cotton Allotment," *Southern Courier,* 20 August 1965, 2; Fay Bennett, "The Condition of Farm Workers, in 1962," in *Report to the Board of Directors of National Sharecroppers Fund,* n.d., 1, 3, MLK Archives, *SNCC Papers,* box 55, folder 14; and Sarah Heggie, "Rural Study Links Poverty with USDA Discrimination," *Southern Courier,* 2–3 December 1965, 4.

23. SNCC, "ASCS Organizers Handbook," 1965, 1–2, MLK Archives, *SNCC Papers*, box 51, folder 2; Department of Agriculture, "ASCS Background Information," *Bulletin*, no. 1 (February 1965): 1–4, MLK Archives, *SNCC Papers*, box 51, folder 2; Eagles, *Outside Agitator*, 135; and Mike Kenny, as quoted in Nelson Lichtenstein, "ASCS: 'A Gut Issue,'" *Southern Courier*, 30–31 July 1966, 1.

24. "Farm Talk: ASCS Committeemen Decide Cotton Allotments," *Southern Courier*, 20 August 1965, 2; Fay Bennett, "The Condition of Farm Workers in 1962," in *Report to the Board of Directors of National Sharecroppers Fund*, n.d., 1, 3, MLK Archives, *SNCC Papers*, box 55, folder 14; and Memo to Friends of SNCC, "ASCS Elections," 5 November 1965, MLK Archives, *SNCC* Papers, box 51, folder 3.

25. Elmo Holder to B. L. Collins, 18 July 1965, MLK Archives, *SNCC* Papers, box 51, folder 1; Edward M. Rudd, "Farmers Plan ASCS Races," *Southern Courier*, 30–31 October 1965, 1; Edward M. Rudd, "New Political Group in Lowndes to Name Own Negro Candidates," *Southern Courier*, 1–2 January 1966, 1; Alabama SNCC Staff Report, August 1965, MLK Archives, *SNCC Papers*, box 94, folder 21; Memo from Janet [Jemott], Tina [Harris] to Silas [Norman], Murial [Tillinghast], September/October 1965, MLK Archives, *SNCC Papers*, box 94, folder 21; and interview with Mathew Jackson Sr. by Robert Wright, 4 August 1968, HU Archives, *CRDP.*

26. Interview with Mathew Jackson Sr. by Robert Wright, 4 August 1968, HU Archives, *CRDP.*

27. SNCC, "ASCS Organizers Handbook," 1965, 9, MLK Archives, *SNCC Papers*, box 51, folder 2; unnamed black farmer as quoted in Edward M. Rudd, "Negro Farmers Must Use the Vote Well to Win in This Fall's ASCS Elections," *Southern Courier*, 25–26 September 1965, 4.

28. Memo to friends of SNCC, "ASCS elections," 5 November 1965, MLK Archives, *SNCC Papers*, box 51, folder 3; Edward M. Rudd, "Moves Hurt Negroes in ASCS Campaign," *Southern Courier*, 13–15 November 1965, 5; Affidavit of Stokely Carmichael taken by Edward Reed Jr., [Special Agent, Office of Inspector General, USDA], 11 March 1966, 1–2, MLK Archives, *SNCC Papers*, box 51, folder 3; and SNCC press release, "Alabama ASCS Elections Held Today," 15 November 1965, MLK Archives, *Papers of Bob Mants*, box 1, folder "Ala Lowndes Co—LCFO ASCS Community Committee Election, 1965."

29. "SNCC Program: ASCS Elections, 1965," October 1965, MLK Archives, *SNCC Papers*, box 51, folder 3; and SNCC press release, 28 December 1965, 2, MLK Archives, *SNCC Papers*, box 35, folder 5.

30. Affidavit of Stokely Carmichael taken by Edward Reed Jr., 11 March 1966, 4; "No Negroes Elected to New ASCS County Committees," Lowndes *Signal*, 8–9 October 1966, 1; Doug Harris and Tina Harris to Reverend Kenneth K. Marshall, 2 December 1965, MLK Archives, *SNCC Papers*, box 149, folder 1b; John Lewis to Orville Freeman (Secretary, Department of Agriculture), 30 November 1965, MLK Archives, *SNCC Papers*, box 2, folder 10; "New ASC Community Committee Elected," Lowndes *Signal*, 9 December 1965, 1; Stokely Carmichael, as quoted in

Edward M. Rudd, "Freedom City, Alabama: Lowndes Families Start Tent Village," *Southern Courier,* 8–9 January 1966, 1; and Rudd, "New Political Group in Lowndes," 1.

31. Interview with Elzie McGill by Wright, 4 August 1968, HU Archives, *CRDP*; and Frank Miles Jr. and Sidney Logan Jr., as quoted in "Lowndes County Freedom Organization Leaders Talk about Their Party," 126.

32. John Hulett, as quoted in Rudd, "New Political Group in Lowndes," 1.

33. *The Black Panther Party. Speech by John Hulett. Interview with Stokely Carmichael. Report from Lowndes County,* 8; interview with John Hulett by Smith, 20 May 1968, HU Archives, *CRDP*; SNCC Research Department, "Background on the Development of Political Strategy and Political Education in Lowndes County, Alabama," 1, MLK, Archives, *SNCC Papers,* box 46, folder 11; Rudd, "New Political Group in Lowndes," 1; "Lowndes County Freedom Organization Leaders Talk about Their Party," 126; and interview with Mathew Jackson Sr. by Wright, 4 August 1968, HU Archives, *CRDP.*

34. John Hulett, as quoted in *The Black Panther Party. Speech by John Hulett. Interview with Stokely Carmichael. Report from Lowndes County,* 8; and Frank Miles Jr., as quoted in "Lowndes County Freedom Organization Leaders Talk about Their Party," 126.

35. Staff Report, "Voting and Political Participation by Blacks in the 16 Alabama Hearing Counties," in U.S. Commission on Civil Rights, *Hearing held in Montgomery, Alabama, 27 April–2 May 1968,* 922–40; "Negroes Urge Court to Bar Alabama Act," *New York Times,* 9 March 1966, 81; John Herbers, "U.S. Sues to Force a Vote in Alabama," *New York Times,* 23 March 1966, 1; interview with John Hulett by Smith, 20 May 1968, HU Archives, *CRDP*; SNCC Research Department, "Background on the Development of Political Strategy and Political Education in Lowndes County, Alabama," 1, MLK Archives, *SNCC Papers,* box 46, folder 11; John Hulett, as quoted in Rudd, "New Political Group in Lowndes," 1; and in "Lowndes County Freedom Organization Leaders Talk about Their Party," 126; and interview with Mathew Jackson Sr. by Wright, 4 August 1968, HU Archives, *CRDP.*

36. John Hulett, as quoted in "Lowndes County Freedom Organization Leaders Talk about Their Party," 126.

37. Jack [Minnis] to Bill Strickland, 21 October 1965, 1, MLK Archives, *SNCC Papers,* box 45, folder 1.

38. Jack Minnis, "The Story of the Development of an Independent Political Movement on the County Level" (Louisville, Ky.: Southern Conference Educational Fund, 1967), 1–2, Duke University, Library Pamphlet Collection.

39. SNCC Research Department, "Background on the Development of Political Strategy and Political Education in Lowndes County, Alabama," 4, MLK Archives, *SNCC Papers,* box 46, folder 11.

40. "Lowndes County Forms Local Political Group," *Student Voice,* 20 December 1965, 2, MLK Archives, *SNCC Papers,* box 51, folder 3; and unnamed movement

supporter, as quoted in Roberts, "Student Rights Group Lacks Money and Help but Not Projects," 37.

41. SNCC WATS Report, 6 December 1965, MLK Archives, *SNCC Papers*, box 41, folder 5; Benson, "A New Freedom Party," 1, 3; and Minnis, "The Development of an Independent Political Movement," 2.

42. SNCC, "News of the Field #4," April 1966, MLK Archives, *SNCC Papers*, box 35, folder 9.

43. "Profile of Alice Moore," MLK Archives, *Papers of Robert Mants*, Box 1, Folder "Lowndes County—LCFO, Profile of Candidates."

44. "Mass Meeting Day Tuesday for Lowndes County Party," 1; and "Lowndes County Freedom Organization Leaders Talk about Their Party," 126.

45. Ivanhoe Donaldson to the Editors of the *New York Times*, October 1966, 1, *SNCC Papers*, MLK Archives; Stokely Carmichael, "What We Want," *New York Times Review of Books*, 22 September 1966; and Stokely Carmichael [Kwame Ture], as quoted in Cheryl Lynn Greenberg, ed., *A Circle of Trust: Remembering SNCC* (New Brunswick, N.J.: Rutgers University Press, 1998), 167.

46. Viola Bradford, "Lowndes: A Good Day to Go Voting, but Black Panther Candidates Lose," *Southern Courier*, 12–13 November 1966, 1; Alice Moore, as quoted in Viola Bradford, "Election Aftermath in Lowndes: 'Sold His People for a Coke,'" *Southern Courier*, 19–20 November 1966, 1; Terence Cannon, "Lowndes County: Candidates Lose, but Black Panther Strong," *The Movement* (December 1966), in Carson, *Student Voice*, 183; Terrance Cannon, "Interview with Sidney Logan, Jr.: 'They'll come on over to us,'" *The Movement* (December 1966), in Carson, *The Student Voice*, 184; and interview with Lillian McGill by Smith, 29 May 1968, HU Archives, *CRDP*.

47. U.S. Commission on Civil Rights, *Hearing Held in Montgomery, Alabama, 27 April–2 May 1968*, 596–603; Cannon, "Lowndes County: Candidates Lose," 183; Cannon, "Interview with Sidney Logan, Jr.," 184; interview with John Hulett by Smith, 30 May 1968, HU Archives, *CRDP*; and interview with Lillian McGill by Smith, 29 May 1968, HU Archives, *CRDP*.

48. The LCFO's strong electoral showing won local people the right to change the LCFO's name to the Lowndes County Freedom Party. For election results and reports on white chicanery, see Bradford, "Lowndes: A Good Day to Go Voting," 1; "How Lowndes County Voted," Lowndes *Signal*, 10 November 1966, 2; SNCC, "Election Reports (Georgia, Alabama, Mississippi)," 10 November 1966, 1, MLK Archives, *SNCC Papers*, box 35, folder 9; "Dallas: DCIFVO Head Not Discouraged," *Southern Courier*, 12–13 November 1966, 1; Fred P. Graham, "Rural Deep South Elects 10 Negroes," *New York Times*, 12 November 1966, 16; U.S. Commission on Civil Rights, *Hearing Held in Montgomery, Alabama, 27 April–2 May 1968*, 594–96; Bradford, "Election Aftermath in Lowndes," 1; Cannon, "Lowndes County: Candidates Lose," 183; Cannon, "Interview with Sidney Logan, Jr.," 184; and interview with Lillian McGill by Smith, 29 May 1968, HU Archives, *CRDP*.

Protest March, Alcorn College. *Front left:* Charles Evers, March 1966. *Courtesy of Mississippi Cultural Crossroads.*

Chapter 7

"God's Appointed Savior"
Charles Evers's Use of Local Movements for National Stature

Emilye Crosby

Charles Evers first garnered national attention in June 1963 when his younger brother Medgar Evers, the NAACP's first field secretary in Mississippi, was assassinated. Charles immediately claimed his brother's job and although Medgar's record and the publicity surrounding his death gave Charles instant legitimacy—among Mississippi African Americans and movement leaders and supporters around the country—he floundered for much of the next two years, failing to establish a viable civil rights program, fighting with other civil rights activists in Mississippi, and alienating his NAACP bosses. His only real success was as a visiting speaker who could draw and captivate audiences, and as a source of legitimacy for liberal white politicians (through the Evers name). That changed in late 1965, when he seemed to stumble on a formula for generating successful local movements in a portion of Mississippi that had been largely untouched by previous activism. Using the newly passed Voting Rights Act as an opening wedge for massive voter registration drives that transformed the political landscape of several black majority counties, Evers also produced considerable excitement and spurred action among local blacks through his impressive speaking ability, forceful articulation of shared grievances, and very visible, public challenges to the powerful white men who had dominated these communities for decades. He was also a magnet for new NAACP members and popularized economic boycotts against white merchants as a tactic for generating leverage for immediate concessions, like desegregation of public facilities, the use of courtesy titles for black customers, and expanded employment for African Americans.

Evers's association with these visible, apparently strong local movements with obvious tangible successes came at a time when the national NAACP was desperate to regain prominence and a toehold in Mississippi. At the same time white segregationists were searching for new ways to maintain the status quo, and the national movement was in transition, with increasing strains between white liberals and the Student Nonviolent Coordinating Committee (SNCC), which had previously dominated the Mississippi movement and recently garnered considerable national attention for the 1964 Freedom Summer project. As a result, Evers's role in and association with county-level movements in southwest Mississippi, particularly the one in Claiborne County, positioned him as a key player, locally, in Mississippi, and around the nation. These local movements secured his tenuous position with the NAACP, provided him with a base for competing with other civil rights organizations and activists, gave him national legitimacy, generated the power he needed to negotiate with white segregationists, and served as the foundation for several nationally celebrated political campaigns. To many, especially movement supporters outside the state, Evers and these local movements, especially the electoral potential of newly enfranchised black communities, appeared to epitomize the promise of the civil rights movement and to represent the final step in securing full citizenship for African Americans.

Because of this, Evers and the local movements in which he was involved were widely perceived as triumphant. Evers was, in fact, extremely important—as a catalyst for widespread black voter registration, as a role model for challenging the mores of white supremacy, and as an inspiration for overcoming the pervasive fear that reinforced white authority. Yet this was only part of the story. At the same time Evers's authoritarian and undemocratic style hampered local leadership, and his personal goals and ambitions quickly undermined his ability to effectively speak and work for the widespread, long-term empowerment of most of the African Americans who filled the ranks of the movements he led. Because he could prosper economically and politically without significantly altering the existing status quo, he saw no need to mount a substantive challenge to that status quo, even though it effectively locked out the majority of blacks. Ultimately it became clear that Evers was always more self-serving politician and businessman than civil rights leader; he actively pursued profit and became a power broker, using movement achievements to enhance his financial well-being and to develop ties with influential liberals and segregationists. Thus while Evers was important to many local people and small communities, especially in southwest Mississippi, and did play a critical role in challenging white supremacy, he ultimately used local movements as a platform for consolidating his personal power and influence. In many respects his success was dependent on keeping others from having the same access.

Although Evers is at the center of this story, he was able to use these local movements to enhance his power largely because, at some level, his vision and use of power appealed to the national NAACP, which was more concerned with its prestige and ability to compete with other civil rights organizations than it was with the larger goals it had been founded to pursue. Even more important is that prominent liberals and segregationists simultaneously embraced Evers. Thus while part of this history is the story of Evers's betrayal of the local people who saw him as a savior, answered his call to act, and, in the process, secured his power, it is also the story of the self-serving actions and shared interests of people who, on the surface, appear incompatible. In the end, it seems that the NAACP, segregationists, and liberals all embraced Evers because, despite his inconsistent actions and outspoken, confrontational style, he helped preserve the economic and political status quo of those in power.

Evers's entrance into the Mississippi movement was abrupt and controversial. When Medgar Evers was assassinated, Charles returned to Mississippi from Chicago, where, by his own account, he had been pimping, running numbers, and bootlegging. Even before his brother was buried, Charles Evers claimed his job with the NAACP by telling several reporters that he was replacing Medgar. Evers later wrote that NAACP head Roy Wilkins "almost slit his throat" shaving when he heard on the radio "that the NAACP had picked Medgar's successor: Charles Evers." Evers added, "The last thing Roy wanted was Medgar's rough, tough big brother coming out of the Chicago rackets to soil Medgar's memory and tarnish the NAACP." In fact, despite reservations, Wilkins did concede Charles the job rather than risk a public confrontation with the slain martyr's brother. Charles Evers asserted, "With the memory of Medgar's murder so close, he just couldn't refuse an Evers."[1] This incident exemplifies the opportunism and ambition that characterized Charles Evers throughout his life.[2]

Three months after Evers took over as the NAACP field secretary for Mississippi, NAACP Director of Branches Gloster Current pointed out to Wilkins that although Evers was "not as well prepared and grounded in our movement as we would like," Current was "impressed by his aggres-siveness and willingness to move out in several directions and not wait to find out what he should do. In other words, he believes in erring by doing rather than erring by inaction." Despite this hopeful tone, Evers and the nation's oldest civil rights organization were a bad match. Evers never saw himself as a cog in the NAACP machine and consistently ignored national policy, embarrassed the organization with his speeches, refused to follow its guidelines for submitting reports, and issued press releases with typing, spelling, and syntax errors. His controversial style and propensity to act on his own without consulting his superiors kept him in hot water. NAACP officials alternately ordered and cajoled him to consult with the national office and to have his speeches pre-approved; they questioned his judg-ment and, where possible, gave him explicit instructions for handling con-troversial situations like the trial of Byron de la Beckwith, accused of mur-dering his brother. Within a year of Evers's hiring, Gloster Current's cau-tious optimism had evaporated, and he wrote Evers, "There are times when I despair of ever being able to obtain from you a clear understand-ing of how an executive functions in the NAACP."[3]

When Charles Evers began his work as NAACP field secretary, the orga-nization had a tenuous presence in Mississippi, with about a dozen branches. Virtually all the civil rights activism in the state was initiated by SNCC and the Council of Federated Organizations (COFO), an umbrella group that coordinated civil rights work in the state from 1962 to 1965. While SNCC/COFO workers moved into communities, encouraging voter registration, teaching in citizenship and freedom schools, and organizing the Mississippi Freedom Democratic Party (MFDP), the NAACP had little to report. During his first two years as state field secretary, Evers was a popular guest speaker around the country but did little at home. Evers's rare reports, a continuing source of contention with the national office, had little to say about NAACP activity, and he initiated little in the strug-gle for civil rights. Evers was actually most active in trying to undermine civil rights rivals, SNCC and COFO, something that Gloster Current praised him for.[4]

Despite their shared antipathy of COFO, Evers's conflicts with Wilkins and Current escalated in October 1964 when he explicitly defied orders and used a Buffalo, New York, NAACP speech to endorse Robert Kennedy in the latter's Senate race. Current complained to Wilkins's assistant, John Morsell, that Evers was acting as "if he were God's appointed savior," and contended, we have "a very real problem which we are going to have to deal with." The following summer when Evers again blatantly ignored the NAACP nonpartisan policy, Current made a case for firing Evers for "gross misconduct" and "incompetence." In addition to his repeated violation of policies and procedures, Current charged that Evers had failed to cooperate with "top-level staff" working on a voter registration project.[5] It appeared that Charles Evers's connection to Medgar, and his work to undermine COFO, were no longer enough to appease the national office.

Ironically the decline of SNCC/COFO and an August 27, 1965, Klan car bomb attack that injured Natchez, Mississippi, NAACP branch president George Metcalf gave Evers a reprieve and the opportunity he needed to save his job. Although he had little or no prior involvement in the Natchez movement, many people in the area were immediately receptive to him as Medgar's brother and he took the community by storm, articulating widespread black anger and publicly warning whites that blacks were armed and ready to retaliate. His bold statements and charismatic speaking captivated many Natchez blacks, who flocked to hear him at mass meetings. After quickly winning popular support, Evers moved to take over the Natchez movement and destroy rival organizations.[6] Evers also increasingly followed the NAACP party line (perhaps because his job was in jeopardy or because, at a fundamental level, he shared more with the New York staff than was initially evident). After his explosive statements about black retaliation were widely publicized, Evers issued a press release calling for peace. Evoking the "ambush killing" of his brother Medgar, he concluded by arguing that "this is a time for reason, a time for honest communication, a time for constructive working together to build a better community. This is not a time for violence." Not surprisingly, the formal statement coincided with a visit from top NAACP officials and reflected their reasoned language, not Evers's angry and impulsive commentary. Similarly, although Evers led several protest marches in defiance of court orders, he called off others and generally undermined sentiment and action directed at massive demonstrations and civil disobedience. In this, and in his willingness to negotiate with white leaders, Evers's actions were generally in line with the aims of the NAACP.[7] When Evers mobilized several busloads of partisans to lobby on his behalf at the NAACP convention where the board was considering his firing, his obvious popularity gave credence to his threat to start a competing organization if he were fired. By undermining the MFDP, winning control of the Natchez movement, gaining favorable national press, and downplaying mass protest in favor of boycotts and negotiation, Evers had made himself, as John Dittmer writes, "indispensable to the national NAACP."[8]

Despite his earlier ineffectiveness as a movement leader, Evers built on his Natchez triumph and initiated successful local movements throughout southwest Mississippi. Despite the persistence of violence and continued collaboration between state officials, law officers, and terrorists, the monolithic defiance for which Mississippi was known had eroded. Moreover, Evers faced little organizational competition; the COFO coalition had disbanded in July 1965, and a significant number of key SNCC organizers had returned to school while others had left the state. Many of the remaining workers struggled with the organization's structure and direction.[9] Ironically, then, even though he had played little positive role in the Mississippi movement, in late 1965, the opportunistic Evers was best positioned to take advantage of both the Voting Rights Act (signed into law in August) and Mississippi political leaders' grudging acceptance of the inevitability of some change.[10]

In November 1965, acting as point man for Charles Evers, Rudy Shields, a Korean War veteran who moved to Mississippi from Chicago to act as a freelance organizer and help blacks register to vote, began organizing in Claiborne County (and its county seat of Port Gibson). Located near the Mississippi River just South of the Delta and about forty-five miles north of Natchez, from its early nineteenth-century history through World War II, the county had been dominated by large cotton plantations; well into the twentieth century black/white interactions were shaped by the legacy of slavery and the system of sharecropping that replaced it. A small white elite dominated the community through economic, political, and legal control couched in the language of benevolent paternalism and backed by the threat of violence. On the eve of the civil rights movement, Claiborne County had about nine thousand residents, 80 percent of whom were African Americans, yet fewer than two dozen black citizens were registered to vote and whites maintained absolute control over the legal and political systems.

On December 12, 1965, Shields reorganized an essentially dormant NAACP branch that had operated in secret with only a handful of members. Despite some fear, at Shields's urging the group agreed to operate openly.[11] By the end of January 1966 hundreds of blacks were attending Tuesday night mass meetings. In mid-April Charles Evers reported that the NAACP branch had more than thirteen hundred adult members. Before the year ended more than seventeen hundred people had joined the organization, more than 40 percent of the county's black residents over the age of twenty-one. By mid-May there was a youth branch with almost five hundred members, and twenty-six hundred African Americans, more than two-thirds of the county's eligible black population, was registered to vote.[12] On April 1, 1966, the NAACP initiated a boycott against white merchants in an attempt to force concessions (like using courtesy titles, integrating public spaces, and hiring African Americans in responsible positions) from recalcitrant white leaders. Although the boycott had almost unanimous black support and immediately cut into merchants' profits, the white community consistently refused to negotiate and the boycott lasted into 1967.[13]

Rudy Shields and a core of workers—dominated by women, teenagers, and young men—were responsible for most of the day-to-day work of the movement, but Evers was the *leader.* His brash fearlessness and flashy oratory drew people into the movement and made him wildly popular. One participant remembers that, at weekly mass meetings, Evers "would make his grand entrance, walk down the aisle, everybody would just stand up and cheer, clap, go on 'ooooh!' and the choir would start singing one of the freedom songs. 'Ain't Gonna Let Nobody Turn Me Around,' . . . that kind of stuff. And you know, by the time he would get up to speak, the crowd would be at a fever pitch." Here Evers was at his best—teaching, encouraging, inspiring. As one man put it: "He got the folks built up to where they were ready to go." Another remarks, "Charles Evers wasn't scared of the Devil . . . [and] he could talk. . . . He would tell those white folks just what he wanted them to know." One of his closest supporters in nearby Fayette practically deifies him, saying, "He came, and we just used him as an earthly God. You know how when you're thirsty, you're hot, you're thirsty, you're run down, and somebody gives you a cool drink of water?"[14]

With Evers's newfound success building large NAACP branches and national press featuring his role in successful voter registration campaigns, especially in Claiborne County, the NAACP's top leaders began to view him in a far more positive light. Although many of their old conflicts persisted, they became convinced that Evers could help the NAACP become the dominant civil rights organization in Mississippi and regain its place of national prominence. In an April 1966 letter to NAACP head Roy Wilkins, Gloster Current combined information about an upcoming trip to Claiborne County with details about thriving voter registration and membership drives in southwest Mississippi, concluding that the NAACP's method of "handling Mr. Evers is going to prove fruitful after all." After his Claiborne County visit, Current wrote Evers that the mass meeting he attended "was fruitful, stimulating and indicated what a great job you are doing." Pleased with expanding membership numbers, Current urged Evers to take care of himself and authorized him to hire temporary help so he could rest for several weeks. Current also wrote NAACP state president Aaron Henry that the Port Gibson meeting made it "apparent how effective our work has been in southwest Mississippi. The audience was overflowing and the spirit was high." Moreover, he asserted that Evers "is our best hope for completion of the task in Mississippi," writing that, "frankly, I believe we have reached the point in our relationship with Charles that he is proven quite valuable to us." Less than a year after he had made a case for firing Evers, Current had reversed his position and was now concerned about keeping Evers on the payroll, especially in light of rumors that the American Federation of Labor was offering Evers a voter registration job.[15]

Current's view was reinforced in May when NAACP lawyer Jack Young reported on Evers's handling of the situation in nearby Fayette, Jefferson County, after a white policeman shot an unarmed black man. Young initially feared that Evers would say something that the "Association would later have to eat." Instead, he saw Evers calm an angry crowd, and wrote Current, "I do not feel that there is any likelihood that any violence will occur because Charles has the people in Fayette completely under his control and domination. If he said, 'march,' they march. If he said 'be quiet,' they are quiet. I believe that they would burn the town if he said burn the town." After seeing Evers's popularity firsthand, Young characterized him as "Our Leader" and argued that Evers "is a great influence for good." He concurred that "the prestige of the National . . . because of Charles' work in Adams, Jefferson and Claiborne Counties, is at an all time high, and that under the circumstances, it would be disastrous for us if he chose to leave at this time." To keep Evers, the NAACP gave him a pay raise, an assistant, and control of a previously autonomous voter registration office. Writing Evers in June to confirm this new arrangement, Current referred to the "heartaches and difficulties of the past three years" and to the "misunderstandings and adjustments we all had to make," but he concluded that "under your leadership the state of Mississippi and especially the NAACP has been going forward. . . . We now stand on the threshold of victory." Several weeks earlier Current was brimming with excitement about the NAACP's Mississippi memberships, led by the almost twelve hundred new Claiborne County members. He wrote the organization's publicity director that "the NAACP is the dominating organization in Mississippi, numerically and spiritually."[16]

As soon as Evers began bolstering the NAACP's membership and reputation, the national staff began to give him more latitude and to overlook actions that violated the organization's policies. However, he remained inconsistent, individualistic, opinionated, and controversial. In February 1966, for example, he was threatened with a libel suit when he implied that the Fayette sheriff was making money from bootleg liquor.[17] Other problems were more troubling and persistent, especially accusations that Evers used civil rights boycotts to make money. From selling sandwiches and loaning money to students during his college days to associating with the Chicago underworld, Evers was always on the lookout for money-making ventures. He was part owner of stores in Jackson and Natchez at the time that he was leading boycotts in those communities, and in 1967 he opened a shopping center in Fayette that drew black customers from around the area, including some who were boycotting white stores in their home communities. In 1965, as part of its ongoing efforts to disrupt the civil rights movement, the Mississippi State Sovereignty Commission "exposed" Evers's connection to a store that he was encouraging black boycotters to shop in.[18] The resulting publicity prompted a flurry of activity within the NAACP. A board member wrote Roy Wilkins that she was "extremely concerned" about the "legal implications" of Evers's actions, and the organization's Committee on Branches specifically recommended that as long as Evers's NAACP work entailed boycotts, he should either avoid involvement in business or resign. Influenced by Evers's recent achievements and his value to the organization, however, the national NAACP ultimately let the matter drop, and Evers continued to pursue profit even when that meant operating businesses at the same time that he was leading boycotts.[19]

The NAACP leadership also ignored complaints that Evers encouraged coercion, including violence, to enforce boycotts. In Claiborne County he set the tone for this approach in a speech announcing the boycott. He told the listening crowd: "If we catch a Negro at any store, we will get his name, address, and phone number and take care of him later. Claiborne County is off-limits to Negroes. Don't even ride around town in your cars." He regularly insisted that boycott violators would be "taken care of" and suggested it was acceptable for the black community to use these coercive methods to police itself.[20] In August 1966 Jackson NAACP member Falba Ruth Conic complained to Gloster Current about Evers's "recent encouragement of violence against other Negroes who did not wish to honor a boycott." She suggested that since the national office had not "discharged him" or even "rebuked him in a public statement," she "assumed that it endorses his administration." She concluded by saying, "[I will] sever my connections with the NAACP" if its "new policy is one of threats of violence and vandalism . . . because it has sunk to the level of the bigoted organizations, black and white, that it has hypocritically denounced." In his reply Current insisted that "it has never been the NAACP policy to use threats of violence or to uphold vandalism," and he argued that Conic had failed to "substantiate" her complaint. After brushing aside the issue of enforcement, Current praised Evers for "carrying on his late brother's work under severe handicaps and with great courage." In an indication of the relationship between positive national publicity and the organization's tolerance for Evers's controversial actions, he directed her to the August 22, 1966, edition of *Newsweek* which included Evers on a list of top Negro leaders.[21] Despite Current's denial, it is likely that he was aware that Conic's complaint was grounded in truth; throughout this period Evers's speeches consistently threatened consequences for blacks who violated boycotts, and a number of local and state leaders insist that the NAACP was aware of Evers's approach to boycott enforcement.[22]

Evers's value to the NAACP was reinforced by his stature among white liberals. He had capitalized on distress over Medgar Evers's murder by forging relationships with powerful national figures. He explained, "I began knocking on people's doors, saying I was Medgar's brother and wanted a favor. They'd let me in." He added, "I met many Negroes in those first years who I wouldn't have met but for Medgar's murder. I also got closer to Nelson Rockefeller. All these people were so outraged by Medgar's killing and wanted so bad to do *something* for civil rights that they were happy to do the little things I asked." During Charles Evers's first two years working for the NAACP when he offered the organization little more than the Evers name, NAACP staff members were troubled by Evers's independent connections to prominent white liberals. In addition to giving him a potential power base outside the organization, Evers publicly acted on these ties even when it meant openly disregarding his employers.[23] By 1966, however, when Evers was staying closer to home and his southwest Mississippi successes were reflecting positively on the national organization, top officials were pleased by his national visibility and flourishing reputation among white liberals.

Evers's standing with both the NAACP and Northern liberals was reinforced by his importance in an emerging political coalition of moderate Mississippi whites and blacks. According to Charles Payne, this "group was repeatedly successful at presenting itself to opinion-makers and policymakers outside the state as the new face of the freedom movement in Mississippi." After the failed challenge of the Mississippi Freedom Democratic Party at the Democratic national convention in Atlantic City in 1964, many white liberals became increasingly antagonistic toward SNCC and its organizational offspring, including the MFDP and the Lowndes County Freedom Organization (LCFO) in Alabama, which were focusing more and more on black nationalism, political alternatives to the Democratic Party, economic critiques of American capitalism, and opposition to the Vietnam War.[24] For white liberals troubled by calls for Black Power and by the far-reaching critique of American society that these organizations were making, Evers, who publicly supported integration, praised mainstream American institutions, and was outspoken in his criticism of SNCC and Black Power, was an appealing alternative. Moreover, Evers's visible accomplishments with voter registration (and the potential for translating that into black electoral power within the framework of a moderate ideology, the national Democratic Party, and mainstream America) offered a seductive contrast to SNCC's disillusionment, and to the problems highlighted by Martin Luther King Jr.'s ineffectual Chicago campaign and the increasingly visible urban violence. Evers offered white liberals reassurance that the movement had succeeded, and he did so without threatening their status quo.

When Kwame Toure's (Stokely Carmichael) use of the phrase "Black Power" during the 1966 Meredith March coincided with a decisive majority vote by Claiborne and Jefferson County blacks in the June 1966 Democratic primary, Evers quickly capitalized, boosting his national reputation. In subsequent months newspapers increasingly praised Evers and acted as if he were *the* representative of the Mississippi civil rights movement. For example, in July 1966 *New York Times* reporter Roy Reed wrote that "one immediate and unintentional effect of the militant march, with its suggestions of 'Black Power,' was to raise the political stature of Charles Evers and the NAACP." Noting that Evers denounces "Black Power" because "it suggests black domination," Reed contrasted him favorably with those leaders affiliated with SNCC who, he asserted, "tend to be more militant." Pointing to the strong black electoral showing in southwest Mississippi in the June primary, Reed called Evers the "most effective Negro leader in the state." He ended by noting that, "unlike some younger Negro leaders, Evers repudiates all black government for predominantly Negro counties."[25] In an August article for *Reporter* magazine, Henry Hurt referred to Black Power as an "alarming cry" but then claimed that "Mississippi's Negro leadership has been generally immune to the appeals of the extremists." He subsequently focused almost exclusively on Evers, as if he alone was "Mississippi's Negro leadership." Observing that Evers opposed Black Power because it advocates "black supremacy," Hurt added that "Evers is almost contemptuous of groups that favor all-black anything." Like Roy Reed, Hurt combined a discussion of Evers's "political control over three Mississippi counties" (including Claiborne) with Evers's opposition to all-black slates. Hurt's article also alluded to, but then glossed over, criticism about Evers's business practices, observing that "Evers, always a good businessman himself, has done very nicely with a food store he purchased during a previous series of boycotts."[26]

In addition to using Evers to critique proponents of Black Power, journalists frequently presented evidence of Evers's political dominance in southwest Mississippi as a hopeful alternative to black-oriented third-party efforts, including those of the MFDP and the LCFO. One of the most obvious examples of the extent of Evers's influence came in the 1966 congressional race. In the June primary, Claiborne County blacks voted overwhelmingly for the MFDP candidate Clifton Whitley, giving him a 1,639 to 1,224 countywide lead over runner-up James Eastland. In the November election when Whitley ran as an independent, however, Evers swung his support to Republican Prentiss Walker. Eastland's vote total stayed relatively consistent, Whitley's dropped from 1,639 to 120, and Prentiss Walker led the county with 1,671 votes. According to Claiborne County NAACP president James Dorsey, most people "were willing to follow Mr. Evers whatever he said at that particular time. They felt like they should do it."[27] Commenting in the *World Journal Tribune*, Rowland Evans and Robert Novak described Evers as "the new South's first Negro political boss" and not just "a responsible civil rights leader." They added that "it is of major significance that Evers, an advocate of biracial moderation, succeeded where prophets of Black Power failed." In contrast, the authors referred to the MFDP's electoral losses and "their self-defeating theory of black separatism." Like most journalists and many white liberals, Evans and Novak presumed that it was inherently preferable for blacks to work with whites and to vote for white candidates. They criticized the MFDP's third-party strategy as "self-defeating," although the MFDP candidate had a platform which addressed major problems facing black Mississippians. At the same time they praised Evers's advocacy of Prentiss Walker, whom they themselves described as "a white supremacist" with Klan support.[28] Given their own analysis of Walker's politics, it is hard to see how voting for him was an effective strategy for black Mississippians.

White Tougaloo chaplain Ed King remarks that, during the late 1960s, "Evers's national credibility was enormous." He argues that liberals were receptive to Charles Evers because of "his brother's name" and because "he would run around with them, talking about what an integrationist he was." Recalling situations before 1964 when Evers "attacked SNCC for being interracial," King insists that Evers's talk of integration was insincere and a calculated part of his opposition to SNCC. He explains that "when [SNCC and CORE have] gone way off into Black Power and separatism, he can talk to the Northern press about black and white together and we're not extremists like them." And he adds, "The northern press loved that."[29] Because liberals found much of what Evers espoused reassuring, most ignored the ways that some of his statements and beliefs actually overlapped with the tenets of Black Power that they found so disturbing. White liberals were often bothered by self-defense when it was part of a Black Power ideology but appeared to accept it from Evers. For example, Roy Reed wrote, in July 1966, that "while other civil rights leaders debate the effectiveness of nonviolence, Mr. Evers has reached a solution that seems to satisfy him and his followers. He carries a pistol everywhere."[30]

White liberals also overlooked Evers's periodic advocacy of violent retaliation against whites. According to historian Adam Fairclough, in 1966 Martin Luther King Jr. and Evers had an encounter in Philadelphia, Mississippi (where three civil rights workers had been killed two years earlier). "Evers had orated on the need for blacks to fight back with guns, evoking an excited response from the audience. But King had interrupted him, pointing out that Medgar's killer . . . was living close by: 'If you're that violent, why don't you go up the highway to Greenwood and kill the man who killed your brother?'" Evers had no response. However, he continued to make similar comments. For example, in August 1966 in the midst of his national popularity as a spokesman for interracial cooperation, he told a Harlem audience, "If a pin scratches a Negro any more in Southwest Mississippi we are going to hunt them down till hell freezes over!" Rebuked by Roy Wilkins, who was sharing the platform, his comments appear to have had little impact on white liberals' embrace of him. Evers reversed himself and parroted King's words to him a few years later when he was traveling with a white writer who was doing a story for *Harper's Magazine*. In this context, he attacked those the writer referred to as black "advocate(s) of violence." According to Evers, "They say to kill, but you don't see *them* shooting anybody. The white people have sat back and let the racists advocate violence and do violence. We're not going to do that."[31]

Evers's talk of interracial cooperation and power sharing were probably just as duplicitous and certainly illusory. In southwest Mississippi, away from the spotlight and oratory, whites clung to power. A few appealed to black voters, but whites and blacks remained polarized. Evers's much-publicized talk of biracial government and integration in southwest Mississippi was at best unrealistic and at worst an accommodation to white supremacy. White liberals and the national media who accepted Evers and his commentary at face value were embracing what they wanted to believe and were overlooking many of the contradictions that lay just beneath the surface. Moreover, like the NAACP, most failed to press Evers about his questionable decisions and tactics, and seemed willing to accept his abuses of power.

During this period many of Mississippi's white political leaders had begun to realize that some changes in race relations were inevitable, and they had also begun to perceive the NAACP and Evers as more acceptable than groups associated with SNCC. In July 1966 reporter Roy Reed noted that Evers's "repudiation of 'Black Power' and his reluctant association with the [Meredith] march gave him increased acceptability among white [Mississippi] leaders."[32] As early as the fall of 1964 Gloster Current told a meeting of civil rights activists that Evers "has rapport" with white officials in Jackson. In December 1965 the Natchez police chief actually expressed concern that Evers was out of town, because he feared that without him no one could "control the Negro civil rights workers." In the 1990s a white Port Gibson Alderman insisted that Evers "wasn't as bad as some of the others," while a merchant observed that "Charles Evers is no fool. I mean you could reason with Charles Evers better than you could with some of these others. You could talk to him."[33] Port Gibson whites felt much less kindly toward Evers in the midst of the 1966 mass movement. But even as they fought Evers and the movement, whites around the state clung to their old patterns and preferred to deal with the black community through a single leader, and, with his influence extending from crowd control to electoral politics, Evers was the obvious choice. White Mississippians found it far easier to negotiate with Evers—whose overriding commitment to most aspects of the status quo and his active pursuit of political power and economic gain made him particularly receptive to bargaining with those in power—than to respond more directly to the broad-based concerns of a diffuse black community.[34]

This is reflected in a November 1966 secret meeting between Sovereignty Commission director Erle Johnston and NAACP leader Roy Wilkins. As the two men discussed their shared antipathy toward other civil rights groups, Wilkins insisted to Johnston that Evers "is important to Mississippi just for the reason of controlling SNCC and not letting them gain a foothold."[35] By the end of 1966 the NAACP and the Sovereignty Commission were also united in their opposition to the Child Development Group of Mississippi (CDGM), an award winning Mississippi Head Start group that many associated with SNCC. Johnston wrote in his memoir, "As strange as it may seem, unwittingly the NAACP (and Evers) and the Sovereignty Commission were working toward the same goal: to get rid of CDGM. . . . The Commission wanted them out because they stirred up trouble and turmoil. Evers wanted them out because he wanted to extend his control and power." In a letter asking Mississippi's NAACP branch presidents to support rival group Mississippi Action for Progress (MAP) in its battle with CDGM, Gloster Current ignored the substantive issues of programming and ideology and, among other things, emphasized that "this marks one of the few times that such men of prominence of both races have agreed to work together on behalf of Negro advancement."[36] Current's comments to Evers a month later once again illustrate the NAACP's overwhelming concern with organizational prominence and reveal their eagerness to work with powerful white Mississippians. Praising Evers extensively for recent national coverage and for his connections to white supremacists, Current wrote, "The fact that the atmosphere has changed decidedly in favor of our organization and that the white power structure is no longer trying to destroy the Association but rather in some instances trying to assist is a wonderful tribute, first [to] the sacrifices of Medgar and secondly to your own ingenuity and efforts."[37]

Although Evers and white Mississippians remained largely antagonistic as 1966 drew to a close, their mutual embrace of practical politics and their shared opposition to other civil rights groups opened the door to future collaboration. Here, Evers's relationship to the Claiborne County movement provided him with critical bargaining power, and on January 26, 1967, Evers and Sovereignty Commission director Erle Johnston struck a deal to end the then ten–month old Port Gibson boycott.[38] This settlement worked to the advantage of both men. Johnston liked to think of the Sovereignty Commission as a racial troubleshooter, and he tried to improve Mississippi's national image by reducing visible racial conflict wherever possible. For Johnston, Evers was an ideal collaborator. For his part, by January 1967, Evers's ability to initiate strong local mass movements and his willingness to openly confront well-known white segregationists had earned him considerable popularity among blacks. These successes and the high numbers of blacks registered to vote had propelled him into the limelight and provided him with a strong constituency and considerable political potential. He had little to gain from continuing the boycott, and, in fact, its successful resolution reinforced his national reputation. A June 1967 *New York Times* article, for example, noted that Evers "has been able to bring white authorities to yield to Negro grievances."[39] Thus, by 1967, Evers no longer needed to engage in confrontational protest, and he preferred to emphasize black political power and concentrate on building his own economic base. The Sovereignty Commission was able to help Evers maintain his reputation—among blacks and Northern liberals—by convincing local whites to make minor concessions.[40]

In fact, the Port Gibson boycott settlement inaugurated a mutually beneficial relationship between Charles Evers and the Sovereignty Commission that added to his growing power in Mississippi politics and bolstered his national prominence. The 1967 commission files are filled with details about conversations, negotiations, and deals involving Evers, the commission, and Southwest Mississippi communities. Almost immediately after the Port Gibson boycott resolution, Evers and the commission worked together to end another boycott in nearby Woodville (Wilkinson County). In March 1967 Evers and the commission conspired again, and Evers postponed a threatened school boycott in Hazlehurst (Copiah County) designed to protest an unpopular black principal.[41] In between these boycott negotiations, Natchez NAACP activist Wharlest Jackson was killed by a Klan car bomb, and Evers and Johnston discussed ways to minimize the possibility of black retaliatory violence. Johnston apprised Evers of the deployment of national guardsmen and praised him for "having marches to give his people an outlet for their emotions." Evers also considered Johnston's requests that he support particular candidates in local and state elections. In one instance, Evers agreed to Johnston's suggestion that he "scatter the Negro vote in the first primary" of the governor's race.[42]

In the 1970s Evers testified that Johnston "had a job to do . . . and I had one to do, too." He added that "we sort of had a thing going." In his memoir Johnston noted that Evers "became a very practical disciple of racial progress" and that they developed a "'behind-the-scenes' relationship of understanding and trust." In a March 1967 memo he assured Governor Paul Johnson that "Evers has shown signs of being more reasonable."[43] Despite efforts to keep their association quiet, Evers's dealings with the white power structure were not particularly secret, at least within the movement community. After asserting that Evers was "conclusively identified with the state Sovereignty Commission," a SNCC organizer observed that "people were talking about that later in retrospect, but we knew that early on." In July 1967 MFDP chair Lawrence Guyot told a reporter that he disagreed "with Evers's tactic of dealing covertly with whites," and when Evers was running for Congress in 1968, a Tougaloo College student criticized him for the way he "dealt with the power structure in Natchez." The author of a 1968 profile of Evers also noted this connection, writing, "For some time at least a few local and state officials have believed that he can be trusted, that his word is good; and they have in effect and in fact worked with him to try to make orderly and peaceful a transition they now know is inevitable."[44]

Evers's close associations with white supremacists strained his relationships with many in the movement. By late 1967 Evers and his organizer Rudy Shields were clearly moving in different directions. Their falling out was probably triggered by Evers's growing connection to the Sovereignty Commission, his preference for negotiation, and his willingness to settle for superficial change. Lawrence Guyot observes that Shields helped "create legitimacy for Evers" within the black community, but that when Evers no longer had effective competition within the civil rights movement, Evers perceived Shields as a threat.[45] The break between Evers and Shields was also closely tied to their divergent leadership styles, tactical approaches, and personal goals and motivations. It also was a reflection of their differing identification with local people and their diverse interests. Although Evers, and not Shields, was a native Mississippian, ultimately Shields, more than Evers, identified with, represented, and was accountable to local African Americans. Ed King believes that Shields came to Mississippi "out of the most noble purposes" and not "to share in the gravy and corruption and loot that Charles was getting." Rick Abraham, who met Shields after the latter had split with Evers, summed up the main difference between the two men, concluding that Shields "wasn't after recognition or credibility and he wasn't looking for a well paying career in public office. And I think Charles Evers was."[46] Abraham also contends that "Rudy did not profit from his leadership of the people," pointing out that "the people he worked with were poor. Rudy stayed poor." Actually Shields and Evers both had symbiotic relationships with local people, but while Evers pursued profit and expanding influence, Shields eked out a subsistence living. He testified in 1973 that "in the 8 years I have been in Mississippi, I have never been employed. Each community supports me." He explained, "I help people . . . and they support me."[47]

Even aside from the issue of profiting from the movement, Shields's day-to-day organizing work in communities gave him an outlook on and approach to change that was almost antithetical to Evers's. By living and working with local people, Shields came to share their experiences and vantage point. With this bottom-up perspective, he had little tolerance for the political posturing that came to define Evers. Unlike Evers, who presumed that change came through "having a powerful leader," Abraham explains that "Rudy's vision was that" change "trickles up from the grassroots to the top." He also believes that Shields was troubled by Evers's "compromises" and "alliances," and argues that one of the most important things about Shields's leadership was his belief that "someone has to be out there on the cutting edge taking strong positions and representing the folks that other folks, other people, leaders, sometimes forget about." He concludes, "Mississippi needed Rudy Shields and he . . . was willing to fight when a lot of people were giving up the fight or being fooled into thinking they didn't need to fight any more."[48] These conflicts between Evers and Shields closely paralleled the longstanding differences between Evers and the organizations affiliated with the SNCC-COFO tradition. Lawrence Guyot explains that Evers "never had any inhibitions about saying" that his approach to the civil rights movement was to "involve as few people as possible in . . . the decision making, and make as much money as possible." Port Gibson NAACP president James Dorsey acknowledged that the organization's executive board was not "democratic" and that members typically made decisions only after Evers had provided guidance. He explains, "On the one hand [Evers] would try to make you think that he wanted you to have a mind of your own, but on the other hand he always wanted to stay in command of things."[49]

In addition to disagreeing with his "autocratic" approach, Evers's critics thought he was too concerned with profit and self-interest. One man in-

sisted, "There's just nothing there. There's no principle. It's all self-aggran-
dizement. It's all self-promotion." A Fayette critic complained that
"Charles Evers is just getting rich off his Brother's name," and explained,
"All these white folks do is offer Charles Evers a pretty good size of money
and he will get just like them and he has." She added, "If Charles Evers had
been the man his brother was he would have been dead." A Port Gibson
woman said, "He say he was trying to help black folk. I don't know.
(Laughter) He was probably working for himself. (Laughter)."[50] Charles
Payne concludes that although "no one doubted his nerve," many found
him "abrasive and egotistical" and believed he was "opportunistic—ex-
ploiting the popularity of a martyred brother, opening a grocery store of
his own when white stores were being boycotted, using poverty funds as a
form of patronage to build his own political machine, [and] making alliances with powerful politicians with segregationist records."[51] Evers's
portrayal of himself was actually very similar to the portrait painted by his
critics, and they differed most not in the details but in the interpretation.
As Payne points out, "What was selling-out from one perspective was just
moving on from another, becoming a part of the structure so that one
could change it even more." This belief, that the entire point of the movement was to "open up the system," epitomized Evers's approach. In 1967 he
told one reporter, "They say I want to become a member of the white
man's world. Of course, I do—that's what my brother died for. . . . I believe in working on the inside," he insisted, "not the outside." A reporter
observed that "for Evers, the transition from civil rights to politics was
natural and inevitable."[52]

Evers's desire to wield influence and be part of the system is clearly evident in his acceptance of the role of political boss. In 1966 a reporter wrote
that Evers "has assumed political control over three Mississippi counties,
and his influence is steadily increasing." Other reporters referred to Evers
as a "political boss" and as "a combination benevolent society and big-
city-styled boss." Newspapers regularly highlighted Evers's political influence and described southwest Mississippi with phrases like "Evers's fief-
dom" and his "political enclave." In 1967 Evers told reporters that "we want
the Negroes' vote in Mississippi to count." He explained, "That doesn't
necessarily mean that we want them to vote for all Negro candidates, but
we want their vote channelled."[53] Whites in Mississippi and around the
country embraced Evers's control, especially since it was combined with
his willingness to support white candidates. One journalist called this
strategy "ostensibly biracial." Since Evers agreed to back white candidates

even when they resisted offering "concessions to Negroes" and cooperated with white Democrats even though they refused to "reciprocate openly," he essentially traded personal influence and prestige for the fundamental interests of his constituents.[54]

After establishing his ability to channel black votes in southwest Mississippi, Evers used this base for his high-profile personal campaigns—to run for a congressional seat in 1968, to try to become the mayor of Fayette in 1969, and to run for governor in 1971. Although he lost all but the mayoral race, his strong showings bolstered his overall political standing. For example, in the 1968 congressional campaign, Evers carried five counties, including Claiborne, to lead the first primary. Although he lost in a runoff, his campaign was featured in national newspapers and magazines, and one reporter noted that he had "developed an important bloc of votes which he can, presumably, deliver." Roy Wilkins wrote Evers that his "excellent showing" in the congressional campaign "enhanced your personal prestige, and reflected great credit upon" the NAACP. According to political scientist Leslie McLemore, the state's white moderates, initially feared that if Evers "were beaten badly" he would lose "his influence with the white power structure" and "be destroyed politically." Instead, Evers proved that he could turn out the black vote.[55]

For many years Evers's national influence was reinforced by his position as the mayor of Fayette, a post he held from 1970 to 1981. Over the years it became increasingly clear, however, that his political ambitions were increasingly distancing him from the local people he claimed to represent. For example, many believe that his 1978 independent candidacy for the U.S. Senate was explicitly intended to enable conservative Republican Thad Cochran to beat out his Democratic opponent. In 1981, after alienating many blacks by supporting then President Ronald Reagan, he was defeated in his bid for a fourth term as mayor of Fayette. In the mid-1960s his popularity among area blacks was so strong and so pervasive that such a loss would have seemed inconceivable. Since then, however, Evers has lost far more political campaigns than he has won. For example, in November 1995, after one term as Jefferson County's chancery clerk (elected in 1991), he ran as a Republican in an unsuccessful bid for a legislative seat representing Claiborne and Jefferson counties. In a July 1995 column, Bill Minor, who covered the civil rights movement for years, commented, "One thing you can always say about LeGrande Charles—wherever the money is, that's where he is. Naturally he's found his home in the Grand Old Party."[56]

In fact, Evers seems increasingly estranged from local people, the African Americans who initially provided the foundation for his political influence. Recently his political activity has been concentrated outside Mississippi where he has attempted to provide legitimacy for conservative white Republicans with segregationist backgrounds. For example, in December 2002, after Mississippi Senator Trent Lott was forced to resign his post as Senate majority leader for publicly suggesting that the country would have been better off had Strom Thurmond won his 1948 bid for president on a segregationist platform, a *New York Times* article noted that Evers was one of a few blacks who expressed support for Lott and attended a reception on his behalf. Almost a year earlier, in February 2002, when civil rights groups were lining up in opposition to Charles Pickering's nomination to the Fifth Circuit Court of Appeals, Evers published a supportive editorial in the *Wall Street Journal*. In the article, and at a subsequent White House reception, Evers claimed that "it's not the NAACP down there (in Mississippi) that opposes Pickering. It's the Yankees up here." Actually, as NAACP national board chair Julian Bond noted, "Evers got that one wrong." According to a summary in the *Black Commentator*, "the Mississippi State Conference of the NAACP, 31 Black state legislators, the Black lawyers' Magnolia Bar Association, Black Congressman Bennie Thompson, and just about every African American Mississippian outside of Evers' clucking little brood on the White House lawn" opposed Pickering.[57]

As this suggests, at some point Charles Evers lost touch with his primary constituency and had stopped representing it long before that. Although his leadership was clearly important to African Americans in Claiborne and other southwest Mississippi counties, it is highly problematic to simply cast him as a heroic leader, a Moses leading his people to the promised land of voting rights and political power. He *was* courageous and charismatic, with a compelling ability to motivate black Mississippians. He was also self-serving and relied on being a power broker instead of building the strength of the larger black community. One result was that in Claiborne County, after Evers turned his attention elsewhere, a handful of prominent individuals replicated his authoritative and self-promoting leadership style, contributing to a culture of jealousy and competition. Thus Evers's leadership model, and the black community's continuing dependence on a handful of people for decision making, created opportunities for abuses and accusations of greed and betrayal. As the high hopes generated by the mass movement and the first black elected officials failed to translate into substantive changes in most people's lives, many blacks began to believe that their leaders were, as one minister put it, in the movement "for what they could get out of it."[58]

Evers's emphasis on bolstering his own status is particularly evident in his ties to and dealings with white liberals, segregationists, and the national NAACP. And perhaps one of the most important things we can learn from looking at the relationship between Evers's leadership and local movements is that these groups, which appeared very different on the surface, were each attracted to Evers because they believed he would bolster their power and because they understood that he actually posed little threat to the economic and political status quo. The national NAACP became so caught up in organizational survival and prominence that they ignored the connections between Evers and boycott coercion and profit. Even more distressing is that the NAACP's rivalry with SNCC and the MFDP led it (like Evers) to try to gain an advantage and destroy civil rights competition through collaborating with the Mississippi Sovereignty Commission. Perhaps even more important, for white liberals threatened by the radical vision of SNCC and the MFDP, Evers was a safe, appealing alternative and they embraced him, despite his questionable tactics and (perhaps even because of) his unwillingness to work for a sustained, broad-based, democratic movement. At the same time Mississippi segregationists were also fairly quick to appreciate that Evers would accept personal power in place of a long-term struggle to remake Mississippi from the bottom up. In the end, it appears that many embraced the view expressed by a reporter covering Evers's 1968 congressional campaign, that Evers might be "Mississippi's 'greatest hope,' and his example a paradigm for the rest of the country." This assessment was almost certainly true for those already in power, but Evers ultimately failed those who had been and remained locked out of the system, especially those African Americans in Claiborne County (and throughout rural Mississippi) who he used as bargaining chips after they helped establish his legitimacy.[59]

NOTES

1. John Dittmer, *Local People: The Struggle for Civil Rights in Mississippi* (Urbana: University of Illinois Press, 1994), 178; Charles Payne, *I've Got the Light of Freedom: The Organizing Tradition and the Mississippi Freedom Struggle* (Berkeley:

University of California Press, 1995), 361; Charles Evers, with Andrew Szanton, *Have No Fear: The Charles Evers Story* (New York: Wiley, 1997), 146, 147.

2. Evers, *Have No Fear,* 7, 56.

3. Gloster Current to Roy Wilkins, Sept. 9, 1963, Current to Charles Evers, July 1, 1964, Wilkins to Evers, Dec. 13, 1964, Current to Evers, Feb. 5, 1964, Current to Evers, Apr. 23, 1964, National Association for the Advancement of Colored People papers, Library of Congress, Washington, D.C. (hereafter, NAACP papers); Charles Evers, interview by Emilye Crosby, Fayette, Miss., Aug. 5, 1992.

4. Dittmer, *Local People,* 242–302; Donald White to Wilkins, Feb. 4, 1964, R. Hunter Morey to Wilkins, Feb. 4, 1964, Current to Evers, Feb. 5, 1964, Evers to Ruby Hurley, Aug. 28, 1964, Current to John Morsell, Oct. 5, 1964, Current to Evers, Oct. 23, 1964, Current to Evers, June 25, 1965, NAACP papers. For examples of Sovereignty Commission reports on Evers's conflict with COFO, see Informant report, May 22, 1964, Report of Operator #79, Aug. 7, 1964, Sovereignty Commission papers, Mississippi Department of Archives and History (hereafter, SCP).

5. Current to Morsell, Oct. 5, 1964, Current to Evers, June 25, 1965, Current to Wilkins, Aug. 13, 1965, NAACP papers.

6. Current to Evers, Oct. 23, 1964, Evers to Hurley, Jan. 25, 1965; *New York Herald Tribune,* Aug. 28, 1965, NAACP papers; Dittmer, *Local People,* 353–54.

7. *Jackson Daily News,* Aug. 28, 1965, *New York Herald Tribune,* Aug. 28, 1965, *Jackson Clarion-Ledger,* Aug. 31, 1965, Current to Publicity Department, Sept. 2, 1965, Evers Press Release, Sept. 1, 1965, Morsell to Henry, Oct. 8, 1965, NAACP papers; Dittmer, *Local People,* 353–62.

8. Dittmer, *Local People,* 356–62; Evers, *Have No Fear,* 149–50; Dixon Pyles, interview by Emilye Crosby, Jackson, Miss., July 31, 1992; Charles Evers, *Claiborne Hardware et al. v. NAACP et al.,* testimony, 414; Informant report, Sept. 7, 1965, Sept. 11, 1965, Sept. 20, 21, 1965, Sept. 27, 1965, and Sept. 30, 1965; Charles E. Snodgrass to Birdsong and A. D. Morgan, Sept. 14, 1965, PBJP; Gene Roberts, "N.A.A.C.P. May Oust Evers as Aide in Mississippi," *New York Times,* Sept. 10, 1965.

9 Dittmer, *Local People,* 314, 315–37, 341–42, 346, 347; Payne, *I've Got the Light of Freedom,* 315, 316, 340, 341, 365–66; Neil R. McMillen, *Citizens' Council: A History of Organized Resistance to the Second Reconstruction* (Urbana: University of Illinois Press, 1971), 266.

10. Neil R. McMillen, "Black Enfranchisement in Mississippi: Federal Enforcement and Black Protest in the 1960's," *Journal of Southern History* 43, no. 3 (1977): 369; Dittmer, *Local People,* 352.

11. Nathaniel Jones (with Julia Jones), interview by Emilye Crosby, Claiborne County, Miss., June 30, 1996; Rudolph Shields, *Claiborne Hardware et al. v. NAACP et al.,* testimony, 429; Evers to Current, Jan. 14, 1966, NAACP papers.

12. Julius Warner, interview by Emilye Crosby, Port Gibson, Miss., June 29, 1992; Current to Wilkins and Morsell, Apr. 20, 1966, "Time to Dig," Aug. 8, 1966, NAACP papers; Thomas Watts file, in *Microfilm Edition of Southern Civil Rights Litigation*

Records for the 1960s, ed. Clement E. Vose (New Haven, Conn.: Yale University Photographic Services), 1977 (hereafter, SCRLR).

13. Current to Wilkins and Morsell, Apr. 20, 1966, NAACP papers; Thomas Watts file, SCRLR.

14. James Miller, interview by Emilye Crosby, Port Gibson, Miss., Feb. 2, 1994; *Vicksburg Citizens' Appeal,* Oct. 19, 1966, Ed King papers, Coleman Library, Tougaloo College (hereafter, EK papers); Ezekiel Rankin, interview by Emilye Crosby, Jefferson County, Miss., May 14, 1992; J. L. Sayles, interview by Emilye Crosby, Claiborne County, Miss., May 20, 1992; James Dorsey, interview by Emilye Crosby, Port Gibson, Miss., Feb. 10, 1994; Leesco Guster, interview by Emilye Crosby, Port Gibson, July 3, 1996; Lillie D. Brown, interview by Emilye Crosby, Fayette, Miss., July 23, 1992.

15. Current to Wilkins and Morsell, Apr. 20, 1966, Current to Evers, Apr. 28, 1966, Current to Henry, Apr. 28, 1966, NAACP papers.

16. Jack Young to Current, May 28, 1966, Current to Evers, June 13, 1966, Current to Henry Lee Moon, May 18, 1966, NAACP papers.

17. Barbara Morris to Young, Feb. 10, 1966, Morris to Robert I. Carter, Feb. 25, 1966, NAACP papers.

18. *Vicksburg Citizens' Appeal,* Feb. 8, 1967, EK papers; Johnston to Tom Scarbrough, Jan. 11, 1966, Tom Scarbrough report, Jan. 14, 1966, Editorial for *Fayette Chronicle,* Jan. 1966, Paul B. Johnson papers, McCain Archive, University of Southern Mississippi (hereafter, PBJP papers); Tom Scarbrough to Johnston, Jan. 11, 1966, Rep. Geoghegan to House of Rep., Jan. 1966, "Evers Denies He Promoted Boycott for Personal Gain," *Jackson Daily News,* Jan. 19, 1966, Hopkins report, Mar. 4, 1966, SCP; Johnston to Glazier, Jan. 17, 1966, Lawrence Guyot papers in author's possession.

19. Maria L. Marcus to Wilkins, Jan. 28, 1966, Current to Morsell, Feb. 10, 1966, Myrtle Johnson to Kivie Kaplan, Feb. 11, 1966, Wilkins to Evers, Mar. 4, 1966, Evers to Wilkins, Mar. 28, 1966, Current to Henry, Apr. 28, 1966, NAACP papers.

20. Snodgrass to Birdsong and Morgan, Apr. 1, 1966, PBJ papers; Charles Evers speech, June 21, 1966, *Claiborne Hardware et al. v. NAACP et al.;* Charles Evers, *Evers,* ed. Grace Halsell (New York: World, 1971); Evers interview; Evers, *Have No Fear,* 187.

21. Roberts, "N.A.A.C.P. May Oust Evers as Aide in Mississippi"; "Civil Rights Leaders Look at Genesis of 'Black Power,'" *Jackson Clarion-Ledger,* Aug. 25, 1966, SCP; Falba Ruth Conic to Current, Aug. 13, 1966, Current to Falba Ruth Conic, Aug. 19, 1966, NAACP papers.

22. Current to Henry, Apr. 28, 1966, NAACP papers; "Evers Calls for Beating of Negroes," *Jackson Clarion Ledger,* July 26, 1966, SCP; Robert Beals in *PGR,* May 12, 1966; James Dorsey, interview by Emilye Crosby, Port Gibson, Miss., Dec. 20, 1994; Ed King, interview by Emilye Crosby, Jackson, Miss., Sept. 4, 1998.

23. Evers, *Have No Fear,* 136; Current to Morsell, Oct. 5, 1964, Current to Evers, June 25, 1965, NAACP papers.

24. Payne, *I've Got the Light of Freedom,* 341, 375–77; Dittmer, *Local People,* 314–18, 325, 340, 341–43, 348–51.

25. Roy Reed, "Negroes and Liberal Whites Score Big Gains in Mississippi," *New York Times,* July 17, 1966.

26. Henry Hurt, "Boycott and Ballot," *Reporter* 35 (Aug. 11, 1966): 23–27.

27. June 9, 1966, *Clarion Ledger,* EK papers; June 9, 1966, Nov. 10, 1966, *PGR;* James Dorsey, Dec. 1994 interview.

28. Rowland Evans and Robert Novak, "New South's First Negro Political Boss," *World Journal Tribune,* Nov. 16, 1966, 37.

29. King interview; Guyot interview.

30. Roy Reed, "Negroes and Liberal Whites Score Big Gains in Mississippi," *New York Times,* July 17, 1966; see also Don McKee, quoted in *Jackson Clarion-Ledger,* Aug. 25, 1966.

31. Adam Fairclough, *To Redeem the Soul of America: The Southern Christian Leadership Conference and Martin Luther King, Jr.* (Athens: University of Georgia Press, 1987), 325–26; "Civil Rights Leaders Look at Genesis of 'Black Power,'" *Jackson Clarion-Ledger,* Aug. 1966, SCP; Robert Canzoneri, "Charles Evers: Mississippi's Representative Man?" *Harper's,* July 1968.

32. Fairclough, *Race and Democracy,* 408; Roy Reed, "Negroes and Liberal Whites Score Big Gains in Mississippi," *New York Times,* July 17, 1966.

33. James Forman, *The Making of Black Revolutionaries* (Seattle: Open Hand, 1972, 1985), 401; [Snodgrass] report, Sept. 22, 1965, Snodgrass to Birdsong and Morgan, Dec. 27, 1965, PBJ papers; "Over 100 Arrested in Natchez March," *Jackson Clarion Ledger,* Oct. 5, 1965, SCP; Charles Evers, *Claiborne Hardware et al. v. NAACP et al.,* testimony, 403; Jimmy Allen, interview by Emilye Crosby, Port Gibson, Miss., Feb. 9, 1994; Bill Lum, interview by Emilye Crosby, Port Gibson, Miss., July 29, 1992.

34. Evans and Novak, "New South's First Negro Political Boss," 37; *Mississippi Independent: Community Newspaper,* Apr. 28, 1967, EK papers; King interview.

35. Erle Johnston, *Mississippi's Defiant Years, 1953–1973: An Interpretive Documentary with Personal Experiences* (Forest, Miss.: Lake Harbor, 1990), 294–95; Wilkins and Erle Johnston meeting, Nov. 12, 1966, in *Southern Regional Council* papers (New York: New York Times Microfilming Corporation of America, 1984).

36. Johnston, *Defiant Years,* 291; Current to Mississippi Branch Presidents, Oct. 14, 1966, NAACP papers.

37. Current to Evers, Nov. 18, 1966, NAACP papers.

38. "Jobs for Negroes Won by NAACP Unit in Miss," NAACP papers; *New Orleans Times-Picayune, Memphis Commercial-Appeal,* Jan. 27, 1967, SCP; Cole report, Jan. 18–24, 1967, PBJ papers; Nathaniel Jones 1996 interview; Alexander

Collins, *Claiborne Hardware et al. v. NAACP et al.*, testimony, 217; James U. Allen, *Claiborne Hardware et al. v. NAACP et al.*, testimony, 1206; Allen interview; James Hudson, *Claiborne Hardware et al. v. NAACP et al.*, testimony, 121; James Hudson notes, *Claiborne Hardware et al. v. NAACP et al.*, 754; Barbara B. Ellis, *Claiborne Hardware et al. v. NAACP et al.*, testimony, 143; Julia Jones, *Claiborne Hardware et al. v. NAACP et al.*, testimony, 539; William Matt Ross, *Claiborne Hardware et al. v. NAACP et al.*, testimony, 927.

39. Oct. 10, 1965, Informant report, SCP; Dittmer, *Local People*, 361; Evers, *Have No Fear*, 156; "Negroes Are Ending Mississippi Boycott," Jan. 27, 1967, "Civil Rights Forces Claimed Victory," *New York Times*, Jan. 28, 1967.

40. "New Mississippi Center Offers Voting Advice in Rights Drive," *New York Times*, May 15, 1967, EK papers; King interview; Cole report, Jan. 18–24, 1967, PBJ papers.

41. Cole report, Feb. 13, 1967, PBJ papers.

42. Johnston to file, Mar. 1, 1967, Cole report, Apr. 21, 1967, PBJ papers; Ken Dean, Memorandum for Council Files, Feb. 20, 1967, SRC; Johnston, *Defiant Years*, 339–40.

43. Charles Evers, *Claiborne Hardware et al. v. NAACP et al.*, testimony, 4696–97; Ken Dean, Memorandum for Council Files, Feb. 20, 1967, SRC; Johnston, *Defiant Years*, 232, 293; Johnston to Paul Johnson, Mar. 13, 1967, SCP.

44. Johnston to Cole, Mar. 31, 1967, SCP; Worth Long, interview by Emilye Crosby, Atlanta, Ga., Jan. 31, 1994; *Washington Post*, July 17, 1967, "Evers Criticized by Students," Feb. 9, 1968, EK papers; Canzoneri, "Charles Evers: Mississippi's Representative Man?"

45. Airtel to Director, FBI, from SAC, Jackson, Sept. 5, 1967, Rudolph Arthur Shields, File number: 157–HQ-7950, FBI files (in author's possession); Guyot interview.

46. King interview; Rick Abraham, telephone interview by Emilye Crosby, Feb. 10, 1999.

47. Rick Abraham interview; Rudolph Shields, *Claiborne Hardware et al. v. NAACP et al.*, testimony, 427–28; Dorothy Brandon, interview by Emilye Crosby, Fayette, Miss., Aug. 5, 1992; James Whitney, *Claiborne Hardware et al. v. NAACP et al.*, testimony, 292, 300; James Miller, interview by Emilye Crosby, Port Gibson, Miss., Feb. 2, 1994; James Scott, interview by Emilye Crosby, Port Gibson, Miss., June 22, 1992; Brown interview.

48. King interview; Rick Abraham interview.

49. Guyot interview; King interview; Henry Hurt, "Ballot and Bullet," *Reporter* 35 (Aug. 11, 1966): 23–26; Roscoe Johnson, Jack Chatfield notes (in author's possession), 58, 62; James Dorsey, Jack Chatfield notes, 58; "From Reporters' Pads," Jack Chatfield notes, 74.

50. Sullivan interview; Elliott Lichtman, interview by Emilye Crosby, May 30, 1996; Guyot interview; Ken Dean, quoted in Johnston, *Defiant Years*, 295; Long in-

terview; Jan. 18, 1968, Jan. 10, 1971, Annie Rankin papers, Coleman Library, Touga-loo College; Gladys I. Watson, interview by Emilye Crosby, Port Gibson, Miss., Feb. 4, 1994; Maurice Landers, interview by Emilye Crosby, Port Gibson, Miss., July 22, 1992; Dan McCay, interview by Emilye Crosby, Claiborne County, Miss., May 19, 1992.

51. Jerry De Laughter, "Evers Scores Northern 'Exploitation' in Look at Future for Negro," *Memphis Commercial Appeal,* Jan. 19, 1967; "New Mississippi Center Offers Voting Advice in Rights Drive," *New York Times,* May 15, 1967, "Evers Criticized by Students," Feb. 9, 1968, EK papers; Rugaber, "The Brothers Evers"; Payne, *I've Got the Light of Freedom,* 360–61.

52. Payne, *I've Got the Light of Freedom,* 358; *Washington Post,* July 17, 1967; "Evers at Millsaps Sees South Ahead in Race Relationships," May 18, 1967, EK papers; Rugaber, "The Brothers Evers."

53. Henry Hurt, "Ballot and Bullet," *Reporter* 35 (Aug. 11, 1966): 23–26; "Inside Report: New South's First Negro Political Boss," Nov. 16, 1966, *New York World Journal Tribune,* 37; *Washington Post,* July 17, 1967, EK papers; "Evers Conducting Negro Vote Drive: Hopes to Elect Candidates in 3 Mississippi Counties," June 25, 1967, *New York Times*; John Dittmer, "The Politics of the Mississippi Movement, 1954–1964," in *The Civil Rights Movement in America,* ed. Charles Eagles (Jackson: University Press of Mississippi, 1986), 91; Frank Parker, *Black Votes Count: Political Empowerment in Mississippi after 1965* (Chapel Hill: University of North Carolina Press, 1990), 5, 71; Leslie Earl McLemore, "Protest and Politics: The Mississippi Freedom Democratic Party and the 1965 Congressional Challenge," *Negro Education Review* 37 (July–Oct. 1986): 404–5; Newsletter of the New Orleans Movement for a Democratic Society, Nov. 1967, reprinted in *Freedom Information Service,* Nov. 3, 1967, *Mississippi Independent: Community Newspaper,* April 28, 1967, EK papers; King interview.

54. "Inside Report: New South's First Negro Political Boss," *New York World Journal Tribune,* Nov. 16, 1966, 37; *Washington Post,* July 17, 1967, EK papers.

55. "Part of the Way," *Time,* Mar. 8, 1968; "Mississippi: The Impossible Dream," *Newsweek,* Mar. 11, 1968; "Mississippi: Closer to Home," *Time,* Mar. 22, 1968; Rugaber, "The Brothers Evers"; Canzoneri, "Charles Evers: Mississippi's Representative Man?"; McLemore, "The Mississippi Freedom," 404–5; Wilkins to Evers, Mar. 13, 1968, NAACP; Leslie Earl McLemore, "The Mississippi Freedom Democratic Party: A Case Study of Grass-Roots Politics" (Ph.D. diss., University of Massachusetts, 1971), 403, 440.

56. Bill Minor, editorial, "Charles Evers has found an unlikely home—the GOP," *Jackson Clarion-Ledger,* July 23, 1995.

57. James Charles Evers, "A Brave Judge's Name Besmirched," *Wall Street Journal,* Feb. 7, 2002; *New York Times,* Dec. 31, 2002; *Clarion-Ledger,* Jan. 23, 2003; John Nichols, "Unspinning the Pickering Push," *The Nation Online Beat,* March 14, 2002 (http://www.thenation.com/thebeat/index.mhtml?bid=1&pid=29, accessed Jan. 16,

2003), *The Black Commentator,* Jan. 16, 2003 (http://www.blackcommentator.com /25/25_issues.html, accessed Jan. 16, 2003).

58. James Devoual, interview by Emilye Crosby, Port Gibson, Miss., July 28, 1992; Albert Butler, interview by Emilye Crosby, Port Gibson, Miss., Feb. 16, 1994; Brown interview; James Miller, interview by Emilye Crosby, Port Gibson, Miss., Feb. 2, 1994; Rachel Wilson, interview by Emilye Crosby, Port Gibson, Miss., June 29, 1992; Willie Wilson, interview by Emilye Crosby, Claiborne County, Miss., May 26, 1992; Sayles interview; James Dorsey interview, Dec. 1994; Hystercine Rankin, interview by Emilye Crosby, Jefferson County, Miss., May 13, 1992; James Miller, interview by Emilye Crosby, Port Gibson, Miss., July 26, 1997; Evan Doss Jr., interview by Emilye Crosby, Port Gibson, Miss., Apr. 7, 1992.

59. Canzoneri, "Charles Evers: Mississippi's Representative Man?"

Chapter 8

Local Women and the
Civil Rights Movement in Mississippi
Re-visioning Womanpower Unlimited

Tiyi Morris

> We were fortunate to have women who had the spiritual-
> ity, economics, education, and charismatic ability to
> unify women, unify people, and motivate them. You
> could see things being accomplished.
>
> —Aura Gary, interview by author,
> May 30, 2001, Jackson Mississippi

Although a national movement that engendered the passage of legislation
to help blacks attain full citizenship rights, the civil rights movement is
perhaps best understood as an assemblage of many small communities of
activism that often emerged to address issues of local importance.[1] Womanpower Unlimited, founded by Clarie Collins Harvey on May 29, 1961, in
Jackson, Mississippi, was one such community. Organized initially to provide aid to the Freedom Riders,[2] who were unjustly arrested, convicted,
and tortured in the Mississippi jails, Womanpower Unlimited (hereafter,
Womanpower) expanded its activism to include such programs as voter
registration drives, youth education, and peace activism. A significant but
largely unacknowledged civil rights organization in Jackson, Womanpower also spearheaded a movement for revitalizing black women's social
and political activism in the state. A group of native Mississippians dedicated to the advancement of civil rights for blacks, they are responsible for

much of the success that the civil rights movement enjoyed in Jackson, Mississippi, between 1961 and 1968.

In attempting to enhance the scholarship concerning local people's and women's participation in the civil rights movement, this essay explores the following issues: (1) What circumstances led to the organization of Womanpower Unlimited? (2) In what types of activities did they engage? (3) What contributions did Womanpower make to the civil rights movement? (4) What are the contributions of local activists to the civil rights movements, and how does understanding local activism enhance our understanding of the Movement? (5) How should we evaluate women's contributions to Black freedom struggles?

The Emergence of Womanpower Unlimited

The origin of Womanpower Unlimited can be attributed to the Freedom Rides. Upon their arrival in Jackson, the Mississippi Methodist Annual Conference was being held in Waveland, Mississippi. When the presiding bishop, Charles F. Golden, learned that ministers of the Methodist Church were detained in this group, he sent a delegation to Jackson to witness the first hearing of the Freedom Riders on May 26, 1961. This delegation was comprised of two ministers, Rev. A. E. Mays and Rev. S. L. Webb, as well as Clarie Collins Harvey, the secretary of the General Board of Christian Social Concerns. Harvey hypothesizes that she was chosen as a member because of her history of activism within the Methodist Church locally and nationally.[3]

At the trial Harvey observed that some of the girls were improperly clothed, without sweaters, and were cold and shivering.[4] She also learned that the Freedom Riders would not be posting bail but instead decided to serve their sentences as they appealed the ruling. The majority would serve sentences of up to thirty-nine days at Parchman Prison, the maximum time they could spend and still appeal the decision. That evening Harvey and Aurelia Young, a professor at Jackson State College (now Jackson State University) and wife of civil rights attorney Jack Young Jr., sent clothes to the jail. Harvey's first response demonstrated a "mothering" instinct—to help these activists in a practical way that would sustain them in their ensuing struggle. She stated in a 1965 interview that "if [the Freedom Riders] were going to remain [incarcerated in Jackson] they were going to have continuing needs and that people within the community, for whom they were making this witness, should have some responsibility for seeing that these needs would be met."[5] Consequently, Harvey sent out a call through the local churches for money, clothing, and other necessities for the civil rights activists. As a result of the groundswell of support she received from the local women to whom she appealed, Harvey was further inspired to create opportunities for them to become involved in the movement by engaging in efforts aimed at improving the quality of life for community residents. In the tradition of nineteenth-century black activists like Nat Turner and Sojourner Truth, who attributed their work to divine inspiration, Harvey says that she was "called" to organize women for the purpose of assisting those who had undertaken God's work of achieving social justice. She also believed that women were inherently suited to fulfill such a purpose. Accordingly Harvey states that the name Womanpower itself gives reference to

> the inner, divine power of women, as all women work together for peace among the people of a given community, nation and in the world. This power is unlimited because it is God's power. . . . Using this power within us, we can help to make life what it should be for any people at any time in any place."[6]

Therefore, on Monday, May 29, Harvey convened a meeting of interested community women at the Central United Methodist Church. And out of this meeting Womanpower Unlimited was born.

Although emerging from efforts to address the immediate needs of the Freedom Riders, Womanpower's activism was based on a much broader platform of pursuing freedom and justice with the primary goals of supporting the civil rights movement and empowering women to engage in social activism. As stated in a 1965 organizational booklet, through Womanpower Unlimited these women proposed "to help create the atmosphere, the institutions, and traditions that make freedom and peace possible. We are all women working together for a peaceful world and wholesome community life."[7] Following in the tradition of their female activist predecessors, such as Charlotte Hawkins Brown and Ida B. Wells, these women were engaging in activism on the local level in the hope that their efforts would have far-reaching positive effects. The members not only desired to contribute to efforts of attaining civil rights for blacks but also to set forth an agenda aimed at creating a beloved community in which freedom, justice, and equality existed indiscriminately among humankind.

Additionally Womanpower adopted a philosophy of organization that emphasized action as opposed to engaging in hampering levels of bureaucracy that plagued other organizations such as the NAACP and sometimes limited their effectiveness. As an extremely centralized organization, the national office often dictated the activities of the local and state NAACP branches. This type of organizational structure could lessen the effectiveness of local branches when time had to be spent securing approval from the national office. In their classic study of protest movements, Frances Fox Piven and Richard Cloward assert that many movement organizers often fail because they direct too much of their energy to creating and sustaining "formally structured organizations" and not into developing the energy that emerges among the populace during incidents of unrest. They state that this failure partially results "from the doctrinal commitment to the development of mass-based permanent organizations, for organization building activities tended to draw people away from the streets and into the meeting rooms."[8] Womanpower avoided this pitfall by maintaining a commitment to respond immediately to movement developments without requiring a series of time-consuming measures to approve actions. Above all, Womanpower remained flexible, declaring that this flexibility would allow them to "move immediately, rather than waiting for a board to convene and to make decisions and all the rest of it. We felt that we needed a relatively free group in the community that could just act, if some action needed to be taken."[9] Such a position was unique not only because it opposed the hierarchical leadership structure that often kept women on the periphery of organizations, as reflected in the limited "titled" leadership roles of women in the black church as well as civil rights organizations such as the National Association for the Advancement of Colored People (NAACP) and the Southern Christian Leadership Conference (SCLC), but also because it provided them with the flexibility to take action quickly around the development and needs of the movement.

Although Womanpower considered itself a movement that could act spontaneously, the organization, nevertheless, had structure. Womanpower was composed of an executive board, committees, and a general membership body. The executive board consisted of a chair, a vice chair, administrative, recording, and publicity secretaries, a treasurer, a chaplain, and a pianist. Committees, established to address the movement's goals, included Membership, Publicity, Hospitality, Prayer Fellowship, and Telephone. Some committees had traditional organizational responsibilities.

For example, the Membership and Publicity committees were responsible, respectively, for increasing and documenting membership and for advertising meetings, news, programs, and publication of the monthly newsletter. There were some committees, however, that were unique to the organization. The Hospitality Committee was responsible for making housing and food arrangements for civil rights activists and speakers coming to Jackson. The Telephone Committee was created to disseminate information quickly. They set up a chain, whereby the committee chairs would contact certain women who each had another group of women to contact. In this way information could be quickly and efficiently communicated to its members. The Prayer Fellowship Committee coordinated Womanpower's efforts to foster interracial fellowship between the members and white women who supported their cause.

Another distinctive aspect of Womanpower's composition was their Chain of Friendship. This Chain of Friendship was the means by which Womanpower allied with white women across the country. From these women, who were contacted primarily through Harvey's travels, Womanpower solicited assistance for the civil rights struggle in Mississippi. This Chain of Friendship increased Womanpower to an affiliation of more than three hundred women committed to social change and working to affect it specifically in Mississippi.

In addition to the success of their programs in attracting others to join Womanpower, members also used their positions in the community as respected professionals and civil rights activists to enlist other women to participate. The general membership body included women of all classes and professions; however, their level of activism varied greatly. Some women, who were schoolteachers and were afraid of losing their jobs, chose to donate money anonymously or to attend meetings irregularly. Regardless of economic class, the women were by and large middle-aged.

The Leadership

While Womanpower Unlimited grew to encompass more than three hundred women nationwide, it was primarily a Jackson-based movement. And, as with most organizations, there were a few instrumental people who are largely responsible for the group's operation. They are Clarie Collins Harvey, A. M. E. Logan, and Thelma Sanders. Because of their prior social and political activism in the Mississippi Federation of Colored Women's Clubs and the NAACP, these women were able to make Woman-power a successful endeavor. Furthermore, their economic independence afforded them an opportunity to openly support the movement, an opportunity that many other middle-class and working-class blacks lacked.

Clarie Collins Harvey was born in Meridian, Mississippi, in 1916, the daughter of Rev. Malachi C. and Mary Augusta Rayford Collins, a school teacher. During the year of her birth, Reverend Collins opened a funeral and insurance business of which Clarie would later become the owner. As the daughter of independent business owners, Clarie was afforded educational opportunities unobtainable to the masses of Southern blacks. She earned a Bachelor of Arts degree in economics from Spelman College in Atlanta, Georgia, a certificate in mortuary technique from the Indiana College of Mortuary Science in Indianapolis, and an M.A. degree in personnel administration from Columbia University in New York City.[10]

Following in the footsteps of parents who were both committed to political and social activism in their church and various other organizations, Clarie's own social and political activism would be instrumental in shaping her ideas on women's activism. Through her participation in the male-dominated NAACP and in Methodist Church organizations, Clarie learned the formal procedures for conducting meetings and how to run an organization effectively. However, she also witnessed the exclusion of women from leadership positions and knew that they needed a forum where their energies could be fully utilized. Her participation in women's organizations, on the other hand, taught her that women's productivity could easily be diminished when they became too engaged in strictly social activities.[11] As a result, she wanted to create a movement in which women would be responsible for creating the agenda and ensuring that their platform would focus on the development of leadership and activist skills, and not simply on organizing social events.

In 1939, as a representative of the national student YWCA, Clarie attended a World Christian Conference in Holland, Amsterdam, where she met Martin L. Harvey, whom she would marry four years later. Martin attended the conference as a delegate of the African Methodist Episcopal Zion Church and leader of the youth delegation. According to Harvey, her husband was "a universal person. He had studied in thirty countries of the world by the time that I had met him, and had an undergraduate degree in religious education from New York University."[12] Their ecumenical activities formed a central aspect of both their individual lives and their marital relationship. Martin Harvey did not believe that social and political activism was a sphere of male engagement, as did some male leaders who were active in civil rights organizations. Consequently Harvey enjoyed her husband's full support of her civil rights activities.

One of the first women Harvey contacted regarding the organization of Womanpower was A. M. E. Logan, whose father was also a minister. Although both were involved in the Jackson chapter of the NAACP, they were primarily acquainted through the work that Logan assisted her husband in as a contractor for Harvey. During Harvey's absences from Jackson, Logan was often responsible for conveying information between her husband and Harvey. Through this personal interaction, Harvey came to regard her as a professional, competent, and reliable woman.[13] This opinion, coupled with the knowledge of her community activism, led Harvey to believe that Logan would be an asset to the organization.

Born in 1906 to the Reverend John Collins Marshall and Nelly Rembert Marshall in Myles, Mississippi, A. M. E. followed closely in her father's footsteps throughout her youth and into adulthood. She, too, was heavily involved in the African Methodist Episcopal Church, "serv[ing] as superintendent of the Sunday school and in every office in the church except the Minister," as well as the NAACP.[14] After marrying Style Logan in 1943, the couple moved to Jackson in the late 1950s, where A.M.E. Logan was employed as a traveling sales representative for a Michigan-based, black-owned company. During this period Logan also became a registered voter, something uncommon for black Mississippians at that time, and began her civil rights activism.

At the organizational meeting of Womanpower Unlimited Logan was elected executive secretary, which meant that she often had the responsibility of overseeing and executing the daily tasks of the organization. Logan recalls that, because she was one of the few who owned a car, she was often the person called upon to transport activists around town. Furthermore, her work as a saleswoman often took her to the rural areas surrounding Jackson, which provided these people with a tangible link to movement participation. Thomas Gaither, field secretary of the Congress of Racial Equality (CORE), recalled,

Mrs. Logan was [able] to extend this entire movement out into the Mississippi countryside. . . . she would actually bring back the items from people in the Mississippi countryside who wanted to contribute to the movement, but were otherwise fearful of really connecting with the movement but they could connect with the movement through Mrs. Logan.[15]

Another prominent businesswoman who comprised this leadership core and whom Harvey was also acquainted with because of her civil rights activism in Jackson was Vice Chair Thelma Sanders. Born in Tougaloo, Mississippi, in 1924, she received her Bachelor of Science degree in home economics from Tougaloo College and attended graduate school in business administration at the University of Southern Mississippi and Mississippi College.[16] Incensed by the discrimination that blacks experienced while shopping in white stores, Sanders, a former home economics teacher, opened a clothing business in 1955 to serve black women, down the street from the Collins Funeral Home.

Prior to her involvement with Womanpower Unlimited, Sanders was actively involved in the NAACP and civil rights activities in Jackson. Therefore, when Harvey requested her involvement and support with Womanpower, she eagerly participated. Despite possible repercussions, Sanders proclaimed her civil rights activism and support for the Freedom Riders. This irked some whites, and in October 1964 her car was bombed.[17] Sanders, however, was steadfast in the face of this type of domestic terrorism and did not let it deter her commitment to the struggle.

Characteristic of many local leaders, who were active before, during, and after the period regarded as the modern civil rights movement, all of these women were veteran activists by the time they became involved with Womanpower. Their experiences with Womanpower were merely an extension and development of their political consciousness and activist agenda. Of equal importance were their positions of economic independence. Unlike teachers and other middle-class professionals whose activism was often prevented or stifled by their white employers, self-employment provided these women a degree of freedom that encouraged their unreserved and open support of the movement.

With the leadership philosophy, economic independence, and active dedication of its members, Womanpower undertook many activities to achieve a just and peaceful society. This activism ranged from organizing mass meetings and providing material and psychological support to civil rights activists to providing material support for local community members who were themselves engaging in civil rights activism or simply in need of financial assistance. This simultaneous dedication to advancing the larger civil rights agenda and meeting the immediate needs of poorer Jackson residents highlights the contributions of local people to sustain both local black communities and the national movement as a whole.

Activities of Womanpower Unlimited

In the weeks following the arrest of the Freedom Riders, Womanpower amassed a great deal of resources for the civil rights workers. The organization collected toiletries and money from community members to purchase small items for the protestors, giving the activists items ranging from shower shoes and soap to candy and magazines. Additionally, upon the Riders' release from Parchman Prison, the women were able to provide them with transportation, food, housing, and clean clothes. Always mindful of the practical ways in which the activists could maintain their dignity and pride, Womanpower also provided them with free beauty and barber services. The organization did everything within its means to take care of the physical needs of the Riders and counter the emotional distress they suffered during their incarceration.

That Womanpower was successful in achieving its goals is apparent in the testimony of many Freedom Riders who attribute their endurance to the women of that organization. Joan Trumpauer Mulholland, a white Freedom Rider from Virginia, vividly recalls their contributions, stating that they "were like angels supplying us with just little simple necessities [and although they were not Freedom Riders] . . . they were doing really equally important things to support us." Mulholland also testifies to the emotional support she received, stating that Womanpower was "great for the morale; things like this really helped people keep going. And if you were having a rough time to see that somebody cared, they knew and thought about you, that was outstanding."[18] Womanpower's work with the Freedom Riders helped to dismantle segregationists' attempts to portray the Freedom Riders as "outside agitators" who were disrupting otherwise content relations between blacks and whites. Such thinking not only underestimated the beliefs of local people but also represented an attempt to undermine the efforts of activists who had come to these communities with the hope of working with and for the local residents. This was also a tactic to promote divisions between local blacks and activists from outside the state in the hope that collaborative efforts would not occur between the two groups. Womanpower, however, dispelled such propaganda, empowering civil rights activists to continue their work and inspiring other Jacksonians to become active in the struggle, even if only through anonymous, monetary support.

After the Freedom Riders left the state, Womanpower turned their activism toward voter education and registration and worked specifically to raise awareness among black women to increase their political power. Harvey states that "The program was unique in that it proposed to stimulate women to meet human community needs, with special emphasis on the registration and voting experiences of themselves and their families."[19] Womanpower sought to empower women by bringing them out of their "homes, local churches and club groups," and encouraging and teaching them how to become agents of change within their communities and the larger society.

Womanpower employed two methods by which to undertake their voter registration efforts—a collaborative effort with other civil rights organizations and an independent initiative funded by the Voter Education Project (VEP) of the Southern Regional Council.[20] This collaborative effort began in the fall of 1961 with the Progressive Voter's League, a nonpartisan group organized in Jackson in the late 1940s to encourage and assist blacks in becoming registered voters. With the assistance of the Voter's League, Womanpower was able to conduct education and registration classes at the Farish Street Baptist Church, which were essential to the voter registration effort. In addition to providing potential voters with instructions on how to fill out the registration form, these classes impressed upon blacks that voting was an act of American citizenship that they rightfully possessed and were being unjustly denied. These organizations also hoped to convey the potential power and opportunity that voting could afford their communities.

This collaborative endeavor soon resulted in the establishment of the Jackson Voter Education Coordinating Committee, which served to streamline resources and create a single plan for black voter education and registration in the Jackson area. In January 1962 this Coordinating Committee—comprised of Womanpower Unlimited, the Voter's League, the Jackson Non-Violent Movement,[21] the NAACP, and other organizations—opened an office on Farish Street. With the hope of reaching larger numbers of blacks by pooling their resources, the Coordinating Committee sought to educate blacks on the importance of the vote and its proper use.

Through workshops they instructed people on how to complete registration forms and how to interpret the constitution (the infamous question #19 on the Voter Registration Form), and trained others to assist in these efforts. The office also served as a location where people could pay their poll tax. This fee, which was required in order to register to vote, had been an effective means of eliminating blacks from politics since its inclusion in the state's 1890 constitution. In addition to the difficulties many blacks had in acquiring the funds, potential voters were also deterred with fewer locations in black areas where the poll taxes could be paid. Therefore a convenient location where blacks could pay this tax made the process easier.

By the spring of 1962 the women of Womanpower believed that their work with the Voter's League and the Coordinating Committee had equipped them with the knowledge and tools necessary to undertake their own program of voter registration directed primarily at women. They applied to the Voter Education Project for financial support and were awarded a grant of $1,000 for a three-month period from September to November 1962. As stated in Womanpower's final report to the VEP, "the unique goal of this special project was to create an awareness among women for social action in the community especially as it relates to registering and voting."[22]

The method employed for Womanpower Unlimited's voter registration campaign was to contact prominent community women in Jackson and the surrounding areas to enlist their support in organizing a group of women to whom Womanpower representatives could speak. This process reached large numbers of women, and the endorsement of the campaign by community leaders gave it more credence. By using the local community's established organizations, such as churches and civic clubs, Womanpower was able to reach a large audience.

Womanpower's efforts were impressive, particularly in ensuring that potential voters' poll taxes were paid. Ironically the actual number of those who registered and voted as a result of their efforts was dismal, reflecting the fear and history of white resistance in the state. While they did not fully achieve their stated goals of registering large numbers of blacks, they recognized how their activities added to the momentum of the movement and, in that sense, were a success. Harvey addressed this issue in a 1965 interview, stating:

> We did accomplish this: we did give people courage and got them thinking
> about registering and voting so somebody would be able to report a year

later that they were able to get so many people registered. If we had not been able to get this spade work, really hard dirty spade work done, of getting people to see why they should register, the good results others had would not have been possible. . . . And so this was our particular contribution to this area.[23]

If people were at least willing to attend the workshops or create a forum for Womanpower to address voting issues, the organization assisted the movement in raising people's consciousness—a precondition for movement participation and sustenance. Womanpower's efforts ensured that more people's consciousness would be changed in the hope that their behavior would soon follow. Womanpower's actions also reveal the local base of voter registration efforts in the state not simply attributable to SNCC's organizing in the state.

This is indicative of the types of efforts displayed by community women that may not initially be viewed as successful endeavors. However, the activities within local communities should be judged not solely by quantitative measures but rather by their contributions to advancing the movement as a whole. Womanpower successfully contributed to the movement's voter education efforts by helping to eliminate some of the apathy and fear that prevented many from attempting to register, and therefore should be credited with enabling the long-term success of the movement.

Another major activity for which Womanpower provided key support was Freedom Summer 1964, which was designed to organize freedom schools and community centers, increase voter registration, and bring national attention to the state of Mississippi.[24] The schools and community centers were designed to provide educational and social resources that the black community lacked. Freedom Summer also sought to solicit support for the newly formed Mississippi Freedom Democratic Party, an independent organization founded to provide an alternative to the standard Jim Crow Democratic gatherings and to challenge the national Democratic Party. Finally, by focusing national attention on the state, civil rights activists hoped to highlight the particular oppression and struggles of blacks in Mississippi and engender federal intervention for their protection and proper inclusion into American political, economic, and social systems.

As they had learned from their experiences with the Freedom Riders, the members of Womanpower were aware of the positive impact that psychological and material support had on civil rights activists. Thus the two essential ways that Womanpower contributed to Freedom Summer were providing basic sustenance—food and housing—for the volunteers. Initially hot meals were served to the project workers at the office of the Council of Federated Organizations (COFO) during June and July. These meals were made possible through donations from Jacksonians as well as from members of the Womanpower "Chain of Friendship" outside the state. In July a formal Community Food Project was established through the Farish Street Baptist Church.[25] The collaboration between Womanpower and the church resulted in serving meals to an average of eighty-five people per day.[26]

Womanpower also maintained the Freedom Houses, which provided free and safe lodging for civil rights volunteers. This was especially important since many volunteers were out-of-state residents. Since hundreds of volunteers filtering into the state needed shelter for the summer, Womanpower members also provided accommodations in their own homes and secured housing in the homes of friends.

These contributions had a profound effect on the activists who benefited from their work as evidenced in a letter by the COFO staff and Womanpower volunteers:

> There is a very important way, perhaps the most important way, that the Mississippi Project has been able to be so successful. That is that all of the workers have been made to feel here that you are really glad for us to be here. . . . And a very important sacrifice . . . was made by the people in Jackson who are housing us and by the ladies in the community who fed us this summer every day for six weeks.
>
> We want to say something special to these ladies. . . . they kept us healthy in a very real way, and we are very grateful to them. . . . We will miss much more than the food, much more than the vitamins—and we thank you for the real sense of being cared for that you gave us this summer.[27]

The volunteers knew that their success was impossible without the collaboration of local people, and it was Womanpower that was responsible for a significant amount of these cooperative efforts and that understood the crucial importance of this behind-the-scenes organizing to maintaining a movement in the state.

As with the Freedom Riders, local women provided a means of mental and spiritual support for the civil rights workers. Womanpower engaged in "othermothering" to support the civil rights movement by providing nurturance as a form of resistance.[28] This helped to prevent the demoralization of outside civil rights activists and to counter negative propaganda and harassment by white resisters hoping to mentally debilitate activists. Bettina Aptheker writes that black women have continuously used nurturing in an effort to raise a community of children who can withstand and fight against societal oppressions. And when this type of nurturing "is done collectively over time it becomes a historically defined resistance."[29]

At the same time they were providing essential resources—like food and shelter—that had been overlooked by the planners. Womanpower members were not merely engaging in traditional caretaking roles, they were filling the gaps that had been left by the organizers—gaps upon which the success of Freedom Summer depended.

Another means by which black women have traditionally sought to achieve empowerment and to be uplifted is through education. With the integration of Jackson public schools in 1964, Womanpower assisted in educational reform for the community. In the fall of 1964 district court judge Sidney Mize issued a mandate that Jackson schools uphold the 1954 *Brown v. Board of Education* decision. Although the integration plan only applied to first graders, this was a significant step for Jackson and one that required a great deal of support from the black community.

Womanpower members sought two avenues by which to assist in this integration effort. First, they participated in the efforts undertaken by community women, black and white, in disseminating information regarding the desegregation plan. Members participated in door-to-door canvassing to encourage those who had children entering the first grade to integrate, and to address questions and concerns anyone had about the school board's plan. Additionally they opened their homes to hold meetings concerning school desegregation with interested parents.

As a result, in September 1964 forty-three black first graders were admitted to previously segregated schools. In order to assist these children and their families, Womanpower "adopted" some of these children to help ensure their success in the new and likely hostile environment. Many of the families of children integrating the schools lived in poverty and had a variety of needs that ranged from clothing and school supplies to a wheelchair for one father. Womanpower made these items known to those whom they appealed for help. They emphasized that academic success would be difficult to achieve if the students lacked either the materials necessary for school or the resources for a decent life at home. Their assistance came in the form of clothes, lunch money, books and supplies, transportation, items family members needed, and extracurricular activities that provided opportunities for students to interact with activists in their community. Womanpower's ultimate goal was to ensure the educational success of these children in the hope that such opportunities would become available for more black youth in the future. With this goal in mind, they understood that adopting a holistic approach to each child's life would be most effective in providing a stable foundation from which the children could develop and mature successfully.

Womanpower Unlimited was a great asset to Jackson in particular but also to the larger civil rights movement in Mississippi, because it generated new forms of activism among uninvolved populations, working with the existing civil rights organizations, and improved the quality of life for members of the community. In addition to its activist efforts within the state of Mississippi, however, Womanpower was also engaged in efforts that connected its members with activists throughout the nation and the world. Internationally, Womanpower took an active role in peace activities while espousing the idea that issues of international peace were as central to the members' lives as domestic issues of civil rights activism. Members believed that it was futile to fight for justice solely in one's own community, particularly if the world at large would not provide a forum for furthering the attainment of equality and the pursuit of understanding among different races. For Womanpower, the struggles for domestic and international human rights were interdependent, and success was not complete unless it was achieved in both areas.

As a representative of Women Strike for Peace and Womanpower Unlimited, Harvey had many opportunities to participate in international peace and anti-colonial conferences. In 1962 she traveled to Geneva, Switzerland, as one of fifty American women and fifty international women representatives to address the "17 Nation Disarmament Conference," and also to Accra, Ghana, for Kwame Nkrumah's "World without the Bomb Conference." In the spring of 1963 Harvey participated in the Vatican Peace Pilgrimage. Her affiliation with Women Strike for Peace and her participation in these international activities provided Harvey and Womanpower with firsthand experience about issues of war and peace. Even though other members of Womanpower were unable to attend these conferences, through Harvey's experiences they were exposed to the ideologies of the peace movement and were thereby equipped with the knowledge to better educate others and intelligently interpret conflicts, such as the Vietnam War. Moreover, this knowledge nurtured their humanistic approach to civil rights activism in seeking broad-based measures of justice. Collectively, Womanpower also responded locally by "reading and studying in depth on peace issues; getting petitions signed; writing letters, articles; speaking, sharing an international peace fest, etc.," and incorporating peace issues into their civil rights forums.[30] This involvement with the peace movement enabled Womanpower to infuse a broader human rights agenda into in their local activism—an agenda that demonstrates that local activism is not merely isolated and parochial. Instead, the local reinforces the national and international, and vice versa.

Although Womanpower had many agendas, the primary aim of its members was civil rights reform. They did not plan to remain a permanent organization; rather, they intended to create the avenues by which significant change could occur locally and nationally, and they believed that with such progress their work would be complete. Womanpower members were certain that they would accomplish their goals, and so they never anticipated a need for permanency. As stated in a January 1966 newsletter, Harvey explained that Womanpower would:

> prepare the way for all of the good and wonderful things that have come and that are coming. With them on the scene, it would be presumptuous of us to continue in the active role we have carried the past years. And so we gracefully move from the center of the stage to the sideline to await our call.[31]

And with such a declaration, Womanpower began to gradually move away from the center of community and civil rights activism in Jackson. This move resulted not only from the members' belief that they had accomplished their goals but also from the waning of the civil rights movement in Mississippi as well as the active role that the National Council of Negro Women (NCNW) was beginning to play in the state. Womanpower Unlimited eventually disbanded in 1968, and many members joined the newly founded Jackson section of the NCNW.

During its brief existence, with its members' unique perspective of activism, derived from black women's historical tradition of survival, uplift, and humanism, Womanpower addressed issues that could be (and were) neglected by other organizations, undertook endeavors focusing on specific issues they deemed important, and generated activism for other civil rights organizations without discrimination. Not competing for resources or seeking authority within a given geographic location or among a particular population, Womanpower sought to engage everyone in the work of universal social justice.

Conclusion

Black women are grounded as members of families, communities, and a unique African culture that embraces women, men, and children. While Womanpower's agenda was primarily directed at attaining civil rights for blacks, its members possessed a humanist vision of activism that did not separate their struggle from other acts of injustice. The idea that despite their local activities, the movement, in general, must be an inclusive and humane one represents the essence of their womanist activism. Improving individual quality of life as well as racial relations in Jackson was merely part of their agenda for attaining worldwide equality and peace. They earnestly believed that rights for blacks in Mississippi, and even throughout the United States, would be futile in a world that did not uphold a belief in the "brotherhood of men." Thus they worked for peace, justice, and understanding on an international level while serving their communities locally. Again, this allows us to see the inextricable connection between the local, national, and international, a connection that does not detract from the significance of fighting on either front but, instead, empowers every level of the struggle.

In asserting themselves as agents of change, Womanpower members challenged the distinction between theory and action, demonstrating that it is only through action that theory is comprehended. And action, in turn, serves to vitalize one's theories. Ideas and actions are mutually dependent on each other, providing avenues for the further development of both. Womanpower emphasized the importance of being able to act in accordance with the evolving theory and direction of the movement, and was able to organize without hesitation to assist and develop strategies to sustain the movement. Thus, in working to achieve the traditional goals of black women's activism, Womanpower Unlimited proceeded from an action-oriented ideology based on "woman power," race consciousness, and humanism.

This essay has attempted to show that black women's leadership and activism at the local level has been a necessary component in the success of

Black Freedom struggles. Although not always recognized as such, black women have constantly been leaders in black liberation movements. While often subject to an existence on the margins of "recognized" leadership circles, black women have nonetheless historically been leaders in their communities as organizers, strategists, and negotiators. Unlike other studies that characterize black women's activism as merely supportive work that coincides with traditional "women's roles," I posit that a gendered analysis of their activism can provide us with an alternate perspective of their participation. The members of Womanpower Unlimited, in fact, saw themselves as occupying the "center stage" of activism in Jackson. They engaged in nurturing and supportive activities as well as "traditional" civil rights endeavors such as voter registration and boycotting, understanding that all were necessary in building an effective movement for justice and equality. Womanpower recognized how the marginalization women experienced because of their gender or tenuous economic position (those women whose economic contribution was a necessity to their family's income and whose employment could be threatened by white retaliation) affected their involvement in the movement, and they created a "safe space" for women to address and work to overcome these obstacles. At the same time they maintained a commitment to larger movement goals and were successful both in empowering black women in their community to become engaged in activism and in accomplishing a civil rights agenda.

Clarie Collins Harvey initially recognized the power she and her peers had as women, as evidenced in the name she chose for her group—Womanpower Unlimited. Womanpower did not accept a marginalized position in the movement but instead created for itself a definition of woman's power that was predicated on action and the necessity of women's leadership. Members recognized the potential ability of women to be a strong force for positive change, and they accepted this responsibility. Furthermore, Harvey recognized the integral role local people played in the freedom movement. When discussing the activities of Jackson residents, Harvey states that they were "pull[ing] together to make the kind of climate in the community [in which] social change could be born."[32] Ultimately the success of the movement relied on the efforts put forth by local people to ensure change in their communities.

Characteristic of the primary organizers, many members were economically independent, middle-aged women who therefore held a unique position that afforded them the autonomy to unreservedly and openly support the movement. Many were housewives or businesswomen, which shielded them from the financial retaliations of whites that many blacks feared. In respect to the larger membership, Womanpower created a sisterhood that connected women across socioeconomic backgrounds. Logan recalls that Womanpower members were from "all walks of life, we had some of the higher ups and some of the lower downs. Any woman that wanted to participate . . . just whoever, if you were a woman you could join because there wasn't no fee that you had to pay. But we just needed your strength, your support."[33]

In addition, many of these women had previous experience in social and political activism and were well-equipped to mobilize resources and inspire others to activism. Womanpower members were respected leaders in their community, who were able to give legitimacy to movement participation. Furthermore, their access to community networks and established organizations and institutions increased their ability to mobilize people to activism and were instrumental in building a movement in Mississippi. These women were able, long-term organizers in their community and represent the tradition of black women's activism that has been a source of strength and leadership in the struggle for black liberation as well as a vital force for social change. Through their efforts they not only sustained a movement for social justice but a legacy of activism as well.

These women incorporated the traditional methods of black women's activism of community uplift into their civil rights agenda. They determined the needs of their local communities and those of the civil rights activists in the state, and then formulated a plan of action to institute efforts to sustain both groups. Realizing the need for both physical and spiritual support, they followed in the footsteps of a long line of women who took responsibility for the survival and progress of the race. These twentieth-century "race women" are a testament to the courage and strength of black women dedicated to social change and racial uplift locally, nationally, and internationally. Although they remain invisible, to some degree, in the chronicles of history, the civil rights struggle in Mississippi owes much to the foresight and action of Womanpower Unlimited. Until we begin more fully to explore the contributions of local people to the civil rights struggle, we will not see the work done internally by local communities or fully understand the contribution of indigenous leadership strategies to the civil rights movement. The story of these local communities shows us that this freedom movement was not entirely about a national agenda of civil rights legislation or outside activists and well-known organizations fighting on the behalf of local people; rather, it was about how local people mobilized and organized to advance the civil rights movement.

NOTES

1. I thank Professors Vernon J. Williams Jr., Nancy Gabin, James Saunders, Sally Hastings, and John Dittmer for their insights and suggestions in the development of this larger project. Special thanks are extended to Professors Kimberly C. Ellis and Judson L. Jeffries for their thorough editing of this piece.

2. The Freedom Riders were an interracial group of civil rights activists who were attempting to integrate interstate transportation terminals as declared by the 1960 Supreme Court decision *Boynton v. Virginia*. Under the leadership of James Farmer and the Congress of Racial Equality, the Freedom Riders planned a journey from Washington, D.C., to New Orleans, Louisiana, in May 1961. For a detailed explanation of the Freedom Riders, see James Peck, *Freedom Ride* (New York: Simon and Schuster, 1962), and August Meier and Elliott Rudwick, *CORE: A Study of the Civil Rights Movement, 1942–1968* (New York: Oxford University Press, 1973).

3. Clarie Collins Harvey, interview by Deborah Denard, July 2, 1976, Jackson, Mississippi.

4. Clarie Collins Harvey, interview by John Dittmer and John Jones, April 21, 1981, Jackson, Mississippi, Mississippi Department of Archives and History, 26.

5. Clarie Collins Harvey, interview by Gordon C. Henderson, August 5, 1965, Jackson, Mississippi, Millsaps College Oral History of Mississippi: Contemporary Life and Viewpoint, 14.

6. Womanpower, *Womanpower and the Jackson Movement* (self-produced pamphlet), 8 .

7. Ibid., 6.

8. Frances Fox Piven and Richard Cloward, *Poor People's Movements: Why They Succeed and How They Fail* (New York: Vintage, 1979), xxii.

9. Ibid., 15–16.

10. George Alexander Sewell, *Mississippi Black History Makers* (Jackson: University Press of Mississippi, 1977), 176–77.

11. Clarie Collins Harvey, interview by Vicki L. Crawford, July 13, 1986, personal collection of Vicki L. Crawford.

12. Harvey, interview by Dittmer and Jones, 16.

13. A. M. E. Logan, interview by author, November 8, 2001.

14. A. M. E. Logan, interview by Vicki L. Crawford, July 16, 1986.

15. Thomas Gaither, "Panel Discussion on the Freedom Rides" at the 1961 Freedom Riders' Fortieth Reunion, Jackson, Mississippi, November 10, 2001.

16. William Brown, interview by author, October 2000. William Brown is the brother of Thelma Sanders.

17. Malcolm Boyd, "The Battle of McComb," *Christian Century* 83 (November 1964): 1398.

18. Joan Trumpauer Mulholland, interview by author, November 10, 2001.

19. Womanpower, *Womanpower and the Jackson Movement,* 14.

20. The Voter Education Project grew out of the Kennedy administration's attempt to foster a "cooling-off" period following the disruption of the Freedom Rides. The VEP was founded to help fund nonpartisan voter education and registration efforts of civil rights groups and was designed to investigate problems encountered by blacks attempting to register.

21. The Jackson Non-Violent Movement was another organization that grew out of the Freedom Rides. Organized primarily by SNCC activists, this new movement sought to organize the increasing desire for activism among Jackson youth. The group organized to challenge segregation through nonviolent direct action protest and participated in activities like boycotting the segregated state fair and buses. Voice of the Jackson Movement Newsletter, August 25, 1961, Clarie Collins Harvey (CCH) Papers, Amistad Research Center; Christian Social Action for Better Community Living, undated, CCH Papers, Amistad Research Center; John Dittmer, *Local People: The Struggle for Civil Rights in Mississippi* (Urbana: University of Illinois Press, 1994), 116.

22. Final Report Womanpower Unlimited, Voter Education Project, January 23, 1963, CCH papers, Amistad Research Center.

23. Harvey, interview by Henderson, 23.

24. For one of the best accounts of Freedom Summer, see Doug McAdam, *Freedom Summer: Political Process and the Development of Black Insurgency, 1930–1970* (Chicago: University of Chicago Press, 1982).

25. United States Civil Rights Commission Report, B85, f12, CCH Papers, Amistad Research Center.

26. An S-O-S, September 10, 1964, CCH Papers, Amistad Research Center.

27. Letter to Ms. Redmond, September 1, 1964, Rosie Redmond Holden Papers, Margaret Walker Alexander Research Center.

28. Not predicated on biological motherhood, black women have engaged in nurturing acts of mothering to ensure the survival of the black community. These "othermothers" (to borrow the term of sociologist Patricia Hill Collins) were often community and political activists, "expressing ethics of caring and personal responsibility . . . [to help] members of the community . . . attain the self-reliance and independence essential for resistance." See Patricia Hill Collins, *Black Feminist Thought: Knowledge, Consciousness, and the Politics of Empowerment,* 2nd ed. (New York: Routledge, 2000), 189–90.

29. Bettina Aptheker, "Direction for Scholarship," in *African American Women and the Vote, 1837–1965,* ed. Ann D. Gordon, Bettye Collier-Thomas, John H. Bracey, Arlene Voski Avakian, and Joyce Aurech Berkman (Amherst: University of Massachusetts Press, 1997), 207.

30. Womanpower, *Womanpower and the Jackson Movement,* 17.

31. Womanpower Unlimited newsletter, January 1966, CCH Papers, Amistad Research Center.

32. Harvey, interview by Dittmer and Jones, 28.

33. Logan, interview by Crawford.

Chapter 9

The Stirrings of the
Modern Civil Rights Movement
in Cincinnati, Ohio, 1943–1953

Michael Washington

Amid the domestic tensions of World War II, in the summer of 1943 a delegation of African Americans in Cincinnati called for a meeting with the mayor. Their purpose was to promote "interracial cooperation and good city administration" by forming a politically independent "citizens committee on unity." The meeting would be a fateful one, for when Mayor James G. Stewart consented to appoint an interracial, interfaith group of leaders to the committee, he gave legitimacy to what would become the vehicle by which African Americans would carry out the struggle for civil rights for the next two decades and usher in the modern civil rights movement in Cincinnati.[1] Functioning in an advisory capacity, but eschewing advocacy, the Mayor's Friendly Relations Committee (MFRC) did not foresee and certainly never endorsed radical solutions to potentially volatile racial issues. Indeed, on issues such as police brutality its ineffectiveness generated more racial animosity than it quelled. It was a cautious approach to issues long simmering in the black community, and it would provoke other groups to assume more radical protest tactics. A coalition of local organizations, including the Congress of Racial Equality (CORE), the National Association for the Advancement of Colored People (NAACP), the Citizens Committee for Human Rights (CCHR),[2] the West End Civic League, the Jewish Community Council, and the Women's City Club, soon mobilized to counter discrimination in restaurants, stores, employment, and colleges of music as well as to counter police brutality, using methods that ranged from back-room negotiating to mass protest.

While historians date the beginning of the modern civil rights movement with Montgomery in 1955, little note has been taken that the radical protest tactics deployed in the Northern city of Cincinnati in the early 1940s and 1950s had already proven effective before Montgomery and the Southern struggles against Jim Crow. Significantly, in the absence of a single charismatic leader like King, Malcolm, or Huey, these seminal struggles in Cincinnati have escaped national attention. In Cincinnati it was unnamed local people, working through organizations and coalitions and sometimes as individuals, who played decisive roles in creating and sustaining the push for civil rights.

While these struggles took place in a Northern border city,[3] they were waged against a system of racial discrimination markedly similar to that found in the South (though many in Cincinnati would repeatedly deny the similarities). This point contradicts the widely held notion of a color line separating de jure segregation in the South and the de facto version found in Northern cities like Cincinnati, Chicago, and Detroit; for in the North residential segregation was a matter of local as well as national policy, enforced by law. Moreover, in the North, as in the South, black voters were frequently disenfranchised by racist political maneuvers. Indeed, it is accurate to describe the racial atmosphere of the North during the postwar period as a state of apartheid, and Cincinnati, a Northern city with Southern sympathies, as an important reminder of the many movements outside the South that have gone unnoticed by historians.

This essay examines the city's civil rights protest movement from 1943 to 1953, from the emergence of the Mayor's Friendly Relations Committee to the desegregation of one of the city's most cherished institutions, Coney Island Amusement Park. The MFRC was a citizens' advisory committee appointed by the mayor to address issues related to human relations and tolerance. Fearful of provoking racial tensions that might arise from the perception that it was a black advocacy group, the committee refused to challenge the status quo, choosing, instead, a conciliatory approach to potentially volatile racial issues. It was the executive director of the Cincinnati Community Chest's Division of Negro Welfare who subverted the gradualist approach of the MFRC by mobilizing local grassroots organizations to mount a direct challenge to racial discrimination throughout the city. Their frontal assault on segregation would culminate in a mass struggle for access to "the largest single public accommodation in Greater Cincinnati," the Coney Island Amusement Park.[4] This laid the groundwork for a full-fledged civil rights movement in postwar Cincinnati and would serve as a testing ground for tactics that would be used by the movement nationwide.

The Mayor's Friendly Relations Committee and the Origins of the Movement, 1943–1948

During a time of intense interracial tensions, the modern struggle for civil rights in Cincinnati did not begin as an angry uprising but rather from a conciliatory effort to prevent such an occurrence. The delegation of African Americans who met with Cincinnati's mayor James G. Stewart on July 8, 1943, included three members of the local NAACP—Harold Snell, the executive director; Sadie Samuels, an elementary schoolteacher; and William Lovelace, a probation officer for the Common Pleas Court—as well as a fourth delegate, Arnold B. Walker, who was the executive director of the Cincinnati Community Chest's Division of Negro Welfare.[5]

In an attempt to prevent Cincinnati from experiencing the type of racial bloodshed associated with the Detroit race riot, where thirty-four people were killed,[6] the delegation suggested that the mayor arrange a special meeting with representatives from a broad cross-section of the community to discuss the necessity for community-wide planning to foster racial tolerance. After considerable delay, on October 7, 1943, the mayor convened a meeting attended by representatives of the Division of Negro Welfare, B'Nai B'rith, Federated Churches, the Cincinnati Recreation Commission, the Congress of Industrial Organization (CIO), Catholic Charities, the NAACP, the Racial Amity Committee, and the Frontiers Club (an African American men's club consisting of businessmen and professionals devoted to community service).[7] As a result of the meeting it was agreed that Mayor Stewart would assume responsibility for naming the committee and that he would submit the matter to the City Council in order to secure its backing and to solicit further suggestions.[8]

On November 17 Cincinnati City Council voted to give the newly formed MFRC official status and affiliation with the city government but limited its role to that of an advisory committee with no enforcement powers.[9] At its first official meeting on December 23, 1943, the committee made clear that it would not function as a black advocacy group, when it issued a statement announcing, "we are not working for the welfare of any one group, but are fostering improvements in conditions, interrelation-ships, and interplay of personalities which will safeguard the rights of all citizens."[10]

From the beginning the African American co-founders of the MFRC felt compelled to project a racially neutral image of the committee, with the disclaimer,

> whatever action is assumed by this committee, it should be clearly under-stood and publicized, we do not regard ourselves as a committee to ward off race riots. We do not expect rioting in Cincinnati. We must regard our job as positive and constructive, looking toward cooperation among all groups and toward equitable opportunities for all races.[11]

Despite their conciliatory language however, African American members of the MFRC viewed it not merely as an impartial advisory committee but rather as a potential vehicle for protecting and advancing the interests of the African American community. Unwilling to be circumscribed by the committee's conciliatory philosophy, its African American members formed advocacy-based coalitions with some of its member organizations, establishing a pattern of effective interracial protest against racial injustice that would be repeated over the next two decades.

This approach was largely the vision of an MFRC board member Arnold B. Walker, who headed the Division of Negro Welfare, a Commu-nity Chest–sponsored social service organization. In that capacity Walker had effectively built coalitions with like-minded organizations such as the NAACP and other social service agencies, as a means of serving and pro-tecting the black community.[12] As a member of the original delegation that urged the mayor to form the MFRC, Walker maintained that white prejudice in the workplace should be one of its primary targets and that the committee should play a role in providing for the "protection of mi-norities in case of racial conflict."[13]

To assist the MFRC in carrying out its goals, in the summer of 1945 Marshall Bragdon was hired as its executive secretary. As a full-time em-ployee of the MFRC, Bragdon was required to keep abreast of relevant is-sues and events in the community. Through his relationships with minis-ters, civic leaders, and black organizations, charges of police brutality against the black community were brought to the attention of the MRFC.[14] Walker, who recognized the importance of holding law enforce-ment officials accountable for the safety and welfare of the black community, proposed that policemen be provided with "training in minority problems" and the "techniques needed to meet them." The police department never implemented his plan, and accusations of racial harassment continued. Just months later it was discovered that the assistant police chief had hung a cartoon on his wall, depicting the body of a gorilla and the head of a black man, with a caption that read "Us'ns Brutalized." It was widely believed that the demeaning image represented two black men, Nathan Wright and Haney Bradley, who had recently been involved in controversial encounters with the police.[15]

The case of Nathan Wright, a leader in the local chapter of CORE, who would eventually earn a Harvard Ph.D. and become an Episcopal priest, provoked outrage in the black community. While a student at the University of Cincinnati, Wright was stopped in November 1946 by two detectives, whom he described as using "abusive and threatening" language. The incident occurred as he was walking along Lincoln Park Drive in the West End with a typewriter he had borrowed from a local church. Assuming that he was stealing the typewriter, the detectives stopped him for questioning. When Wright insisted on seeing their badges, one of them is reported to have remarked, "Oh, you're one of those God damn smart niggers." As Wright was about to be taken away in the patrol car, he called out to neighborhood children to get the minister from the church from which he had just come. Reverend Maurice McCrackin rushed to the police station, where he was threatened with incarceration for interfering with the prosecution of the law.[16] Although the Reverend's presence angered the police, it had the desired effect, and Wright was soon released without charges.[17]

Wright reported his case to city officials, but city manager Wilbur N. Kellogg twice refused to censure the detectives, further inflaming racial tensions.[18] Six months later, in June 1947, the issue of police brutality resurfaced when Haney Bradley was beaten by two police officers and charged with disorderly conduct. After Judge William D. Alexander dismissed the disorderly conduct charge against Haney, the City Safety Director retaliated by refusing to discipline the officers.[19] Bragdon's suggestion that the rookie officers receive race relations instruction was similarly dismissed.[20]

Without enforcement powers, the MFRC had no authority to resolve such incidents. When the MFRC proved ineffective in addressing the issues of greatest concern to African Americans, a handful of justice-minded organizations within its ranks began to function as a splinter coalition to provide the necessary advocacy for the black community on the issue of police brutality. The coalition, comprised of the NAACP, the Federated Churches, the Woman's City Club, the Jewish Community Council, and the West End Civic League, threw its support behind Walker's efforts to hold the police accountable for their actions and issued a statement to the City Council condemning police mistreatment in the Bradley case. The letter charged the safety director and the chief of police with acting to "protect" the officers while showing "little interest in social attitudes and tensions in the community."[21]

Although the letter failed to effect changes in police policy, it galvanized the justice-minded coalition within the MFRC and helped sustain the momentum that had been building around the issues of discrimination in the workplace and public accommodations. In September 1943 a white investigator from the Fair Employment Practices Committee (FEPC), in his report on blacks in war industries, had found that discrimination in Cincinnati was not only widespread but also supported by the local War Manpower Commission (WMC) and the United States Employment Service (USES). Upon interviewing fourteen personnel managers from the city's largest firms, the FEPC official found that they claimed to refuse blacks because integrating their companies would produce work stoppages and perhaps a race riot.[22] Indeed, on June 5, 1944 approximately five thousand white workers at the Wright Aeronautical Corporation staged a wildcat strike to protest the integration of the machine shop, and a day later, ignoring the pleas of the CIO, Wright, and the National War Labor Board, another ten thousand walked out.[23] In May 1945, after other "hate strikes" at Delco Products and the Lunkenheimer Company, the MFRC pledged to seek the cooperation of the WMC and the FEPC in an effort to work toward the successful integration of black workers.[24]

In March 1945 the FEPC heard discrimination cases against a number of Cincinnati employers. During the hearings spokespersons for the Crosley Corporation, the F. H. Lawson Company, the Baldwin Company, the Streitmann Biscuit Company, and Victor Electric Products sought to justify their practices, citing labor unions' threats to strike if their plants became integrated.[25] When the FEPC examiner asked the head of the International Brotherhood of Electrical Workers local at Crosley, which was part of the American Federation of Labor, if his "union had taken any affirmative position on the issue of the employment of Negroes at the Crosley Corporation plant," the union leader answered, "we present the voice of the people. The voice of the people is that they will not work with niggers." Following the hearings only three of the participants altered their wartime discriminatory employment policies.[26]

When the MFRC, relying on a policy of gradualism and diplomacy, met with little success in convincing white employers to integrate their work-forces, the all-black West End Civic League[27] mobilized its membership to adopt a more aggressive approach. Reasoning that inner-city neighbor-hood businesses would be more vulnerable to agitation than large corpo-rations, in 1946 the West End Civic League began approaching white busi-ness owners in their community to persuade them to hire black workers. Their strategy was to begin with diplomacy and then to resort to picketing and distributing handbills outside the businesses if diplomacy failed. As a result of these tactics the owners of Stein Department Store and Laurel Cleaners agreed to hire a black worker in each of their establishments, and four black workers were hired in the Central Five Cents to One Dollar Store.[28] Hence a decade before the Southern civil rights movement would popularize such pressure campaigns, they had already proven successful in Cincinnati's black ghetto.

It was the issue of discrimination in public accommodations that galva-nized local activism and ultimately led to the desegregation of one of Cincinnati's most cherished icons—Coney Island. Despite the fact that an Ohio law of 1884 prohibited discrimination in public accommodations and restaurants, as late as the 1940s it remained common practice for the major downtown restaurants to refuse service to African Americans. The MFRC was characteristically reluctant to take decisive action on this issue. Sensing that the committee was "fighting a losing battle" to integrate the restaurants, Arnold Walker urged the MFRC to hold a conference with representatives of the NAACP, the Division of Negro Welfare, and a newly formed organization called the Conference on Human Relations (CHR) to "discuss the next stage of the current restaurant-visiting campaign."[29]

The campaign to which Walker referred had been initiated by CCHR, which, in the mid-1940s, had begun challenging the discriminatory poli-cies of the restaurant owners by initiating what they called visitation cam-paigns. These consisted of dispatching teams of interracial diners to the targeted establishments. For the most part it appears that these efforts were successful, as African Americans were dining regularly in more than ten downtown restaurants. Still, some establishments continued to intimi-date black diners with impunity, even though they allowed them to eat on their premises. Because neither the police nor the MFRC was prepared to bring an end to such discrimination, Walker pressured the committee to sanction a second stage of visitation campaigns.[30] Although he was unsuccessful in persuading the MFRC to assume an advocacy role, his agency, together with the CHR, helped to develop a local constituency base that would not hesitate to use radical tactics, such as nonviolent direct action, to challenge racial discrimination and segregation.

The early organization was comprised of members of the all-black West End Civic League and of a predominantly white chapter of CORE, composed of students from the Hebrew Union College.[31] Around 1948 the Cincinnati Committee on Human Relations (CCHR) was formed and absorbed most of the members of the CHR. The individuals credited with co-founding the CCHR were Wallace Nelson, his wife Juanita, and Reverend Maurice McCrackin. Nelson, the son of a black Methodist minister, grew up in Little Rock, Arkansas. While attending Ohio Wesleyan University he became an active member in the Christian pacifist movement. As a conscientious objector during World War II, he was imprisoned for thirty-three months for walking out of a civilian public service camp. While incarcerated in Cleveland, Ohio, he waged a protest against prison conditions and smuggled out information to the *Cleveland Call and Post.* Two years into his sentence he was released after a three-and-a-half-day hunger strike protesting prison conditions. Nelson's wife, Juanita Morrow, had been the reporter for the *Cleveland Call and Post* who helped Nelson to expose the inhumane conditions of the prison. He found his way to Cincinnati, after a friend in Covington, Kentucky, encouraged him to meet Reverend Maurice McCracken. After Nelson's release, the two began a lifelong partnership in pursuit of social justice.[32]

It was serendipitous that their paths would cross that of the Reverend Maurice McCrackin. Born in Storms, Ohio, in 1905, as a young child McCrackin and his family moved to Illinois where he graduated from Monmouth College in 1927 and McCormick Theological Seminary in 1930. In the early 1930s he spent five years as a missionary in Iran. The white Presbyterian minister arrived in Cincinnati from Chicago in August 1945 to accept a position as co-pastor of a newly federated Presbyterian-Episcopal congregation called Cincinnati–St. Barnabas in the predominantly black West End of Cincinnati. There he shared pastoral responsibilities with Albert Dalton, a member of the Episcopal Church Army, in carrying out an experiment in ecumenical inner-city mission work between two dying parishes. In 1948 Reverend McCrackin would join with the Nelsons and the local West End residents to form the CCHR,[33] which, in contrast to the conciliatory MFRC, would embrace an activist role that the earlier CHR established with the initiation of its effective visitation campaign to integrate downtown restaurants. The merger of these two organizations produced a number of activists who would form the nucleus of the mass movement to desegregate public accommodations citywide.[34]

The CCHR and the Challenge to Segregation
in Cincinnati's Colleges of Music

Unlike the Mayor's Friendly Relations Committee, the CCHR was unrestricted in its methods to achieve nonviolent social change. In 1948 the organization set concrete goals to challenge the most blatantly segregated institutions in the city. Two local music colleges became the first targets. At a time when Oberlin, Eastman, and Julliard had long been integrated, the Cincinnati Conservatory of Music and the Cincinnati College of Music, predecessors of the College Conservatory of Music of the University of Cincinnati, excluded African Americans from their student bodies on the grounds that integration would alienate their Southern students.[35] CCHR's strategy was first to publicly expose the issue of racial discrimination by the music schools; then to engage in ameliorative negotiations with school officials; and, if face-to-face negotiations failed, to picket as a last resort. By 1950 no progress had been made, and the intransigent posture of both music institutions left the organization no choice but to picket.

By then several active members in a national organization called Peacemakers had joined CCHR in the effort to integrate the colleges. The Peacemakers came into existence in Chicago in 1948 as a result of A. J. Muste's call to build a radical pacifist coalition willing to engage in bold, direct action on such controversial issues as resistance to militarism and the draft, and refusal to pay war taxes.[36] Each member was expected to accept nonviolence as a necessary way of life for resisting totalitarianism and achieving social change, and members were expected to refrain from service in the armed forces, even if it meant resisting conscription.[37]

The founders of the Peacemakers included such well-known pacifists as David Dellinger, Bayard Rustin, Milton Mayer, and A. J. Muste. Among its lesser-known members were Wallace Nelson and Ernest and Marion Bromley,[38] a white couple from Ohio, who introduced the Peacemakers' methods into the movement to integrate the music colleges. In the spring of 1948 the Bromleys, then residing in Wilmington, Ohio, about fifty miles north of Cincinnati, met Reverend Maurice McCrackin. Their meeting resulted in the initiation of a three-pronged action plan called "Operation Brotherhood," which included CCHR's campaign to integrate Cincinnati's two music colleges; a campaign to desegregate the schools in Wilmington, Ohio; and a campaign to support an African American teacher unjustly dismissed from the schools in Xenia, Ohio.[39]

In the spring of 1950 McCrackin and ten other ministers published an article in the national *Peacemaker* newsletter to bring exposure and support to the issue of integrating the music schools. In the article they encouraged people to sign a statement of concern and to write letters to both colleges of music demanding a change in their admissions policies. The article also appeared in other local newspapers and was broadcast on local radio stations. Working in tandem with the Peacemakers, the CCHR organized a well-orchestrated mobilization effort, which resulted in the collection of eight thousand signatures, but the music schools did not concede.[40]

The music school campaign scored a victory in 1951 when the CCHR resorted to a new tactic—public ridicule. The group organized a public hearing to focus attention and public outrage on the administrators of the music schools. The hearing, held on September 6, was moderated by local labor attorney James Paradise and included testimonials from such prominent artists as Walter F. Anderson, a composer and head of the music department at Antioch College, and Pulitzer Prize–winning literary artist Josephine Johnson Cannon. Also testifying were a number of local civic leaders, rejected applicants to the schools, and representatives of other music schools.[41] The persistent activism paid off when both colleges capitulated and agreed to allow African American students to enter their programs, and eventually to reside at their campus residences.[42] Buoyed by their victory and confident in their ability to sustain a long campaign, CCHR members prepared for a more formidable battle—the integration of Cincinnati's Coney Island Amusement Park.

The Coney Island Campaign

Early in 1952, after much deliberation, CCHR decided it was time to tackle the city's beloved—and segregated—Coney Island Amusement Park. The bold decision to integrate the popular attraction was controversial, drawing opposition even from some of Cincinnati's respected African American leaders, including members of the Urban League and the NAACP. Ernest Bromley would later recall,

> Some people told us you [sic] would never be able to do anything there. You ought to be working on something else, like employment. To us it was the · other way because Coney was such a sacred cow. The little [black] kids saw all the advertisements on TV and heard all the stuff on the radio and all of these enticements to come to Coney Island—and they couldn't go. It seemed like a terrible thing.

Notwithstanding Bromley's conviction, many thought that such a challenge would "set race relations back fifty years."[43]

The TV advertisements that Bromley referred to prominently featured local television personality "Uncle Al," who, along with his wife "Captain Wendy," served as an enticement for youngsters to come to the park. Privately owned by Edward Schott, Coney was a Cincinnati institution, built on sprawling grounds on the banks of the Ohio River at the far eastern edge of the city. When Marian Spencer, a mother of two young boys, heard one of the commercials in 1952, she called the park to inquire whether her own children would be welcomed. Learning that they were not, and unaware of the CCHR and its plans to challenge Coney's Jim Crow policy, she brought the matter to the NAACP. When the group suggested involving prominent African American attorney Theodore Berry, Spencer, not one to shrink from such a challenge, insisted on organizing a campaign to integrate the park herself.[44]

A 1942 graduate of the University of Cincinnati, with a degree in English, Spencer had gained valuable leadership experience when she organized to integrate the college prom.[45] While she was preparing to mobilize against Coney, McCrackin and a group of other ministers were engaged in meetings with the owner and president, Edward Schott, to persuade him to abandon his segregationist policy.[46] He refused, and members of the NAACP and the CCHR began picketing the amusement park.[47]

One strategy employed by the CCHR involved cars of interracial riders who attempted to enter the park via its two auto gate entrances. Once refused admission, they would turn off their engines, toss the keys under the seats, and wait to be let in. Because the location of the amusement park overlapped law enforcement jurisdictions, Coney was patrolled by Cincinnati police, Hamilton County Deputy Sheriffs, Anderson Township police, and Coney's private police force, the Solar Rangers. On May 17, 1952, all these law enforcement agencies responded to the park when an interracial group of approximately fifteen CCHR members tried to enter the park in cars. After blocking both the ticket window and the entrance, the protesters were engaged by the police, who arrested Marion Bromley and Wallace Nelson, releasing them a few hours later.[48] The following month, on June 22, the CCHR made its fourth appearance at the gate. The confrontational protest techniques employed by the Nelsons and Marion Bromley in this demonstration were particularly significant in that they would later become popular in the Southern struggles in the 1960s. On that day cars containing interracial groups were turned away from the entrance gates. A constable dragged McCrackin out of his car, and towed it and the vehicle of another protester from the entrance. The Nelsons, Marion Bromley, and art supply store owner Hal Goldberg refused to abandon their posts. As they were thrown into the back seat of a police car, they went limp, employing an effective tactic of nonviolent noncooperation. After being charged with "breach of the peace and resisting an officer," the protesters were locked up in the Hamilton County Jail where Goldberg's wife posted his bail, but the Nelsons and Bromley, true to their nonviolent lifestyles, refused bail and initiated a nine-day hunger strike. When they were bound over to a grand jury they "stood mute," refusing to answer questions. After they were released on their own recognizance, their case was ultimately dismissed.[49]

Although the protesters acted spontaneously, their concerted action represented the culmination of years of collective training and leadership experiences.[50] As co-founders of the national Peacemakers in 1948, both the Bromleys and the Nelsons were devoted to its tradition of nonviolent resistance to injustice and to a willingness to go to jail, if necessary.

Moreover, Nelson brought skills to the Coney Island campaign that were honed from his experiences as field director for national CORE. In 1951 CORE's attempt to provide effective coordination between the national office and the local groups resulted in the creation of a new position, referred to as the full-time "subsistence" fieldworker. In this position Nelson directed CORE's summer workshops. By training potential community leaders in the theories and techniques of nonviolence, the workshops were an important aspect of CORE's efforts to develop a strong national program. In turn, these workshops and the protest methods employed by CORE had a direct impact on Nelson's work with the CCHR.

Although the arrest and jailing of Marion Bromley and the Nelsons temporarily stalled the CCHR, the struggle to integrate Coney Island resumed in July. On July 19, 1952, while distributing leaflets in front of Coney's corporate offices, Ernest Bromley was knocked to the ground by a passer-by as the police stood by and watched.[51] During the same month, as a result of CCHR prodding, a subcommittee of the Cincinnati City Council began an investigation into Coney's admission policy. Convinced that the City Council did not take the matter seriously, the Reverend Maurice McCrackin prepared his own report on Coney Island, but he was denied permission to read it into the City Council record. McCrackin then circulated his report throughout the community to publicize the fact that Coney's Solar Rangers encouraged intimidation and violence against the demonstrators while ignoring vigilante attacks on the protesters. In September 1952 the City Council presented a preliminary report on Coney's admission policies. According to the *Peacemaker*,[52] the City Council's subcommittee found: "1) that Coney Island admission gates are entirely without the territorial limits of Cincinnati; 2) that officials have been informed by their legal counsel that they are operating entirely within the law; 3) that amusement park dignitaries are extremely sympathetic.[53]

In October 1952 concerned citizens representing CCHR and other organizations raised the issue of Coney's segregationist admission policy before the City Council. Rev. McCrackin was joined by Rev. Frank B. Lauderdale of the NAACP, by Charles Posner, head of the Fellowship House, and by Marian Spencer in urging the City Council to pressure Coney to end its policy of racial segregation.[54] In January 1953 the City Council heard a motion that Coney and other city-licensed businesses should be compelled to admit all people without discrimination. While the white majority on the Council voted to postpone the motion indefinitely, its two African American members, Theodore M. Berry and Jessie D. Locker, offered dissenting votes.[55] Ultimately Berry proposed an ordinance permitting the city to close the park for thirty to ninety days if it was found guilty of racial discrimination, but this proposal failed.

The African American Council members were not always in agreement on issues related to the black community. Locker was a Republican who tended to toe his party's line, while Berry was an Independent who sought the total inclusion of African Americans into all aspects of Cincinnati life. Berry's proposed ordinance in 1953 was not the first of his attempts to strike down Coney's policy of racial segregation. In 1951 he had requested that the MFRC investigate Jim Crow practices at the park. He pointed out that notwithstanding the state code making it illegal for such establishments to bar citizens on account of race, creed, or color, the City of

Cincinnati, in effect, endorsed Coney's violation of the law when it annually renewed Coney's license. He threatened that if no effort was made to end segregation at the park, the Council would be forced to take drastic measures.[56]

By 1953 the Coney Island struggle was bearing fruit. The direct action approach of the CCHR had led to dramatic demonstrations, arrests, and fasts that drew public attention to the issue and empowered many local people as well as politicians like Berry to act.

By the summer the NAACP, after initial hesitation, made use of its legal resources to end segregation at the park.[57] On July 2, and again on July 4, NAACP member Ethel Fletcher, an African American social worker, attempted to gain admission to the park. Having recently moved to Cincinnati from Lancaster, Pennsylvania, she would later recall, "I was shocked beyond all words, because you always found that [racial segregation] below the Mason-Dixon Line, you didn't think you would find it in Cincinnati."[58] After filing a class-action suit with the NAACP, on July 20, 1954, Fletcher won an injunction against the park when Common Pleas Court Judge Charles F. Weber ruled that Coney could not deny her admission. It was a partial victory; the judge made it clear that the ruling applied to Fletcher alone, as the case did not qualify as a class action.[59]

Following the ruling, public protest mounted. Local ministers drew up a petition demanding an end to Coney's Jim Crow policy. In August 1954 an interracial group of fifty NAACP members, comprised of adults and children, was denied admission. When sixty-five clergymen issued a "Statement of Concern" in which they insisted that Coney change its admission policy, the threat of economic losses from these protests became a serious concern to the park's management. After a series of backroom negotiations between Edward Schott, the park's managers, executive secretary of the Cincinnati Urban League Joseph A. Hall, and NAACP president Webster Posey, Schott finally consented to loosen the admission policy, opening all but the swimming pool and dance pavilion to black patrons. It was also agreed that the NAACP would, for a period, handpick those blacks who would attend the park. Finally, it was also agreed that publicity and "fanfare were unwise in contrast to a quiet, unpublicized well-planned job" of partial integration.[60] When the park opened on April 30, 1955, for the first time in its history African Americans were allowed to enter. Among the first of approximately twenty black visitors to the park that weekend were Marian Spencer and her two sons.[61]

Over the next several years very small numbers of African Americans patronized the park, as protesters continued to pressure Coney to integrate its swimming pool and dance hall. On May 20 and 25, 1961, members of CORE and the NAACP attempted to use the pool. After a number of arrests, Coney officials finally "acceded to [the] demonstrations" and initiated the process that resulted in the total desegregation of the park by May 30, 1961.[62] The struggle initiated by the CCHR almost a decade earlier had finally come to fruition.

Conclusion

In the fall of 1963, two years after the integration of Coney's swimming pool and dance hall, and after twenty years of protest about the issue of discrimination in the city, the *Cincinnati Enquirer* asked, "What's wrong? Why are the Negroes protesting? Isn't all that discrimination and segregation the South's worry? What are all these meetings and pronouncements about? Why the demonstrations, the picketing, the boycotting, here in fair-minded Cincinnati?"[63] The article was prompted by the rash of local CORE demonstrations that had occurred months earlier about school desegregation and discrimination in retail stores and industry. What the conservative newspaper portrayed as a sudden uprising by African Americans, however, was, in fact, the culmination of twenty years of struggles waged by local people and their organizations to bring racial segregation in the city to an end.

The upsurge of local protest reflected the heightened consciousness and increased activism of the very organizations that had led the Coney struggle. Indeed, the Coney campaigns had empowered local activists like NAACP president William Bowen to challenge Jim Crow throughout the city. Bowen had taken part in 1961 in the final protest that persuaded the Coney management to integrate the entire park. Later the same year he led the local NAACP in a boycott against three local breweries, two dairies, and the Canada Dry Company because of their refusal to employ substantial numbers of African Americans.[64] By the end of 1963 the NAACP and CORE had mounted several demonstrations at school construction sites, exposing discriminatory practices in the building trades.[65]

When, in May 1963, a caravan of local protesters accompanied Theodore Berry to the state capital to challenge Governor James Rhodes for his failure to support fair housing, many among the delegation were veteran activists—Abe Goldhagen, longtime treasurer of the NAACP, and Bill Mason, who held membership in both the NAACP and CORE.[66] Joining them were Dr. Bruce Green and his wife Lucille. Dr. Green, a practicing dentist in Cincinnati, who had been arrested and jailed during the Coney Island campaigns, would later, while president of the local NAACP, be arrested again, during a sit-in at the Building Trades Council to protest employment discrimination.[67] Green's predecessor at the NAACP, William Bowen, was another significant figure in the movement; as NAACP president, Bower had been arrested in 1961 while picketing at Coney in the final protest that persuaded the Coney management to integrate the entire park. Another member of the 1963 delegation to the state capital, Lloyd Trotter, had been a leader of the West End Civic League decades earlier.[68]

In the 1940s Trotter and his organization had largely comprised the membership of the CCHR, whose radical methods of civil disobedience not only helped bring an end to segregation at Coney Island but also gave impetus to a wave of activism that would eventually sweep the entire city and ultimately the nation. In 1960, eight years after the Coney Island struggle began as a challenge to Jim Crow in Cincinnati, protesters picketed a Woolworth store to support the actions of their Southern brethren's sit-in movement.[69] What the *Cincinnati Enquirer* failed to recognize in 1963 and what continues to elude many historians today is that Cincinnati's decade-long Coney Island struggle against Jim Crow, which predated by three years the Montgomery bus boycott, gave birth to tactics that would prove decisive in the national struggles to come.

NOTES

1. Robert A. Burnham, "The Mayor's Friendly Relations Committee: Cultural Pluralism and the Struggle for Black Advancement," *Race and the City: Work, Community, and Protest in Cincinnati, 1820–1970,* ed. Henry Louis Taylor Jr. (Urbana: University of Illinois Press, 1993), 259.

2. CCHR is referred to in the literature as (1) Citizens Committee on Human Rights, (2) Cincinnati Committee on Human Rights, (3) Citizens Committee on Human Relations, and (4) Cincinnati Commission on Human Rights.

3. For a discussion of Cincinnati's unique status as a border city with a "Northern/Southern personality," see Taylor, *Race and the City,* xiv–xviii.

43. According to the Reverend Richard Moore, pastor of Greenhills Presbyterian Church and participant in the Coney Island demonstrations, "As Coney Island went so went the restaurants, bars, and bowling alleys that catered to the general

public" (Judith A. Bechtel and Robert M. Coughlin, *Building the Beloved Community: Maurice McCrackin's Life for Peace and Civil Rights* [Philadelphia: Temple University Press, 1991], 80).

5. Burnham, "Mayor's Friendly Relations Committee," 259.

6. Thomas J. Sugrue, The *Origins of The Urban Crisis: Race and Inequality in Postwar Detroit* (Princeton, N.J.: Princeton University Press, 1996), 29.

7. "Notes on Mayor Stewart's Committee," October 7, 1943, Cincinnati Urban League of Greater Cincinnati (hereafter, ULGC), box 24, folder 5, Cincinnati Historical Society, Manuscripts Collection; also Burnham, "Mayor's Friendly Relations Committee," 260.

8. "Notes on Mayor Stewart's Committee," October 7, 1943, ULGC.

9. Burnham, "Mayor's Friendly Relations Committee," 260–61.

10. "Mayor Stewart's Friendly Relations Committee, December 23, 1943, 1, 2, ULGC, box 24, folder 6.

11. "Statement . . . FOR: Mayor Stewart's Committee, FROM: Negro Organizations Interested in Racial Amity and Good City Government, October 7, 1943, 1, ULGC, box 24, folder 5.

12. Ibid., 3.

13. Bulletin, Number 3, August 1943, 4; ULGC, box 24, folder 6.

14. Burnham, "Mayor's Friendly Relations Committee," 263–65.

15. Ibid., 267.

16. Bechtel and Coughlin, *Building the Beloved Community,* 60; Floyd B. Barbour, ed., *The Black Power Revolt* (Boston: Porter Sargent, 1968), 255.

17. Bechtel and Coughlin, *Building the Beloved Community,* 60.

18. *Cincinnati Time-Star,* December 31, 1946; and Burnham, "Mayor's Friendly Relations Committee," 265, 266.

19. *Cincinnati Enquirer,* July 11, 1947; August 22, 1947.

20. Burnham, "Mayor's Friendly Relations Committee," 267.

21. Ibid., 265, 266.

22. Andrew Edmund Kersten, *Race, Jobs, and the War: The FEPC in the Midwest, 1941–46* (Chicago: University of Illinois Press, 2000), 90.

23. Robert B. Fairbanks and Zane L. Miller, "The Martial Metropolis: Housing, Planning, and Race in Cincinnati, 1940–1955," in *The Martial Metropolis: U.S. Cities in War and Peace,* ed. Robert W. Lotchin (New York: Praeger, 1984), 196.

24. Burnham, "Mayor's Friendly Relations Committee," 270.

25. Ibid., 269; Kersten, *Race, Jobs, and the War,* 91.

26. Kersten, *Race, Jobs, and the War,* 91.

27. Meier and Rudwick, CORE, 58.

28. Burnham, "Mayor's Friendly Relations Committee," 269–71.

29. Ibid., 268–69. Historians have not recognized that there were actually two organizations with the letters CHR in the acronym. The Conference on Human Relations (CHR) was the earlier organization, formed around 1945, and the

Cincinnati Committee on Human Relations (CCHR) was later formed around 1948. Juanita Morrow (Nelson) supplied me (the author) with a number of primary source documents after our March 10, 2004, interview. Among the documents was letterhead from the Conference on Human Relations (CHR). The letterhead listed as "Joint Committee Co-Chairmen" Lloyd C. Trotter and Maurice McCrackin. The office was listed as being located at "916 Poplar St., Cincinnati 14, MAin 0041." There were twelve organizations listed under the word "Sponsorship," including the "American Jewish Congress, American Veterans Committee, Division of Negro Welfare of the Community Chest, Fellowship of Reconciliation, Hillel Foundation, National Association for the Advancement of Colored People, Quadres, Race Relations Committee of Council of Churches, West End Civic League, with the cooperation of Mayor's Friendly Relations Committee, Central YWCA, and U. C. Campus YWCA." This material may be found in the Cincinnati Historical Society under Juanita Morrow (Nelson's) Letters.

30. Ibid.

31. August Meier and Elliott Rudwick, *CORE: A Study in the Civil Rights Movement, 1942–1968* (Urbana: University of Illinois Press, 1975), 58. Bechtel and Coughlin, *Building the Beloved Community*, 71.

32. Meier and Rudwick, *CORE*, 44; Bechtel and Coughlin, *Building the Beloved Community*, 70.

33. Burnham, "Mayor's Friendly Relations Committee," 267.

34. Maurice McCrackin Papers, Manuscript Collection, Cincinnati Historical Society; see also Barry M. Horstman, *100 Who Made a Difference: Greater Cincinnatians Who Made a Mark on the 20th Century, Cincinnati Post*, Cincinnati, 232–33; Bechtel and Coughlin, *Building the Beloved Community*, 58. Cincinnati Committee on Human Relations July 1952 Newsletter (which was provided to the author by Juanita Morrow [Nelson] and will be donated to the Cincinnati Historical Society.

35. Bechtel and Coughlin, *Building the Beloved Community*, 71.

36. Ibid., 74.

37. "The Disciplines," *Peacemaker*, June 5, 1949, 5.

38. Interview with Juanita Nelson, October 18, 2003, Smith College.

39. Bechtel and Coughlin, *Building the Beloved Community*, 74–75.

40. See "Tackling Segregated Education" and "Ask Support in Combating Racism," *Peacemaker*, April 25, 1950, 2; and *Peacemaker*, April 21, 1951, 5, respectively.

41. "Discrimination to Be Aired," *Peacemaker*, September 1, 1951, 2.

42. Bechtel and Coughlin, *Building the Beloved Community*, 76.

43. Ibid., 80.

44. Ibid., 79.

45. Almost fifty years after the Coney Island campaign, Marian Spencer was honored as a recipient of the University of Cincinnati's McMicken College of Arts

and Sciences Distinguished Alumni Award of 2003. By then she had become an accomplished leader, having served as the first woman president of the Cincinnati chapter of the NAACP from 1980 to 1982 and the first African American woman to be elected to the Cincinnati City Council in 1983 (*Cincinnati Herald*, April 26, 2003). Fifty years later, when local civil rights activists were boycotting downtown Cincinnati after the fifteenth African American man was killed by police within a seven-year period, the NAACP relocated its major fund-raiser from the downtown Hyatt Regency Hotel to Moonlite Pavilion at Coney Island. Although Spencer purchased a $60 ticket for the banquet weeks in advance, she refused to attend because, at age eighty-two, she still remembered how hundreds of African Americans were turned away at the front gate—sometimes by force. "My history is such that I still don't feel comfortable there, even though the legal barriers have been taken down," she told a newspaper reporter from the *Cincinnati Enquirer* (*Cincinnati Enquirer*, October 11, 2002).

46. Bechtel and Coughlin, *Building the Beloved Community*, 80.

47. Nina Mjagkij, "Behind the Scenes: The Cincinnati Urban League, 1948–63," in Taylor, *Race and the City*, 283.

48. Bechtel and Coughlin, *Building the Beloved Community*, 81.

49. Ibid., 84, 85; Meier and Rudwick, CORE, 58; interview with Juanita Nelson.

50. Interview with Juanita Nelson.

51. Bechtel and Coughlin, *Building the Beloved Community*, 85.

52. It appears that Coney Island's significance as a cultural icon was such that, in the early years, the campaign challenging its admission policy would not make local news. None of the dramatic and courageous protest through 1952 was reported by the local media. According to Judith Bechtel and Robert Coughlin, "even though a news reporter witnessed the attack on Ernest Bromley at the Coney headquarters and brought a policeman to the scene, the incident never made the paper" (*Building the Beloved Community*, 85). When CCHR invited Carl Rowan, an African American who at the time was a nationally known syndicated columnist, it was reported in the news that he spoke about race relations with no mention of the topic of racial segregation at Coney Island. It is likely that the suit by the NAACP provided the first local press coverage on this issue. Had it not been for the early coverage provided by the *Peacemaker* and the *CORElator*, the organ of the Congress of Racial Equality, the demonstrations may not have been published as news.

53. *Peacemaker*, September 27, 1952, 4; see also Bechtel and Coughlin, *Building the Beloved Community*, 86.

54. Bechtel and Coughlin, *Building the Beloved Community*, 86–87.

55. Jacques, *Coney*, 140–41.

56. *Call and Post*, June 16, 1951.

57. Bechtel and Coughlin, *Building the Beloved Community*, 87.

58. Jacques, *Coney*, 141.

59. Bechtel and Coughlin, *Building the Beloved Community*, 87; Mjagkij, "Cincinnati Urban League," 284; Jacques, *Coney*, 141.

60. Mjagkij, "Cincinnati Urban League," 284–86.

61. Bechtel and Coughlin, *Building the Beloved Community*, 89.

62. Mjagkij, "Cincinnati Urban League," 288.

63. *Cincinnati Enquirer*, September 15, 1963.

64. *Cincinnati Herald*, November 10, 24, 1961; Michael Washington, "The Black Struggle for Desegregated Quality Education: Cincinnati, Ohio, 1954–1974" (Ph.D. dissertation, University of Cincinnati, 1984), 139.

65. Washington, "The Black Struggle," 141.

66. *Cincinnati Enquirer*, September 30, 2003, Obituaries B4.

67. Ibid., June 7, 1994, Obituaries, B4.

68. Interview with Juanita Nelson; see also interview with State Representative William Mallory, October 23, 2003.

69. Mjagkij, "Cincinnati Urban League," 288–89.

Chapter 10

"We Cannot Wait for
Understanding to Come to Us"

Community Activists Respond to Violence at
Detroit's Northwestern High School, 1940–1941

Karen R. Miller

On Tuesday, February 27, 1940, racial tensions that had been brewing on Detroit's West Side exploded into violence at the area's high school. Three hundred white and black youths participated in a racially charged "fracas" outside Northwestern High School. Six young men and one policeman were injured, and eleven people were arrested. The *Michigan Chronicle,* one of Detroit's black weeklies, reported that gangs of white youths had gathered around the high school that afternoon, waiting for students to be let out of their classes. Soon after school was dismissed, one African American and one white girl "engaged in a fistic fight." Their brawl "ignited sparks," and instantly black and white youths "began hurling snow balls, bricks and sticks at each other."[1]

Activists from neighboring black churches and civil rights groups responded to the violence at Northwestern by mobilizing members of community-based organizations that they had been building over the previous few years. They worked to draw parents, students, and neighborhood residents into these groups and ultimately into a larger effort to push the city and the school board to respond to their concerns. These relatively new community-based organizations developed more confrontational and grassroots political styles than most prominent African-American leaders and organizations had maintained throughout the 1930s. Younger black activists, who had become community and labor leaders during the early 1940s, had been refining their ideas about protest and civil rights and building political coalitions to fight together against police brutality, for union recognition, workers' rights, and equal access to welfare and city resources. The clashes at Northwestern High School were an opportunity for this newer group of activists to develop leadership and build support for their increasingly popular approach to organizing and local politics. In fact, the political networks and organizational style that these groups used and continued to develop were part of a move toward a new kind of activist style upon which the city's civil rights movement would ultimately be built.[2]

Community activists' responses to the Northwestern riots helped solidify and expand the political networks upon which Detroit's larger Black Freedom movement would be built during the 1940s and into the 1950s. The men, women, and young people who participated in these organized responses to discrimination and violence were part of what Angela Dillard calls an "emerging civil rights community."[3] The city's labor movement and recent fights against police brutality had drawn activists fighting for racial equality into closer alliances with the white and black Left. This article explores how members of Detroit's "emerging civil rights community," alongside students from Northwestern High School, organized responses to the mounting violence and persistent discrimination that African Americans faced in their neighborhoods and schools during the early 1940s. Furthermore, it shows that the disturbances at Northwestern High School were among the first in a series of clashes to which community activists responded and through which they began to build a more clearly defined and more grassroots movement for racial justice in Detroit.

Recently historians have produced a number of studies that have exposed the mechanics through which white residents worked to maintain segregation and sustain their political dominance in the urban North during and after the Second World War. These studies have done an excellent job exploring white intentions and examining strategies that white citizens used to mobilize political power. However, they have paid little attention to black resistance and have even suggested that African Americans were effectively politically immobilized by racial clashes instigated by white city residents. Detroit has served as an important case study for scholars interested in the history of white racism. *The Origins of the Urban Crisis*, by Thomas Sugrue, has attracted considerable attention for its nuanced and well-researched portrait of white Detroiters' organization against integration and black political power. However, Sugrue's story, which begins in

1940 and ends with the city's famous rebellion of 1967, sheds little light on grassroots black activism in the city. In fact, it portrays African Americans largely as victims of white racism; Detroit's black community, the book suggests, had little meaningful political power.[4]

This portrait stands in sharp contrast to recent scholarly work that has highlighted the growing—and consequential—power of Detroit's black community activists before, during, and after the Second World War. Rather than quietly accepting second-class citizenship, the city's black residents refused to comply with white supremacist dictates that prescribed a limited role for them in Detroit. In fact, as Heather Thompson explains, during the same period that white residents were fighting to "defend" their neighborhoods from African American homebuyers, black Detroiters were building substantial political alliances within the city's labor movement and urban institutions. Indeed, the organizations and connections that African Americans developed during this earlier period laid important groundwork for a large and politically vibrant civil rights movement in the city.[5]

Scholars have paid less attention to how violent racial clashes, like the conflict at Northwestern High School in 1940, helped spur organizing among African Americans. Furthermore, few have examined school violence in this light; because it has been so consistently dismissed as nihilistic, impulsive, and ultimately irresponsible, black participation in that violence, either defensive or offensive, has been especially derided as unwise. Rather than *dis*-organizing or *dis*-empowering students and activists, this article demonstrates that the clashes at Northwestern helped to inspire and mobilize these women, men, and young people in their fights for racial equality. In fact, this study is an effort to explore how the clashes at Northwestern—an example of school violence in which black students participated—helped to stimulate and foster mobilizations for African American equality.

The routine violence of discrimination that students experienced every day did not raise the ire of community members and leaders high enough for them to be called to action. However, the more dramatic and public *physical* violence of the riots pushed people toward action because it helped to crystallize the problems they were confronting. There were some calls for black students to reexamine their behavior and make sure that they were not attracting negative attention, but these nods toward a politics of respectability were drowned out by far more prominent calls for city politicians to protect and provide for black students and residents.

This indicates a change in sensibility from a previous generation of leaders and activists.[6]

Finally, community activists' responses to the Northwestern riots in 1940 are important because they provide historians with an example of a significant struggle for desegregation and equality in Northern, urban schools before the *Brown v. Board* decision. In fact, organizing community members to respond to school-related concerns was, in some ways, an ideal campaign for a group of activists who were working to build a grass-roots civil rights movement. Schools themselves were already a focus of community concern—black parents in Detroit took a consistent and abiding interest in their children's education. Furthermore, since public schools maintained geographically defined districts, concerns about specific schools could help activate neighborhood-based interest in a campaign for social justice. Public schools were also a state resource. Residents who may not have felt comfortable making claims about their own needs, could see their children's safety as urgent; unsafe schools were an affront to black residents' sense of themselves as equal, tax-paying citizens.

The Riots

Northwestern High School sat right outside the black West Side, a neighborhood that had been majority-black since the 1920s and that boasted higher property values than most other predominantly African American areas in the city. Grand River Avenue, one of Detroit's main thoroughfares, acted as an imaginary line that had separated this neighborhood from adjoining white areas. Northwestern's school district disrupted the clarity of this boundary, drawing students from both sides of Grand River. Furthermore, by the mid-1930s, more parts of the school district had become "areas of transition," with white residents moving out and selling their homes to middle-class African American families.[7] By 1940 the school had maintained the same racial balance for the last three or four years; approximately 18 percent of the student body—seven hundred of the school's four thousand students—was African American.[8]

It is unclear what, exactly, ignited the violence at Northwestern High School in the winter of 1940. A number of participants told reporters that the conflict had begun the previous Friday when white and black boys had gotten into a fight at a neighboring store. There had been more "sporadic fighting" on Monday, but tensions exploded on Tuesday after school. That day two policemen were on duty near Northwestern, and eventually fifty officers moved into the area. Police broke up the initial skirmishes and "led the Negroes . . . in the direction of their homes." However, two large groups of white youths followed the black students. Fights began again in front of Wingert Elementary School, whose student population was 85 percent black, and younger students started to get involved in the fray. Teachers and police fought to maintain the peace through the rest of the afternoon, but groups of black and white youths continued to attack each other. Finally, by evening, the fighting had ended, but tensions remained high.[9]

The next day special police squads were assigned to the area "from early morning until late in the afternoon." They arrested twenty-two more young men and one young woman, most of them African American, after more fights broke out around Northwestern and Wingert schools. These brawls were far smaller and easier to manage, but the police had trouble dispersing the crowd of between three thousand and five thousand spectators who were hanging around to watch the melee. Most of the people arrested were standing in the crowd with makeshift weapons. By Thursday the "fracas" had ended.[10]

Northwestern's principal, B. J. Rivett, claimed that the clashes were instigated by "outside elements" and that few Northwestern students were involved in the fighting. Rivett blamed a group of "hangers-on" who had been coming by and lingering around the school for the past two or three years. However, he did not associate their presence, or the fights they picked, with racial tensions. "They come in and start playing foot ball when regular students are practicing and try to take over the games. Minor fights result and sometimes the students have taken it upon themselves to drive the others away."[11]

"Participants in the fighting" maintained a different outlook about the underlying tensions that caused the "near-riot." They reported that "trouble had been brewing" between African American and white students for some time. A number of white youths insisted that the fighting was merely the first violent expression of a "smoldering discontent" that had been building up since January, when the new semester began. They believed that an unusually large influx of African American students had transferred to Northwestern from other schools that term and had prevented white students from being able to attend the high school. Raymond O'Hara, for example, explained that his "interest in the affair" was rooted in his concern for his younger brother who had been denied a spot at

Northwestern. Black students understood the "riot" as an extension of the individual and institutional discrimination and harassment that they faced at Northwestern. Harold Erickson, a student at the school who was injured in the clashes, reported that the violence had been the cause of mounting white aggression; "white boys," he explained, "had been chasing Negroes home from school" for some time.[12]

Principal Rivett dismissed white students' claims that they were being "crowded out" of the school as "ridiculous"; he explained that anyone who lived in the district was free to enroll at Northwestern. He was equally unsympathetic to the concerns of black students. He maintained that he had not been aware of "racial trouble of any kind or description" at the school before the day that the violence began. In fact, he explained, "there is hardly any racial feeling among the students whatsoever." Rivett was thus unwilling to sympathize with white concerns *or* to recognize the persistence of racism at the school.[13]

Community Responses

Local leaders drew on existing networks of community activists to craft a response to the violence. Concerned about the mounting problems, Reverend Malcolm Dade, vicar of nearby St. Cyprian Episcopal Church, led a "committee of colored citizens" to meet with Principal Rivett on Tuesday morning, before the violence turned into a schoolwide riot. Dade was accompanied by Dr. James McClendon, president of the local branch of the National Association for the Advancement of Colored People (NAACP), Reverend Charles A. Hill, pastor at Hartford Avenue Baptist Church, and three members of the West Side Human Relations Council (WHRC). In their effort to "nip the disturbance" in the bud, this group urged Principal Rivett to do something about the escalating violence and warned him that the "threatening racial turmoil" could become a serious problem. Rivett paid little attention to the council of these black leaders and did nothing to forestall the coming conflict.[14]

The men and women who participated in this meeting with Principal Rivett were part of an emerging group of black leaders who maintained close ties to the labor movement and who were interested in pushing for a more confrontational political stance toward the city government. Reverend Dade was relatively new to Detroit. He had become the minister at St. Cyprian's in the late 1930s and had been involved in local politics since his arrival. He and his wife, Esther Dade, became active members of the civil rights community in Detroit soon after they moved to the city. Esther Dade was a member of the executive board of the NAACP in 1937 and 1938. Malcolm Dade joined the Association's executive board in 1939. Reverend Dade was also an early supporter of the efforts of the UAW-CIO (United Auto Workers–Congress of Industrial Organizations) to organize black workers. In November 1939, a few months before the Northwestern riots, he and Reverend Charles Hill had been the only two ministers to join a committee of twenty-five prominent black leaders in condemning the practices of Chrysler Corporation in its fight with the union.[15]

Reverend Charles Hill was the pastor at Hartford Avenue Baptist Church, one of the largest and most popular churches on the city's black West Side. During the 1930s he had been an active participant in the city's "emergent left" and by the early 1940s had become a prominent figure in Detroit's civil rights community. He was an active member of the NAACP but focused more of his political energy working with the National Negro Congress and the Civil Rights Federation, both of which were connected to the city's labor movement.[16] The members of the West Side Human Relations Council who attended the meeting were Emmala Cabule, the chairperson of the "Character Building" committee and the vice president of the organization, Bettie Ellington, and James Jones. Reverend Charles Hill was also an active member of the WHRC and served as chairperson of its "Adjustment" committee. Founded in 1936, the WHRC was a project of the area's interchurch fellowship and was established to address what it identified as the growing problem of juvenile delinquency on the black West Side. The group articulated two goals for itself: to work to improve and uplift black youth while fighting to ensure that the community received "all the protection and benefits [it] deserved from city, county, and state government."[17]

Dr. James J. McClendon had been the president since 1938 of Detroit's NAACP chapter—the largest branch in the country. Under his leadership the branch had become a far more visible participant in civil rights struggles in the city; it had moved from a supporting role to a leadership position in fights against police brutality, discrimination in public welfare, and exclusion from public accommodations. By 1939 the association's office secretary, Carolyn Dent, reported that interest in the work of the branch was increasing as "more and more letters come in from people who are anxious to tie up with a progressive movement bringing better conditions to their race."[18]

These black leaders were discouraged and displeased by Rivett's unwillingness to listen to their recommendations, but they refused to be stymied by the principal's unresponsive stance. Instead, they continued to pressure city officials to respond to their concerns. On Wednesday morning, the day after the racial tensions exploded into riotous violence at Northwestern, most of the membership of the Northwestern Pastor's Association, along with representatives from the NAACP, met with the mayor, the police commissioner, the city prosecutor, and the police superintendent. This group pushed city officials to create an interracial committee to study and address the problems behind the Northwestern clashes. In fact, Dr. McClendon, head of the NAACP, had already convened a group of white and black leaders to "deal with the situation." He urged the mayor to make this group an official governmental organization.[19]

The Northwestern Pastor's Association, an organization of twenty-one black ministers from churches on the black West Side, had held its founding meeting in October 1939, just a few months before the Northwestern riots. The group was convened initially to fight for more jobs for black workers in the stores along Milford Avenue, one of the major shopping districts in the area that had "practically no colored employees." It also focused attention on the Grenada Theater, a movie theater with a majority-black clientele that maintained segregated seating and employed no African American workers. The group's initial meeting was presided over by Reverend Charles Hill and included representatives from local organizations, such as the NAACP, the West Side Human Relations council, and the Detroit Civic Rights Committee (CRC).[20] Its formation provides a significant example of the proliferation of new community organizations designed to address civil rights abuses in the black community in Detroit.

The occurrence of the Northwestern riots was not the first time that Detroit's civil rights leaders had taken an interest in discrimination in the city's schools; they were well aware of the problems black students faced and their difficulties in securing jobs within the school system. The CRC, an organization headed by "Snow Flake" Grigsby, had taken the lead on fighting for equal access to education and to jobs in the school district throughout the 1930s. Frank Cody, superintendent of Detroit's schools through the decade, had been a receptive and polite audience for their concerns. An advocate of tolerance, he expressed his own concerns about racial "problems" when he spoke to the CRC in February 1934. Cody was not willing to consider solutions that challenged the status quo in any meaningful way, but the CRC kept pushing him to respond to their concerns. In June 1934 the CRC met with the school board and received a mixed reception. One member of the board expressed his interest in segregating Detroit's school system, but others were more willing to listen to the committee and slowly began to respond to its activism. In August and September the board hired nine African American men and women as teachers.[21]

Snow Flake Grigsby and the CRC recognized the power of public schooling as an issue that could mobilize Detroit's black residents. They are also examples of the kinds of leaders and organizations that would ultimately become the foundations for the emerging civil rights community in Detroit. Grigsby, a tireless campaigner against discrimination, refused to settle for the small gains he won through the CRC and constantly criticized established black leaders for their accommodationist positions.[22] Grigsby and the CRC had taken the lead in pushing the school board to hire black teachers and to begin teaching black history and literature. The CRC could claim a small victory in the fall of 1935 when the Garfield Intermediate School, a predominantly African American public school, approved a list of books by black authors for use in classrooms.[23] The CRC continued to pressure the school board to hire more staff and teachers throughout the decade. By the end of the 1930s pressure from black activists had had some effect on the school board, but overall only limited progress had been made.

The CRC started to meet modest success in the period after the mobilization of the Northwestern High School riots. In 1939, before the riots, Detroit schools employed only five black high school teachers and eighty black teachers in grade schools, all of whom worked in majority-black schools.[24] By 1941 the district had hired thirteen more black teachers, which was an improvement, but black teachers still only represented 1.3 percent of all teachers in the district. Nonteaching staff faired a little better, with eighty-five workers representing 2.5 percent of all nonteaching school employees. The community response to the Northwestern conflict was an important element in pushing the city to finally respond to the concerns Grigsby raised over discriminatory hiring.[25]

Black leaders and residents had thus been well aware of the problems black students faced before the Northwestern riots. However, the violence at the high school focused their attention on that discrimination and mobilized them to action. Reverend Dade called an open meeting for the Saturday night after the fighting "for the purpose of peacefully solving the racial disturbance at Northwestern High School." To discuss the problems, he invited black and white community members, students, parents, and teachers to his church, an African American congregation in the heart of the black West Side. The meeting attracted a "large throng," although it is unclear how many whites attended.[26]

This meeting provided a space for neighborhood residents to discuss the recent events, produce ideas about what the violence meant, and discuss how they wanted to handle it. These residents and activists saw the escalating violence at Northwestern as a symptom of the discrimination and animosity that black students faced at school and black residents confronted in the surrounding district. They were mobilized in a way that they had not been mobilized by the more mundane acts of discrimination that laid the foundations for the Northwestern riots. Ultimately those attending the meeting adopted a resolution that made a number of demands and proclamations. First, they "flayed" the police department for its "partiality" and criticized police officers for their "wholesale arrests of colored." Competent witnesses, the resolution explained, had testified that African American students were not the aggressors, yet police continued to interrogate and arrest black youths, many of whom were merely spectators. The meeting also called on the Common Council to investigate the causes of the crowded conditions at the school and to increase Northwestern's appropriation in order to reduce class size. Both these demands demonstrate that community residents placed the clashes at Northwestern High School into a larger context within which they understood race and politics in the city, and this sparked them to action.

The community resolution accused Principal Rivett of "having knowledge of the brewing trouble" and ignoring past complaints registered by black students and community members about racial discrimination and animosity. A number of people explained that they had warned the principal of potential problems "on numerous occasions." These residents had already seen Northwestern as a problem and had taken responsibility for pushing its administrators to respond to their concerns. Furthermore, they charged Rivett with "rank hypocrisy" for his declaration that the fights were instigated by "outsiders" and accused him of using this claim as a ploy designed to "mislead the public." Finally, Rivett and his administration were severely criticized for practicing racial discrimination themselves. Community members demanded the removal of Rivett and of four other teachers whom they identified as consistently discriminatory.

In a speech at the meeting Reverend Horace White, pastor of Plymouth Congregational Church, connected white students' attacks on African

Americans to the generally bad community relations that "real estate dealers" had been working to aggravate. He explained that realtors had been trying to keep black homebuyers from moving into white neighborhoods north of Tireman, another street that served as a stark dividing line between integrated and all-white neighborhoods. White students, the Reverend explained, had picked up on this brewing, neighborhood-based animosity and translated it into their own experiences.[27] He thus suggested that white students were mimicking their parents' concerns and anxieties about residential integration by directing their resentment toward their black classmates. White had arrived in Detroit in 1936 and, like Reverend Dade, quickly became active in civic organizations like the NAACP. He was also interested in local politics and had taken an active role in the city's Democratic Party.[28] He saw the Northwestern riots as an opportunity to draw connections between housing discrimination and white animosity toward black students.

Activists were mobilized by the Northwestern incident to push for resources and political power that they were already fighting to gain on a number of fronts. They used the riots to provide city officials with an added incentive to respond to their demands. For example, men and women who took an interest in electoral politics had been pushing Mayor Jeffries to appoint an African American person to a high-profile position in the city government. One week after the Northwestern High School incident, Jeffries appointed Reverend White to sit on the Housing Commission. For many, however, this token gesture seemed hollow; they remained frustrated with Jeffries's disinterest in their community, especially after the work so many had put into his campaign.[29]

Although black activists pushed city officials to establish permanent committees to address and study racial discrimination, only the school board set up a lasting body to examine these issues. The mayor consistently reassured activists that he "intend[ed] to protect the rights of our Negro citizens," but he refused to comply with their demands to even study the problem. When a small race riot occurred that summer on Belle Isle, the city's largest public park, activists continued to pressure the mayor to do something more substantive than simply pronounce his commitment to equality. Senator Charles Diggs, an African American Democrat in the State Senate, reconstituted the interracial committee that the NAACP had convened after the Northwestern incident and urged the mayor to make that body a government-sponsored institution. The mayor complied with Diggs's request, but he proceeded to neglect the Committee on Inter-Racial Problems, which quietly disbanded soon after it was established. Diggs built on the networks developed in response to the Northwestern High School violence. He pushed for a series of meetings between black community leaders and city officials that were similar to the meetings that had been held the previous winter. Like the Northwestern High School incident, the Belle Isle riot of the summer of 1940 produced no permanent committee to examine racial tensions. However, Northwestern had clearly laid a foundation for future activism.[30]

In hindsight, black leaders' tireless efforts to push government officials to study the problem of racial discrimination may seem ill-conceived. Reports themselves seldom created needed changes to the systems that maintained inequality. However, activists' interest in pushing for these reports should be understood as central to their effort to gain official recognition that discrimination indeed existed. It should also be seen as their attempt to expose the ways that discrimination and inequality were maintained through public and private bureaucracies. These reports were usually written by black sociologists who worked for the Urban League and were hired by government commissions to study racial tensions. Official reports thus confirmed activists' assertions that discrimination shaped African Americans' access to city resources and limited their ability to achieve full equality in the city. Furthermore, white officials, even self-identified liberals, consistently resisted pressure to study racial problems. White officials' aversion to collecting statistics, let alone addressing discrimination, stands as an implicit recognition of the extent to which calls for such studies effectively challenged the racial status quo.[31]

Youth Organizing

Black students were not immobilized by these clashes. Whether or not they initiated any of the fighting—and it is unclear how the conflicts began—black students participated in the violence at Northwestern High School. Black youths worked to protect themselves and their friends, and fought back against white attacks. Lorenzo Pack, a professional heavyweight boxer and graduate of Northwestern, for example, came over to the school on Wednesday afternoon to "escort a cousin home." As he was standing and talking to Clarence Reading, a probation officer (who was also the son of former Mayor Richard Reading), police approached Pack, frisked him, discovered that he was carrying a "heavy club" under his coat, and arrested him. Reading protested, declaring that Pack was "a leader of Negro youth" and was there "to calm his people down," but to no avail. A young African American woman and a number of young black men were also arrested for carrying weapons that they were not using.[32] A number of black youths thus made the decision to defend themselves, their friends, and their family members from attack that day.

During the week of the violent clashes at Northwestern, a group of black students at Northwestern worked to intervene in the fighting by drafting a petition. They began circulating it in school on Wednesday, the day after the first and largest outbreaks of violence. The petition, which the students had started "on their own initiative," pledged its signers to "do all in their power to promote good racial relationships and prevent strife."[33]

Although the newspaper article that reported on this petition identified the students who circulated it as African American, it gave no further information about who they were. It is likely, however, that they were either members of the NAACP Youth Council or influenced by its activism.[34] Detroit's NAACP Youth Council, which historians August Meier and Elliot Rudwick described as "the most active [youth council] in the country," was an organization of young women and men between sixteen and twenty-five years of age. It was founded in 1936, after a delegation of youth attended the Association's first national youth conference in Baltimore, Maryland, in July. Over the next year the group established six councils across the city, including one on the West Side, in the same neighborhood as Northwestern High School.[35]

The Central Youth Council, the body to which all officers and leaders of the neighborhood councils belonged, had taken an interest in discrimination and inequality in the city schools. It sponsored an "Educational Inequalities Mass Meeting" in November 1936 and invited Snow Flake Grigsby, from the Civic Rights Committee, to speak. Grigsby delivered a lecture outlining the discrimination faced by African American students and teachers in Detroit's schools, and "launched an attack upon the local adult body's inactiveness toward all the situations known to exist." The Youth Council sponsored a similar mass meeting in November 1937 and attracted a crowd of three hundred youth to come and discuss "educational inequalities."[36] By the summer of 1938 the Youth Council had shifted its organizational focus. Instead of sponsoring informational meetings and debates, the group began to use direct action to fight for change. It initiated a "Job Opportunities Campaign," which included picketing and boycotting several white-owned stores that refused to hire African American workers. By the spring of 1939 the council had pushed local businesses to hire at least thirty-four black workers around the city.[37]

The West Side NAACP Youth Council had been quite active in 1937, when Detroit's NAACP branch sponsored the national meeting of the association. Members of the West Side Council worked on the national meeting that year. They also met success collecting signatures on a petition to install a new stop sign on a local street and in their effort to push the management of the Beechwood theater to improve its sanitary conditions. At the end of that year its president, Pauline Dotson, and one of its most active members, Helen White, became officers in the Central Youth Council, and Horace Sheffield became the president of the West Side Youth Council.[38]

Sheffield pushed the West Side Youth Council in a more explicitly political direction. When he became president of the organization he produced a pamphlet designed to attract young people to Youth Council meetings. The pamphlet, which he called "Negrissipation," lambasted the "lack of organization among older members of our race" and described "Negrissipation" as the state of disappointment faced by black youth when they realize that "we are economically dependent upon the white man and must assume the guise of a clown for practically everything we get." He explained that the Youth Council was working to "stamp out the devastation of Negrissipation and in united fashion bring about equality for the Negro economically, socially, and politically."[39]

Predominantly white youth organizations with politically leftist views also responded to the Northwestern High School riots. On the Thursday night after the riots representatives from "four youth organizations" met to produce a leaflet to distribute to Northwestern students the next day. These leaflets made "an appeal to reason and tolerance as a solution" for the friction that caused the "disturbance" at the school. Youth involved in producing the pamphlet began to distribute it at Northwestern on Friday morning, March 1, but were quickly arrested by the police. At least eight youths were arrested, the majority of whom were white and were not from the neighborhood. These young men and women saw the incidents at Northwestern as part of a larger, citywide problem which they wanted to help address.[40]

Discrimination persisted at Northwestern High School and at other schools on the West Side. In the winter of 1941 the Detroit Urban League reported that there was "dissatisfaction expressed over a popularity contest held at the school." One African American and one white girl were candidates for Miss Northwestern. When it became clear that the race was very close, a group of teachers cast a "great number of votes" in order to ensure that the white girl won the contest.[41] In January 1941 the principal of McMichael Intermediate School, which was close to Northwestern, convened a meeting to discuss racial tensions at that school. E. J. Corrigan, the assistant principal, appealed to John Dancy, head of the Detroit Urban League, for help in managing the problems. He explained that conditions at McMichael were "worse than they were before the riot." In fact, the school had had "more cases of fighting between the races in the last six weeks and with increasing frequency than ever before."[42] The effort to force Northwestern to hire black teachers persisted with little advancement. In the spring of 1941 residents of the black West Side presented the Board of Education with a petition protesting the "non-employment of Negro personnel" at Northwestern. Furthermore, residents complained that their efforts to start a parent-teacher association had been stymied by the school's administration every time they tried to pull one together.[43]

The persistence of racist incidents at Northwestern and the fighting at McMichael mobilized an organization called the Greater Detroit Youth Assembly, an interracial, citywide federation of progressive young people, to sponsor a neighborhood meeting which they called the "Northwestern Institute." The Institute was well attended by white and black youth, teachers, neighborhood residents, civil rights activists, and members of a range of groups from across the city. The Youth Assembly, "a cooperating center for youth organizations," received wide support for its initiative. For example, the Detroit Council of Churches, an interracial organization headed by Clarence Hill Frank, an African-American pastor, wrote a letter to its members urging them to attend the institute. Frank Cody, superintendent of the city's school district, also wrote a letter of support for the Youth Assembly.[44]

The Youth Assembly focused on Northwestern because of the riots that had flared up there the previous spring, which it saw as "symptomatic" of the "inter-racial problems of the young people in this area." Members of the Assembly believed that the incidents at Northwestern, and the continuing problems students faced there, represented the "crying need in our community." Bridget Paulson, one of the organizers of the Institute, explained that she did not believe that the problems they were addressing were particular to the West Side. However, the Youth Assembly was taking advantage of the citywide attention the riots had received in order to gain support for their work.[45]

The Northwestern Institute was the Youth Assembly's effort to pull together representatives from organizations across the city, including community organizations, branches of the city government, religious groups, unions, and social agencies. The Youth Assembly extended invitations to the Police Department, the West Side Human Relations Council, the UAW-CIO Education Department, the Federation of Settlements, the Urban League, the West Side NAACP Youth Council, among others. Its "partial list" of invitees spanned thirty-eight groups, including eight youth organizations, seven African American groups, six social agencies, four government departments, four religious organizations, and seven groups affiliated with the labor movement.[46]

As many as 182 people, including representatives from 64 organizations, attended the Youth Assembly on March 30, 1941. A person from almost all the organizations on the partial list of invitees came, as well as people from a host of other, similar groups. George Mogil, a student activist, opened the meeting with an invitation to action. "We cannot wait for understanding to come to us," he explained, "we must seek it."[47] Conditions had not improved since the rioting of the year before. Discrimination continued to be an enormous problem. The high school maintained segregated seating in its auditorium, showed movies "depicting a distorted picture of the Negroes," employed no African American teachers or administrators, and rarely allowed black students to participate in extracurricular activities. Furthermore, Northwestern remained overcrowded, with an average of thirty-seven students in a class, inadequate numbers of lockers, and too few seats in the lunch room and auditorium.[48]

LeBron Simmons of the Detroit branch of the National Negro Congress helped to facilitate the first part of the meeting, which was an open conversation. Participants held a range of opinions: black students expressed dismay about the continual discrimination they faced, alongside a handful of white students who willingly attended the meeting but did not believe that discrimination was a problem. After the first plenary, the Institute divided into panels to discuss the "three channels through which conditions could be improved." Reverend Charles Hill facilitated a panel on "What the Administration Can Do," Louis Altshuler of the State, County and Municipal Workers of America led a panel on "What Parents and Community Organizations Can Do," and finally Kenneth Jenkins, from the Michigan District of the American Student Union, led a panel on "What Students Can Do." Jenkins was one of the students arrested for distributing leaflets outside Northwestern on the Friday after the riots.[49] These panels each developed a series of "findings" and recommendations that the entire body voted to accept. Many of the Institute's findings were similar to those articulated by attendees of the meeting held at St. Cyprian soon after the riots. They included calls to hire more African American teachers, to organize a Parent-Teacher Association at the school, to take disciplinary action against teachers, students, or administrators who practice discrimination, and to build better facilities in the school that could accommodate all its students. Finally, their recommendations included demands for citywide changes, such as an end to police brutality against African Americans, as well as the prosecution of groups who "incite race hatred or chauvinism."[50]

Activists who attended the Northwestern Institute continued to put pressure on the school board. In August 1941 Reverend Charles Hill, Reverend John Miles of the West Side Human Relations Council, and Bridget Paulson from the Northwestern Institute attended a school board meeting to push the body to hire more black teachers at Northwestern.[51] The next month a black student was stabbed at the high school, and the Youth Assembly responded with a call to convene a meeting at Hartford Avenue Baptist Church. The stabbing, George Mutnick of the Northwestern Institute exclaimed, "proves the failure of the policy of delay which has hitherto prevailed."[52]

A few days before the Northwestern Institute convened its first mass meeting, Mayor Jeffries began to pull together an Interracial Committee. It is unclear whether the Institute helped to push him finally to heed the advice of activists who had been pressing for just such a committee for the past year. However, the timing and the broad-based support the Institute was receiving suggest that it indeed had an impact on his decision. The group was "composed of members of both White and Colored groups," and was chaired by William Norton, a white leader in the social services community in Detroit, who was the head of the Children's Fund of Michigan. The Committee commissioned a study of "conditions among Negroes," which was conducted by Warren Banner of the National Urban League, and which included a discussion of Northwestern High School. In his study Banner facetiously observed that "the first impression to be gained from the result of interviews with [school] officials is that of a beautiful harmony existing between Negro and white children and between teachers and pupils of all races." However, he ultimately concluded that white principals, teachers, and students were regularly "alienating" black students, parents, and community residents.[53]

Mayor Jeffries conceded to activist pressure by forming the interracial committee and sponsoring Banner's study, but once pressure lifted, he proceeded to neglect the committee and the problems it was designed to address. Ultimately it would not be until the city exploded in an enormous race riot in 1943 that the mayor would pull together a permanent committee of citizens to look at race relations and interracial violence.

Both adult and youth activists from across the city saw the events at Northwestern as a call to organize a movement against discrimination, and used tactics that they had been developing in the previous decade to respond to the violence. The attention the Northwestern riots received from city officials was a direct result of the pressure from the city's "civil rights community" and is evidence that Detroit's activists had effectively mobilized more political power than they had been capable of assembling previously. Activists understood the problems at Northwestern as products of the racial tensions that animated the lives of all black residents in the city. They explicitly connected their concerns about the school with their frustrations about blockbusting, red-lining, segregation, and school funding. While city officials continued to minimize the impact of discrimination on black residents and play down its very existence, as this story demonstrates, they could no longer ignore activist pressure to address these problems.

NOTES

1. "Students in Race Riot at Northwestern High," *Michigan Chronicle*, March 2, 1940.

2. For a discussion of the transition from a more accommodationist to a more confrontational political style among Chicago's NAACP members, see Beth Tompkins Bates, "A New Crowd Challenges the Agenda of the Old Guard in the NAACP, 1933–1941," *American Historical Review* 102 (April 1997).

3. Angela Dillard argues that Detroit's "civil rights community" had "taken on a coherent and recognizable shape by the late 1930's." During World War II, she argues, the civil rights community "reached a level of maturity and effectiveness unmatched either before or after in the history of the city's left" ("From the Reverend Charles A. Hill to the Reverend Albert B. Cleage, Jr.: Change and Continuity in the

Patterns of Civil Rights Mobilizations in Detroit, 1935–1967" [Ph.D. dissertation, University of Michigan, 1995]).

4. See Thomas Sugrue, *The Origins of the Urban Crisis: Race and Inequality in Postwar Detroit* (Princeton, N.J.: Princeton University Press, 1997). Arnold Hirsch has also looked closely at white motivations for struggles against residential integration in the urban North in the postwar period. See Arnold Hirsch, *Making the Second Ghetto: Race and Housing in Chicago, 1940–1960* (Chicago: University of Chicago Press, 1982).

5. Heather Thompson, *Whose Detroit? Politics, Labor, and Race in a Modern American City* (Ithaca, N.Y.: Cornell University Press, 2001). For a discussion of black political power and organizing before, during, and after the Second Great Migration, see Dillard, "From the Reverend Charles A. Hill to the Reverend Albert B. Cleage, Jr."; Victoria Wolcott, *Remaking Respectability: African American Women in Interwar Detroit* (Chapel Hill: University of North Carolina Press, 2001); and Richard Thomas, *Life for Us Is What We Make It: Building Black Community in Detroit, 1915–1945* (Bloomington: Indiana University Press, 1992).

6. For a discussion of the politics of respectability in Detroit and its general decline at the end of the 1930s, see Wolcott, *Remaking Respectability.*

7. Warren M. Banner, "Observation on Conditions among Negroes in the Fields of Education, Recreation and Employment," 1941, Detroit Urban League Papers (hereafter, DUL), box 74, folder: "History: Observation on Conditions among Negroes in the Fields of Education, Recreation and Employment," 9.

8. "Riot Blamed on Outsiders," *Detroit News,* February 28, 1940.

9. This account of the first day of skirmishes is taken from the following newspaper articles: "Riot Blamed on Outsiders"; "Seven Injured as Youths Riot at High School," *Detroit Free Press,* February 28, 1940; "One Stabbed in Disturbance at School"; "Students in Race Riot," *Detroit Tribune,* March 2, 1940.

10. "23 Are Seized in New Fights at High School," *Detroit Free Press,* February 29, 1940; "School Heads Act in Rioting," *Detroit News,* February 29, 1940; "Police Patrols Halt Fisticuffs at High School," *Detroit Free Press,* March 1, 1940.

11. "Riot Blamed on Outsiders."

12. White youths involved in the Northwestern violence explicitly connected the problems faced by Detroit's school system, such as overcrowding, with African Americans. The story they told about why they participated in the race-based clashes—that African American students had crowded whites out of the school—indicated that they believed black students had taken away resources that should have belonged to them ("Seven Injured").

13. "Seven Injured."

14. "Students in Race Riot at Northwestern High"; "One Stabbed in Disturbance at School."

15. Esther Dade's name appears as a member of the executive committee on NAACP letterhead in 1937 and 1938; Malcolm Dade's name appears as a member

of the executive committee on NAACP letterhead in 1939. See National Associa-
tion for the Advancement of Colored People (hereafter, NAACP), Branch Files,
Detroit, Michigan, 1917–1939, part 12, series C, reel 13. In their discussion of the
Chrysler strike and its resolution, August Meier and Elliot Rudwick identify the
Reverends Malcolm Dade and Charles Hill as "militant black supporters of the
union" (Meier and Rudwick, *Black Detroit and the Rise of the UAW* [New York:
Oxford University Press, 1979], 69).

16. See Dillard, "From the Reverend Charles A. Hill to the Reverend Albert B.
Cleage, Jr."; and interview of Charles Hill by Roberta McBride, May 8, 1967, used
by permission of Herbert Hill, Archives of Labor and Urban Affairs (hereafter,
ALUA).

17. Quoted in Wolcott, *Remaking Respectability,* 225. Jeanette Worlds to John
Dancy, March 4, 1938, DUL, box 4, folder 12, Bentley Historical Library (BHL).

18. The NAACP had become more active toward the end of the 1930s than it
had been previously. In 1937 Gloster Current, a leader in the city's NAACP youth
councils had remarked that "the senior group is practically dead as far as activity is
concerned and cannot see any farther than their noses." Carolyn Dent to Dean
William Pickens, March 30, 1939; and Gloster Current to Juanita Jackson, January
16, 1937, NAACP, part 12, series C, reel 13.

19. "School Heads Act in Rioting."

20. "Ministers Chart Fight against Injustice," Detroit Tribune, October 7, 1939.

21. "Our Local School Problems," *Detroit Tribune,* February 24, 1934; "Board of
Education South in Behalf of Race Teachers," *Detroit Tribune,* June 16, 1934; "Lloyd
M. Cofer Is Appointed to Post in Detroit School System," *Detroit Tribune,* August
25, 1934; "Bradfield Named to Local School Post," *Detroit Tribune,* September 1,
1934; John C. Dancy to Charles S. Johnson, September 28, 1934, DUL, box 3, folder
10.

22. Snow F. Grigsby, *An X-Ray Picture of Detroit,* Detroit, Michigan, December
1933, NAACP, part 12, series C, reel 12; interview of Snow Flake Grigsby by Roberta
McBride, May 8, 1967, used by permission of Herbert Hill, ALUA.

23. "Detroit Starts Fight for More Teachers, Wants Race History Taught in City
Public Schools," *Chicago Defender,* February 23, 1935; "Local Public Schools Ap-
prove Books of Negro Authors," *Detroit Tribune,* October 19, 1935. The list of
books approved included *Opportunity,* the monthly magazine of the National
Urban League; Carter G. Woodson, *African Myths* and *Negro Makers of History;*
Willis Richardson, *Plays and Pageants;* and the *Negro Yearbook.* Previously, no
black history or literature was taught at any of the Detroit Public Schools. John C.
Dancy to George Longe, November 13, 1934, DUL, box 3, folder 12.

24. "Protest Lack of Elevation for Teachers," *Detroit Tribune,* April 16, 1938; John
C. Dancy to Norman O. Houston, November 22, 1939, DUL, box 4, folder 26.

25. Banner, "Observation on Conditions among Negroes."

26. "Police Rapped for Partiality," *Detroit Tribune,* March 9, 1940.

27. It is possible that White was describing a "blockbusting" campaign. Instead of a sincere effort on the part of realtors to keep the neighborhood north of Tireman white, they may have been working to scare white families into selling their homes by whipping up concern about a possible "invasion" of African Americans. Thomas Sugrue identifies a neighborhood north of Tireman and west of Grand River as a "defended" neighborhood in the postwar period. In other words, Sugrue argues, this area was one of the sites where white residents were persistently attacking black families who were attempting to move into the area. Sugrue, *The Origins of the Urban Crisis*, 236.

28. "Report of the Election of Officers of the Detroit, Michigan, Branch," December 13, 1937, NAACP, part 12, series C, reel 13.

29. "Rev. Horace A. White Is Named to the Detroit Housing Commission," *Detroit Tribune*, March 16, 1940. Charles A. Roxborough, the former State Senator, wrote to the mayor in his role as president of the United District Congressional Organization. Roxborough explained that he had been criticized by other members of the organization because he had worked to secure an endorsement from its members, but "nothing has been done for them politically since you have been in office" (Charles A. Roxborough, President of the United District Congressional Organization, to Mayor, April 18, 1940, Mayor's Papers [hereafter, MP] 1940, box 4, folder: "Interracial Comm. 1940"). Beatrice M. Fleming of the Republican State Central Committee of Michigan wrote to the mayor detailing the work that she and her organization had done for his campaign. She complained that other "groups" had received their due from the mayor but that African Americans had not been recognized for their contributions. "Due to the fact that so many changes have been made during your four months in office for many groups, and nothing done for our group," she declared, "I am wondering when we are to expect recognition." Beatrice M. Fleming, Republican State Central Committee of Michigan, to Mayor, April 18, 1940, MP 1940, box 4, folder: "Interracial Comm. 1940."

30. Mayor Edward Jeffries to Henry Murray, March 16, 1940; Charles Diggs to Mayor Edward Jeffries, July 11, 1940, MP 1940, box 4, folder: "Interracial Comm. 1940," Detroit Public Library. Police Commissioner Frank Eaman advised the mayor *not* to establish an interracial committee. He explained that his "own personal feeling is that everyone interested in preventing a recurrence can do it through private contacts." Frank D. Eaman to Mayor, July 15, 1940, MP 1940, box 4, folder: "Interracial Comm. 1940."

31. Even when white officials caved in and agreed to allow commissions to sponsor studies of racial discrimination, they often "buried" the reports. For example, a 1926 report, "The Negro in Detroit," was sponsored by the city's Community Fund, but one person financed the publishing, printed one hundred copies, and "gave them about as he saw fit." In other words, the city's officials took little responsibility for distributing or publicizing the document. John Dancy to Cecil C. North, May 4, 1928, DUL, box 1, folder 23, BHL.

32. "23 Are Seized in New Fights at High School." Pack was found not guilty of disturbing the peace. Clarence Reading testified at his trial. "Police Rapped for Partiality."

33. "23 Are Seized in New Fights at High School."

34. Meier and Rudwick, *Black Detroit*, 80.

35. Special Assistant to the Secretary to Miss M. L. Beasley, June 8, 1936. Two hundred people attended a planning meeting for Detroit's NAACP Youth Council in October 1936. Gloster Current to Juanita Jackson, October 5, 1936; Gloster Current to Charles H. Houston, October 13, 1936, NAACP, part 12, series C, reel 13. Gloster Current was one of the driving forces behind Detroit's NAACP Youth Council when it began in 1936. Current was in his early twenties at the time. He played in and directed his own orchestra of "radio artists" from 1930 to 1939, and in 1939 left Detroit to attend college at West Virginia State University. After his education Current returned to Detroit and became the executive secretary of the Detroit branch of the NAACP from 1941 to 1946, and then became the director of branches for the National NAACP from 1946 to 1977.

36. Gloster Current to Juanita Jackson, November 21, 1936; "Detroit Educational Inequalities Mass Meeting," November 1937, NAACP, part 12, series C, reel 13.

37. Meier and Rudwick, *Black Detroit*, 81.

38. Gloster Current, "Report of Detroit Central Youth Council Chairman to Senior Branch of the N.A.A.C.P.," October 11, 1937; "Detroit N.A.A.C.P. Youth Council Holds Election," November 14, 1937; Gloster Current to Juanita Jackson, May 14, 1937; Gloster Current to Juanita Jackson, December 9, 1937, NAACP, part 12, series C, reel 13.

39. Horace Sheffield, "Negrissipation," 1938, NAACP, part 12, series C, reel 13. Sheffield, who was twenty-three years old in 1940, worked at Ford's River Rouge Plant and attended college in the evenings. The summer after the Northwestern riots, he joined the UAW and became a volunteer organizer in the campaign to win recognition for the union from the Ford Motor Company. Sheffield continued to work as the president of the West Side Youth Council, and when Ford workers walked out on strike, he convinced the council to support the walkout. The Youth Council borrowed a sound truck from another UAW local, made a sign that said, "The West Side Youth Council of the NAACP supports the strike," and drove around the plant urging black and white workers to walk off their jobs. Interview of Horace Sheffield by Herbert Hill, July 24, 1968, used by permission of Herbert Hill, ALUA. Horace Sheffield went on to work as an International Representative for the UAW from 1942 to 1967. He also continued to fight for civil rights and for fair representation of African Americans in the union throughout his career.

40. "On the morning of March 1," March 24, 1940, Civil Rights Congress Papers (hereafter, CRC), box 80, folder: "Northwestern Riot Arrests." Organizations that participated in these actions had youth members who were affiliated with the Civil Rights Federation (CRF). The CRF, which was established in 1935 to pull to-

gether the city's political Left into a better-coordinated coalition, was closely tied to the labor movement, and, along with the city's white Left, began to take more of an active interest in racial discrimination toward the end of the 1930s. In 1939, for example, the CRF established its "Negro Rights Committee." Reverend Charles Hill was an early and active member of the CRF. Catherine Hartley, International Labor Defense Press Release, March 13, 1940, CRC, box 80, folder: "Northwestern Riot Arrests," ALUA. The Civil Rights Federation included racial justice as part if its initial platform, but racial justice only became a major focus of its activism later in the 1930s. Historian Angela Dillard has demonstrated that the CRF "increased its standing" among black activists because of its close connection with the National Negro Congress (NNC). For a discussion of the CRF and the NNC in the 1930s, see Dillard, "From the Reverend Charles A. Hill to the Reverend Albert B. Cleage, Jr." 75–122.

41. "Board Minutes," 1941, DUL, box 61, folder: "Executive Board Materials."

42. E. J. Corrigan to John Dancy, January 10, 1941, DUL, box 71, folder: "Race Relations 1941–1942."

43. Banner, "Observation on Conditions among Negroes," 11.

44. A. L. Goddard to Friend, DUL, box 71, folder: "Race Relations, 1941–1942."

45. "Youth Seek to Solve Racial Problems at Northwestern," *Detroit Tribune,* April 5, 1941.

46. Bess Schmidt to Friend, March 1941; "Partial List of Organizations which have been asked to assist in the Northwestern High School Institute," March 1941, CRC, box 80, folder: "Northwestern Riot Arrests."

47. "Meeting at Northwestern High School," March 30, 1941. Lewis B. Larkin Papers, box 7, folder 6, ALUA.

48. "Meeting at Northwestern High School," March 30, 1941. Lewis B. Larkin Papers, box 7, folder 6, ALUA.

49. Murray Korngold, Statement about his arrest on March 1, 1940 in front of Northwestern High School, March 5, 1940, CRC, box 80, folder: "Northwestern Riot Arrests."

50. The Northwestern Institute, "Recommendations," CRC, box 80, folder: "Northwestern Riot Arrests."

51. "Petition Board of Education for Negro Teacher At N. W. High," *Detroit Tribune,* August 30, 1941.

52. George Mutnick, "An Emergency Call," September 17, 1942, CRC, box 80, folder: "Northwestern Riot."

53. Edward Jeffries to John C. Dancy, March 28, 1941, DUL, box 71, folder: "Race Relations, 1941–1942;" Banner, "Observation on Conditions among Negroes."

Milwaukee, Wisconsin, Autumn 1968. NAACP march. Father James Groppi (*center*), walking east along Wisconsin Avenue. *Photography by Howard M. Berliant, WHi(X3) 36107, State Historical Society of Wisconsin.*

Chapter 11

"Not a Color, but an Attitude"

Father James Groppi and
Black Power Politics in Milwaukee

Patrick Jones

In late September 1967 Father James Groppi, five members of the NAACP Youth Council "Commandos," and two other local white clergymen set off from Milwaukee, Wisconsin, to Washington, D.C., to lobby liberal politicians for a national "fair housing" law and to attend the "Conference on the Churches and Urban Tension."[1] The conference, organized by the Methodist Church with the support of several other liberal denominations, sought to bring greater national attention to the explosive open housing drama unfolding on the streets of Milwaukee. For a month hundreds of civil rights advocates had clashed with thousands of white, working-class residents on the city's South Side. Just across the 16th Street Viaduct, linking "Africa to Poland," as the local joke went, angry white mobs chanted white power slogans, threw rocks, firecrackers, and feces, and pummeled nonviolent marchers with their fists. Milwaukee was only the latest in a string of housing clashes that rocked urban America during the mid-1960s, marking the issue as a key civil rights battleground in the North. Conference organizers in the nation's capital hoped to dramatize the need for national action on this pressing issue by spotlighting the Milwaukee campaign.

At a session on the first day featuring Fr. Groppi and the Commandos, leaders of Pride, Inc., a local black nationalist organization founded by Marion Barry, opposed Fr. Groppi's close relationship with the Commandos and his role as primary spokesperson for the Milwaukee open housing campaign. A line of critics rose to castigate the white priest and his young black companions with a list of derogatory names and Black Power barbs. "Fr. Groppi has one thing wrong with him," one member of Pride, Inc., declared, "his color. It's the same old case of whites using Negroes."[2] During this verbal onslaught, Groppi said nothing, but instead retreating to a corner of the room. The five Commandos stepped forward to defend the young priest and to explain that, in fact, *they* were the leaders of the Milwaukee campaign and Groppi was their adviser. They went on to reaffirm their conviction in Black Power but also their commitment to what they called a "not-violent," interracial, church-based movement in Milwaukee. Following a series of testy exchanges, the meeting degenerated into chaos. It ultimately took a wedge of Commandos to get Fr. Groppi out.[3]

Over the next two days the local militants continued their efforts to undermine the conference. As Groppi and the Commandos met with legislators, members of Pride, Inc., told reporters that the Commandos were not authentic Black Power leaders because they allowed a white man to advise them. The group also tried to block the Milwaukee activists from participating in a scheduled march and prayer vigil at the Washington Monument. Their challenge divided the conference into black and white caucuses and few African Americans participated in the public actions. In the end, the conference broke upon the rocky shoals of competing visions of Black Power. The organizers' attempt to bring the Milwaukee campaign to a broader national audience fizzled as the media focused more on the internal strife than on the issue of housing.[4]

Yet the confrontation solidified the alliance between Fr. Groppi and the Commandos, and reaffirmed their commitment to their own brand of Black Power politics. "Fr. Groppi and ourselves are together," one Commando told reporters after the conference ended. "We would die together, even if it meant going to hell. This movement is black and white. It contains people of all colors. We do not turn anyone away who is seeking justice for the blacks and who is willing to work and sacrifice to bring it into existence."[5] Another wrote as they left the capital city, "I advocate Black Power, but not to the point that it stops any people or any man from identifying himself with a Black Power movement, even if he be white, yellow or green."[6] When the Milwaukee delegation returned home, an interracial throng of several hundred met them at the airport, chanting Black Power slogans, "We love Fr. Groppi!" and "Freedom!" Later, at St. Boniface Church, the delegation received a standing ovation as they reaffirmed the principles of their campaign. Vel Phillips, Milwaukee's lone African American Common Council member, called the interracial open housing campaign "beautiful" and warned that Milwaukee might prove to be "a last ditch stand for non-violence, a last ditch stand for the church and a last ditch stand for an integrated movement." Comedian Dick Gregory argued that Black Power advocates nationwide were becoming less anti-white because of the Milwaukee demonstrations. "What we are doing here in Milwaukee," he said, "is convincing a lot of cats that black nationalism is not a color, it's an attitude." When Groppi rose to speak, several Commandos swept him onto their shoulders as the crowd roared, a powerful affirmation of the priest's role in the local movement.[7]

The Milwaukee movement makes us think once again about the Black Power story and challenges us to ask new questions.[8] Milwaukee was not the only city where the National Association for the Advancement of Colored People (NAACP) played a major role in the local development of the Black Power movement.[9] And we have not paid nearly enough attention to the youth and student branches of the NAACP. Moreover, we are just beginning to appreciate the complex roles of Catholic civil rights activists throughout the urban North, an important dynamic considering the large proportion of Catholics throughout the region. The Milwaukee story forces us to look beyond simple slogans and orthodoxies to find out just what Black Power meant on the ground; to find out how local activists combined direct action and nonviolence with armed self-defense, civil rights with Black Power, and demands for housing and school integration with expressions of social and cultural autonomy. In short, it challenges us to consider how local civil rights activists fashioned their own version of Black Power politics that made sense in the context of their community.

Father James Groppi's Road to Civil Rights

The African American community in Milwaukee remained extremely small until the 1920s when it began to undergo a slow but steady increase. In the wake of World War II the black community grew more quickly as the industrial base of the economy heated up. In 1910 fewer than 1,000 African Americans lived in Milwaukee. By 1950 the black population had grown to 62,458, and by 1970 it numbered 105,088, or more than 10 percent of the city's overall population. Yet African American opportunity remained severely circumscribed throughout the fifties and early sixties. A mixture of choice, economic necessity, discriminatory real estate and loan practices, and overt racism restricted more than 90 percent of African

American residents to an overcrowded seventy-two–block area on the city's North Side, commonly known as "the inner-core." Employment discrimination, substandard public education, police brutality, and crumbling infrastructure were prevalent. Young black people bore a disproportionate amount of the everyday burden of racial inequality in Milwaukee. Most lived in dilapidated housing in this segregated neighborhood, were surrounded by poverty, and attended inferior, segregated schools. Summer youth unemployment was a chronic problem in the inner-core. Many felt that this explained rising crime statistics and simmering tensions with police. Under these circumstances young black Milwaukeeans were ripe for political mobilization. A white Catholic priest would help unlock the potential of this youthful activism.

James Groppi was born in 1930 to Italian immigrant parents in Bay View, Wisconsin, a white, working-class neighborhood dominated by Irish and Slavic immigrants located a few miles south of downtown Milwaukee. Although quick to note that his experience paled in comparison to the "terrifying discrimination" faced by African Americans, Groppi recalled feeling isolated and bullied as a youth and often said his experiences gave him an appreciation for what it was like to be an "outsider."[10] Throughout adolescence and early adulthood Groppi found himself pulled toward religion. He told one reporter, "To me, life, in order to have meaning, had to have religion. The brevity of life is one thing that always hit me—the shortness. You've got to do something in this short expanse of time in order to make eternity meaningful."[11] In 1950, at the age of twenty and with only tepid support from his parents, James Groppi entered Mt. Calvary Seminary in rural southern Wisconsin. In 1953 he transferred his religious studies to St. Francis Seminary, a few miles from his boyhood home.

It was during his years as a Catholic seminarian that Groppi's interest in race relations and the African American community crystallized. Beginning in 1956 Groppi spent three successive summers working at an urban camp for children, almost all of them poor and black. White Capuchin priests with a long-standing commitment to the local African American community ran the camp at Blessed Martin Parish near the Hillside Housing Project on the city's impoverished North Side. "For us, in the 1950s, for the first time we came into contact with and directly experienced discrimination and racism," explained Patrick Flood, one of Groppi's fellow seminarians at the camp, "That whole experience brought about a conversion experience . . . or a change of will in all of us where we became . . . very committed to social justice around the issue of race."[12] From that point forward Fr. Groppi's reaction to racism and discrimination was immediate, emotional, and personal, not abstract or intellectual. For Groppi, the face of a young African American girl stung by a racial slur held "the pain of Jesus Christ as he hung on the cross."[13]

Although he requested an assignment in Milwaukee's inner-core, the Archdiocese initially sent Fr. Groppi to St. Veronica, a primarily white, working-class parish located in a South Side neighborhood similar to the one where he grew up. Following a 1963 clash with parishioners over their opposition to plans to build low-income public housing in the area, the Chancery transferred Fr. Groppi to St. Boniface, one of five Milwaukee central city parishes struggling to remain relevant to the increasingly African American community around them. St. Boniface, located adjacent to the predominately black North Division High School, proved to be a supportive place for Groppi's growing interest in civil rights. It was "a live church,"[14] democratic, experimental and committed to social justice through social action. During the tempestuous open housing campaign of 1967–68 St. Boniface emerged as the primary "movement center" in Milwaukee, home base for hundreds of civil rights activists from across the city and nation.

One Capuchin friar, Fr. Mathew Gottschaulk, played a particularly important role in the civil rights development of a small group of young priests, including Fr. Groppi. "[Fr. Mathew] knew the inner city as a sociologist as well as a clergyman," Fr. Patrick Flood recalled. "He knew all the families. Everybody knew him."[15] Gottschaulk engaged the local black community directly and reached out to a small circle of young priests to join him. When the Southern civil rights movement made national news during the late 1950s and early 1960s, Fr. Mathew rounded up his young friends and traveled South to participate.

These experiences brought the young clergymen face to face with Southern-style racial inequality. In 1961, and again in 1963, Fr. Mathew led a group of Catholic priests—including Fr. Groppi and Fr. Flood—South to bear witness to racial discrimination.[16] "We went and visited areas [in Mississippi and Alabama] where people were involved in [civil rights] and there was a Catholic church," Flood explained. "And usually the Catholic church was getting it on both sides. In the South, to be Catholic wasn't the greatest thing on earth anyway, and [Catholics] were also working with the black community."[17] Fr. Groppi next traveled to Washington, D.C., in 1963, to participate in the March on Washington; the following summer he drove to Jackson, Mississippi, with Milwaukee NAACP Youth Council member Nathan Harwell to work with the Mississippi Freedom Democratic Party on voter registration.[18] The next spring a group of Milwaukee priests set off for Selma, Alabama, heeding Martin Luther King Jr.'s ecumenical call for support after the "Bloody Sunday" violence. While in Selma the clergymen attended marches and rallies, learned the techniques of militant nonviolent direct action, registered voters, conducted teach-ins with parents, knelt in inter-faith prayer protests, and heard Martin Luther King, Ralph Abernathy, and James Forman speak. Selma convinced many Northern activists, including those from Milwaukee, of the need to bring the struggle for racial justice home to their local communities. For Catholics, Selma seemed to fulfill the reform spirit that had captured the Church during the Second Vatican Councils.

This direct exposure to the Jim Crow South forced Fr. Groppi to clarify his commitment to the movement at home. Groppi explained the process as a conversion: "What happened was that as you went along in the movement, you got swallowed up in the cause. And the cause was the cause of righteousness. Pretty soon your fear was gone."[19] At a civil rights rally at St. Boniface shortly after his return from Selma, Fr. Groppi told more than two hundred people, "In the South there is a constant working to overcome [racial discrimination]. This is something we need to learn in the North. . . . Bigotry is not confined to any one state. It is present here in Wisconsin."[20]

After Selma, Fr. Groppi and a small coterie of Milwaukee Catholics plunged deeper into the local school desegregation campaign that had been building since 1963. The Milwaukee public school system was skewed sharply along racial lines. The NAACP defined integrated education as a 15–40 percent African American student body in each school. In Milwaukee one high school, two junior high schools, and eleven elementary schools were more than 90 percent black. Four other elementary schools were 60–90 percent black, and two high schools, one junior high school, and four elementary schools had an African American enrollment of 50 percent and rising.[21] In part, this reflected segregated housing patterns. But civil rights activists contended that school board members—almost exclusively white—also consciously drew district lines and allocated resources unequally to reinforce these racialized housing patterns and protect white students, thereby ensuring substandard educational opportunities for black students. In 1964 school desegregation advocates, led by state NAACP chairman Lloyd Barbee, formed an umbrella organization, the Milwaukee United School Integration Committee (MUSIC), to press for change. As education officials and white politicians failed to act, the school desegregation campaign moved from reason and moral suasion to direct action and civil disobedience. In the spring of 1965 members of MUSIC elected Fr. Groppi vice chairman. In a city with a population approaching 50 percent Catholic, the curious sight of a white priest confronting racial inequality attracted increasing media attention. By the fall of that year local newspapers no longer felt it necessary to introduce Fr. Groppi, instead referring to him knowingly as "a local civil rights leader."

The NAACP Youth Council Comes of Age

The school desegregation campaign played a pivotal role educating and organizing young inner-core African Americans. MUSIC placed thousands of black youth at the center of their growing campaign against segregated public education and gave many their first taste of political action. Their endless meetings, lectures, fliers, dances, rallies, "Freedom Institutes," "Hootenannies," and "Freedom Camps" gave young African Americans a political education in racial inequality and told them that they had a crucial role to play in changing those conditions. On May 18, 1964, MUSIC successfully mobilized an estimated fifteen thousand inner-core students to support a one-day, citywide school boycott. During the boycott more than eleven thousand students attended one of thirty-three "Freedom Schools" set up mainly in church basements and extra rooms throughout the inner-core. A second boycott the following year turned out between five thousand and seven thousand students, this time for three consecutive days. Despite the outpouring of grassroots pressure, the school board refused to address the yawning racial gap in public education.[22]

The school desegregation campaign also provided a vehicle for the Milwaukee NAACP Youth Council (YC) to become more active in the movement. A small nucleus of YC members had worked since the early 1960s to move the organization from its traditional focus on membership recruitment and social activities to militant direct action. The YC's first successful action came in 1963 when several dozen members picketed against employment discrimination at three inner-core restaurants and forced a settlement with the owner. Following the campaign, however, the YC adviser resigned because a majority in the adult NAACP branch opposed their direct action tactics. This institutional resistance kept the activist embers burning low until MUSIC arrived on the scene and in the schools.[23]

In 1965, behind the leadership of Direct Action chairman DeWayne Tolliver, YC members attended planning meetings, made phone calls, went door to door, passed out flyers, marched, picketed, sat-in, boycotted, sang, and chanted, all in the name of ending segregation in Milwaukee's public schools. The campaign provided the YC an activist outlet away from the resistant adult branch of the NAACP. As the school desegregation campaign became more militant, the YC played an increasingly prominent role.

It was at this point that the YC began its search for a new adviser. In the crucible of the school desegregation movement and amid changing national and local circumstances, the YC and Fr. Groppi found each other. During the spring of 1965 YC members elected the young priest as their adviser. The alliance brought together the energy and spirit of African American youth, the charismatic leadership of Fr. Groppi, and the organizational structure and resources of the NAACP and the Catholic Church. For many Milwaukeeans, rooted in a traditional understanding of religion and social relations, it seemed incongruous that a group of inner-city black youth would connect with a white, Catholic priest for militant civil rights leadership. Yet the links were clear to those who had been paying close attention.

For Groppi, the YC offered an institutional vehicle to formalize and focus his work with young people in the inner-core outside the formal confines of the Catholic Church. Having known many YC members for years because of his work in the community, Groppi possessed the ability to relate to their experiences. He saw civil rights activism as a way to build leadership skills and self-esteem, and provide inner-city black youth with a constructive outlet for their boredom, frustration, and anger. Meanwhile, the YC had been searching for an adviser to fit its growing activism. MUSIC organizing activated inner-core students and filled them with new possibilities. No local African American minister had demonstrated the same commitment to direct action and personal sacrifice that Fr. Groppi had displayed.

Once united, Fr. Groppi and the YC played a central role in MUSIC's fast-evolving school desegregation campaign. In May police arrested several YC members, including Tolliver and Nathan Harwell, for their part in a prolonged demonstration against construction of the MacDowell School, a new site that civil rights activists complained would be segregated. Police arrested Harwell again on June 4, along with Fr. Groppi and four other clergymen, when they blocked a bus at the Seifert Elementary

School with a "human chain." In October Fr. Groppi stood at the center of a fierce public controversy over the use of church facilities to support a second citywide school boycott. Afterward, it was Groppi and the YC that announced plans for continued MUSIC demonstrations, including marches to the homes of Mayor Henry Maier and school board president John Foley. In December the duo led a final MUSIC-sponsored civil disobedience campaign at the MacDowell site. Police again arrested Fr. Groppi and others when they chained themselves to heavy construction equipment to block work on the project. By the end of 1965 the NAACP Youth Council and Fr. Groppi had moved to the forefront of the local movement for racial justice.

From the Eagles Club to Open Housing

But arrests and civil disobedience still failed to move school administrators to address the racial divide in Milwaukee's public schools. As a result, the school desegregation campaign moved from the streets to a protracted court battle, leaving Fr. Groppi and the YC to seek new issues for their activist energies.[24] In early 1966 they decided to target the local branch of the Fraternal Order of Eagles, a national organization that restricted its membership to "Caucasians." With fifty-four hundred members, the Milwaukee chapter of the Eagles Club was the second largest local in the country and an important network for the city's white power brokers. Blue-collar industrial workers, labor leaders, politicians, judges, and business professionals all mingled at Eagles Club events. In this way membership was an imperative for ambitious local leaders.

The YC and Fr. Groppi saw the Eagles Club policy as a source of grave injustice. How could African Americans expect to get unbiased treatment from judges, politicians, real estate brokers, labor leaders, and business executives who maintained their membership in the racially restrictive Eagles Club? Arguing that the club was not, in fact, a private association, and thus exempt from civil rights laws, but rather a quasi-public organization under those laws' jurisdiction, the YC sought to have the racially exclusive membership policy changed or to encourage public officials to resign their memberships.

A series of pickets outside the Eagles Club in February and March 1966 failed to attract significant television or newspaper coverage. The lack of media attention made it difficult for the YC to articulate its case clearly to the public. Reactions to the protest focused primarily on the membership policy, a constitutionally protected practice, ignoring local public officials' affiliation with the group. Employing the ubiquitous rhetoric of the Cold War, Eagles Club leaders branded the YC "a left-wing extremist organization," and even some liberal civil rights advocates questioned the wisdom of challenging the Eagles' policy when more pressing issues, like employment and housing, remained on the table.[25] To them, however lamentable, the law seemed clear on the issue. But Fr. Groppi and the YC remained undaunted.

On August 9, 1966, as the YC debated its next move, a bomb blast rocked the offices of the Milwaukee NAACP, no doubt in retaliation for the rising tide of civil rights activism and black self-assertion in the city. Police arrested two members of the Wisconsin Ku Klux Klan and Milwaukee Citizens Council, along with the Grand Dragon of the Illinois KKK, in connection with the explosion. Moderate leaders of the adult branch of the NAACP urged local African Americans "not to retaliate," while state chairman Lloyd Barbee called the blast "a planned effort to destroy a symbol of established civil rights activists."[26] The morning after the bombing, Milwaukeeans awoke to news that several YC members, most in their late teens, had armed themselves with a loaded carbine and stood guard over their inner-core "Freedom House" where they held meetings and recruited members. Fr. Groppi told reporters that the armed self-defense was his idea, after the Freedom House and St. Boniface rectory received a series of telephone threats. "[We] will not remain non-violent in the face of some bigot coming at night and placing a bomb beneath the window," Groppi explained. "That is where [our] non-violence ends."[27]

Less than two weeks after the bombing, the YC resumed its Eagles Club protest by picketing the home of Judge Robert Cannon in the western suburb of Wauwatosa. The Council targeted Cannon because of his liberal record and public support of civil rights, believing he would quickly cave in and resign from the club, initiating a cascade of defections. What the YC did not anticipate was a confrontation with thousands of hostile white residents. For eleven straight nights Fr. Groppi loaded up an old beat-up bus that St. Boniface owned and ferried civil rights demonstrators to the sidewalk in front of Cannon's large brick colonial house. Chanting anti–Eagles Club slogans and singing freedom songs, the YC led pickets, prayer vigils, and parades. Their numbers grew steadily from 30 to more than 250 over the full course of the protest. But the YC underestimated Judge Cannon's resolve. The jurist stood firm, stating, "I will remain in the Eagles as long as I live."[28]

As the judge dug in his heels and the demonstrations continued in Wauwatosa, white reaction also grew vociferous. Roughly one hundred white onlookers and counterdemonstrators showed up over the first few nights. Their numbers mushroomed to more than a thousand by the following weekend, stretching for several blocks down Wisconsin Avenue. With each passing day the hostility and intensity became more menacing. Most of those that came out just watched, but others shouted and hurled obscenities, like "Nigger lover!" "Go back to the zoo, nigger," and "Kill 'em, kill 'em! This is a white man's town. We don't want any cannibals here!" Some held signs stating "Groppi, Go Home," "Keep Tosa White," and "Burn, Barbee, Burn." A few threw eggs, bricks, cherry bombs, rocks, and debris. Several robed Klansmen showed up, and an increasing number of police officers and sheriff's deputies, in full riot gear, struggled to maintain public order. After nine days of swelling crowds, Wauwatosa Mayor Ervin Meier asked Governor Warren Knowles to dispatch four hundred National Guardsmen to protect the civil rights demonstrators.[29]

At an October 4 news conference Fr. Groppi announced that the YC had formed "a militant commando force" to aid in the group's civil rights activism. "This is a direct action force that goes into very intense situations, that's very militant," he explained. "They will be a police force. They will not be armed." The following day local newspapers carried photographs of several young African American men, clad in black berets, black ascots, green army fatigues, and black boots. But cultural conservatism ran deep in Milwaukee, and most white residents and city leaders preferred a slow, studied approach to municipal problems and charged that the "Commandos" were an example of "extremism." Responding to these accusations, Groppi stated, "We are militant. We are a vigorous direct action group. I don't think this is extremism."[30] Yet, to many in Milwaukee, the tactics employed by Fr. Groppi and the YC overshadowed the issues they sought to address.

The creation of the Commandos sprang from several sources. It was a direct reaction to the bombing of the NAACP office in August and the violent attacks on YC members during the Eagles Club protests in Wauwatosa. YC members felt that law enforcement did not adequately protect civil rights demonstrators—many of whom were children—in the face of violent white opposition and thus felt the need to create their own self-defense corps. In addition, the formation of the Commando unit reflected the rising tide of Black Power politics nationally.[31] Fr. Groppi hoped to use the group to further cultivate leadership and self-respect among poor, young African American men in the inner-core and to channel their rage in constructive ways. In retrospect, Groppi commented, "The Commandos . . . were a very chauvinistic group. There were no women that were in the Commando group. It was looked at as a very macho thing."[32] Ed Thekan, the lone white Commando, explained, "It was men and there was a perceived need, I think, to identify with the black male who had . . . been emasculated, downgraded by the white society. . . . Here is a case to [exult] the black man as the leader in the sense of protector."[33] The rhetoric and style of the group also represented an attempt to inject greater militancy into the Milwaukee movement. Although the Commandos were almost exclusively black, they adhered to a biracial philosophy and practiced "not-violence." "'Not-violence' meant we didn't carry weapons and we didn't start nothing, but we also didn't take nothing," explained Commando leader Joe McClain. "If the police or white crowds came after us or the marchers, we weren't afraid to mix it up. We fought back."[34] Commandos flanked marchers during demonstrations and enforced discipline within the lines.

Often, lying just behind the public face of nonviolent direct action and unarmed "not-violence" was the presence of weapons. For example, on the second day of the Wauwatosa protests, as white resistance grew, Fr. Groppi and lawyer Tom Jacobson loaded up the old bus with YC members, many of whom would go on to become original Commandos. Nervous tension filled the air. The previous day Groppi had called Jacobson to ask if he would represent the YC in the event of arrests and confided that he was fearful of white violence. Jacobson agreed to help. When the two men boarded the bus, Jacobson told the group that he could only represent them and defend their rights if they adhered to nonviolence. "If you have any weapons, you need to get rid of them now before we leave," he said. No one stirred. Again he spoke: "I'm going to get off the bus and come back on." Jacobson exited and Fr. Groppi walked up and down the aisle. Clink. Clink. Clink. Brass knuckles, knives, and chains all appeared in a pile. Jacobson was shocked but relieved that the youths had relented.[35] Ed Thekan explained, "You were dealing with street people who basically found a need in their own daily lives to protect themselves from . . . threats, assaults, etc. So, they carried a bicycle chain, or . . . a switchblade or whatever was hot that day. But [we began to] see where that wasn't required on the picket line." Throughout the rest of the direct action era in Milwaukee, nonviolent direct action would coexist alongside "not-violence" and a behind-the-scenes version of armed self-defense. Originally the Commandos functioned as a subgroup of the YC but later took on the central leadership role during the volatile open housing campaign.

The armed defense of the Freedom House and the formation of the Commandos was just one aspect of the YC and Fr. Groppi's more general embrace of Black Power. At marches, rallies, and meetings during the winter of 1966–67 civil rights activists chanted Black Power slogans, held Black Power signs, sported Black Power T-shirts, and donned buttons emblazoned with the slogan, "Burn Baby Burn." At St. Boniface priests placed banners in both Swahili and English around the church, they laced sermons with Black Power rhetoric, and Fr. Groppi refused to wear colorful priestly vestments during mass, preferring instead to wear black on the alter as a sign of racial solidarity. Spirituals, civil rights songs, and Black Power slogans replaced traditional Catholic hymns in the liturgy. Groppi also used "dialogue homilies" to teach neighborhood children about the tenets of Black Power and self-determination.[36]

These and other unique features of Black Power in Milwaukee highlighted the way Groppi and the YC fit national Black Power ideology to their particular local circumstances. To many, the sight of a white Catholic priest leading chants of Black Power from the altar and the picket line no doubt seemed peculiar.[37] And it was, in that it stood against national trends. The leading role of Fr. Groppi as a Black Power advocate and spokesman ran counter to the growing racial separatism of Black Power in other areas. In addition, the Commandos' persistent embrace of interracial cooperation and "not-violence," as well as their refusal to brandish weapons publicly, even as a symbolic act, also set them apart from many other local Black Power organizations.

The chain of events that began with the bombing of the NAACP office and extended through the Wauwatosa protests and the creation of the Commandos frayed relations between the YC and Milwaukee police. Harold Breier, the white chief of the force, did not sympathize with the local civil rights movement and saw nonviolent direct action as a threat to civil order. During the Eagles protest he turned the department's "Tactical Squad," a group of six to eight detectives that grew out of the city's decades-old vice squad, against movement activists. The squad took hundreds of photographs of marchers, wrote down license plate numbers at rallies, meetings, and church services, and generally kept a menacing watch over movement leaders. "We called them the Goon Squad," recalled one Commando leader. "Their job was to monitor the activities of the NAACP Youth Council, especially those people who were viewed as leaders."[38] This conflict was further stoked by a series of violent, after-hours incidents between Milwaukee police officers and inner-core youth. As the cry of "police brutality" swept the movement in the urban North and West, these clashes took on increasingly menacing proportions. Tensions smoldered as the summer of 1967 approached. With little concrete action taken by city officials on a host of civil rights issues, more and more Milwaukee leaders issued riot warnings. "The seeds are planted. The fire is under the pot," Fr. Michael Neuberger warned reporters. Milwaukee was primed for "riot, bloodshed, suffering and mayhem."[39]

Tensions were compounded in late June when the YC and Commandos announced that they would target racial discrimination in housing and work for a citywide open housing ordinance. Alderman Vel Phillips had introduced the measure to the Common Council three separate times, and each time her fellow council members defeated it by a vote of 19 to 1. Mayor Henry Maier deflected responsibility away from city leaders and to suburban and county governments by urging passage of a law covering the entire metropolitan area. Civil rights leaders hoped that a confrontational direct action campaign would foster the "creative tension" necessary to force legislative action by the Common Council. "We're going to march," Fr. Groppi told a rally at St. Boniface. "We're coming off the reservation. We're going to move where we want. We're going to live where we want. . . . Either we get what we want in this city, or we're going to turn [it] upside down. If it takes the National Guard out all summer, that's what the Youth Council's going to do."[40] The YC held regular rallies at St. Boniface and picketed the homes of aldermen who opposed the ordinance. At one gathering the group threatened to cross the Menominee River Valley, the city's "Mason-Dixon Line," a natural buffer between the segregated African American inner-core and the overwhelmingly white, working-class neighborhoods on the South Side. A few days later Fr. Groppi told the Common Council that, without action on housing, Milwaukee could be turned into a "holocaust."[41]

As the local showdown grew, national events fueled the fire. On July 12, 1967, four days of full-scale racial violence erupted in Newark, New Jersey; when the gunfire, burning, and looting subsided, 23 African Americans lay dead, more than 1,500 were injured, 1,300 were arrested, and over $10 million in property lay charred and ruined. Two weeks later, closer to home,

Detroit burst into flames. Again hundreds of National Guardsmen were needed to quell the rebellion. In the end, three days of unrest claimed 43 African American lives, 1,189 injuries, and 7,231 arrests. The nation looked on in horror. Suddenly the whole urban calculus had dreadfully changed. Behind the scenes Milwaukee officials drew up plans to confront racial unrest.

On July 30, only a few days after the Detroit uprising ended, racial violence came to Milwaukee's inner-core. Young people clashed with police. Stores were looted, cars were overturned, and roving mobs menaced inner-core residents and white passers-by. Mayor Henry Maier gained national notoriety by moving quickly, instituting a citywide curfew and calling out hundreds of National Guardsmen. Fr. Groppi, the NAACP YC, and Commandos worked the streets, urging calm and order. In the end the violence claimed three lives and caused more than on hundred injuries, as well as nearly $600,000 in physical damages. Mayor Maier called rioters "hoodlums." Many white Milwaukeeans condemned the violence, which confirmed their preconceptions of black residents as lawless criminals. Some blamed civil rights activists, particularly Fr. Groppi and the YC, for the troubles. The major media outlets and a number of civic leaders similarly condemned the rioting, but also saw it as a strong indication that more vigorous official action was needed to address the problems of the inner-core. Civil rights leaders and many African Americans viewed the outburst as the inevitable, if regrettable, result of mounting frustrations and anger in the face of chronic inequality and half-hearted official action. Perhaps most ominous, the riot stoked the flames of a generalized white reactionary impulse throughout the city.[42]

Going South: Open Housing in Milwaukee

The civil disturbance in Milwaukee brought a new degree of cooperation between civil rights and community organizations. Three weeks after Milwaukee's riot, with the community still reeling, the YC, backed by the state NAACP, the Milwaukee Urban League, the Milwaukee *Star,* and a variety of liberal religious and community organizations, announced that it would take its open housing crusade into the heart of white opposition on the South Side.[43] The day before the demonstration, local newspapers printed a map detailing the march route, a move that no doubt contributed to the vigorous white response. On August 28 two hundred civil rights advocates, flanked by police, Commandos, and media crews, set off from St. Boniface across the 16th Street Viaduct. The group held a permit for an open housing rally in Kosciuszko Park, located inside a largely Polish neighborhood, a few blocks from the hall where hundreds of local people had enthusiastically welcomed segregationist Alabama governor George Wallace during the 1964 Democratic presidential primary. At the other end of the viaduct, more than three thousand white residents came out to observe and oppose the open housing demonstration. Many were simply curious. Others held signs that read, "Polish Power" and "A Good Groppi Is a Dead Groppi." Still others shouted obscenities and slogans like, "Niggers go home!" "Go back to Africa!" and "Sieg heil." Soon bottles, garbage, and chunks of wood rained down on the peaceful marchers. The crowds pressed menacingly against police cordons. At the park an estimated five thousand white locals met the demonstrators, resulting in an outburst of scuffling. The violence injured twenty-two people, and police arrested nine. As the battered civil rights activists left Kosciuszko Park, Fr. Groppi vowed to return the following night. Even so, Common Council members still refused to act on an open housing ordinance.

The mood was tense as the demonstrators set out again for the South Side. Trailed by a cadre of local and national media, Fr. Groppi, the YC, and Commandos led freedom songs and Black Power chants to try to steel their supporters against what lay ahead. As the group neared the other side of the bridge, they could hear a low growling clamor rise in front of them. At Crazy Jim's used auto lot, rock and roll blared from mounted speakers and an effigy of a white priest, defaced by a swastika, swung by the neck from a rope. Several hundred young, white toughs hurled threats and obscenities. Two men held a Confederate flag while others waved signs that read, "White Power," "Bring Back Slavery," and "I Like Niggers: Everybody Should Own a Few." A detachment of Milwaukee police rushed forward to head off trouble. Beyond the auto lot, thousands of hostile white spectators lined the sidewalks opposite marchers and filled the blocks around Kosciuszko Park. Children wore George Wallace stickers. Bottles, eggs, rocks, wood, firecrackers, urine, and spit flew. Shouts of "kill . . . kill . . . kill . . . kill" were reported. Police commanders quickly passed out shotguns, rifles, and gas masks to the officers protecting the march. The demonstrators refused to back down, defiantly pressing their way through the threatening crowds, protected by both well-armed police and unarmed Commandos. At the nearby Police Safety Building, local officials conferred with the Wisconsin National Guard about a possible call-up of troops.

Police continued to shove their way through mobs of white spectators at every intersection. At one corner more than one thousand angry whites broke free, swarming over marchers, reporters, and police, beating huddled and fleeing demonstrators, and battling openly with the Commandos who stepped forward to meet them. Bedlam had erupted on the South Side of the 16th Street Viaduct. Riot-clad police moved quickly to quell the disturbance by pumping shotgun blast after shotgun blast into the air above the crowd. Other officers lobbed tear gas into the crowd and then moved in to disperse them. Fr. Groppi and the YC refused to turn back. Singing "Ain't Gonna Let Nobody Turn Me Around," they pressed on to Kosciuszko Park, determined to hold their rally. Once there, however, violence again broke out, and the civil rights demonstrators beat a hasty retreat toward the viaduct. Feeding on the sense of panic, a core of six hundred angry counterdemonstrators pursued and attacked the open housing advocates as they scurried toward safety. Tear gas still hung thick in the air when the marchers finally reached the security of the 16th Street Viaduct. When Fr. Groppi, the YC, and the Commandos finally reached their Freedom House, they found it engulfed in flames. Milwaukee police had fired incendiary tear gas canisters inside the old wooden structure and had then blocked fire trucks from putting out the blaze.

The violence in Milwaukee received national press coverage and drew comparisons to the 1965 "Bloody Sunday" massacre of nonviolent voting rights advocates by state troopers near the Edmund Pettus Bridge in Selma, Alabama. Like Martin Luther King Jr. in 1965, Fr. Groppi put out an ecumenical call for religious and laypeople to come to Milwaukee to bear witness to the turbulent white reaction and march. Hundreds heeded his plea, including Dick Gregory and Jesse Jackson. Martin Luther King wired his support. For nearly a year afterward, Milwaukee became a central site of the national effort to achieve open housing legislation. Thousands of civil rights advocates from across the country and all over Milwaukee rallied, marched, protested, boycotted, and battled with hostile whites in a campaign that stretched for more than two hundred consecutive nights. "Closed housing" groups organized in opposition to the campaign, and a number of far-right associations like the John Birch Society, the American Nazi Party, and the Ku Klux Klan also joined the fray.

Fr. Groppi was the lightning rod through which much of the raw emotion on both sides of the open housing issue flowed. Public attention often fixed on his leadership role. Because he was a Catholic priest, Fr. Groppi commanded attention. Whereas a black leader may have been dismissed out of hand, a white Catholic priest—a traditionally privileged position of respect and obedience within the Church—could not as easily be ignored. Many white Catholics had trouble understanding how "one of them" could betray both his race and religion for the civil rights of black people. Conversely, for liberal Catholics, Fr. Groppi represented the fulfillment of Christ's work and a more activist stance by the church combating urban inequality. There were few who did not hold a strong opinion about the priest from Bay View. Groppi's presence brought divisive issues to the forefront of public debate and flushed white hostility to racial equality into the spotlight. Yet at times Fr. Groppi's central role in the movement and the disproportionate amount of media attention it brought him overshadowed the primary issue of racial inequality.

It was out of this cacophony of struggle and strife that the Milwaukee contingent traveled to Washington, D.C., in late September 1967, to attend the "Conference on the Churches and Urban Tension." Groppi and the five young Commandos felt secure in their strategy and tactics, which had been ground out of local circumstances. Despite criticism from the leaders of Pride, Inc., Groppi and the Commandos felt that they *were* Black Power advocates. Born out of official intransigence and violent white opposition, their version of Black Power emanated from the ethnic, racial, and class relations in Milwaukee.

In large measure, the Milwaukee vision of Black Power was a rhetorical style and political posture, but it did have solid feet. To Fr. Groppi, the YC, and Commandos, Black Power was linked more to consciousness than to skin color. It embraced militant confrontation with entrenched local power structures. Cultivating indigenous African American leadership, particularly among young, black men, and projecting a masculinist verbosity and toughness of style, it included building African American institutions and encompassed race pride, self-determination, and "not-violence." But it also meant a pragmatic, interracial approach to coalition politics in a city where angry white working-class residents far outnumbered African Americans and their allies. It allowed space for sympathetic whites and religious people to participate in their movement and acknowledged that a more public display of armed self-defense might court slaughter. Practical experience had taught Milwaukee's civil rights leaders that their best chance for success lay in this mix of approaches.

But even in Milwaukee the Black Power impulse was not monolithic. During the late 1960s a small Black Panther Party branch appeared in Milwaukee but was unable to sink deep or lasting roots.[44] The two African American newspapers in the city took a decided turn toward cultural nationalism and came to level criticisms against Fr. Groppi's leadership in the movement similar to those that had been voiced in the nation's capital. The Commandos ultimately split into two factions, one that continued to advocate a militant "not-violent" approach to social change and another that embraced a community-organizing model linked to federal funding and institutional relationships. In the end, Fr. Groppi parted ways with the NAACP Youth Council and Commandos, convinced that the time had come for the group to function on its own, outside the intense media glare that his unusual presence invariably attracted. Following the open housing campaign, the era of direct action in Milwaukee declined.

Yet for more than three years a white Italian-American priest and a group of young, inner-core African Americans led a militant movement for racial justice in Milwaukee, a movement they understood to be informed by Black Power. During the spring of 1968, in the wake of Martin Luther King's assassination, the Common Council finally relented and passed a citywide open housing ordinance. Federal legislation that same year also contained a strong fair housing component, no doubt a reaction to the turmoil in cities like Milwaukee. Milwaukee would remain one of the most segregated cities in the United States, but white citizens and local officials could no longer ignore the experiences, hopes, and aspirations of the black community.

Conclusion

The story of Fr. James Groppi, the NAACP Youth Council, and the Commandos suggests the need for a closer, more nuanced examination of local Black Power politics and a greater appreciation for the way that local people took the raw materials of this more militant approach to civil rights and applied them to their own circumstances. Such a view of Black Power suggests that it may be much more variegated, contested, and localized than we have assumed in the past. The leading role of Fr. Groppi as a Black Power advocate and spokesman challenged the growing racial separatism engulfing the movement in other cities. In addition, the Commandos' persistent embrace of interracial cooperation and "not-violence" set them apart from many other local Black Power organizations. In these and other ways the YC and the Commandos refashioned the national slogans and trends of the Black Power movement to the unique dynamics of Milwaukee's social relations in order to make it relevant to their lives. If we view Milwaukee through this lens, then a white Catholic priest heading up a Black Power movement might, in fact, make sense.

But despite the national attention the "Selma of the North" generated between 1965 and 1968, the story has largely fallen from public memory. Unlike the 1965 campaign for voting rights in Selma, Alabama, the campaigns of the YC and the Commandos against segregated urban education, the Eagles Club's exclusionary membership policy, police brutality, and unfair housing practices offered no clear moral divisions, nor did they hold forth a tidy redemptive narrative of American institutions overcoming an obvious injustice. Competing ideas of private property, free association, individual rights, and the American dream collided with an insurgent racial militance, resulting in a series of explosive clashes. Race relations, civil rights insurgency, and Black Power were, in many ways, considerably more murky in the urban North than in the Jim Crow South. And because many of these issues persist, the story of the civil rights movement in places like Milwaukee requires a reckoning with contemporary racial issues that historians and the public have been reluctant to entertain. To be sure, we are still early in the process of excavating important movement stories outside the South. Perhaps with time this imbalance will change and the Northern movement will take its place alongside the more well-known stories of the South.

NOTES

1. In addition to Groppi, the delegation included five Commandos—Richard Green, Lawrence Friend, Jerry Sims, Raymond Blathers, and Charles Harper—as well as Fr. Patrick Flood of the Council on Urban Affairs and Rev. David Owen of the Milwaukee Methodist Church.

2. *Milwaukee Journal,* October 1, 1967, 12.

3. *Concern,* October 15, 1967, 8; *Milwaukee Journal,* September 29, 1967, 1; *Milwaukee Journal,* October 1, 1967, 1.

4. Ibid.

5. *Concern,* October 15, 1967, 9.

6. Ibid., 10.

7. Ibid.; *Milwaukee Journal,* October 1, 1967, part 2, 1; *Catholic Herald Citizen,* October 7, 1967, 5; *Milwaukee Journal,* October 9, 1967, pt. 2, 1.

8. In its broadest sense, the Black Power movement strove to express a new African American consciousness. To some, it represented race dignity and self-reliance. Others thought of Black Power mainly in economic terms. Black Power encouraged the improvement of African American communities, rather than working for integration. It also looked to black cultural heritage and history for the roots of African American identity. To cultural nationalists, Black Power related primarily to the arts and cultural expression. Furthermore, most Black Power advocates felt a necessity for black people to define the world for themselves, in their own terms, free from white control or domination. For some, this took the form of a political struggle against racism and imperialism, and a more confrontational, demanding style. Many Black Power militants increasingly identified with pan-African struggles for liberation around the world. With this political evolution came a growing repudiation of nonviolent direct action and an embrace of armed self-defense, or even offensive violence, as a "revolutionary tool."

9. In particular, the story of Robert F. Williams, president of the Monroe, North Carolina, branch of the NAACP in the 1950s has made us reconsider the origins of the Black Power movement. See Timothy B. Tyson, *Radio Free Dixie: Robert F. Williams and the Roots of Black Power* (Chapel Hill: University of North Carolina Press, 2001); Robert F. Williams, *Negroes with Guns* (Detroit: Wayne State University Press, 1998).

10. See "Father Groppi," typescript of the first chapter of an autobiographical sketch, n.d. but ca. 1971, Groppi Papers, State Historical Society of Wisconsin (SHSW), Madison, Wisconsin, box 14, folder 7, 7–8 (hereafter, "Groppi Autobiography"). See also James Groppi interview with Frank Aukofer, October 13, 1967, in Aukofer Papers, SHSW.

11. Frank Aukofer, *City with a Chance* (Milwaukee: Bruce Publishing, 1968), 89–90.

12. Fr. Patrick Flood interview with Patrick Jones, March 13, 2000.

13. "Groppi Autobiography," 14–15.

14. Squire Austin interview with Patrick Jones, October 7, 1999.

15. Flood interview.

16. Fr. Mathew Gottschaulk interview with Patrick Jones, April 15, 1999.

17. Flood interview.

18. "Groppi Autobiography," 19–20. On February 15, 1984, one year before Groppi's death, there was a slide show presentation and Youth Council/Commandos reunion at East Library in Milwaukee, Wisconsin. The reference to Harwell's trip came from this source. Hereafter, I refer to this transcript as "Groppi Lecture at East Library." It appears that Fr. Groppi may have taken other trips South as well. Later in the East Library lecture, Groppi alluded to a trip South with Youth Council member DeWayne Tolliver, but no details were provided. It is unclear whether this was the same trip in which Harwell participated or a separate journey.

19. "Groppi Lecture at East Library," February 15, 1984.

20. *Milwaukee Journal,* April 4, 1965, 2.

21. Special Committee on Equality of Educational Opportunity Minutes, December 10, 1963, Lorraine Radtke Papers, State Historical Society of Wisconsin; Lloyd Barbee interview with Patrick Jones, January 30, 1999; *Milwaukee Journal,* December 11, 1963, 31.

22. See Milwaukee United School Integration Papers, SHSW, Madison, Wisconsin. See also Lloyd Barbee Papers, SHSW, Madison, Wisconsin.

23. Tom Jacobson interview with Patrick Jones, November 1, 1999; John Givens interview with Patrick Jones, November 17, 1999; *Milwaukee Sentinel,* March 26, 1963, 8; *Milwaukee Journal,* March 26, 1963, 14; "Why We Demonstrate," Milwaukee NAACP Youth Council flyer, ca. March 1963, Milwaukee NAACP Papers, SHSW, Madison, Wisconsin; *Milwaukee Sentinel,* March 28, 1963, part 2, 1; *Milwaukee Journal,* March 28, 1963, part 2, 2; *Milwaukee Star,* April 6, 1963, 2.

24. For more than a decade Lloyd Barbee spearheaded a legal fight to integrate the Milwaukee Public Schools. In 1976 a federal court judge ruled that Milwaukee public schools were indeed segregated. Two years later the court ruled that the segregation was the result of intentional policies by the school board, not simply housing patterns, and ordered the two sides to come up with a remedy. Barbee and Milwaukee school officials agreed to a broad-based desegregation plan, including limited busing. For a full documentary overview of the school desegregation case, see the Barbee Papers. Also see Jack Dougherty, "More Than One Struggle: African-American School Reform Movements in Milwaukee, 1930–1980" (Ph.D. dissertation, University of Wisconsin–Madison, August 1997); and William Dahlk, "The Black Educational Reform Movement in Milwaukee, 1963–1975" (M.A. thesis, University of Wisconsin–Milwaukee, 1990).

25. *Milwaukee Eagle,* March 19, 1966, 1; see also *Milwaukee Journal,* March 16, 1966, part 2, 1.

26. *Milwaukee Journal,* August 9, 1966, 1, 10.

27. *Milwaukee Journal,* August 10, 1966, 1; August 11, 1966, part 2, 2.

28. *Time* magazine, September 9, 1966, 23–24.

29. *Milwaukee Journal,* August 25, 1966, part 2, 10; Aukofer, *City with a Chance,* 101.

30. *Milwaukee Journal,* October 6, 1966, part 2, 1; *Milwaukee Courier,* October 8, 1966, 1.

31. Militant self-defense groups also existed in Bogalusa, Louisiana; Oakland, California; Tampa Bay, Florida; Dayton, Ohio; New England; and Long Island. In Bogalusa and Oakland these groups carried weapons and often shot it out with the KKK or local police. In the other cities these groups did not carry weapons but rather sought to defend civil rights activists from hostile crowds and violent police. *Milwaukee Journal,* October 6, 1966, part 2, 1; June 16, 1967, 4; June 17, 1967, 8.

32. "Groppi Lecture at East Library," February 15, 1984. In fact, Betty Martin was

the only official female Commando. During the open housing campaign, the Commandos also elected Vel Phillips an "honorary Commando" as a symbolic link between their direct action campaign and her work in the Common Council. By and large, though, the group was exclusively male.

33. Ed Thekan interview with Arlene Zakhar, ca. 1984. In author's possession.

34. Joe McClaine interview with Patrick Jones, March 29, 1999.

35. Jacobson interview.

36. "Groppi in Black for Yule Mass," *National Catholic Reporter,* January 3, 1967, 7; Karen Kelly, "The Scene—Milwaukee," *Community,* October 1967, 3; Aukofer, *City with a Chance,* 83–84.

37. In part, this peculiarity comes from the fact that we have yet to explore the Christian roots of Black Power, even though there are a number. For example, see Angela Dillard, "Religion and Radicalism: The Reverend Albert B. Cleage, Jr., and the Rise of Black Christian Nationalism in Detroit," in Jeanne Theoharis and Komozi Woodard, eds., *Freedom North: Black Freedom Struggles outside the South, 1940–1980* (New York: Palgrave Macmillan 2003).

38. Prentice McKinney interview with Patrick Jones, January 11, 1999.

39. *Milwaukee Journal,* May 8, 1967, part 2, 1.

40. Ibid., June 22, 1967, part 2, 1.

41. Ibid., July 26, 1967, part 2, 1; *Milwaukee Courier,* July 29, 1967, 1; *Milwaukee Star,* July 29, 1967, 1.

42. Henry Maier, *The Mayor Who Made Milwaukee Famous* (Lanham, Md.: Madison Books, 1993), 8; see also Karl Flaming, "The 1967 Milwaukee Riot: A Historical and Comparative Analysis" (Ph.D. dissertation, Syracuse University, 1970); and idem, *Who Riots and Why? Black and White Perspectives in Milwaukee* (Milwaukee: Milwaukee Urban League, 1968).

43. The following narrative of open housing activism relies on various news accounts and personal interviews with participants. See *Milwaukee Journal,* August 30, 1967, 1; *Milwaukee Sentinel,* August 30, 1967, 1; *Milwaukee Star,* September 2, 1967, 1; and *Milwaukee Courier,* September 2, 1967, 1. In addition, see Betty Martin interview with Arlene Zakhar, January 20, 1984; Vel Phillips interviews with Patrick Jones, December 3, 1999, and April 20, 1999; Joe McClaine interviews with Patrick Jones, December 3, 1989, and March 29, 1999; Prentice McKinney interviews with Patrick Jones, January 11, 1999, and March 27, 1999.

44. Andrew Witt, "Self-Help and Self-Defense: A Reevaluation of the Black Panther Party with Emphasis on the Milwaukee Chapter" (M.A. thesis, University of Wisconsin–Milwaukee, 1999).

Chapter 12

Practical Internationalists

The Story of the Des Moines, Iowa, Black Panther Party

Reynaldo Anderson

Yeah my mother sent me to stay out of trouble, but while I was out there I met a guy named Bunchy Carter in Los Angeles that summer. Bunchy Carter was a leader of the Los Angeles chapter of the Black Panther Party and was attempting to transform the five thousand member Slauson gang into a revolutionary force.

—Mary Rem, founder of the
Des Moines Black Panther Party,
July 10, 2002 (personal communication)

The newspaper has always targeted me as the chairperson and I was never the chairperson, in fact, I was the organizer. For example, when the party started in Des Moines, it was a sister . . . Mary Rem, her name is Hadishar now. She was the one who actually started the thing and I joined. She had been to California and she talked with people. She actually was around recruiting and fighting against police brutality. I had been a VISTA volunteer and we met up on the street passing out leaflets. And that's how I joined the party.

—Charles Knox, Deputy of Education
of the Des Moines Black Panther Party,
August 21, 2000 (personal communication)

Leaving Des Moines, Iowa, in 1967 just after her high school graduation, Mary Rem headed for Oakland, California, and the headquarters of the fledgling Black Panther Party (BPP) for Self-Defense founded by Bobby Seale and Huey P. Newton in October 1966. While in California visiting relatives, Mary Rem ignored her mother's advice about "staying out of trouble" and began her life as a black revolutionary. She gained some political training in the Black Panther Party and was very much inspired by the example of another organizer, the legendary Los Angeles gang leader turned revolutionary Bunchy Carter. Mary Rem was searching for answers to the deepening urban problems she had experienced in her hometown in the Midwest. Looking at the Los Angeles model of organizing where Bunchy Carter had demonstrated his extraordinary aptitude for explaining political matters to ordinary people, Mary Rem observed his success at radicalizing thousands of youthful members of the infamous Slauson Street gang through community programs and political education.

Rem began to think about taking those organizing lessons back to Iowa and founding a Black Panther Party in Des Moines. Although Des Moines did not have a major ghetto like Los Angeles, the heartland city had serious urban problems such as racial unrest, segregated education, and police brutality. Armed with that political training, the young Mary Rem returned to her hometown and began the work of door-to-door canvassing in her community in order to organize and politicize young people around several burning issues, including police brutality. Rem yearned for a new kind of organization in the Midwest that would organize for political change and mobilize against the oppressive conditions in the black community. While going door to door in Des Moines to solicit support, she met Charles Knox, who was working in VISTA (an anti-poverty program).[1] That meeting of Mary Rem and Charles Knox was the genesis of the Des Moines BPP in the heartland. By 1968 Rem would legally incorporate a Black Panther branch in Des Moines that was prepared to defend the black community against violent attacks whether by local police or by the paramilitary Minute Men, a right-wing terrorist group that would ultimately bomb the Panther headquarters.

In terms of the published history of the Black Panther Party, this story from the heartland is distinct and largely overlooked. For one thing, hurdling over the formidable gender barriers in a male-dominated arena of Black Power politics that excluded many women from political leadership and that marred their equal participation, Mary Rem became one of the very few women ever to initiate a chapter of the Black Panther Party.[2] Gender barriers in the Black Freedom movement had created difficulties for women leaders in the North, but in the tradition of Southerners Ella Baker and Gloria Richardson, Northern women such as Mary Rem forged their own liberation.[3] Second, while a growing body of scholarship exists on the Panther leaders in major urban centers such as the Los Angeles and the Bay Area of California, very little is known about how the Black Panthers developed in America's heartland: Kansas, Nebraska, and Iowa.[4]

In Iowa the Des Moines Panthers worked alongside Panther activists in Kansas City and Omaha, Nebraska; in fact, those three chapters worked together so closely that they even rotated members in order to develop Black Panther politics and programs. This chapter seeks to situate the local activities of the Des Moines chapter of the Black Panther Party in a context that connects them to the larger struggle for freedom of Africans and African Americans taking place globally. It reveals that the Black Panther Party was not only national but local, taking on the issues and character of the members in each city. It also suggests that the heartland branches of the Black Panther Party had ideas of their own about women's oppression and women's liberation, about sexual liberation, about issues of drug and alcohol abuse, and about international affairs.

The rise and fall of the Black Panther Party in Des Moines occurred roughly between June 1968 and January 1971. The Iowa chapter emerged during a period of phenomenal growth of the BPP that some scholars have defined as the Black Panther Party's "Revolutionary Nationalist" phase; however, many of the political and ideological conflicts between the Des Moines branch and the national headquarters developed after that early phase as the national party changed its political line to intercommunalism, a fragmentary philosophy espoused by Huey Newton toward the end of his incarceration and subsequent release from prison.

The Des Moines Black Panther Party developed when young activists in the black community decided to organize in response to burning urban issues: unequal educational, school busing, urban renewal, unemployment, and police brutality. The problems of African Americans in Des Moines were longstanding. According to one historian, Victor Cools, traditionally whites and blacks lived in separate worlds in Des Moines. There were three major waves of African American migration to Iowa. First, during World War I the U.S. coal industry imported blacks from several Southern states to break labor strikes in Iowa. Following the war and the Great Migration, African Americans were discriminated against in public accommodations such as restaurants, hotels, and theaters and were profoundly segregated, in one instance creating a nearly all-black town called Buxton.[5] A second major migration of African Americans to Iowa took place during the war boom of World War II. Third, the postwar black migration between 1950 and 1960 was by far the largest movement. By the mid-1960s rising discontent over segregation and black urban problems prepared the soil for the birth of the Black Panther Party in Des Moines. Ninety-three percent of the African American population was concentrated in two precincts.[6] Educationally African American students had lower test scores and graduated at lower rates than white students. In addition to educational problems black residents were concerned about such issues as urban renewal, school busing, unemployment, and police brutality.

Urban renewal became a burning issue when the federal government financed two slum clearance and construction projects in a Des Moines "model cities" area. Those projects threatened black neighborhoods with widespread displacement including areas that were designated for clearance to make way for the construction of a freeway through the inner city. One resident, BPP member Clive De Patton, recalls:

> The Blacks; they used to occupy on the west side an area called Center Street. . . . It was very close to downtown so they brought in urban renewal. The people were paying taxes for $5,000 or $6,000. Urban renewal came by and said, "We will give you $4,500 for it." For the people this was more money than they had ever had and they said OK, but when the [officials] came and paid the people, the people got $2,500 or $3,000, you know. That was to get the Black people away from downtown. Then to get them further away from downtown they came in with the freeway.

Center Street, the so-called black section of town, was directly impacted by the plan. Center Street was the cultural and small business center of black life in Des Moines until it was eliminated through the "Model Cities" plan.[7]

Rallying young people around such burning issues as urban renewal, a relatively small black population of Des Moines, about twenty thousand, built a BPP chapter with a large membership of about one hundred at its peak.[8] Despite its relatively large number of cadre, according to Rem, it was more difficult for the police and the FBI to infiltrate the Des Moines BPP because, in such a small community, everyone knew one another.[9] The rank-and-file membership was especially young, with many of its cadre under the age of twenty. Not only were the Des Moines recruits young, but most of them were drawn from the ranks of recent high school graduates, students, working-class, and impoverished African Americans.[10] However, other members like Clive DePatton were children of the black middle class in Des Moines. DePatton's father, Hobart, owned several small businesses in the Center Street and University Street area until the property was confiscated through eminent domain by the city of Des Moines.[11] Finally, the average educational level of the membership was rather limited. Although the founder, Mary Rem, had finished high school, and the Deputy of Education, Charles Knox, had attended college, many of the rank-and-file activists were high school dropouts.[12]

The Des Moines chapter required that its members either work or attend school in order to learn the needs of the people and understand where they lived and worked. In the minds of the Iowa leadership, since members had to get up early in the morning to participate in programs for the community, the work or school requirement attracted only the most dedicated individuals to the Des Moines BPP. According to Andre Rawls, Kansas City chapter member, the Black Panther Party was neither "a social organization" nor "a political organization in the sense of American . . . politics"; rather, it was a way of life:

> You would have us getting up at 5:00 in the morning to get the kids fed then give them whatever job, whatever school task we had, come back in the evening, go out into the community, politicize, sell newspapers, do political education classes, and end our day at about midnight. It was a way of living. It is very difficult sometimes to get people to understand that the Black Panther Party was not a social organization, nor was it a political organization in the sense of American electoral politics. But it was a military revolutionary organization that you actually lived in.[13]

Since the majority of the members were young people, the discontent of black students was an important part of the chapter's agenda. The quality of education that blacks received in the Des Moines public school system was poor. Eventually black students—led by Edward Smith, president of the Black Committee for Student Power, and following the BPP directives—presented sixteen wide-ranging demands to the school board.[14] According to the *Des Moines Register*, these demands included the following: (1) Have black teachers teach African–African American history; (2) instruct students about the true fighting history of minorities and poor whites; (3) establish community control boards; (4) hire more black teachers; (5) refer to students as African American or black rather than Negro; 6) involve students in the decision-making process; (7) include minorities on Student Councils; (8) reevaluate the Department of Pupil Services; (9) eliminate the Tracking System; (10) inform all students of available scholarships regardless of academic standing; (11) remove racist teachers; (12) overhaul teacher in-service training; (13) provide greater academic freedom; (14) give teachers a decision-making role in education; (15) allow students with voting power to be on the school board; and (16) do not release information about students without their consent.[15]

According to Knox, "Some of those young people went to jail for staging that kind of sit-in. But, it was worth it because in the end you got the teachers with a union. And the teachers in Des Moines should be thanking those students right now."[16] The black students were supported by a handful of white students. For example, a white student, Robert Wallace, said, "many White students back their Black brothers and sisters 100 percent." However, the increased militancy of the black students attracted a backlash in certain sections of Des Moines's white community. According to the *Des Moines Register,* when the segregationist governor of Alabama, George Wallace, visited the Midwest in October 1968, on his campaign for the presidency, enthusiastic, large white crowds greeted his arrival.[17]

Charles Knox proved instrumental in helping the Panthers mobilize resources. In line with that, the Des Moines branch secured the use of a house in the local community that was owned by the Catholic Church with the promise to use the facility to help the local black population. Charles Knox explains how he challenged and persuaded the BPP chapter to consider this offer:

That's when I posed the question to them: "If they were serious about organizing, if you are serious lets go get this house from these Catholics." That's how we started. And when we got the house it was amazing because they didn't think it was going to happen. I did the pre-negotiation for the house. You know, telling the people if they were serious they would let the young folks come on in and let us take it and run it.

Once he secured an office for the chapter, Knox focused on political education for the membership. Cadres were instructed in the BPP's theoretical terminology but were also instructed on how to adapt theory to the practical everyday reality for midwestern blacks. All members were required to view the Panther film "Off the Pig" as a primer on how the Party was founded in Oakland in 1966.[18] According to Mary Rem, the main reason that the Heartland chapters had to tailor BPP programs a little differently from other Panther chapters, such as the one in Chicago, was because the Panthers did not have a large black population to draw on in those regions of the country.[19]

But the differences in Des Moines were not restricted to demographics; there were differences in political style as well. Cadres wanted to know how general political ideas related to their particular situations in the heartland. Knox explained:

> The mid-west was down with the Political Education to the extent that it was very practical. How did it really work for us? So that was a big difference from just reading a line and saying that this works. When we start talking about the raising of consciousness we ask well, what is this? And how do we do it? So again, we were raising those kinds of questions. That was in a sense unique to the mid-west. Because when we went to other places our people weren't doing that. That was a practical thing so that we would not have mistaken ideas, as Mao talks about. How do you correct mistaken ideas? Criticism and self-criticism.[20]

The Des Moines BPP attempted to pursue the goals of the Black Revolution in several ways by including national programs, political education, regional cooperation, local solidarity, and national solidarity. For example it adopted the revolutionary nationalist philosophy of the central committee headquartered in Oakland, California, but its political education classes focused on literacy and the concept of freedom with cadres and community people, which were issues of particular concern to the black community of Des Moines. Many of the rank-and-file cadres were functionally illiterate and had to be taught how to read in order to understand and promulgate the party line. Knox described the situation:

> You have to remember that the folks that came to the party, many of them couldn't even read. This is very important. They couldn't even read. They couldn't distinguish letters. The political education classes taught them to read. We would take the Red Book and ask brothers to read a paragraph out of the book. Dictionary and Thesaurus next to us, and we read and we read and we learned to read. And we learned analysis.[21]

Part of what the Panther Party did was to make reading relevant and accessible. Knox continued, "That was so great to see. Young people who couldn't read, all of a sudden learning to read. They didn't read because they didn't have a reason to read. Now they have a reason to read. What is the reason? The reason is our freedom. The reason is our liberation. The reason is for your mother, for the family, for us."[22]

In addition to its political education program for fighting illiteracy, the Des Moines BPP adopted key national programs but tailored them to local needs: a Drug/Alcohol Program and a Free Breakfast Program. The Drug and Alcohol Program emerged out of the insistence that cadres not consume alcohol while conducting Panther business, for an intoxicated Panther could not be effective and function for the people, and the assertion that alcohol caused the body to deteriorate. Knox explained how the heartland handled those issues as a regional organization:

What happened out of that was a series of lectures on alcoholism grows out of this . . . need to talk about treating people who did have the problem and launched us into, say, Des Moines bringing people, taking people, to Kansas City to get treatment for drugs, for drug addiction—*right*—because Des Moines did not have a center. Or Kansas City when the person can't go there, go into Des Moines if Des Moines had something or Omaha. So you see we moved into those areas because of necessity.[23]

The Des Moines BPP also successfully developed a Free Breakfast Program which was not a simple task, given that many of the city's African American leaders did not like to discuss the level of hunger in the black community:

Because they were going to school inadequately nourished and cold . . . we were at the bottom of the system and we understood the problems better than anyone else. And how did we address them? We went ahead and established a breakfast program and didn't have any money. So look at how it works, if we can establish a breakfast program with no money—by donation and the system has all of the money with taxes, why don't they have a national free breakfast program for children? Which happened after the party established a free breakfast program for the children.[24]

Seventy-five to one hundred elementary and junior high school children of different races and backgrounds were fed by the Free Breakfast

Program in Des Moines.[25] The Free Breakfast Program was supported by other churches including white denominations. According to Reverend Robert Kanagy, pastor of the (predominantly white) Forest Avenue Baptist Church:

> We feel it's worthwhile or we wouldn't be involved in it. It serves a need that is real. I would hope that next year it might be done by the schools, where it ought to be.[26]

By means of the Free Breakfast Program and the student demands, the Des Moines Panthers linked the concerns of African Americans with poor whites.

The Des Moines BPP strengthened its ties to the local community by demonstrating that it practiced what it preached. By establishing common interests with ordinary people, the party criticized social programs that exploited people. For example, the Des Moines BPP worked with the National Welfare Rights Organization to address the concerns of poor women who were receiving a government check but had unresolved problems related to poverty and racism.[27] According to Knox and Andre Rawls, the Heartland chapters articulated issues that the traditional organizations either would not or could not address. The Des Moines BPP criticized the welfare system for breaking up black families and discouraging family formation:

> like the system was oppressing . . . to the extent that they were taking children from mothers for example, the welfare system. The welfare system was not adequately addressing problems of the mothers and not giving what they need and not only to exist but to really function as a family.

The Des Moines chapter was able to take such a bold stance because it did not share the worry traditional groups had of losing their funding.[28] According to Knox, the BPP's financial independence also made it threatening in the eyes of certain people because there was no reliance on government or state aid. Knox noted:

> So this is what we raised that other people were afraid to raise, that your organizations were afraid to raise because they would lose their money. But since we were not funded by anybody (laughter) we had no accountability to anybody but the people. This is why the masses of people had gravitated

towards us. While the system saw a need to try to move to destroy us try to infiltrate us and destroy us, because it would rise to a popular movement because to the kinds of problems that we were addressing.[29]

While Des Moines was making headway in its local organizing, a growing crisis emerged in its relationship to the regional and national centers of authority in the Black Panther Party. There was a brief attempt to coordinate regional activities with the Chicago chapter of the BPP, led by Fred Hampton. The Chicago chapter was the authority for the entire Midwest region by virtue of the city's strategic location and the size of the chapter.[30] The problem, Knox believed, between the heartland chapters and the Chicago leadership seemed to stem from the perception that Fred Hampton and the leadership were more concerned about the relationship with the national committee in Oakland than about the connection to the heartland. The former communications secretary for the Kansas City chapter, Andre Weatherby, recalls traveling extensively between the heartland chapters and attempting to maintain a cordial relationship with the Chicago chapter and Hampton, while attending the Chicago Seven trial and observing the prosecution of Panther leader Bobby Seale:

> I was on the west side at Madison and spent two nights there, three weeks before Freddy had got killed in that apartment. Fred wanted us to relate more. Cause he had heard about Des Moines and Kansas City. He sort of reached out to us. And we were supposed to be trying to coordinate something and he was killed after you know, after we had talked somewhat about doing something.[31]

The significance of the Hampton assassination was that soon thereafter communication problems between the national headquarters and heartland chapters began to deteriorate. Previously Hampton had mediated some of the concerns of the heartland chapters with the central committee. However, following Hampton's death an important link to the region was eliminated. The Des Moines chapter of the BPP developed friction with the national BPP because of the national committee's directive that the Des Moines chapter needed to sell more copies of the Panther paper and to increase the circulation. Moreover, the Des Moines BPP chapter and other heartland chapters felt that the national committee was insensitive to the concerns of their region and was not putting revolutionary theory into practice. Knox recalls,

Distribution had become such a financial crutch. They [the national committee] were pushing paper distribution over any other works for the party. And that was part of the issue that all of the separation turned on. If you were going to call yourself a member of the National Black Panther Party then you were going to have to sell papers. It was a quota kind of thing. I remember that, and that is why [Sam] Napier [representing national headquarters on newspaper sales] came to the mid-west and because we had cut distribution down and he was having a problem with that.[32]

For the Des Moines chapter, the national Panther paper was an educational tool for the local population, and the local leadership insisted on thoroughly familiarizing Des Moines cadre members with the information in the paper during education classes, which would not only educate the rank and file but would enable members to become more effective organizers based on revolutionary theoretical principles. For example, the more education the cadres received, the more effectively they could persuade people in the black community about the soundness of the party line. According to Knox, it was that thorough examination of the paper that led to disagreements:

We studied the paper. We didn't just distribute it. And that was the point of being in classes all day. We weren't just trying to sell a paper we felt that if we were going to be serious about this then we need to make sure we studied the articles and had an understanding of what the paper was about. And that created a big risk as it related to [the] national office.[33]

The tension with the central committee emerged from the reality that David Hilliard was in charge of the BPP during Huey Newton's incarceration and Bobby Seale's legal problems. The party was having problems raising money in 1969, was increasingly dependent on newspaper distribution, and was immersed in an ideological conflict over the requirement to read and teach Eldridge Cleaver's book *Soul on Ice.*

These internal and external tensions were also occurring at a time when the national organization was under increasing government repression and ideological flux. Some larger issues emerged when the Iowa Panthers examined the political content of the newspaper. For one thing, the issue of drugs sparked a debate; for another, there was the issue of "revolutionary rape."

The heartland chapters of the BPP were more culturally conservative than their Bay Area counterparts. The rift or ideological difference with the national BPP emerged out of a set of circumstances that included issues of drugs, ideological differences, and a breakdown in communication. Given their work in drug and alcohol intervention, the Heartland members were disturbed by reports of drug use in moderation from the national leadership.[34] Andre Rawls recalls,

> The brothers on the West Coast were doing drugs. I remember when Pete O'Neal (deputy chairman of Kansas City) went out there we had serious no drug, no alcohol policies and Pete came back and said . . . in Moderation. And that to me was a part of the downfall when people started making exceptions and started augmenting the theory.[35]

There was also concern that theory was being bastardized and that concepts were being introduced that were not applicable to the reality of the Des Moines social milieu. By the fall of 1970 the central committee, under Huey Newton's influence, was moving away from revolutionary nationalism and adapting Marxism to accommodate changing global conditions of capitalism, and the belief that national borders were increasingly unimportant.[36] Also, the required reading of Eldridge Cleaver's book *Soul on Ice* caused tension with the Heartland leadership (Rawls). The book was supposed to be a guide for the psychological transformation of black men into revolutionaries and for the revolutionary potential of the black community. However, for the Des Moines chapter the controversy over Cleaver's book involved his statement on the necessity of raping a black woman to learn how to deal appropriately with a white woman. Des Moines members pointed out contradictions between this notion and other statements of central committee members that endorsed the idea of women's liberation and equality. After some members of the Des Moines cadre read *Soul on Ice*, the question was raised as to why the book was required reading by the national committee. According to Knox:

> We thought he [Eldridge Cleaver] was brilliant until when people really read *Soul on Ice* then we banned the book. Because we took a position that this guy talking about raping a black woman to practice on, to deal with a white woman, I mean we thought he was a nut then.[37]

The required reading of the book widened the rift between the Des Moines chapter and the national BPP. According to Knox, other members of the Des Moines chapter predicted that Cleaver's psychological behavior as represented in his book would later lead to a division in the BPP and Cleaver's ultimate exit from the party. The reaction of the heartland chapters to *Soul on Ice* represented the cultural conservatism of many of the members. Knox explained:

> The Midwest was almost like very conservative. We were all opposed to fornication. It almost got to that level with us we said wait a minute *you don't do women like this*. We were always up into this, well, *why would you do women like this?* This doesn't make sense to us.[38]

The ultimate demise of the Des Moines BPP resulted from the combined forces of attempted assassination and repression, incarceration, and dissension with the national committee BPP members. The attempted assassination of the Des Moines BPP leadership occurred when the Panther headquarters was bombed on April 27, 1969. The bombing of the Des Moines Panther headquarters was the last in a series of bombings that had taken place in the black community that month, beginning in a power substation, an interracial community program called "Soul Village," and finally the BPP's house.[39] The chapter had faced increasing hostility from the Minutemen, a paramilitary organization that operated in the Midwest similar in style to their Southern manifestation, the Ku Klux Klan. According to Rem, it was not unusual to receive death threats from the Minutemen via local media, particularly the radio. Thus the Des Moines BPP suspected that the police, along with the Minutemen, were part of the bombing assassination attempt because of comments made by officers who arrived on the scene within seconds of the explosion and because of the types of plastic explosives used. Charles Knox recalls:

> Because the police walked in there, and the reason we felt they had something to do with it, and believe it or not, not because we want to talk about the police not none of that. But here are the words that they uttered when they walked into the house, "We know, we know all the niggas up in here are dead," that's how we knew. Otherwise we could speculate, but when that policeman said, uttered those words, I then knew that they were involved with the bombing.[40]

According to the *Des Moines Register*, forty-eight homes in the black community were damaged as a result of the explosion and three other homes were destroyed. Fortunately no one was injured by the blast, although three officers were injured following the explosion in scuffles with Panther members and rock-throwing black youth.[41] The Des Moines Panthers were forced to relocate to another house and establish a new headquarters. The Des Moines chapter of the BPP faced mounting legal problems in order to stay active because of the incarceration of its leader, Mary Rem, and its cadres Archie Simmons, David Colton, and Mike Smith, who were collectively referred to as the Des Moines Four in the national Black Panther paper the week of May 31, 1970. According to the Black Panther paper, the Des Moines Four were incarcerated for allegedly blowing up a police station, and Archie Simmons was held for allegedly blowing up the Panther's own headquarters. The Des Moines imprisonment, along with the incarceration of many members around the country, decimated the ranks of the party. The plight of the Des Moines Four was symptomatic of what was going on in the national organization around the country. By May 1970 the effectiveness of the FBI's COINTELPRO program (a program initiated by the federal government to neutralize and eliminate black activists) and internal dissension within the BPP were decimating the ranks of the party and reducing its effectiveness. Also, the repression of the BPP hampered its ability to raise funds for the legal defense of incarcerated members.

The Des Moines BPP, along with the heartland chapters of Omaha and Kansas, broke away from the national BPP in the fall of 1970 largely over ideological differences but also for not adhering to the rules and regulations of the national party. Knox recalls the split and the chapter's commitment to continue the struggle:

> We decided to leave the Panther Party and just do something else because we felt that they were misguided, that they were not putting theory into practice as it relates to the whole dialectical material and thus we formed the Black Revolutionary Party. That was associated with Marxism and all that kind of stuff. We sort of like elevated ourselves from the, as you say from the party.

After the Des Moines chapter of the BPP left the national organization in the fall of 1970, Knox and other cadre members of the heartland chapters founded the Black Revolutionary Party (BRP) in January of 1971. The

Black Revolutionary Party served as the umbrella organization for several political entities, and it engaged in international politics and programs before it began to dissolve in the summer of 1972.[42]

The BRP guided or influenced several organizations and individuals, including local Black Student Unions (BSUs) at colleges in Omaha, Des Moines, and Kansas City; returning black Vietnam veterans; the Venceremos Brigade (an organization dedicated to supporting the Cuban Revolution); Operation Spearhead (a black tutorial program); the Free Angela Davis Committee; and the Black Methodists for Church Renewal (BMCR) and Rev. Phil Lawson; as well as the Cairo, Illinois, Black United Front, with Rev. Charles Koen.[43] The Des Moines Black Revolutionary Party was also very involved in struggles for international justice. For example, it demonstrated international support for other oppressed minorities when the chapter openly supported the independence of the province of French-speaking Quebec in neighboring Canada. Knox explains the Quebec solidarity work:

> We traveled to Canada to support the Quebecois in their struggle for self-determination and actually made some contact with people there who were interested in our cause, however, we were not able to pursue any serious commitments because of government repression.

The Des Moines BRP successfully contacted the Chinese and North Korean governments to procure political education materials to help promulgate the Black Revolution. Although heartland chapters were relatively isolated and in minor locations in contrast to international cities like Chicago or New York, the Des Moines BRP successfully engaged in international politics with its limited resources. Knox explained:

> We were practical internationalists. We did not believe in this pseudo shadow diplomacy, it was real or nothing. And so the way we dealt with internationalism in carrying out goals. Like, We related to China. For example, I wrote a letter to Chairman Mao. If y'all are serious send us some Red books to Des Moines. Scared Des Moines and the mid-west, scared them to death cause Chairman Mao sent us the books! He sent us thousands of Red books! Before Nixon went to China we were distributing the books. We said we wanted a Red book in every house. If we are serious about this track, let's put one in every house in Des Moines and in Kansas City. So we got the Red books.[44]

Following its success with the importation of Red books from China, the Des Moines chapter of the BRP contacted the North Korean government and procured materials to politically educate the local population in Des Moines. By this time North Korea was considered to be among the international revolutionary vanguard because, although the Chinese leader Mao Tse Tung had established relations with the United States, North Korean leader Kim Il Sung maintained his country's revolutionary stance. However, the Des Moines Black Revolutionary Party also believed in democratically approaching the political education of the local population because community referendums were held to vote on political education materials. Knox recalls the party's reasoning:

> We believe in learning from the people. So we took it and we talked about it, that was how our internationalism worked. We wrote to Kim Il Sung, in Korea, and got his books, *all right?* And distributed his books to see exactly whether or not any of this could be applicable to us. Because let me tell you, if it was not applicable we didn't care what it said. We didn't, it had no bearing. It was real for us. Because it had no meaning if we could not use it. You know, there are some things in there that we couldn't use and some things were [becoming] very impractical for us so it didn't make sense for us to use that. So we tried to use what we could in terms of the internationalism and we talked about Canada.[45]

The fragmentation of the BRP began in the fall of 1972 when cadre members attempted to redefine their political direction. The ideological position of the members split into three general directions: Pan Africanism, Maoism, and Marxist Leninism.[46] Charles Knox was unable to persuade the cadres of the BRP to organize under a single ideology.[47] The Kansas City faction of the BRP developed the Amilcar Cabral Political Study Group (a Black Anti-imperialist Collective) that supported several causes to include the African Liberation Support Committee, the Chilean Solidarity Committee, the Leavenworth Brothers Defense Committee, the Anti-imperialist Film Group, and the Boycott Gulf Oil Campaign. The Des Moines faction of the BRP was later influential in the development of a black radio station and later founded the Fred Hampton Community Law School in Chicago, Illinois.

In conclusion, the story of the Des Moines Black Panther Party represents the Black Revolution from a distinctly local perspective and conclusively demonstrates that the Black Panther Party was far from one monolithic entity. Instead, the Des Moines BPP was an example of how ideas were related on a local level by revolutionaries committed to their constituents. Also, this BPP chapter illustrates how fluid social change was during this period in the black liberation struggle and that there was a high degree of intellectual sophistication among cadres of the BPP that worked outside the major cities. Finally, this story of the Des Moines BPP assists in putting to rest the idea that, by the time of Huey Newton's release from prison, the BPP was no longer a unified entity from coast to coast.

NOTES

1. Mary Rem, personal communication, July 10, 2002.

2. Another major exception to that exclusively male narrative is Erika Huggins who started the New Haven chapter, and there was perhaps another woman leader in another New England branch.

3. A major barrier for women inside the Black Panther Party was the cultural nationalist belief that women needed to adopt a "complementary" role to black male leadership. Another challenge was that Black Panther women wanted to distinguish themselves, and remain autonomous, from the Women's Liberation movement. As far as they were concerned, the Women's Liberation movement that emerged out of activities with the Southern civil rights movement was primarily focused on the goals and interests of white middle-class women, and many Panther women believed that black women had distinctly different relationship dynamics with black men and thus a socialist revolution would be necessary to free black women and the entire community. See Tracye Matthews, "No One Ever Asks, What a Man's Role in the Revolution Is": Gender and the Politics of the Black Panther Party (1966–71)," in *The Black Panther Party (Reconsidered)*, ed. Charles Jones (Baltimore, Md.: Black Classic Press, 1998), 267–304.

4. See, for example, Jones, *Black Panther Party (Reconsidered)*; and Kathleen Cleaver, ed., *Liberation, Imagination, and the Black Panther Party* (New York: Routledge, 2001). The political life of local branches was also a major topic at the June 2003 Black Panther History Conference at Wheelock College organized by professors Jama Lazerow and Yohuru Williams.

5. James L. Hill, "Migration of Blacks to Iowa ,1820–1960," *Journal of Negro History* 66, no. 4 (1982): 289–303.

6. Ibid.

7. Gayle Narcisse, *They Took Our Piece of the Pie: Center Street Revisited* (Des Moines: Iowa Bystander, 1996), 3–11.

8. Charles Knox, personal communication, August 21, 2000.

9. Rem, personal communication, July 10, 2002.

10. Knox, personal communication, August 21, 2000.

11. Narcisse, *They Took Our Piece of the Pie*, 3–11.

12. De Patton, in congressional hearing (1971).

13. Andre Rawls, personal communication, August 21, 2000.
Des Moines Register, October 16, 1968, 6.

14. Knox, personal communication, August 21, 2000.

15. *Des Moines Register,* October 16, 1968, 6.

16. Knox, personal communication, August 21, 2000.

17. *Des Moines Register,* October 20, 1968, 1.

18. De Patton, in congressional hearing (1971).

19. Rem, personal communication, July 10, 2002.

20. Knox, personal communication, August 21, 2000.

21. Ibid.

22. Ibid.

23. Ibid.; *Des Moines Register,* April 23, 1969, 1.

24. Knox, personal communication, August 21, 2000.

25. *Des Moines Register,* April 23, 1969.

26. Ibid.

27. De Patton, in congressional hearing (1971).

28. Knox, personal communication, August 21, 2000.

29. Ibid.

30. Ibid.

31. Rawls, personal communication, August 21, 2000.

32. Knox, personal communication, August 21, 2000. Sam Napier was later killed in a Black Panther internal conflict.

33. Ibid.

34. Ibid.

35. Rawls, personal communication, August 21, 2000.

36. Knox, personal communication, August 21, 2000.

37. Ibid.

38. *Des Moines Register,* April 28, 1969.

39. Knox, personal communication, August 21, 2000.

40. *Des Moines Register,* April 28, 1969.

41. Art Bronson, personal communication, July, 11, 2003.

42. Ibid.; Knox, personal communication, August 21, 2000.

43. Knox, personal communication, August 21, 2000.

44. Ibid.

45. Bronson, personal communication, July, 11, 2003.

46. Ibid.

47. Ibid.

Chapter 13

Inside the Panther Revolution

The Black Freedom Movement and the Black Panther Party in Oakland, California

Robyn Ceanne Spencer

The publication of John Dittmer's *Local People: The Struggle for Civil Rights in Mississippi* and Charles Payne's *I've Got the Light of Freedom: The Organizing Tradition and the Mississippi Freedom Struggle* in the mid-1990s laid the groundwork for scholarly analyses of the Black Freedom movement that did not revolve around the actions of charismatic national leaders or government officials. Instead, Dittmer and Payne crafted richly textured historical narratives centered on the process of political empowerment that led ordinary local people, far away from the spotlight or the headlines, to become active participants in the struggle for civil rights. In their analyses local people were important not only because of the political changes their activism set into motion but also for the lessons about participatory democracy, collective action, experiential learning, and grassroots leadership evident in the flowering of their political consciousness. Although many scholars have elaborated and expanded on Dittmer's and Payne's bottom-up approach to re-analyze the civil rights movement, few have extended their methodologies or analytical frameworks to study the thousands of African Americans who fought for dignity, self-determination, and social justice in the Black Power movement. While civil rights historiography has focused on dramatic and transformative events and highlighted individual and collective triumphs on the national and local level, Black Power has only recently been analyzed by scholars as a local phenomenon that revolutionized grassroots politics in urban America,

and as a mass movement in which the *process* of change was just as important as the *outcome* of change.[1] Instead, many scholars have characterized
the civil rights movement and the Black Power movement as two distinct
entities with dissimilar goals, strategies, tactics, and movement cultures. In
this conceptualization Black Power was a divisive backlash born out of
disillusionment with the shortcomings of the civil rights movement; characterized by anger and violence; and spearheaded by Northern blacks
who, according to one leading historian, were "filled with rage and looking
for a way to affirm themselves."[2] When local people have been poor black
youth in prisons, high schools, colleges, and street corners in inner-city
areas stigmatized as dysfunctional and pathological, their attacks on entrenched power and privilege have not been valorized. Yet it is precisely
these local urban struggles that so clearly demonstrate the inability of
scholarly analyses of black protest premised on impermeable boundaries
between civil rights and black power to capture the complexity of the
Black Freedom movement.

This essay analyzes the impact of the Black Panther Party, one of the
leading organizations of the Black Power movement, on the people and
politics of Oakland, California. It argues that the Panthers' political impact was multilayered—not just measurable in their actions but also in-
scribed in the way they lived, the revolutionary values they tried to emulate, and their attempts to empower, educate, and politicize oppressed
people. The Black Panther Party was a political vehicle created by local
people who drew on Southern resistance traditions and the contours of
their urban experience to defy police brutality, housing shortages, unemployment, racism, poverty, and their own fear and apathy, and to take collective action to transform their conditions. Founded by Huey Newton
and Bobby Seale, two streetwise community college students in 1966, the
Panthers captured the imagination of a generation of American youth and
inspired them to drop out of school and brave alienation from their families and friends to work for social change. They were committed to remaking the world—and themselves—or literally die trying, and they created
alternative lifestyles premised on the notion that the personal was profoundly political. Despite the ravages of a powerful campaign of political
repression unleashed against them by the FBI in 1968, the Panthers successfully challenged Republican dominance of local politics, created and
staffed innovative free social programs that cushioned the blow of poverty
for hundreds of families, and registered thousands of voters in the quest
for community control. Perhaps most important, this work was done by a

committed cadre of rank-and-file members whose courage and vision changed the face of grassroots politics in the United States.

Local Context

By the mid-1960s blacks in Oakland, like Newark, New Jersey, Detroit, Michigan, and other urban centers nationwide, were in the throes of a socioeconomic crisis. The roots of black poverty were laid during World War II, when thousands of African Americans migrated from Louisiana, Texas, Oklahoma, and Arkansas and other parts of the South to Oakland, an essential port and naval shipyard that was home to large transportation and manufacturing industries such as Kaiser Industries, Bank of America, and Safeway Corporation.[3] Between 1940 and 1944 Oakland's black population soared from 8,462 to over 20,000.[4] New migrants brought their own cultural morays, distinctive speech patterns, protest traditions, and strong sense of community, radically transforming the character of Oakland's black communities. They altered the fragile racial balance brokered between the historic black community and the white majority by flouting the social boundaries that governed interracial relations. West Oakland became home to 85 percent of Oakland's African American population, who were unable to move into other locales because of white property owners' refusal to rent or sell to blacks, racial discrimination in the private market, the banking industry's discriminatory policies in allocating real estate loans, and restrictive covenants barring black people from model suburbs created by federally sponsored wartime construction programs.[5]

By the 1950s the economic policies of Oakland's deeply entrenched conservative Republican political machine had decimated the economic base of the inner city. Local business elites encouraged industrial development outside the city. Capital flight and white flight soon followed. Between 1950 and 1960 approximately one hundred thousand white middle-class homeowners left Oakland and were replaced by an equal number of black and Chicano renters.[6] The Nimitz Freeway, completed in 1958, cut through the heart of West Oakland, dividing it in half and destroying many homes and businesses in the process. Two years later train service to Oakland was discontinued, resulting in the loss of a traditional source of employment for blacks.[7] The economic center of the West Oakland community, the business district around Market Street and 7th Street that was once known as the thriving "Black Downtown," never recovered from these losses. By

1959 one-quarter of all families in Oakland earned less than $4,000 a year and almost half the families in the city lived in deprivation or worse.[8] By 1966 unemployment in Oakland was more than twice the national average and almost half the entire work-eligible flatland population was unemployed or sub-employed.[9]

Owing to residential segregation the Oakland hills were a predominantly white enclave, and 60 percent of blacks and approximately 8 percent of Mexican Americans made their home in the dilapidated and overcrowded flatlands. Educational institutions serving flatland residents were overcrowded and underfunded. In 1966 the Ad Hoc Committee for Quality Education in Oakland chronicled ten years of racial inequality in local schools, including the push by both the Congress of Racial Inequality (CORE) and the National Association for the Advancement of Colored People (NAACP) for high school boundaries to be changed to facilitate integration in 1962, the Fair Employment Practices Commission report exposing "discrimination in hiring practices and attitudes of Oakland schools" in 1964, and parent protests about inadequate hot lunch programs in the schools in 1965.[10]

Oakland's black newspapers chronicled many accounts of police brutality against African Americans throughout the 1950s, a decade that began with the acknowledgment by a crime commission that there had been numerous instances of police brutality and misconduct aimed at Oakland's non-white residents.[11] Much of the city's police force had been recruited from the Deep South, and police officers frequently held racist attitudes.[12] Police brutality worsened as Oakland activists launched civil rights protests and demonstrations in the late 1950s and early 1960s. There were more than twenty demonstrations protesting police violence in Oakland between 1965 and 1966, a time when black police officers made up less than 3 percent of the total Oakland police force.[13]

In the absence of black-led progressive organizations and the paucity of black elected officials to address the city's escalating economic problems, black protest erupted from below. Vibrant grassroots political organizations, led by children of migrants, attempted to fill the leadership vacuum in Oakland's black communities. Newton and Seale were two of these children. Seale was born in Dallas, Texas, and migrated to Oakland with his family in 1942. Newton was born in Monroe, Louisiana, and migrated to Oakland with his family in 1945.[14] Both men had firsthand experience with poverty and housing shortages growing up, and were influenced by Malcolm X's advocacy of armed self-defense and black nationalism, as well as revolutionary theorists such as Mao Tse-tung, Frantz Fanon, and Fidel Castro. They both cut their teeth in local nationalist political formations in the early 1960s before coming together in 1966 in an Anti-Poverty Center to create the Black Panther Party. Newton wrote in his autobiography that he and Seale "recognized that the rising consciousness of Black people was at the point of explosion."[15] They collaborated to write the ten-point platform and program demanding full employment, reparations from the federal government, decent housing, education representative of the black experience, and the exemption of all black men from military service. Point 7 called for an end to police brutality and affirmed black people's right to organize self-defense groups. It took its justification from the second amendment's guarantee of the right to bear arms. Point 8 called for freedom for black prisoners, and point 9 called for a jury of peers for black defendants, as guaranteed in the Fourteenth Amendment. Point 10 demanded "land, bread, housing, education, clothing, justice and peace."[16] This ten-point platform and program, a program of radical reform rooted in visceral experiences of discrimination in Oakland, would become one of the Panthers' most valuable organizing tools.

Emboldened Local People

The local people that Panther co-founders Seale and Newton attempted to recruit to the Black Panther Party were "black brothers and sisters off the block," "mothers who had been scrubbing Miss Ann's kitchen," and "brothers and sisters in college, in high schools, who were on parole, on probation, who'd been in jails, who'd just gotten out of jail, and . . . who looked like they were on their way to jail."[17] Seale and Newton initially practiced an open-door membership policy, hoping to shape recruits into a disciplined, politically astute cadre through political education. Early party members had usually grown up in the Bay Area and often came into the party through their association with someone else. Membership spread throughout social and political circles, in what one member described as "waves of curiosity, interest, acknowledgement, concern."[18] These early recruits came from many different paths and from all levels of income, education, and political consciousness, and were attracted to the party for different reasons. Some wanted the sense of "doing something" to change the conditions around them and were drawn to the concept of black people standing up for themselves. Others were attracted by the party's ten-point platform and program, while others were drawn in by the party's armed stance. As young people who had come to political age during the sixties, these young men and women were immersed in the process of self-discovery and self-exploration, and were filled with optimism and a sense of possibility.

Sherwin Forte was one of the Panthers' first recruits. Forte became involved in the party in early 1967, when he was in his late teens. His family had migrated from Birmingham, Alabama, to Berkeley, and then to North Oakland. He grew up with a consciousness of police brutality and frequently witnessed the police harassing black teenagers. The politically charged atmosphere of the sixties had raised his awareness even further, and he had become an avid admirer of Malcolm X. Forte recalled the atmosphere of that time:

> The Vietnam War was happening, and I had a choice whether I would go and fight the country's battles in Vietnam or whether I wanted to take my life and use it to redress some wrongs in this country. I didn't see the Vietnamese as the enemy. I saw the enemy as racist America. . . . And you know, when you are young, you have a lot of fervor, a lot of strength. I think I felt like the way a majority of young people felt at that time given the riotous atmosphere, the killings, the National Guard, the helicopters, the protest in Berkeley, the anti-draft movement. It was a period of action and tension, and a lot of blacks focused on the political system.[19]

The Panthers' emphasis on the issue of police brutality resonated deeply with Forte, and he was attracted to the self-defense aspect of the party's program and the potential of having "the same tools that the oppressor had—guns." At the time he joined, he was a student at Merritt College. The Panthers had opened their first office at 5624 Grove Street, a few blocks away. Merritt was a hub of political activity, and Forte recalled spending a lot of time in "these little sessions, these arguments, these discussions about the black man in America, the draft, what Stokely Carmichael was saying, what H. Rap Brown was saying. I guess the general term was 'bull sessions.'"[20] Forte met Seale at one of these sessions, and was intrigued by the Panthers. Forte and his younger brother Reginald attended a meeting and experienced an "instantaneous connection" with the fledgling organization. By the second meeting, they were both committed members.

One of Newton's and Seale's first actions was to dauntlessly monitor the actions of the Oakland Police Department, poised to intervene with tape recorders, cameras, law books, and legally carried firearms.[21] These police patrols were random and incorporated into their daily movements and activities as they drove around Oakland's black communities. Typically Newton and Seale would observe police officers as they arrested people to make sure that the police were not breaking any laws or using excessive force. Their goal was to educate the community about its legal rights, to legitimize the idea of self-defense, and to gain the attention of Oakland blacks. Facing down agents of the state in this way was not very dissimilar from going down to the courthouse in the rural South to attempt to vote—it required the same courage and self-assurance, and held the same potential of bloody retribution. The sight of young black men, with guns in their hands, loudly asserting their right to bear arms and warning the police not to be the aggressors, repeatedly drew a crowd. The Oakland police repeatedly reacted with shock and surprise at the sight of the armed youths but were powerless to strip the Panthers of their weapons. Although patrolling often consisted of reading the penal code or simple observation, there were several major confrontations and stand-offs with the police in which the Panthers refused to back down. Onlookers reacted with elation and victory when the police would retreat after being bested in verbal confrontations by Newton's rapid-fire rhetoric and Seale's wisecracks. In addition to the drama of the bravado, onlookers also were being schooled in active citizenship. According to Panther Emory Douglas, onlookers also observed "the way the Panthers articulated the law," "the way the Panthers were able to bail them out of jail if they were arrested. The way the Panthers explained to them what their rights were when they were being arrested: that all they had to do was give their name and their address and they didn't have to answer all the questions."[22] Not only were these patrols laboratories for observers, they also served as powerful workshops for participants on overcoming fear. When Sherwin Forte went on patrols and saw Newton explain the law to the police and saw their reaction of frustration and shock, he felt empowered. It "confirmed that we could gain respect, command respect," and "bolstered our egos, made us feel very powerful, like we were a force to be reckoned with and it was something that we became less and less afraid of doing."[23] Many others were inspired by the Panthers' example of standing up.

Membership in the organization grew at a slow but steady pace. Women began to join the party as members in the spring of 1967. Despite the Panthers' macho public image and the traditional gendered associations surrounding the defense and protection of community, black women drew on their own protest traditions to demand a space for themselves within the organization. For some Panther women, involvement in the party gave them the tools to contest the Panthers' gender politics and provided a space where they could develop their own consciousness. Tarika Lewis, sixteen years old at the time, was the first young woman to join the Panthers. Like Reginald Forte, she was a student at Oakland Technical High School and an activist in the Black Student Union. Lewis grew up in North Oakland and would often sit in on classes at Merritt College. Joining the Black Panther Party was part of her search for self-knowledge, and a reflection of her concern with Oakland's pervasive police brutality.[24] Elendar Barnes joined the party in the spring of 1967 after learning about the organization through Laverne Williams, her best friend and Huey Newton's girlfriend. For Barnes, Panther membership was a continuation of her activism as a Merritt College student involved in the Black Student Union, and a natural evolution of the politics she had grown up with:

I became very involved in that level of politics because it was an extension of what I knew, an extension of what they called the Deacons [for Defense] down South. And my grandfather wasn't necessarily a member of the Deacons but our family's stance was, you know, you protect your family by any means necessary and, you know, you use guns. My grandfather was the first person to buy land on what was considered the white part of town. I'd go visit him in the summers and I remember that the Ku Klux Klan burnt a cross on his yard because they opposed him living on that side of town. And I think a lot of people in Oakland have these southern roots and that whole connection with the idea of protecting your own. People were used to using and keeping guns because that's what they did in the country. My grandfather always kept a gun; it was invisible but it always was in the back of the car, or up in the window in the back of the truck and they always said in the South that they were for hunting but he said it was for the white man. And it wasn't for the white man who wasn't bothering you. It was for the KKK and the others. And that's what moved me into the Panthers.[25]

The Panthers soon evolved from local organization to social movement. On May 2, 1967, the Panthers led an armed delegation of thirty men and women to Sacramento, California, to highlight their opposition to the Mulford Bill, which prohibited carrying unconcealed firearms in public.

The Panthers' received national and international publicity after the delegation mistakenly walked onto the floor of the state legislature. Requests began to pour in from people around the country who wanted to establish Panther chapters, and the Panthers received increased scrutiny from the police and from the FBI, who saw them as emblematic of the urban unrest sweeping the country.[26] In October 1967 Newton was arrested and accused of killing one police officer and wounding another in an early morning melee. The Free Huey movement, launched to raise awareness about his case, was the catalyst for the Panthers' nationwide expansion.[27] The assassination of Martin Luther King, and the subsequent police killing of Bobby Hutton, the Panthers' first recruit, several days later confirmed the tactical viability and necessity of armed self-defense to many in the black community. The *Black Panther,* the publication founded by the Panthers in 1967, had grown into a full-scale political organ, filled with news articles, commentary, speeches, and bold political graphics, and was read by thousands of people around the country. By 1969 there were more than forty Panther chapters nationwide. These chapters were a result of local people rooted in what Kathleen Cleaver, Panther communications secretary, described as "pre-existing . . . local relationships," who had identified themselves with the image of "Black Power and popular rebellion and resistance . . ." that the Panthers represented. The party's transition from a tightly knit band of Bay Area residents to a web of loosely interconnected local activists across the country changed the nature of the Oakland Panthers. They were now not just a local organization filled with people who "somebody knew who they were or had gone to school with them [and could] . . . vouch for them" but rather the national headquarters of a movement of local people nationwide working to change the conditions in their communities.[28]

The Politics of Community Empowerment

The Panthers launched community programs in 1968 which included a Free Breakfast Program, Liberation Schools, and a Free Clothing Program. These programs empowered people to pool resources to address the lack of social services in their communities. This was no lesson in self-reliance but instead a trenchant critique of the government's unwillingness to provide for its poorest citizens, and an attempt to embody a socialist ethos and model alternative institutions. The Panthers' pioneering community program, the Free Breakfast Program, drew on established institutions and longtime activists in Oakland's black community. The Panthers approached Reverend Earl Neil of St. Augustine's Church to provide facilities to house the program and attempted to obtain lists of black elementary school students in West Oakland and to contact parents.[29] Ruth Beckford, a community activist and a member of the Panthers' Community Advisory Committee who became involved in the planning and implementation of the Free Breakfast Program, helped plan the logistics of the program in terms of food, frequency of merchant donations, and staff. Beckford recruited Parent Teacher Association (PTA) mothers to cook for the breakfast program in shifts. Despite the rigors of volunteering, including arriving at the church at 6:00 A.M. to cook in bulk and lay out the food, "those women were happy to do it. They felt that this was a very positive program for the Panthers. Where others might have been afraid of any association with the Panthers 'cause they thought that they were violent, this program was their strongest point and was able to rally people from all sections of the community."[30]

Newton's release from prison in 1971 precipitated heightened repression against the organization and brought to the surface simmering internal debates about the direction of the. COINTELPRO, the FBI-launched counterintelligence program against black nationalists, had been squarely aimed at the Panthers in late 1968. The Panthers were classified as "most violence-prone organization of all the extremist groups not operating in the United States," and the FBI vowed to "not only accelerate our investigations of this organization and increase our informants in the organization but that we take action under the counterintelligence program to disrupt the group" by creating "factionalism between not only the national leaders but also the local leaders, steps to neutralize all organizational efforts of the BPP [Black Panther Party] as well as create suspicion amongst the leaders as to each other's sources of finances, suspicion concerning their respective spouses and suspicion as to who may be cooperating with law enforcement."[31] This precipitated a violent period of internecine warfare, resignations, and expulsions that almost destroyed the organization.

The Panthers regrouped with fewer than one thousand members and concentrated organizational resources in Oakland, hoping that the city would become a model for grassroots organizing and community activism all over the country. They self-consciously reassessed the organization as a political vehicle and created a vibrant movement culture that nourished and sustained members' activism. Although the Panthers remained a top-down organization, democracy had flowered at the base of the organization, where a collective structure facilitated members' total commitment. The Panthers attempted to meet the needs of its membership for food, clothing, shelter, and even health care. They created a Health Cadre whose job included keeping track of ill comrades and children, and tracking epidemics of the flu and other contagious illnesses that could spread quickly in a collective living situation. The close-knit nature of the collective gave the Panthers all the trappings of a family. Agenda items for central committee meetings included comrades' appearance and clothing needs, interpersonal conflict, and the maintenance of cleanliness in work areas.[32] A memo to central body members dated August 16, 1972, brought up the need for a dialogue on planned parenthood within the party, policies for expectant mothers, the creation of an infirmary, and the teaching of remedial reading and math skills.[33] The Panthers adopted collective parenting, providing a space for women to be both mothers and active political organizers. Panther James Abron fondly recalled that the party "basically took care of you from dusk to dawn if you had kids." Parents were "given their kids on the weekends, but Monday through Friday, we would teach 'em, feed 'em, take 'em to our dormitories and wash 'em, help them with their homework, put 'em to bed, clean their clothes, wipe their butts and then [laughter] the process would start over again.[34] The collective structure also facilitated internal dissension as party members grappled with sexism, classism, individualism, and materialism in the attempt not only to create alternative structures and institutions but also alternative lifestyles.

Panther Bobby McCall described this dynamic:

> We ate together. We slept together. We lived together. We did everything together like a family, like an organization should. . . . We were a bunch of disciplined, organized young brothers and sisters who were determined to uplift the black community. It wasn't no joke being in the Party. It might have been called a party, but it was no party. We had a lot of fun with each other because we loved each other. We had a lot of family affairs. We always celebrated each other's birthdays, . . . in a big way. We didn't celebrate holidays but we did celebrate life with each other.[35]

The Panthers' recommitted themselves to local activism, building relationships, and working for the long haul, key themes of the community organizing tradition described by Payne.[36] Panther Ericka Huggins proclaimed the organization's commitment to doing "the hard, drudgery, boring, day-to-day, no-reward, you-can't-see-the-future kind of work." This might involve going "door to door every day all day long and ask people 'Do you—?' and not get to finish the sentence," trying "to educate people that have no understanding of what you're talking about because they don't have any food, they don't have any shoes, they don't know where their children are going to be in the next minute, they can't get their welfare check, don't know what their social security number is, don't know where the office is, can't get to the office, and don't want to, anyway. And are having family problems on top of that." The Panthers hoped that this work would "lead to an eventual understanding of why there is a need for alternative institutions."[37]

The Panthers sought political power in Oakland as a tactic to mobilize and organize the black community, which would also provide them with a legitimate voice in the Oakland political scene. Although Oakland blacks had mobilized to elect Ron Dellums to the House of Representatives in 1971, local politics remained dominated by conservative whites. By 1972, a time when the city had a black voting population larger than 25 percent, only one in eight members of the Oakland City Council was black. The Panthers were poised to move into this political vacuum. They began to engage in strategic endorsement and campaigning for Democratic candidates, and actively sought municipal and county appointments. In May 1972 four Panthers won seats on the Berkeley Community Development Council, a twenty-four-member antipoverty board with a multimillion dollar federally funded budget.[38] One month later the Panthers issued a press release stating that they were running candidates for the West Oakland Planning Committee (WOPC), which was to facilitate citizen participation in Oakland's $4.9 million budget "Model City" urban renewal project because voting was the "Power of the People: the only means to begin implementing community control."[39] In August 1972 Panther members and supporters ran for seats on the West Oakland Planning Committee,[40] winning six out of eighteen seats on the West Oakland Model Cities governing board.[41]

In 1973 Seale ran for mayor and Panther Elaine Brown ran for City Council on the Democratic Party ticket. Seale's and Brown's campaign platform centered on social programs such as housing, preventative medical health care, childcare, educational improvement, and environmental protection. The Panthers' array of free social services was central to their political vision and a cornerstone of their campaign. They expanded the range of programs to include a free plumbing and maintenance program, a free food program to "supplement the groceries of Black and poor people until such time as economic conditions allow them to purchase good food at reasonable prices," and opened a health clinic in Berkeley to provide free medical attention, medication, referrals, sickle cell anemia testing, immunization, prenatal instruction, first aid kits, and community health surveys.[42] The Oakland Community School (OCS), a model for community-based education, was one of the Panthers' strongest programs. The OCS began as the Intercommunal Youth Institute in 1971, a school program catering to the children of party members. OCS students, ranging from two to eleven years of age, received full tuition, health care, and individualized classroom attention. The staff of twenty-seven full-time accredited teachers taught students art, music, science, Spanish, environmental studies, and physical education.[43] In the summer students participated in a structured program of trips, classes, and recreational activities.[44] By May 12, 1976, approximately 125 children attended the OCS, which had earned a nationwide reputation for excellence in community-based education.[45]

Brown and Seale spoke out against secrecy in government and the negative impact of urban renewal on local communities; they also advocated transferring the economic resources from the port of Oakland to the city itself. This campaign transformed the Black Panther Party into a political machine. The party closed down many local chapters nationwide and brought their cadre to Oakland to work on this campaign. Voter registration was the main task of these campaign workers and the linchpin of the Panthers' strategy. Between November 8, 1972, and March 18, 1973, the Panthers registered 14,662 people to vote.[46] In the spring of 1973 white supporters formed "Whites for Bobby Seale and Elaine Brown"; the Gay Men's Political Action Group of Oakland created fliers supporting Brown and Seale;[47] and Cesar Chavez and the United Farm Workers endorsed Seale and Brown.[48] By March Seale was one of the recognized front runners in the mayoral campaign. As Election Day drew near the Panthers increased the pace of their campaign. Brown won more than thirty-four thousand votes but lost her bid for City Council. Seale received forty-five thousand votes, 37 percent of the total vote—enough to put him in a run-off election with incumbent John Reading.[49] Although Seale lost the run-off, he considered his campaign an example of the power of blacks and of working and progressive people when they are organized "into a mighty political thrust." In his victory speech, he stated:

We organized to make our power known and felt. That knowledge, for us and those who oppose our right to the expression of our humanity, can no longer be kept from us. For, this election has made an historic decision, here in the midst of this most powerful country: Black people, especially, as well as the majority of people have decided that together we can move mountains and turn the tide of reaction, so that we all may live and be free from exploitation, slavery and the many ills we have faced. [50]

The Panthers were unable to retain campaign machinery in local communities to build on their momentum after the campaign. By 1974 there were fewer than one hundred members and the organization was filled with internal contradictions and structural weaknesses. Hilliard and Seale both left the organization, and Newton had fled into exile to escape felony charges. As a result of focusing all their resources on the election, other aspects of the Party's program, such as their newspaper, and the community survival programs, inevitably suffered. Although the Brown-Seale campaign did not result in grassroots empowerment or the long-term organization of the Oakland community, the Panthers did become an important voice in local politics. Between 1974 and 1977 the Panthers made significant inroads into Oakland's local political scene. The Panthers supported John George in his successful bid for election as the first black county supervisor in Alameda County. When Governor Jerry Brown ran for president in 1976, Panther leader Elaine Brown served as a Democratic delegate. In 1977 the Panthers campaigned for Lionel Wilson, a longtime Panther ally, for mayor of Oakland. Wilson's campaign built on Seale's successful showing in 1974. The Panthers played an important role in voter registration, mobilization, and get-out-the-vote actions around his campaign. Wilson won, becoming Oakland's first Democratic mayor in thirty years and the first black mayor ever.[51] After Newton's return from exile in 1977, and his descent into substance abuse and criminal activity, more and more Panthers resigned from the organization. The Oakland Community School, the Panthers last remaining survival program, closed its doors in 1982, and the Black Panther Party officially came to an end.

Conclusion

Two of the Panthers most important and perhaps most overlooked contributions to the Black Freedom movement were their attempts to nurture oppressed people's political consciousness and revolutionize their daily personal and political praxis. The Panthers' determination to provide not only a philosophy of liberation but also to embody the world they were trying to create, despite all its shortcomings, reflected the same ethos as Martin Luther King's Beloved Community. This community was a work in progress, frequently derailed by cult of personality, lack of accountability of the leadership, breakdown in internal political education, and other flaws that would prove fatal to the organization long after the juggernaut of political repression had receded into the past. The process of bringing local people to political consciousness, which was at the heart of the Black Freedom movement organizing tradition, eluded the Panthers as they became more insular, and rigid structural hierarchies increasingly muffled rank-and-file members' most persistent calls for democracy and organizational reform. This slow process was chronicled in the complaints of party members: that comrades did not "love and respect each other as human beings instead of males and females";[52] that members were unable to "do any consistent door to door work around the subscription drive, voter registration or any of the other activities that are done to hold the previously established and to build new face-to-face relationships with the people on the precinct level";[53] that insularity hindered community organizing and Panthers "barely see the masses much less have a chance to educate them."[54] In 1979 party members demanded that the organization "firmly embrace the principle of criticism and self-criticism," warning that "without this our leadership becomes separated from our party body as is the case now, consequently isolating the party from the people." Their poignant plea, that "our party must be a microcosm of the kind of society we want to create to replace the old" went unanswered.[55] However, their efforts at reform embody just how successful the Panthers had been in creating empowered political activists committed to change, even though the organization was ultimately not able to live up to the expectations it had produced. The power of the Panthers' history is not in the how and why of their failures or even in the tally of their successes; it is in the process by which they swept young black men and women off street corners and away from college campuses all around the nation to partake in the work of social justice—what Newton once described as "the attempt to make more freedom."[56]

NOTES

1. See Komozi Woodard, *A Nation within a Nation: Amiri Baraka (Leroi Jones) and Black Power Politics* (Chapel Hill: University of North Carolina Press, 1999); Timothy B. Tyson, *Radio Free Dixie: Robert F. Williams and the Roots of Black Power* (Chapel Hill: University of North Carolina Press, 1999); Yohuru Williams, *Black Politics/White Power: Civil Rights, Black Power and the Black Panthers in New Haven* (New York: Brandywine, 2000); Jeanne F. Theoharis and Komozi Woodard, eds., *Freedom North: Black Freedom Struggles outside the South, 1940–1980* (New York: Palgrave Macmillan, 2003).

2. Darlene Clark Hine and Kathleen Thompson, *A Shining Thread of Hope: The History of Black Women in America* (New York: Broadway Books, 1998), 297.

3. Rod Bush, ed., *The New Black Vote: Politics and Power in Four American Cities* (San Francisco: Synthesis, 1984), 320.

4. Marilynn S. Johnson, *The Second Gold Rush: Oakland and the East Bay in World War II* (Berkeley: University of California Press, 1993), 52.

5. Donald Hausler, "Blacks in Oakland: 1852–1987," [photocopy], 122, Public History Room, Oakland Public Library, Lakeshore Branch, Oakland, California; Johnson, *Second Gold Rush*, 214; Hausler, "Blacks in Oakland," 117.

6. Edward Hayes, *Power Structure and Urban Policy: Who Rules in Oakland?* (New York: McGraw-Hill, 1972), 108.

7. Hausler, "Blacks in Oakland," 125–26.

8. Hayes, *Power Structure and Urban Policy*, 44–45.

9. Hausler, "Blacks in Oakland," 176; Hayes, *Power Structure and Urban Policy*, 46.

10. Ten Years of Segregation in Oakland, folder: "Oakland Schools Racial Problems—Other Than Clippings," Oakland Public Library, Lakeshore Branch, Public History Room, Oakland, California.

11. "Crime Commission Reveals Local Cops' Brute Methods," *California Voice*, 13 January 1950, 1, 2; The police chief at the time did not acknowledge that a problem existed and few reforms were made; see Hausler, "Blacks in Oakland," 122. The *Sun-Reporter* was at the forefront in reporting complaints of brutality. See "Police Brutality, Old Story," *Sun-Reporter*, 26 February 1955, 8; "What's Wrong with Our Police Department," *Sun-Reporter*, 7 June 1958, 6; "New Police Brutality Cases Anger Parents: Ask Police Chief and Mayor 'Stop Brutality,'" *Sun-Reporter*, 14 November 1959, 1; "Victim of Police Brutality?" *Sun-Reporter*, 4 March 1961, 1, 5.

12. Hayes, *Power Structure and Urban Policy*, 36–39.

13. Personnel Division, Oakland Police Department to Chief C. R. Gain, 16 February 1973, folder: "Vacancy Projection and Recruiting Data," Oakland Public Library, Lakeshore Branch, Public History Room, Oakland, California.

14. Bobby Seale, *A Lonely Rage: The Autobiography of Bobby Seale* (New York: Times Books, 1978), 19; Bobby Seale, *Seize the Time: The Story of the Black Panther*

Party and Huey P. Newton (Baltimore, Md.: Black Classic Press, 1991), 4; Huey Newton, *Revolutionary Suicide* (New York: Writers and Readers, 1973), 13–15.

15. Newton, *Revolutionary Suicide*, 110.

16. Seale, *Seize the Time*, 59–63.

17. Ibid., 64–65.

18. Judy [Hart] Jaunita, interview by author, 20 October 1997, tape recording, Oakland, California.

19. Sherwin Forte, interview by author, 9 October 1997, tape recording, Oakland, California.

20. Ibid.

21. Their actions were not without precedent. Other community groups had also begun to monitor police activities in Oakland. The Oakland Direct Action Committee (ODAC), founded by Mark Comfort, began patrolling Oakland's black communities in the summer of 1966. Mark Comfort, "Conditions in the Oakland Ghetto," Interview by Elsa Knight Thompson," 1967, cassette E2BB1309, Pacifica Radio Archives, Los Angeles, California.

22. Emory Douglas, interview by author, 9 October 1997, tape recording, San Francisco, California.

23. Forte, interview by author.

24. Tarika Lewis, interview by author, 16 October 1997, transcript, Oakland, California.

25. Elendar Barnes, interview by author, 25 September 1997, tape recording, Brooklyn, New York.

26. Newton, *Revolutionary Suicide*, 151.

27. Ibid., 187.

28. Forte, interview by author.

29. Bobby Seale, interview by author, 13 October 1997, tape recording, Oakland, California; "FBI Intelligence Summary—Nov. 15–22, 1968," box 65, Huey P. Newton Foundation Papers, Special Collections, Green Library, Stanford University, California (hereafter, HPN Papers); n.b.: I accessed the HPN Papers at Stanford University in 1996 when the archival recording process was just beginning, and therefore box and folder titles, contents, and so on, may be different.

30. Ruth Beckford, interview by author, 16 October 1997, tape recording, Oakland, California.

31. Ward Churchill and Jim Vander Wall, *The COINTELPRO Papers: Documents from the FBI's Secret Wars against Domestic Dissent* (Boston: South End, 1990), 124–25.

32. Memo re: Agenda Items to be discussed, May 22, 1973, folder: "Central Committee Info," box 10, HPN Papers; "Notes from Central Body Meeting, October 2, 1972," folder: "Central Committee Info," box 10, HPN Papers.

33. Folder: "Central Committee Info," box 10, HPN Papers.

34. James Abron, interview by author, 6 October 1997, tape recording, Oakland, California.

35. Bobby McCall, interview by author, 14 October 1997, tape recording, San Francisco, California.

36. Charles Payne, *I've Got the Light of Freedom: The Organizing Tradition and the Mississippi Freedom Struggle* (Berkeley: University of California Press, 1995), 364.

37. Michele Russell, "Conversation with Ericka Huggins. Oakland, California, 4/20/77," 12–13, box 1, HPN Papers.

38. "Panthers Elected to Berkeley Anti-Poverty Program," box 2, HPN Papers.

39. "Bobby Seale campaign info," box 14A, HPN Papers.

40. "Innerparty Memorandum #3," box, 14, HPN Papers.

41. "Panther Protection: Party Will Start Escort Service: Officials Ponder Motives," *Sacramento Bee*, 10 December 1972, folder: "US v. Hilliard re: Wiretap," box 26, HPN Papers; "Panthers elected to Berkeley Anti-Poverty Program," box 2, HPN Papers.

42. Black Panther Party, ed., *CoEvolution Quarterly*, no. 3 (fall 1974): 29; "Budget, 1971," folder: "Black Panther Party No-Profit Corporations Including Black United Front," box 34, HPN Papers.

43. February 1976 article, folder: "OCS Brochure," box 4, HPN Papers.

44. "July 1977 Corporate Overview EOC," folder: EOC, box 4, HPN Papers.

45. Folder: "Montclair Article," box 5, HPN Papers.

46. Voter Registration Counts, folder: "Voter Registration Elections Committee," box 7, HPN Papers.

47. Folder: "Bobby Seale Campaign Info," box 14A, HPN Papers.

48. Ibid.

49. "Seale's 'Revolt' Plans," *San Francisco Examiner*, 12 November 1972, 1.

50. "Election Victory Statement," folder: "Bobby Seale Campaign Info," box 14, HPN Papers.

51. Folder: "Wilson's Donation List," box 17, HPN Papers.

52. "Memo to: The Servant From: Comrade JoNina Abron," folder: "Reports on Comrades," box 14, HPN Papers.

53. Section Progress Reports, 6 September 1973, box 2, HPN Papers.

54. "Memo to: Huey, From: Dale re: Women in the Perty [*sic*]," 4 October 1977, folder: "Reports on Comrades," box 14, HPN Papers.

55. 1 May 1979 Report, folder: "Reports on Comrades," box 14, HPN Papers.

56. Box 15, HPN Papers, folder "West Magazine Interview with Huey P. by Digby Diehl—*LA Times*," 30.

About the Contributors

Reynaldo Anderson received his Ph.D. in Communication Studies at the University of Nebraska–Lincoln and is a lecturer in communication at Fontbonne University.

Katherine Mellen Charron is a Ph.D. candidate at Yale University. She is co-editor of *Recollections of My Slavery Days* by William Henry Singleton.

Emilye Crosby is Associate Professor of History at the State University of New York–Geneseo. She is author of "Teaching about Self-Defense in the African-American Freedom Struggle," in *Teaching the Civil Rights Movement.*

Hasan Kwame Jeffries is Assistant Professor in the Department of History and at the Kirwan Institute for the Study of Race and Ethnicity at Ohio State University.

Patrick Jones is Assistant Professor of History and Ethnic Studies at the University of Nebraska–Lincoln.

Peter B. Levy is Professor of History at York College of Pennsylvania. His publications include *Civil War on Race Street: The Civil Rights Movement in Cambridge, Maryland* and *America in the Sixties—Right, Left, and Center: A Documentary History.*

Karen Miller is Assistant Professor of Urban Studies at LaGuardia Community College.

Tiyi Morris is Assistant Professor of History at DePauw University.

Charles Payne is the Sally Dalton Robinson Professor of African American Studies, History, and Sociology and the director of the African and African American Studies Program at Duke University. He is the author of *I've Got the Light of Freedom: The Organizing Tradition in the Mississippi Civil Rights Movement*, co-editor of *Time Longer Than Rope: A Century of African American Activism, 1850–1950,* and co-author of *Debating the Civil Rights Movement.*

Brian Purnell is a Ph.D. candidate in history at New York University.

Robyn Ceanne Spencer is Assistant Professor of African and African American studies and history at Pennsylvania State University.

Jeanne Theoharis is Assistant Professor of Political Science at Brooklyn College of the City University of New York. She is co-author of *These Yet to Be United States: Civil Rights and Civil Liberties in America since 1945* and co-editor, with Komozi Woodard, of *Freedom North: Black Freedom Struggles outside the South, 1940–1980.*

Michael Washington is Professor of History and founding director of the Afro-American studies program at Northern Kentucky University. He is the author of "A Dream Deferred for Quality Education: Civil Rights Legislation and De Facto Segregation in the Cincinnati Schools, 1954–1986," in *Dream and Reality: The Modern Black Struggle for Freedom and Equality.*

Komozi Woodard is Professor of American History and Public Policy and of Africana Studies at Sarah Lawrence College. He is the author of *A Nation within a Nation: Amiri Baraka (LeRoi Jones) and Black Power Politics,* editor of *The Black Power Movement, Part 1: Amiri Baraka: From Black Arts to Black Radicalism and Beyond,* and co-editor, with Jeanne Theoharis, of *Freedom North: Black Freedom Struggles outside the South.*

Index